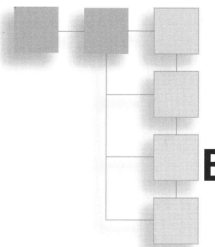

Microsoft®
Excel® 2013 *for the*
Business Analyst

Larry Rockoff

Cengage Learning PTR

CENGAGE
Learning®

Professional • Technical • Reference

Australia • Brazil • Japan • Korea • Mexico • Singapore • Spain • United Kingdom • United States

Microsoft® Excel® 2013 for the Business Analyst
Larry Rockoff

Publisher and General Manager, Cengage Learning PTR: Stacy L. Hiquet

Associate Director of Marketing: Sarah Panella

Manager of Editorial Services: Heather Talbot

Senior Marketing Manager: Mark Hughes

Senior Acquisitions Editor: Mitzi Koontz

Project Editor: Dan Foster, Scribe Tribe

Technical Reviewer: Keith Davenport

Interior Layout Tech: MPS Limited

Cover Designer: Luke Fletcher

Indexer: Sharon Shock

Proofreader: Megan Belanger

For product information and technology assistance, contact us at **Cengage Learning Customer & Sales Support, 1-800-354-9706**

For permission to use material from this text or product, submit all requests online at **cengage.com/permissions**

Further permissions questions can be emailed to **permissionrequest@cengage.com**

Microsoft, Excel, and Access are registered trademarks of Microsoft Corporation. All other trademarks are the property of their respective owners.

All images © Cengage Learning unless otherwise noted.

Library of Congress Control Number: 2013948718

ISBN-13: 978-1-285-77888-4

ISBN-10: 1-285-77888-X

Cengage Learning PTR

20 Channel Center Street

Boston, MA 02210

USA

Cengage Learning is a leading provider of customized learning solutions with office locations around the globe, including Singapore, the United Kingdom, Australia, Mexico, Brazil, and Japan. Locate your local office at: **international.cengage.com/region**

Cengage Learning products are represented in Canada by Nelson Education, Ltd.

For your lifelong learning solutions, visit **cengageptr.com**

Visit our corporate website at **cengage.com**

Printed in the United States of America
1 2 3 4 5 6 7 15 14 13

For Lisa

Acknowledgments

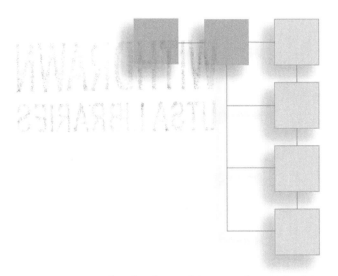

A general thanks goes to all at Cengage Learning who had anything to do with this book, from the proofreader to the indexer. As with my two prior books, I'd especially like to thank Mitzi Koontz, my acquisitions editor, for giving me the opportunity to proceed with this third project. Keith Davenport, my technical reviewer, did a splendid job, as usual. I would also like to praise the work of Luke Fletcher, who created such an aesthetically pleasing cover. Lastly, Dan Foster, my project editor, was superb in asking the right questions, correcting subtle errors, and adding stylistic flourish to many of my sentences.

I'd also like to acknowledge and thank the many readers who have contacted me on my website, larryrockoff.com, with comments or questions on my two prior books. It's both humbling and thrilling to realize that your thoughts can assist someone halfway around the world.

Finally, and most especially, I would like to thank everyone in my immediate family for their encouraging words as I've dedicated myself to this endeavor. Thank you… Lisa, Kyle, Emily, Steve, and Dan.

About the Author

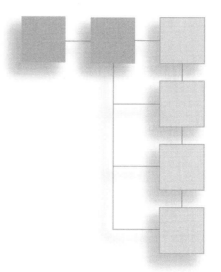

Larry Rockoff has been involved with Microsoft Excel and Business Intelligence development for many years. His main area of interest is with using reporting tools to explore and analyze data in complex databases. He holds an MBA from the University of Chicago, with a specialization in Management Science.

His two prior books, *The Language of SQL* and *Data Analysis with Microsoft® Access® 2010*, are available worldwide in both paper and electronic form.

He also maintains a website with occasional commentary on computing issues at:

- larryrockoff.com

Please feel free to visit that site to contact the author with any comments or questions. You are also encouraged to follow his Facebook author page or Twitter site at:

- facebook.com/larryrockoff
- twitter.com/larryrockoff

Contents

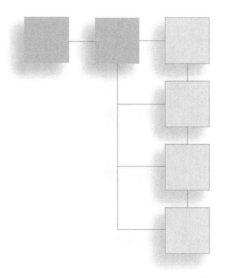

Introduction

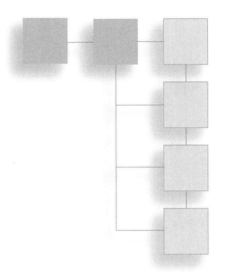

Used by millions around the world, Microsoft Excel has become synonymous with the word *spreadsheet* and both defines and dominates that software category. One would be hard-pressed to find any business analyst who doesn't use or interact with Excel in some manner. One reason for Excel's popularity is that it is a very easy tool with which to get started. Its intuitive user interface simply requires the user to enter some data in some cells and perhaps add a few formulas. The results are immediate and understandable.

The purpose of this book is to help the beginning Excel user move beyond the basics and become more comfortable with some of Excel's more complex features. The focus is on helping the business analyst use Excel as a data analysis tool. The full realm of Excel features is considered. Besides the commonly used tactic of entering numbers and formulas in cells, special emphasis is given to the use of Excel tables, charts, pivot tables, and pivot charts. We also emphasize procedures that allow you to interact with external data, whether that is with text files or your entire corporate database.

Topics and Features

The topics in this book are many and varied, but in essence, we'll focus on one main objective:

- How to use Excel to analyze data

Our definition of data analysis includes the ability to summarize and manipulate data, but excludes the use of advanced quantitative analysis.

With this objective in mind, we'll emphasize the following aspects of Excel:

- Performing calculations with formulas and functions
- Creating pivot tables to summarize and interact with data
- Representing data via charts and graphs
- Interacting with external data

We assume no prior knowledge of Microsoft Excel. In other words, this is an introductory book on Excel, but one that focuses on topics that will be useful for the business or data analyst.

A number of features make this book unique among Excel books:

- **The emphasis is on data analysis**

  Microsoft Excel can be used to store data, analyze data, and then present data to other individuals. Our emphasis is on using Excel's various features to analyze data. We spend relatively little time on storing data, since that is best left to desktop databases such as Microsoft Access.

- **Pivot tables are covered extensively**

  Most introductory books on Excel give little or no mention to pivot tables. For the business analyst, however, the pivot table is an essential tool that allows you to easily interact with your data and gather quick summaries of what it contains. We therefore cover this important topic early in the book and devote two full chapters to its use.

- **The visual representation of data is discussed**

  Our interest in data analysis includes the use of charts and pivot charts to explore and represent data via purely visual means. In doing so, we provide tips on how to select the right chart type for your data. We also explore the visual aspects of using pivot tables. By utilizing the many layout options for pivot tables, we'll show you how to arrange your data to create the clearest possible presentation.

- **You will not be required to sit with a computer as you read the text**

  It will not be necessary to download data or run through exercises as you read the text. The text includes small data samples that allow you to understand how Excel works simply by reading the book.

With our emphasis on data analysis, several topics receive little or no mention. These include:

- Installation
- Visual Basic and Macros
- Inferential Statistics
- Trigonometric and Engineering Functions

When statistics is discussed, we will cover much of what is referred to as descriptive statistics, and very little of inferential statistics. This means that, while we discuss ways to use statistics to summarize data via counts, averages, sums, and percentiles, we won't cover the more complex mathematics that are involved in inferring results for a population from sample data. Similarly, we'll stay away from the more complex mathematical functions, such as those involving trigonometry or matrix arrays. Finally, we won't cover Excel add-ins that are available only with Office Professional Plus versions of Excel, such as PowerPivot and Inquire.

Excel 2013 has many exciting enhancements over what was available in Excel 2010. New features of Excel 2013 that are covered in this book include:

- Data models and relationships
- Pivot table drill down and drill up commands
- Pivot table timelines
- Table slicers
- Flash fill

Of particular note is the new capability of Excel 2013 to establish relationships between multiple data sets to create a data model. This feature, once available only through the PowerPivot add-in, allows the analyst to combine the data from multiple tables in a single pivot table or pivot chart.

Plan of the Book

This book presents its material in a unique sequence. The majority of Excel texts run through their topics with an early and primary emphasis on understanding worksheets and cells, and how to create formulas for worksheet cells. Those topics are covered in this book, but they are left to the later chapters. After providing a conceptual overview of Excel, we start right off with ways to summarize data with tables, pivot tables, and pivot charts. Only after covering summarization techniques do we delve into the more detailed task of using functions to further analyze data.

The 14 chapters in this book are organized and sequenced as follows:

Chapters 1 and 2 provide an overview of Excel. Chapter 1 focuses on a conceptual overview as it briefly describes Excel's main components and how they relate to each other. This provides the big picture of how Excel worksheets, cells, pivot tables, and charts relate to each other. Chapter 2 gets more specific, as it covers the Excel user interface and begins to explore basic functionality of the more important commands on the Ribbon.

Chapter 3 focuses on interactions with external data. After discussing basic ways to import text files and data from databases, we place considerable emphasis on Microsoft Query—an important tool within Excel that allows you to extract data from multiple tables in external databases, and bring that data into Excel for analysis.

Chapters 4 through 7 discuss Excel tables, pivot tables, and pivot charts. Chapter 4 shows how you can use Excel tables to filter and sort data. Chapters 5 and 6 cover pivot tables in detail. This all-important tool allows you to interact with and present data in an intuitive and flexible manner. Chapter 5 explains the basics of the pivot table interface, and Chapter 6 discusses advanced calculation and summarization options. Chapter 7 covers charts and pivot charts, with emphasis given to pivot charts. We discuss the various chart types and layout options to enable your data to become easily understandable with a visual representation.

Chapters 8 and 9 return the focus to worksheets and cells. Chapter 8 discusses the general ways in which data can be organized in worksheets, via sorting, filtering, and grouping. Chapter 9 presents the basics of how to specify relative or absolute references to cells, and the fundamentals of using formulas and functions. It also covers the Name Manager—an important tool for referencing arrays of cells with your own names, thus simplifying the task of creating and understanding formulas.

Chapters 10 through 13 are all about Excel functions. These chapters cover, respectively, text, numeric and date, aggregate and statistical, and logical and lookup functions. Through the use of numerous examples, you'll gain practical knowledge of how to apply the most useful of these functions to your analysis work.

Finally, Chapter 14 discusses a number of Data Analysis tools that address different types of analysis problems. Three of the tools—Data Tables, the Scenario Manager, and Goal Seek—offer powerful what-if functionality. Two of the tools—Data Analysis and Solver—are Excel add-ins that assist with statistical and optimization analysis.

Companion Website Download

Although we do not require you to utilize any data files while reading the book, we do provide one Excel workbook that may be of interest to those who want to experiment with the data referenced in this book. The workbook contains numerous worksheets that correspond to some of the figures in this book. Again, it's not at all necessary to download this file. It is provided solely as a convenience. The file can be found at www.cengageptr.com/downloads. Once on that site, you can find the file by searching for the author or title.

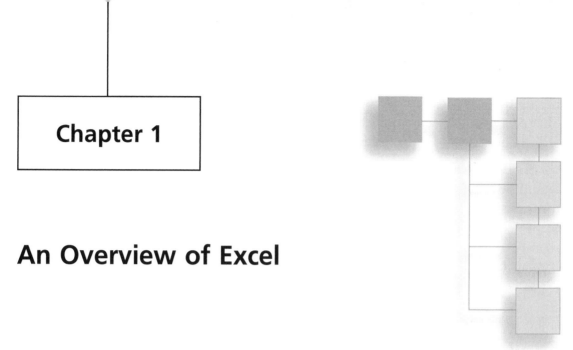

Chapter 1

An Overview of Excel

As the most widely used spreadsheet in the world, Microsoft Excel holds a unique position in the realm of business analysis. With its ubiquitous presence on innumerable laptops and desktops, Excel is nearly indispensable as a tool for the analysis of data. Furthermore, as the de facto spreadsheet standard, dozens of reporting tools and databases allow users to export data directly into Excel, allowing it to serve as a complementary counterpart to numerous other software packages.

The idea of a spreadsheet burst on the scene back in 1979, with the invention of Visi-Calc for the Apple II by Dan Bricklin. VisiCalc formulated the concept of a rectangular array of cells in which individual cells are identified by numbered rows and lettered columns, and which may contain formulas that reference other cell addresses.

The popularity of VisiCalc was quickly superseded by Lotus 1-2-3 when it was introduced in 1983. Lotus 1-2-3 introduced numerous improvements to the spreadsheet model, including the ability to create charts and formulate a rudimentary database. Over time, Lotus 1-2-3 found its way to the dustbin of software history, and was eventually replaced by Microsoft Excel, which was first introduced for the Macintosh computer in 1985, and then for Microsoft Windows in 1987.

Excel Components

Loaded with features, Microsoft Excel is like the Swiss army knife of computer software. As one of the most complex pieces of software ever devised, Excel comprises a number of components, each serving its own purpose and with a unique user interface.

In addition to the basic arrangement of cells into rows and columns, there are numerous other elements in Excel to consider, such as charts, tables, and pivot tables. In addition, Excel interfaces with data in the outside world in numerous ways. For example, Excel can communicate with relational databases, text files, xml files, and OLAP cubes, just to name a few.

Our first objective, therefore, will be to provide an overview of Excel that discusses and illustrates its various components. Not only do we want to understand these elements separately, but we also want to grasp how they interact with each other. Each of these components will be discussed in depth in later chapters, but for now, we want to focus on the big picture. We'll begin our discussion with these five basic components of Excel:

- Cells
- Charts
- Tables
- Pivot Tables
- Pivot Charts

As a minor note, you might notice that pivot tables and pivot charts are referred to as PivotTables and PivotCharts in Excel. These are trademarked Microsoft terms for these components. We use the more generic terms, pivot tables and pivot charts, in this book.

Figure 1.1 illustrates how data can move between these five different components.

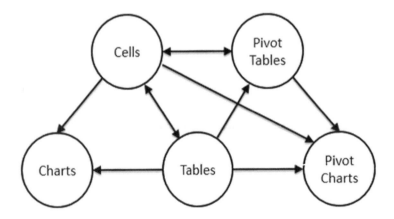

Figure 1.1
Excel components.
© 2014 Cengage Learning.

The arrows in Figure 1.1 indicate the flow of data. For example, the arrow pointing from tables to charts signifies that charts can be created from data in tables. The reverse, however, isn't true. Tables can't be created from charts. The double-sided arrow between cells and tables reveals that tables can be created from data in cells, and data in cells can be created from tables.

Most of the remainder of this chapter will introduce each of these five components. In brief, the cells component refers to the most commonly used feature of Excel, in which users can arrange data in an array of cells on a worksheet. These cells are referenced by row and column. In Excel nomenclature, a rectangular array of cells is usually referred to as a range. Tables can be created from a rectangular array of cells and provide some useful features with additional functionality. Pivot tables are a markedly different type of component, in which data can be arranged in a crosstab or matrix-type structure and manipulated by the user in an interactive manner. Pivot charts are related to pivot tables, in that they allow you to view the data in pivot tables in a graphical format. Charts have a similar appearance to pivot charts, but they are based on data in cells or tables.

The methods for converting data between these components will be covered later in this book. The important point for now is that each of these five components has distinct formats and interfaces.

Cells

Excel files are referred to as *workbooks*. Since the introduction of Excel 2007, Excel workbooks are normally given a suffix of *.xlsx*. Upon first opening Excel, one is immediately shown the basic element of Excel: a rectangular array of cells. Figure 1.2 shows the upper left corner of such an array.

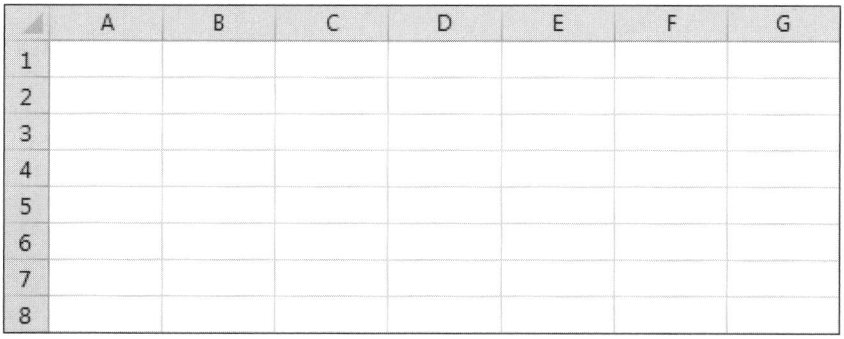

Figure 1.2
Array of cells.
Source: Microsoft® Corporation.

The array is composed of rows and columns, the rows being referred to by numbers and the columns by letters. Each cell in the array is identified by its row number and column letter. For example, B3 refers to the intersection of the second column (B) and the third row (3). The entire array of cells is referred to as a *worksheet*. Each worksheet can contain up to 1,048,576 rows and 16,384 columns. For the mathematically inclined, this is over 17 billion cells.

Each Excel workbook can contain any number of worksheets. In fact, there is no absolute maximum number of worksheets that an Excel workbook can include. The number of worksheets is limited only by the amount of available memory. By default, when a new Excel workbook is created, it will be made up of a single worksheet, named Sheet1. Worksheets can be identified and selected by tabs in the bottom left corner of the screen. Figure 1.3 displays this portion of the screen, revealing the worksheet of a new workbook. When a workbook contains more than one worksheet, additional tabs appear along the bottom, each with the name of a worksheet.

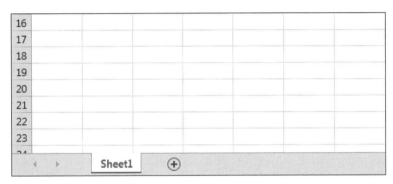

Figure 1.3

A worksheet.

Source: Microsoft® Corporation.

An Excel worksheet offers tremendous flexibility because each worksheet really consists of three overlapping layers: a data layer, a formula layer, and a presentation layer.

The data layer allows users to enter any desired value into a cell. For example, if you enter the value 52 in a cell, that cell holds that value and will normally display that number. Data in cells can be numeric or alphabetic.

The formula layer of a worksheet is what gives Excel its unique power and potential. The cleverness of formulas is derived from their ability to reference values in other cells. For example, at its most basic, a formula in cell E5 might contain the value:

   = C5

This means that the value of cell C5 is automatically copied to cell E5. Even more remarkably, these cell references are *relative*. This means that as new rows or columns are inserted into a worksheet, the references you already have in place continue to be valid. If you were to add a new row above row 5, what was in row 5 now becomes row 6, and all formulas are instantly adjusted. As a result, the above formula in cell E5 would now be found in cell E6 and would contain the value:

    = C6

In other words, all existing formulas continue to be valid as rows or columns are added or deleted.

Formulas can be much more complex than just a simple reference to another cell. For example, the following formula specifies to multiply the value of cell A2 by the value of cell B2, and then add 50 to the result:

    = (A2*B2) + 50

In addition, formulas can also invoke built-in functions to yield even more powerful calculations. For example, the following formula utilizes the SUM function to specify that the values in cells B1 through B25 should be added together:

    = SUM(B1…B25)

The data and formula layers of a worksheet allow you to enter values in any cells and create formulas from those values. The presentation layer takes the end result of the data and formulas and adds in visual elements. For example, you can specify that a cell contain a light green background with a red border. More significantly, you can define the format for numeric and data values. This means that you can stipulate that the numeric values in a particular cell always display with one decimal place, regardless of the true underlying value of the cell. That is, even if the value of a cell is 52.345, the presentation layer can result in a visual display of that data as 52.3.

The intricacies of formulas and functions will be covered much more fully in Chapters 9 through 13. Chapter 9 provides an overview of formulas and functions, including the important topic of the Name Manager, which lets you simplify your formulas by using meaningful names in place of cell references. Chapters 10 through 13 cover functions in detail. While we don't cover all of the more than 450 functions available in Excel, we discuss those functions that have the greatest value for the business analyst. Chapter 10 focuses on text functions, a class of functions that permits you to manipulate text within words and phrases. Chapter 11 covers numeric functions, allowing you to accomplish a wide variety of quantitative transformations. And we also cover date functions in this chapter. Interestingly, Excel stores dates as numbers but relies on the presentation layer of a worksheet to display dates in any of the usual formats. Chapter 12 discusses aggregate and statistical functions, providing the ability to summarize data in a wide variety of ways, from simple counts to additive sums to percentiles and standard deviations. Finally, Chapter 13 explains logical functions, a class of functions that can add a great deal of flexibility and power to your repertoire.

Tables

Data can be placed in worksheets in a completely free-form manner, with any type of data in any cell, without regard to how it relates to anything else. As we mentioned, cells can contain either raw data or formulas. Furthermore, data entered in cells can be a meaningful value or merely a comment or heading. Consider the worksheet shown in Figure 1.4.

	A	B
1	Meals	
2		
3	Date	
4	5/1/2014	had cereal for breakfast (150 calories), turkey for lunch (300 calories)
5		and a salad for dinner (500 calories)
6	5/2/2014	had eggs for breakfast (200 calories), salad for lunch (300 calories)
7		and hamburger for dinner (600 calories)
8	5/3/2014	ate same foods as yesterday

Figure 1.4
Unstructured data in a worksheet.
Source: Microsoft® Corporation.

This worksheet has a mixture of data, informal information, and comments. The values in cells A3 through A8 provide information on the date of each entry. The value "Date" in cell A3 is header information, and the values in cells A4 through A8 contain the actual dates. The data in cells B4 through B8 is much more informal, merely relating some information on what happened during each day of the diet. Cell A1 is an additional comment, stating the topic of the entire worksheet.

As seen, this data is relatively unstructured. With a little effort, however, this worksheet can be reorganized into an arrangement that looks like Figure 1.5:

	A	B	C	D	E	F	G
1	Date	Breakfast	Lunch	Dinner	Breakfast Calories	Lunch Calories	Dinner Calories
2	5/1/2014	cereal	turkey	salad	150	300	500
3	5/2/2014	eggs	salad	hamburger	200	300	600
4	5/3/2014	eggs	salad	hamburger	200	300	600

Figure 1.5
Data arranged into an array.
Source: Microsoft® Corporation.

Notice a number of significant changes. First, we removed all the unnecessary comments. We restructured the data so it appears in a neatly organized array of cells where different attributes are placed in separate columns. The information and measurements for each day of the diet appears in a single row. The first row contains the names of the attributes, and all subsequent rows contain data values. To make the data easier to understand, we've utilized the presentation layer of the worksheet to apply a bold font to the first row. This convention clearly identifies the first row as header information for the array of data.

As for the columns, the first column, Date, uniquely identifies each row. The subsequent columns provide data on the various attributes of the diet, such as breakfast, lunch, and so on. Notice that we've separated the item eaten for breakfast from the number of calories consumed during breakfast, placing them into different columns.

This arrangement of data into an array of rows and columns is the standard and preferred method to represent a set of data. In Excel terminology, such an arrangement of data is referred to as a *range*. It must be said, however, that the convention of placing attributes in columns and entities or events in rows is somewhat arbitrary. For example, we might have represented the same data as shown in Figure 1.6.

	A	B	C	D
1	Date	5/1/2014	5/2/2014	5/3/2014
2	Breakfast	cereal	eggs	eggs
3	Lunch	turkey	salad	salad
4	Dinner	salad	hamburger	hamburger
5	Breakfast Calories	150	200	200
6	Lunch Calories	300	300	300
7	Dinner Calories	500	600	600

Figure 1.6

An alternate arrangement of the same array of data.

Source: Microsoft® Corporation.

Figure 1.6 presents the same data as Figure 1.5, but with attributes in the rows and data values in the columns. Rather than four rows and seven columns, we now see the data transposed into seven rows and four columns. Although technically accurate, this is not the preferred way to present tabular data. The convention is to lay out data as in Figure 1.5.

At this point, it must also be said that there is yet another way to display this set of data. In Figure 1.5, each row contains information about what occurred on a single day.

Another alternative would be to present the data with one row per meal. This configuration appears in Figure 1.7:

	A	B	C	D
1	Date	Meal	Food	Calories
2	5/1/2014	Breakfast	cereal	150
3	5/1/2014	Lunch	turkey	300
4	5/1/2014	Dinner	salad	500
5	5/2/2014	Breakfast	eggs	200
6	5/2/2014	Lunch	salad	300
7	5/2/2014	Dinner	hamburger	600
8	5/3/2014	Breakfast	eggs	200
9	5/3/2014	Lunch	salad	300
10	5/3/2014	Dinner	hamburger	600

Figure 1.7
An array of data with one row per meal.
Source: Microsoft® Corporation.

The advantage of this arrangement of data is that it reduces the number of attributes. As such, we consider this a preferable way to present this data. In Figure 1.5, there was one row per day. The Date value in column A defined the date. There were six attributes for each date: Breakfast, Lunch, Dinner, Breakfast Calories, Lunch Calories, and Dinner Calories. In contrast, the array of data shown in Figure 1.7 has one row per meal. The specific meal is defined by the date in column A and the meal in column B. We now have only two attributes: the food eaten (in column C) and the number of calories for the meal (in column D).

Once we have data as shown in Figure 1.7, it is a simple matter to convert that set of data into an entity that Excel calls a *table*. Excel tables have been designed to offer capabilities similar to tables in full-fledged databases. To sidetrack for a moment into the broader topic of databases, the type of software known as *relational databases* allow one to organize data into distinct entities known as *tables*. The common custom is to create tables to represent entities that are of interest to an organization, such as customers, products, sales, and so on. Each table is defined with any number of attributes, and can hold information about instances of those attributes. By convention, the attributes are referred to as *columns* and the instances are called *rows*. For example, a table named Customers might have attributes such as Name, Age, and Sex. Each row in the table would represent a different customer. When portrayed visually, the rows and columns of each table are displayed, as expected, into vertical columns and horizontal rows.

As a repository for data, relational databases typically allow users to access that data via a computer language called SQL, short for *structured query language*. This lingua franca of relational databases allows the user to access data in a highly efficient and logical manner. In fact, SQL allows the user to retrieve large amounts of data from multiple tables with a single query.

As an Excel user, it's important to understand the ways in which Excel complements and sometimes requires interaction with relational databases. Although data can be stored entirely within Excel workbooks, an organization's data is often stored in a relational database. Fortunately, Excel provides a tool called Microsoft Query that allows Excel users to retrieve data directly from external databases. This tool will be discussed in Chapter 3.

Returning to our discussion of Excel tables, this component allows us to store and access data in ways similar to the tables found in full-fledged relational databases. As in relational databases, Excel tables assume that data is laid out in a rectangular array, with attributes in columns and entity instances in rows. Figure 1.7 portrays data in this type of layout.

With a single command, Excel can transform the data shown in Figure 1.7 into an object referred to as a table. After it's turned into a table, the data appears as in Figure 1.8.

	A	B	C	D
1	Date	Meal	Food	Calories
2	5/1/2014	Breakfast	cereal	150
3	5/1/2014	Lunch	turkey	300
4	5/1/2014	Dinner	salad	500
5	5/2/2014	Breakfast	eggs	200
6	5/2/2014	Lunch	salad	300
7	5/2/2014	Dinner	hamburger	600
8	5/3/2014	Breakfast	eggs	200
9	5/3/2014	Lunch	salad	300
10	5/3/2014	Dinner	hamburger	600

Figure 1.8

An Excel table.

Source: Microsoft® Corporation.

Notice that the column names in row 1 are now highlighted, indicating a header row that names each attribute. Furthermore, each cell in row 1 now has a drop-down indicator that, when selected, brings up additional functionality for that column. When any of the drop-downs in row 1 are selected, it displays a set of additional filter and sort commands that allow you to filter or sort the data in the table based on values in that column. For example, one could choose to view only rows where the meal was breakfast. The data would then appear as in Figure 1.9.

	A	B	C	D
1	Date ▼	Meal ▼	Food ▼	Calories ▼
2	5/1/2014	Breakfast	cereal	150
5	5/2/2014	Breakfast	eggs	200
8	5/3/2014	Breakfast	eggs	200

Figure 1.9
Table with a filter.
Source: Microsoft® Corporation.

The result of the filter is that we see only the data in rows 2, 5, and 8. The data in the other rows is still in the worksheet. However, we have temporarily chosen not to view them. The functionality of tables will be covered in detail in Chapter 4, but for now, the main point is that tables provide functionality that allows the user to manipulate tabular data in an interactive manner.

Looking back at Figure 1.1, we can see that tables can be created from data in cells. The opposite is also true. Data in a table can also be converted back into an array of cells. Tables can also be converted into pivot tables, which is the next component to be discussed.

Pivot Tables

Excel tables represent data in a rectangular array, where attributes are in columns and instances of the entity are in rows. By using filtering, we can choose to view or hide rows. However, we can't view or hide columns in a similar manner. In a sense, the presentation of data is fairly static; there are only a limited number of ways that data can be manipulated.

Pivot tables hugely extend the potential for data manipulation over what can be done with simple tables. Pivot tables are like tables on steroids. First introduced with Microsoft Excel 5 in 1993, pivot tables allow one to view data in a completely flexible and interactive fashion. Let's illustrate by using the data in Figure 1.8 and presenting that same data as it might appear in a pivot table. Figure 1.10 shows the result.

Date	Meal	Food	Sum of Calories
5/1/2014	Breakfast	cereal	150
	Dinner	salad	500
	Lunch	turkey	300
5/2/2014	Breakfast	eggs	200
	Dinner	hamburger	600
	Lunch	salad	300
5/3/2014	Breakfast	eggs	200
	Dinner	hamburger	600
	Lunch	salad	300

Figure 1.10

A pivot table.

Source: Microsoft® Corporation.

One key feature of a pivot table is its ability to let users arrange the fields in any desired manner. Notice that Figure 1.10 doesn't include the usual column and row labels seen in the previous figures. This is because the creation and manipulation of a pivot table isn't accomplished with formulas in cells. Instead, when a pivot table is first created, one is presented with a special "PivotTable Fields" pane that lets the user arrange the available fields as desired, in the various areas of a pivot table. Figure 1.11 shows the PivotTable Fields pane that corresponds to the data in Figure 1.10.

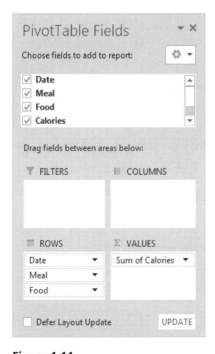

Figure 1.11

PivotTable Fields.

Source: Microsoft® Corporation.

In this example, the four available fields are: Date, Meal, Food, and Calories. We've chosen to place the Date, Meal, and Food fields in the *Rows* area of the pivot table, and Calories in the *Values* area. We've placed nothing in the *Columns* or *Filters* areas of the pivot table. As a result, we've created a hierarchical structure in the rows, showing us the meals that fall under each date, and the foods that were eaten during each meal. Calories are displayed in their own column.

Notice how interactive the presentation of data is in pivot tables compared to tables. In regular tables, the number of rows displayed is determined by the selection specified by the table filters. However, the columns displayed are predetermined and static. In contrast, pivot tables dynamically determine both the rows and columns that need to be displayed, based on filtering and the type of layout that's specified.

When using pivot tables, the way in which data is displayed is very fluid. With one quick adjustment, we can rearrange the layout of the pivot table by moving the Date field to the columns area. The result is shown in Figure 1.12.

Sum of Calories		Date		
Meal	Food	5/1/2014	5/2/2014	5/3/2014
Breakfast	cereal	150		
	eggs		200	200
Dinner	hamburger		600	600
	salad	500		
Lunch	salad		300	300
	turkey	300		

Figure 1.12
Alternate arrangement of pivot table.
Source: Microsoft® Corporation.

In this arrangement, the data for our three dates appears in separate columns. The numbers displayed are the same. Only the layout has changed.

In a sense, the arrangement of fields in Figures 1.10 and 1.12 is fairly routine. The true power of pivot tables becomes more apparent when we arrange the fields as shown in Figure 1.13.

Date	Sum of Calories
5/1/2014	950
5/2/2014	1100
5/3/2014	1100

Figure 1.13
Alternate arrangement of pivot table.
Source: Microsoft® Corporation.

In Figure 1.13, we've chosen to place the Date field in the rows area of the pivot table. Once again, the Calories field is in the values area. However, we've left the Meal and Food fields completely out of the pivot table. This provides a more summarized view of the data, with the pivot table showing us the total calories consumed on each date. Notice that data is automatically summed up for us. We didn't need to enter any formulas or do anything special to sum up the data. The pivot table does the summation automatically.

In Figure 1.13, we summed up the data by date. If we wanted to sum the calories by meal, we can simply replace the Date field with the Meal field. The result is shown in Figure 1.14.

Meal	▼	Sum of Calories
Breakfast		550
Dinner		1700
Lunch		900

Figure 1.14

Alternate arrangement of pivot table.

Source: Microsoft® Corporation.

We now see how many calories were consumed during each meal, irrespective of day.

This brief illustration has only touched on some of the possibilities and features of pivot tables. This topic will be covered in depth in Chapters 5 and 6.

Charts and Pivot Charts

Just as pivot tables add a dynamic element to the more static portrayal of data in cells, Excel charts and pivot charts add an interesting visual element to the portrayal of data, transforming a bunch of numbers into a visual presentation that can be understood at a more intuitive level. Excel charts can be created from either an array of cells or from tables. Excel pivot charts can be created from an array of cells, tables, or pivot tables.

Although charts and pivot charts have a similar appearance, their means of manipulating data is quite different. Like cells and tables, regular charts are quite static. After they're initially created, it takes a bit of work to alter the display of the chart. In contrast, pivot charts make use of a PivotChart Fields pane similar to the PivotTable Fields pane previously seen in Figure 1.11. Thus, just like pivot tables, the elements in a pivot chart can be easily rearranged after creation.

One aspect of pivot charts not apparent in our depiction of Excel components in Figure 1.1 is that pivot charts are always coupled with pivot tables. If, for example, one creates a pivot chart from data in cells or a table, Excel will also create a pivot table at the same time. In other words, pivot charts don't exist apart from pivot tables. When fields are manipulated in a PivotTable Field List for a pivot chart, that interaction also affects the associated pivot table.

Let's illustrate with a pivot chart that has been created directly from the pivot table seen in Figure 1.10. The result is shown in Figure 1.15.

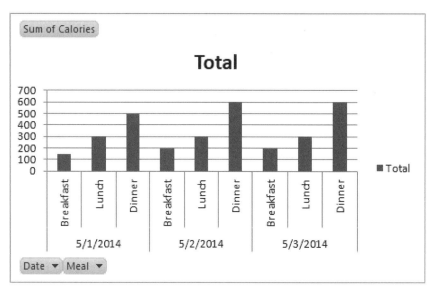

Figure 1.15

A pivot chart.

Source: Microsoft® Corporation.

In creating this pivot chart, a few minor adjustments were made. First, we modified the labels so Dinner appears after Lunch. Pivot tables and pivot charts normally display items in alphabetical order, unless otherwise altered. In a visual representation, it would be somewhat confusing to list Dinner before Lunch.

Second, we chose to remove the Food field from the pivot chart. We're only displaying Date, Meal, and Calories. We've elected to place Date and Meal in the rows area of the pivot chart. We mentioned that pivot charts use the PivotChart Field List similar to that used in pivot tables. However, there's one minor difference. Whereas pivot tables lay out fields in rows and columns, pivot charts refer to rows as categories, and columns as series.

Pivot charts offer the same flexibility and interactive capabilities of pivot tables. With one quick adjustment, we can make this chart more appealing by moving the Meal field from the categories area to the series area of the pivot chart. The result is shown in Figure 1.16.

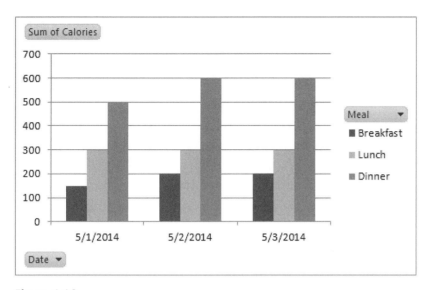

Figure 1.16

A rearranged pivot chart.

Source: Microsoft® Corporation.

To further illustrate the ease with which pivot charts can be modified, let's make one more adjustment. Pivot charts can be designed in over 40 different chart types. The pivot chart shown in Figure 1.16 is called a Clustered Column chart. With a simple modification, we can transform this to a Stacked Column chart type, shown in Figure 1.17.

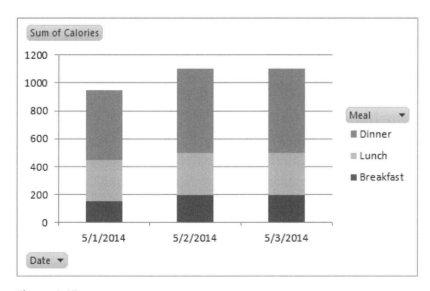

Figure 1.17

A pivot chart with stacked columns.

Source: Microsoft® Corporation.

As a Stacked Column pivot chart, we can now perceive this data with greater insight. The data has been visually compressed into three columns. Each column shows the distribution of calories consumed during that day. We can see the relative distribution of calories by each meal, as well as the total number of calories consumed during each day.

The prior three charts were all pivot charts. It's entirely possible to create similar representations as a standard chart on a worksheet. To illustrate with one example, we'll create a chart that's the equivalent of the pivot chart shown in Figure 1.15. The pivot chart of Figure 1.15 was created from the pivot table of Figure 1.10. However, standard charts can't be created from pivot charts. They can only be created from a range of data in cells, or from tables. Therefore, we'll go back to the table shown in Figure 1.8 and use that as the source for our chart. Keep in mind that this table was also the source for the pivot table of Figure 1.10.

Figure 1.18 shows a chart created from the table of Figure 1.8.

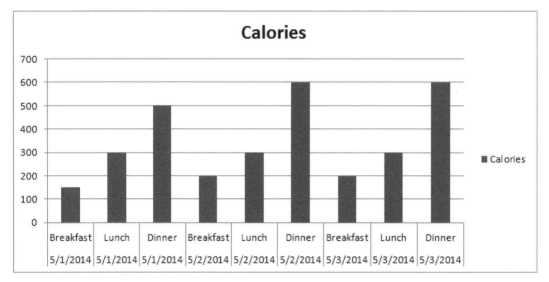

Figure 1.18
An Excel chart.
Source: Microsoft® Corporation.

In comparing the chart of Figure 1.18 to the pivot chart of Figure 1.15, we can observe that the basic presentation is nearly identical. The only differences are with some of the labels. More significantly, though, the ability to modify this chart further is substantially more complex than would be the case if this were a pivot chart. The intricacies of charts and pivot charts will be covered in detail in Chapter 7.

External Data

Thus far, we have placed some data on an Excel worksheet and then transformed that data into tables, pivot tables, charts, and pivot charts. All data started with and remained within Excel. However, in the real world of the business analyst, very often the data will either originate from an external source or be moved to an external location after analysis is accomplished in Excel.

Therefore, in addition to understanding Excel components and the relationships between them, we must also consider how those components relate with data outside of Excel. Figure 1.19 expands on Figure 1.1 to indicate how external data can interact with Excel.

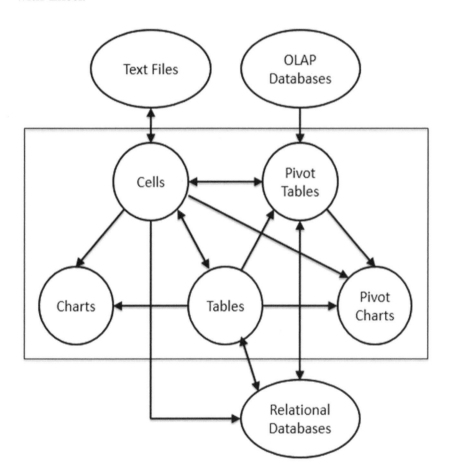

Figure 1.19

Excel components and external data.

© 2014 Cengage Learning.

The large rectangle in Figure 1.19 indicates the boundaries of Excel. The five components within the rectangle were previously shown in Figure 1.1. The three types of data placed outside the rectangle exist apart from Excel. Note that these three indicated data types are not an exhaustive list. Numerous other types of external data can interact with Excel. However, we consider text files, OLAP databases, and relational databases to be the most significant and widely used types of external data.

Of these three external data types, text files are the simplest. Text files can be imported into Excel as an array of cells or exported out from cells in a worksheet. Text files are simple devices that allow us to store data without a lot of fuss. It's merely a matter of storing an array of data as text. Each row of text represents one row in the array. Special characters, referred to as delimiters, are used to delineate the separation of data into columns. For example, one might have a text file with these rows of data:

```
FirstName,LastName,City,State
John,Smith,Cincinnati,OH
Becky,Gold,Akron,OH
Colin,Harwood,Philadelphia,PA
```

This data represents three individuals, indicating their first name, last name, city, and state. The first row provides column names. If this text file is imported into Excel, it will be placed into the normal arrangement of cells, as shown in Figure 1.20.

◢	A	B	C	D
1	FirstName	LastName	City	State
2	John	Smith	Cincinnati	OH
3	Becky	Gold	Honolulu	HI
4	Colin	Harwood	Philadelphia	PA

Figure 1.20
Excel data imported from a text file.
Source: Microsoft® Corporation.

Our second external data type, the relational database, is considerably more complex. In our discussion earlier in this chapter, we mentioned that relational databases are sophisticated structures that store data in any number of tables. Unlike text files, which can only be imported into worksheet cells, data in relational databases can be moved to either Excel tables or pivot tables.

When data is moved from a relational database to a table or pivot table, the usual procedure is to transfer one table at a time. However, Excel provides a powerful tool called Microsoft Query that allows users to retrieve data from multiple tables at once, and import that data into Excel. This is accomplished by formulating SQL statements that join relational tables together on common elements. These queries also permit the user to summarize data prior to its being imported into Excel. Microsoft Query will be covered in detail in Chapter 3.

In addition to importing data from relational databases, one can reverse the process and export certain types of data out of Excel into a table in a relational database. This is generally done from within the external database. For example, Microsoft Access includes commands that allow you to import data from Excel into Access. From Access, one can import Excel data that resides in Excel tables and pivot tables. Additionally, one can import Excel elements called *named ranges* into Access tables. Named ranges are an array of cells in an Excel worksheet that have been given a specific name. Named ranges will be covered later in Chapter 9.

Figure 1.21 shows an example of a table in an Access database that was created by importing the data from Excel. In this particular example, we've imported the data seen in Figure 1.20.

FirstName	LastName	City	State
John	Smith	Cincinnati	OH
Becky	Gold	Honolulu	HI
Colin	Harwood	Philadelphia	PA

Customer Table

Figure 1.21
An Access table imported from Excel.
Source: Microsoft® Corporation.

Notice the difference in appearance between the Excel data of Figure 1.20 and the same data in Access in Figure 1.21. Whereas Excel relies on column letters and row numbers to identify intersecting cells, Access merely names each column with an appropriate label. For example, the first column in the Access table is named FirstName. The data in each of the three rows is not uniquely identifiable by a cell name. Instead, Access uses the language of SQL to select and manipulate data. For the casual Access user, SQL operates strictly behind the scenes. Access users generally rely on its graphical interface to generate SQL statements for them automatically. As an example, the following SQL statement in Access selects the same data that was found in cell C3 in Figure 1.20.

```
SELECT City
FROM 'Customer Table'
WHERE LastName = 'Gold'
```

In both cases, the value of C3 in Excel and the result of the above SQL query is the value "Honolulu."

The differences between manipulating data in Excel worksheets and Access databases should be emphasized. In Excel worksheets, data items are identified by the column letter and row number. Formulas can be applied to any cell to further select and modify data. Users can also create multiple worksheets in a single Excel workbook to organize data in any desired manner.

The process of entering data in individual Excel cells and creating formulas to alter that data is somewhat of a manual process. In contrast, Access provides far greater capabilities in terms of organizing data. As a relational database, data in Access can be separated into any number of related tables. Users can create queries that can retrieve, modify, or delete data from multiple tables. Queries also provide built-in functions that allow you to summarize data.

Whereas Access offers numerous ways to organize data, Excel's strong suit is in its far greater capabilities with respect to functions. Thus, even though the Excel data of Figure 1.20 and the Access data in Figure 1.21 are identical, the constructs of Access and Excel result in different capabilities of what you can do with the data.

The final external data type that we'll discuss are OLAP (online analytical processing) databases. Also referred to as cubes, OLAP databases are special structures that reorganize an underlying relational database into elements known as *dimensions* and *facts*. In this data structure, facts are summable quantities, and dimensions present ways to view those facts. For example, an OLAP database might allow one to view sales facts by several dimensions, such as customer, product, or geography. Whereas a physical cube has three dimensions, a multi-dimensional OLAP database (also called a cube) can have any number of dimensions.

The usual procedure in creating an OLAP database is to first organize the underlying relational database into dimension and fact tables. Earlier in this chapter, we mentioned that the data in relational databases is usually organized into tables that represent the important entities in an organization, such as customers, products, and orders. The process of designing a relational database in such a manner is referred to as *normalization*. In contrast, a relational database (or data warehouse) that has been organized into dimension and fact tables has a somewhat different structure. The process of converting *normalized* relational databases into a structure with dimensions and fact tables is known as *denormalization*.

In a denormalized database, fact tables hold quantitative values that can be summed. Dimension tables hold information about broad entities. Once the denormalized relational database has been built, an OLAP database can be defined and created by referencing that database. It should be emphasized that OLAP databases usually exist completely apart from the underlying relational database.

OLAP databases generally feature a special *time dimension*. This defines attributes that allow users to perform calculations specific to time, such as being able to compare the same month across two fiscal years.

To give an example of the difference between a normalized relational database and an OLAP database, let's say that we have a collection of data about customers, the orders they place, and the products they can purchase.

In a normalized relational database, one might separate this information into these four tables:

- Customer
- Product
- Order Header
- Order Detail

The Customer table would contain attributes about each customer. The Products table defines the various products that are sold. The Order Header table has summary information about the order, such as the Customer ID and total tax. The Order Detail table has information about each item sold in the order, such as the Product ID and the quantity sold.

In an OLAP database, the same data might be organized into these elements:

- Customer Dimension
- Product Dimension
- Time Dimension
- Sales Facts

The characteristic of OLAP databases that makes them particularly compatible with Excel is that these dimension and fact elements correspond nicely with the areas of Excel pivot tables. In Figure 1.11, we saw that the four main areas of pivot tables are report filters, rows, columns, and values. When Excel pivot tables are connected to an OLAP cube, all of the fields in the cube are organized and displayed as belonging to the dimensions and facts that are defined in the cube. In other words, the structure of the cube is clearly portrayed in the pivot table. The dimension fields can be moved into the filter, rows, or columns areas of the pivot table. The facts of the cube can be moved into the values area of the pivot table. All of the normal features of pivot tables, such as the ability to drill down from summary to detail data, correspond nicely to the way that cubes are defined.

When a pivot table is connected to an OLAP cube rather than to a normal Excel worksheet or relational data, the pivot table can exhibit some additional functionality that doesn't ordinarily appear. This includes predefined hierarchies that may be defined in cube dimensions, and special formulas that may be defined in the underlying cube. Figure 1.22 gives an idea of what this can look like.

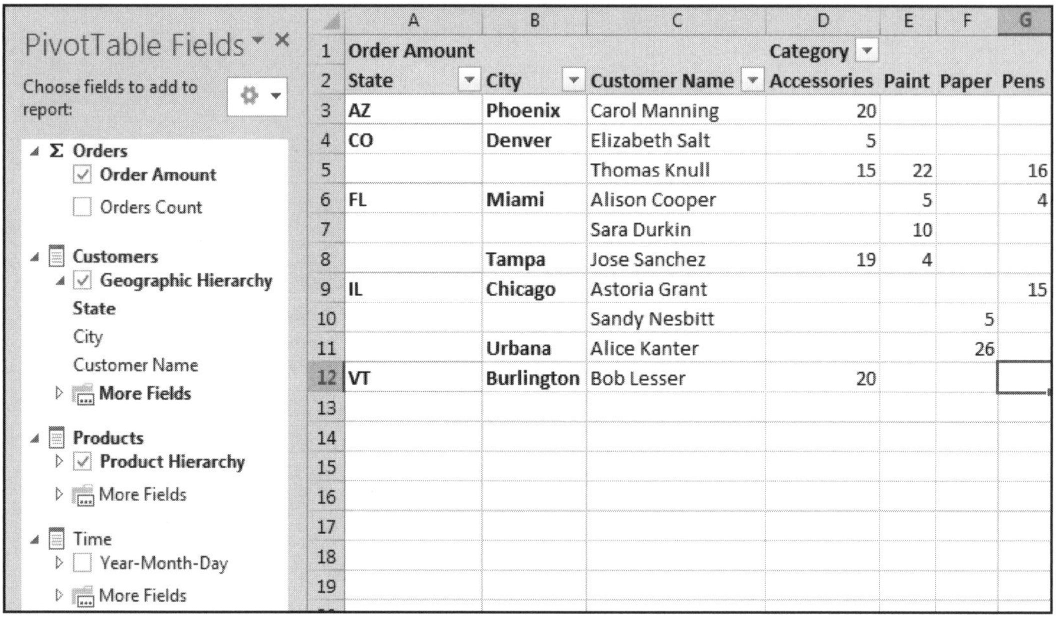

		A	B	C	D	E	F	G
	1	Order Amount			Category ▾			
	2	State ▾	City ▾	Customer Name ▾	Accessories	Paint	Paper	Pens
	3	AZ	Phoenix	Carol Manning	20			
	4	CO	Denver	Elizabeth Salt	5			
	5			Thomas Knull	15	22		16
	6	FL	Miami	Alison Cooper		5		4
	7			Sara Durkin		10		
	8		Tampa	Jose Sanchez	19	4		
	9	IL	Chicago	Astoria Grant				15
	10			Sandy Nesbitt			5	
	11		Urbana	Alice Kanter			26	
	12	VT	Burlington	Bob Lesser	20			
	13							
	14							
	15							
	16							
	17							
	18							
	19							

PivotTable Fields ▾ ✕

Choose fields to add to report: ✿ ▾

⊿ Σ Orders
  ☑ Order Amount
  ☐ Orders Count

⊿ ▦ Customers
  ⊿ ☑ Geographic Hierarchy
    State
    City
    Customer Name
  ▷ ▦ More Fields

⊿ ▦ Products
  ▷ ☑ Product Hierarchy
  ▷ ▦ More Fields

⊿ ▦ Time
  ▷ ☐ Year-Month-Day
  ▷ ▦ More Fields

Figure 1.22
A pivot table connected to an OLAP cube.
Source: Microsoft® Corporation.

Notice that the list of fields in the PivotTable Field List in the left pane is organized into a number of sections. The Orders section contains the facts of the cube. The cube also shows three dimensions: Customers, Products, and Time. Each of these dimensions can contain structures that organize the various attributes into predefined hierarchies that let you drill down into the data with ease.

OLAP cubes, dimensions, and facts are generally beyond the scope of this book. This is because the process of creating OLAP cubes takes place entirely outside of Excel, in tools such as Microsoft Analysis Services. We bring up the topic only to make you aware of some of the more advanced capabilities of Excel.

Add-Ins

In addition to the innumerable features present in Excel itself, Microsoft has allowed Excel to accept add-in software that extends its abilities. This book discusses two such add-ins that come shipped with Excel.

- Data Analysis
- Solver

The first of these, Data Analysis, extends the capability of Excel to perform statistical analysis. Excel provides nearly 100 functions that it classifies as statistical functions. We'll cover the more basic of these functions in Chapter 12, "Aggregate and Statistical Functions." The ability to use Excel as a working tool for statistical analysis is a topic that is beyond the scope of this book. Furthermore, most working statisticians prefer to use dedicated statistics tools for analysis, such as SAS (from SAS Institute) or SPSS (from IBM). However, the Data Analysis tool provides a somewhat more accessible view into the world of statistics for the average user.

Rather than rely on Excel's statistical functions, the Data Analysis add-in offers a self-contained statistical analysis tool that takes data from an Excel worksheet and produces statistical results. When invoked, the Data Analysis tool appears as in Figure 1.23.

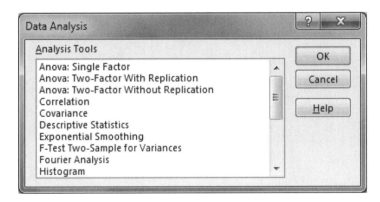

Figure 1.23
The Data Analysis add-in.
Source: Microsoft® Corporation.

Figure 1.24 shows some sample data and the selection of the Descriptive Statistics portion of the Data Analysis tool. In this selection, we're specifying the data in column B of the worksheet as the Input Range for the analysis.

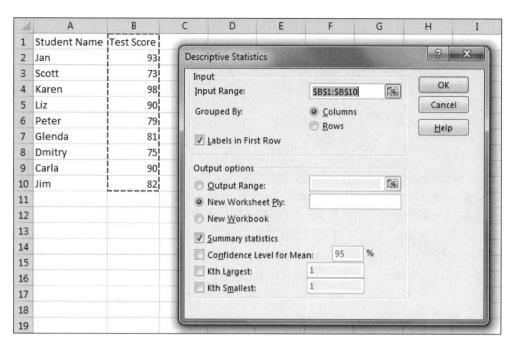

Figure 1.24
Descriptive Statistics selection.
Source: Microsoft® Corporation.

After clicking OK, a new worksheet is created with the data shown in Figure 1.25.

	A	B
1		*Test Score*
2		
3	Mean	84.55555556
4	Standard Error	2.853414675
5	Median	82
6	Mode	90
7	Standard Deviation	8.560244026
8	Sample Variance	73.27777778
9	Kurtosis	-1.237365526
10	Skewness	0.180991793
11	Range	25
12	Minimum	73
13	Maximum	98
14	Sum	761
15	Count	9

Figure 1.25
Descriptive Statistics results.
Source: Microsoft® Corporation.

These results give some basic descriptive statistics, such as the mean (or average), the median, and mode. It's important to note that these results do not interact with the underlying data in any way. If one were to change any of the data values in Figure 1.24, the statistics shown in Figure 1.25 would not change at all. In other words, the values calculated in the Data Analysis tool are simply a static snapshot. This is very different from what is available in Excel functions or pivot tables, which do interact with the underlying referenced data.

To sum up, the Data Analysis add-in provides some complex functionality that isn't easily obtainable via normal Excel functions. However, the downside is that the tool is not interactive. When the underlying data changes, the statistical results remain the same.

Like the Data Analysis add-in, the Solver add-in is another tool that provides complex quantitative calculations, but of a very different sort. The basic idea of the Solver is to analyze a set of data and provide a value that optimizes some desired goal. In mathematical terms, this type of analysis is known as *optimization*. For example, one might want to look at the various components used to manufacture a set of related products and determine how many of each product should be produced to maximize profits, given constraints that may exist on the availability of the various inputs. Or, one may want to calculate the schedules of restaurant employees in such a way as to minimize labor costs, given the needs of the business and the availability of each employee.

Like the Data Analysis add-in, the Solver takes data from an Excel worksheet and uses it to do its computations. However, the format in which data needs to be laid out in the underlying worksheet is considerably more complex.

Like statistical analysis, the mathematics utilized in the Solver require a high degree of knowledge and is not for the faint at heart. As such, this topic is generally beyond the scope of this book. However, we'll run through an example of using the Solver in Chapter 14, "Analysis Tools."

Data Analysis

Before delving further into Excel, we'd like to take a step back and present some thoughts about the nature of data analysis. When one asks what the business analyst hopes to accomplish when he or she looks at data, the following objectives might come to mind:

- To find meaning in the data
- To understand relationships between data elements

- To transform data into an interesting format for a presentation
- To make a specific decision or validate a decision already made

To be more concrete, the analyst might have a specific task to perform, such as:

- Compare the same data in different time periods to discover trends
- Drill down from summary data to the underlying detail
- Split or combine text data to put it in a more readable format
- Create subtotals and totals
- Apply financial formulas to data
- Use what-if analysis to determine ways to maximize profit

Looking at these objectives and tasks from the broadest perspective, we can observe that all of these activities involve transforming data in some way. To be more succinct, we can surmise that there are generally three different types of transformations involved:

- Data transformations
- Mathematical transformations
- Visual transformations

We might say that data analysis starts with raw data and involves modifying the structure of the data itself, applying any needed mathematics, and sometimes visualization, to obtain the end result. Earlier in this chapter, in our discussion of cells, we noted that Excel worksheets are composed of overlapping data, formula, and presentation layers. This corresponds to the data, mathematical, and visual transformations just mentioned. The genius of Excel is that it can address data, mathematical, and visual elements simultaneously, giving the analyst great flexibility in how data can be transformed.

Let's now talk about each of these three elements in a bit more detail. Data transformation can refer to any way that data is reorganized. It can be something as simple as combining a first and last name together to display a person's full name. Or, it might mean adding subtotals and totals rows to raw data. To these purposes, Excel has numerous tools that address data transformation. Chief among these is the pivot table—a method for quickly summarizing and transforming raw data. At the more micro level, Excel provides numerous functions that address the need to transform text to a different format. It must be said, however, that Excel has certain limitations when it comes to data transformation. Compared to database software such as

Microsoft Access, Excel is a less structured tool. In other words, the flexibility of Excel has a certain downside. Unlike Excel, Access allows the analyst to reorganize data in a more organized way. Whereas Excel structures its data into cells, worksheets, tables, and pivot tables, Access requires that all data first be placed in tables. After tables are defined, queries can be created that create views into one or more tables. We mentioned earlier that Access uses SQL, or structured query language, to retrieve data from its tables. This is all accomplished through Access's graphical user interface, so the user doesn't actually need to know SQL to use Access effectively. This gives the Access user the ability to transform and combine data in ways that are often simpler than what's available in Excel. For example, the task of combining data from two tables can be a daunting task in Excel. In Access, this is a simple procedure.

When it comes to mathematical transformation, however, Excel clearly outshines Access. With its more than 450 functions, many of which are quantitative, Excel offers many ways to apply the power of mathematics to data transformation. This includes counts, sums, and numerous statistics. Complex financial and statistical calculations are built into Excel via available functions. The pivot table provides a powerful means of quickly summing data in an easy to use interactive manner. Also, Excel provides a number of additional mathematical tools, such as its Data Analysis and Solver add-ins.

Visual transformation is addressed in Excel in numerous ways. Besides its obviously important charts and pivot chart tools, visualization plays a strong role in many other components. For example, there is an important visualization aspect to pivot tables besides its ability to summarize data. Looking again at Figures 1.10 and 1.12, we see that these two pivot tables present the same data in two different layouts. In Figure 1.10, the Date, Meal, and Food data items are in the rows area, with nothing in the columns area. In Figure 1.12, Meal and Food are in the rows, but Date has been moved to the columns area. The numbers in the two Figures are identical, but the two layouts lend a different level of understanding to each of the alternatives. Thus, the visual presentation of data is significant.

Looking Ahead

The intent of this chapter was to present a conceptual overview of Excel. From this bird's-eye height, we've seen that Excel can be thought of as consisting of five distinct components: cells, charts, tables, pivot tables, and pivot charts. Data can move freely between these components in various ways. For most users, the ability to calculate and manipulate data in individual cells is the prime reason for using Excel. The flexibility of relative cell references, combined with a plethora of available functions, provides substantial computing power, even for the average user. Of the remaining components, pivot tables are perhaps the most significant. Pivot tables provide a great deal of interactivity and allow users to directly manipulate data without having to resort to formulas or functions. Pivot charts are a close relation of pivot tables, allowing users to apply a visual element to their data.

We also looked at interactions between Excel and external data sources, such as text files, relational databases, and OLAP databases. In order to use Excel as an analysis tool, one generally has to first either import or connect to external data in some way. Finally, we looked at a number of important add-ins to Excel that increase the functionality of pivot tables and extend its quantitative analysis capabilities.

After wrapping up our discussion of these basic Excel components, we took a brief diversion to examine some general concepts related to data analysis. In our observation of the three major types of transformations—data, mathematical, and visual—we saw that each plays a role in the quest to create understanding from a mass of data. The objective of turning data into information is an old cliché, but one which nevertheless is fundamental to the task of the business analyst. In this endeavor, it's useful to distinguish between the various methods of data, mathematical, and visual transformations.

Although this chapter has purported to be an overview of Excel, we've actually said very little about the mechanics of getting around in the software. In our next chapter, we'll focus on important elements of the Excel user interface, including worksheets, cells, and the Ribbon. This will allow us to move from concepts to practice, as we begin to understand some of the specifics of how to accomplish a number of basic tasks in Excel.

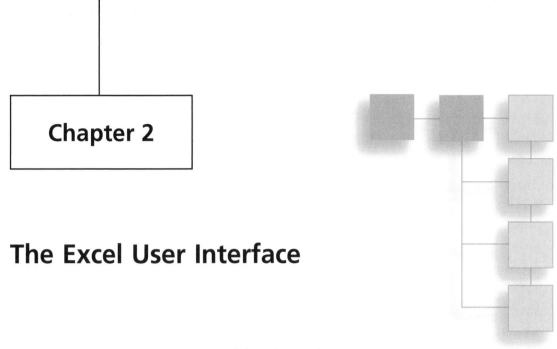

Chapter 2

The Excel User Interface

The Excel user interface consists of four basic elements:

- Worksheets
- Cells
- The Ribbon
- The Backstage View

Excel files, referred to as workbooks, can include any number of worksheets. Worksheets contain cells, identified by a column letter and numbered row. One can enter data or formulas in individual cells, but even if a worksheet contains no data in cells, it can still hold other Excel components such as pivot tables, pivot charts, tables, and charts.

As seen in the prior chapter, the most elemental use of Excel involves entering data and formulas in cells. Other Excel components make use of cells in varying ways. Excel tables allow for the direct entry of values and formulas in cells. However, pivot tables use cells in a more limited fashion. Although pivot table data is displayed in cells, one can't directly enter values or formulas in those cells. Pivot tables rely on a Field List pane to manipulate the values and layout of the pivot table. Charts and pivot charts make no use of cells at all. Charts and pivot charts exist in a separate pane that sits on top of a worksheet, but without any direct connection to the cells that lay underneath.

The Ribbon, a feature found in all Microsoft Office products, displays all available commands. Introduced with Office 2007, the Ribbon is a flexible structure that dynamically shows commands that are appropriate to the task at hand. The commands on the Ribbon are divided into different categories, made available by clicking any of the tabs on the top of the Ribbon. Finally, the Backstage View is a special set of commands that pertain to file management and Excel configuration options. This includes commands such as Save and Print, as well as commands to configure all aspects of Excel, including the Ribbon itself.

Worksheets and Cells

Worksheets and cells make up the heart of Excel. Figure 2.1 shows the bottom left corner of the Excel screen.

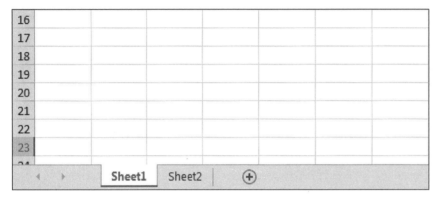

Figure 2.1
Worksheets.
Source: Microsoft® Corporation.

In this figure, we see that this particular workbook has two worksheets, named Sheet1 and Sheet2. Sheet1 is currently selected. That means that everything we do, whether it be entering data in a cell, or creating a table, pivot table, or chart, will remain on this worksheet.

New worksheets can be created by clicking the Insert Worksheet tab, found just to the right of Sheet2 in Figure 2.1. Worksheets can also be created by using the Insert Sheet command found under the Home tab on the Ribbon. Worksheets can be renamed by double-clicking the name or by right-clicking on the worksheet tab and selecting the Rename command from the context menu that pops up. Finally, worksheets can be moved around. This is accomplished by selecting any worksheet tab and dragging it, left or right, to a different position.

Just as cells on a worksheet can be uniquely identified by a column letter and row number, the name of each worksheet can be used to uniquely identify a cell in an entire Excel workbook. For example, the cell named E5 identifies the cell in row 5 of column E of the current worksheet. Cell names can also include the name of the worksheet it's in. In this example, Sheet1!E5 identifies cell E5 on the worksheet named Sheet1. Additionally, worksheet names can include absolute or relative references, a topic that will be discussed in Chapter 9, "Formulas."

Entering data into cells on a worksheet can be accomplished in two basic ways. First, one can click on any cell on any worksheet and directly enter a value or formula in that cell. Second, one can enter the same value or formula in an area of the screen known as the Formula Bar. Figure 2.2 shows the word "Hello" that was entered into cell D2.

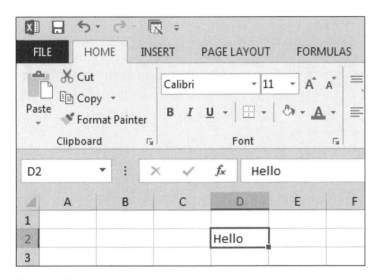

Figure 2.2
Entering a value in a cell or in the Formula Bar.
Source: Microsoft® Corporation.

The data shown in Figure 2.2 could have been entered either by typing directly in cell D2 or in the Formula Bar. The Formula Bar is the rectangle directly to the right of the *fx* symbol. Notice that the label D2 appears in the Name Box, which is the rectangle to the left of the *fx* symbol. This indicates that the name of that cell is D2. Chapter 9, "Formulas," will discuss options for giving a cell a user-defined name, allowing it to be referenced in a formula by a name rather than by its column and row label.

Entering a value is simple enough, but it gets somewhat more complex when one enters a formula in a cell. Let's say that we want to multiply 13 by 21. This is accomplished by entering this formula in a cell:

=13*21

Figure 2.3 shows this formula in cell D3.

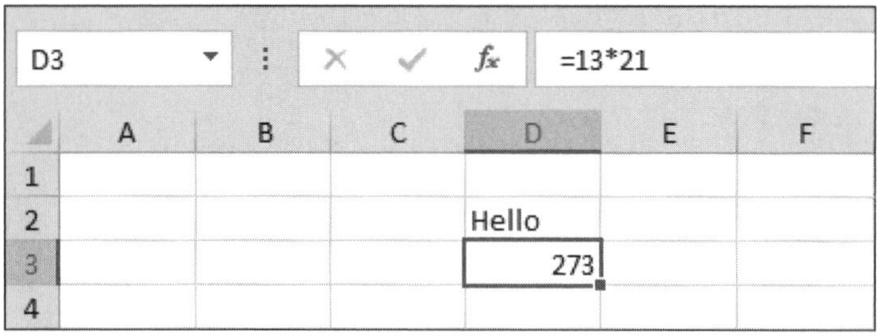

Figure 2.3
Entering a formula in a cell or in the Formula Bar.
Source: Microsoft® Corporation.

In this example, we entered the formula directly in cell D3, and then hit Enter on the keyboard. Alternatively, we could have typed the formula into the Formula Bar. After hitting Enter, we moved the cursor back to cell D3. We now see the formula in the Formula Bar, and the resulting value in cell D3.

It's critical to remember that after they're entered, formulas are not displayed in cells. Cells only show the resulting value. One must usually look at the Formula Bar to see the formula for any particular cell, although in Chapter 9, "Formulas," we'll demonstrate the use of the Show Formulas command to accomplish the same thing.

It's also important to note that it was necessary to type the equals sign (=) in order to tell Excel that this is a formula and not just a bunch of words. If we had left the equals sign out, the screen would have looked like Figure 2.4.

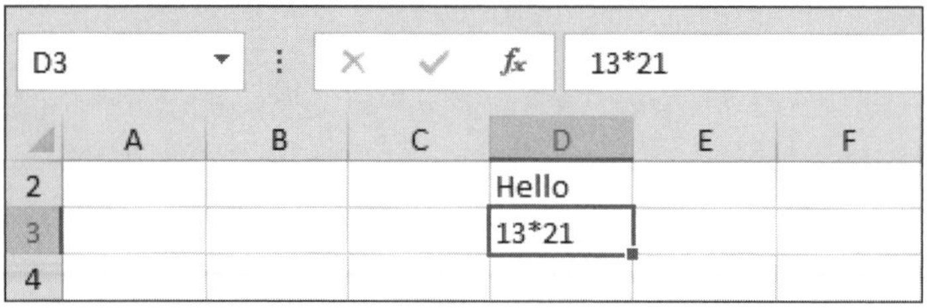

Figure 2.4
A formula without an equals sign.
Source: Microsoft® Corporation.

The subject of entering formulas and functions in cells will be covered extensively in Chapter 9, "Formulas." For now, we just want to leave you with the idea that values or functions can be entered in cells by typing in that cell or by using the Formula Bar.

One additional element of the worksheet and cell interface bears noting. Excel displays a Status Bar at the bottom right corner of the window that provides a number of automatic summarizations of values found in cells. Figure 2.5 illustrates this feature.

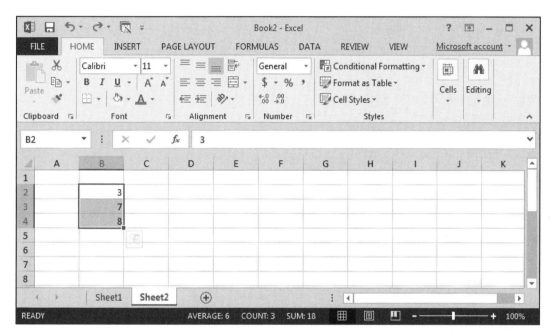

Figure 2.5
The Status Bar.
Source: Microsoft® Corporation.

In this example, we have selected cells B2 through B4. The Status Bar analyzes these three cells and tells us that there is a total count of 3 cells that sum to 18, with an average value of 6. The attributes displayed on the Status Bar can be customized by right-clicking on the bar, and then selecting the desired items to display.

The Ribbon

When you open Excel or create a new Excel workbook, your screen appears as in Figures 2.6 and 2.7. Figure 2.6 shows the upper left side, and Figure 2.7 displays the right side.

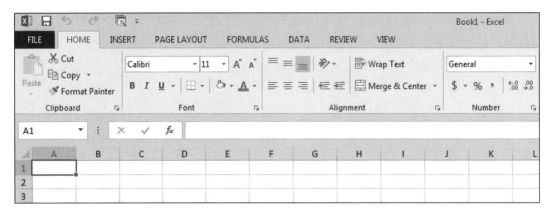

Figure 2.6

Left side of the Ribbon under the Home tab.

Source: Microsoft® Corporation.

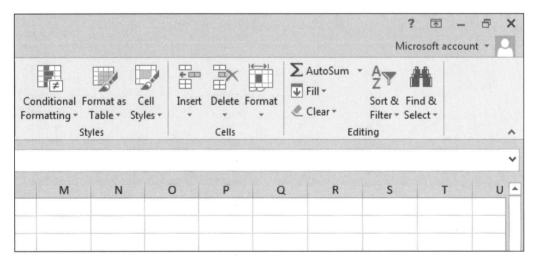

Figure 2.7

Right side of the Ribbon under the Home tab.

Source: Microsoft® Corporation.

The salient feature we want to discuss is the Ribbon. Introduced with Office 2007, the Ribbon is a dynamic tool that displays a set of available commands. The specific commands that are displayed vary, depending on the size of your screen and the size of the Excel window. As currently displayed, we see eight different tabs across the top, with these names: File, Home, Insert, Page Layout, Formulas, Data, Review, and View. By clicking on any of these eight tabs, different commands appear in the Ribbon. Figures 2.6 and 2.7 display the commands on the Home tab of the Ribbon.

The File tab is somewhat different from the other tabs. Also referred to as the Backstage View, the File tab displays some basic file operations and options for configuring Excel. When the File tab is selected, the Ribbon itself disappears and a separate set of commands becomes visible. The Backstage View commands will be covered at the end of this chapter.

The commands under each tab in the Ribbon are divided into *groups*. As seen in Figures 2.6 and 2.7, the commands under the Home tab are organized into these seven groups: Clipboard, Font, Alignment, Number, Styles, Cells, and Editing. Furthermore, each group can optionally contain a special *Dialog Box Launcher* located at the bottom right corner of the group. When selected, the Dialog Box Launcher displays a pane with additional or reorganized commands pertaining to that group. For example, when one clicks the Dialog Box Launcher at the bottom of the Alignment group, one is presented with a Format Cells dialog box with the focus set on an Alignment tab, as shown in Figure 2.8.

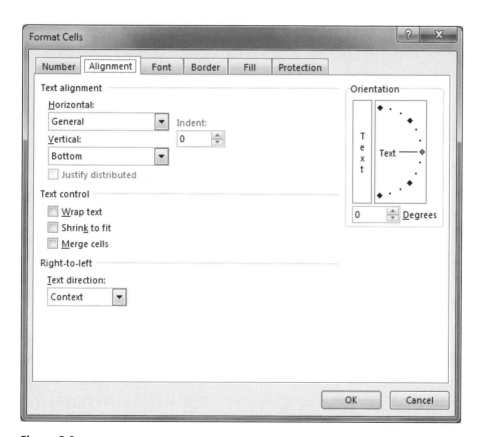

Figure 2.8
Format Cells dialog box.
Source: Microsoft® Corporation.

This Format Cells dialog box presents the Alignment commands in a slightly differ-ent format. It's a matter of personal preference as to whether you might want to make use of these dialog boxes.

The eight tabs seen in Figures 2.6 and 2.7 are always visible, no matter what you're doing in Excel. In addition to these tabs, Excel provides additional *contextual* tabs that display when you're using special elements. For example, if you're working with pivot tables, you'll see two new tabs that appear under a PivotTable Tools head-ing. This is shown in Figure 2.9.

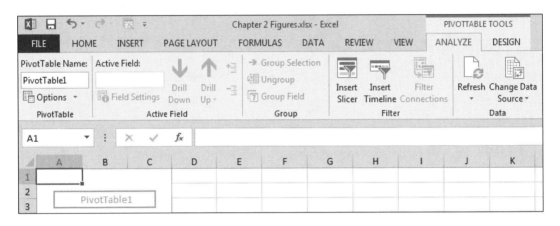

Figure 2.9
Contextual tabs in the Ribbon.
Source: Microsoft® Corporation.

The two new tabs that appear are named Analyze and Design. In Figure 2.9, the Analyze tab is selected, displaying a special set of commands relevant to pivot table options. The Analyze and Design tabs appear only when a cell in the pivot table is selected. If you select a cell outside of the pivot table, the two pivot table contextual tabs disappear. Notice that a PivotTable Tools label appears above the Analyze and Design tabs to indicate that these sets of Ribbon commands are associated with pivot tables.

Another characteristic of the Ribbon is that the actual commands that are displayed vary, depending on the size of your computer screen and the Excel window. As the window widens, more commands are displayed. With a smaller window, command names are abbreviated and combined together. This means that the commands you see on your screen may vary somewhat from the commands shown in this book.

Finally, the display of the Ribbon itself can be altered via a number of display options. Figure 2.7 shows some icons in the upper right corner of the Ribbon. The Ribbon

Display Options icon, which is the fourth icon from the right, lets you select from these three options:

- Show Tabs and Commands
- Show Tabs
- Auto-hide Ribbon

The Show Tabs and Commands option is the normal choice, and is used throughout this book. This displays the entire Ribbon. The Show Tabs option shows only the tabs, hiding the commands until a tab is selected. The Auto-hide option hides the Ribbon entirely unless you click at the top of the application window.

In the remainder of this chapter, we'll discuss the most important commands found under these Ribbon tabs:

- Home
- View
- Page Layout
- Review

The Backstage View commands found under the File tab will be discussed at the end of the chapter. The commands under the Insert, Formulas, and Data tabs will be covered in the remainder of the book.

Home Commands

The commands under the Home tab are primarily about ways to display data within cells. We're going to start with some important commands found in the Cells group on the Ribbon. As seen in Figure 2.7, these commands are viewed by clicking on the keywords Insert, Delete, or Format. When any of these labels are selected, available commands are then displayed in a drop-down menu. The commands under the Insert label are:

- Insert Cells
- Insert Sheet Rows
- Insert Sheet Columns
- Insert Sheet

The Insert Sheet Rows command inserts a row above the selected cell. You can also insert multiple rows by first selecting multiple rows, then selecting the command.

One can insert columns in a similar fashion. The Insert Cells command allows you to insert an individual cell, shifting all cells to the right on the same row, or up in the same column. The Insert Sheet command inserts an entire worksheet to the left of the current worksheet. The commands under the Delete label are analogous to the Insert commands, allowing you to remove rows, columns, cells, or worksheets.

The numerous commands under the Format label in the Cells group are equally important. Of prime interest are the AutoFit Row Height and AutoFit Column Width commands. These commands allow you to make sure that cells are the correct size for the data they contain. To illustrate, let's start with the data shown in Figure 2.10.

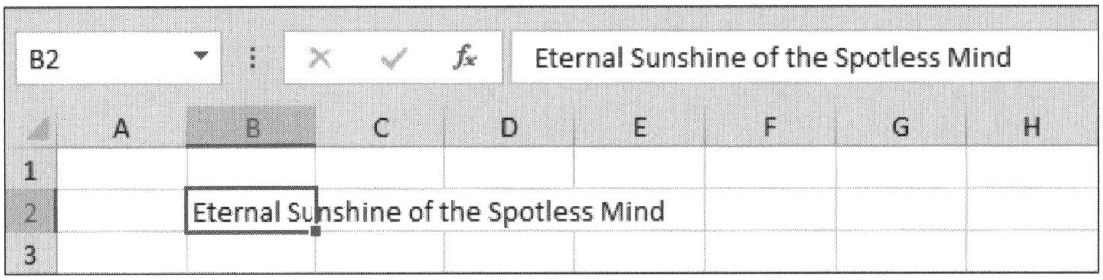

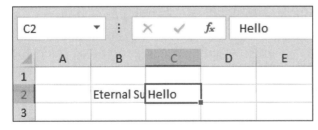

Figure 2.10
A cell with a long text value.
Source: Microsoft® Corporation.

As seen, a lengthy text value has been entered into cell B2. Since the entire text doesn't fit neatly within the cell, it spills over into cells C2, D2, and E2. The problem with this is that it might discourage someone from entering data into cell C2, since that would overlap the text in B2. For example, if one entered the word Hello in cell C2, the worksheet would look like Figure 2.11.

Figure 2.11
Two cells with overlapping text.
Source: Microsoft® Corporation.

One solution to this problem is to apply the AutoFit Column Width command to columns B and C. The result is shown in Figure 2.12.

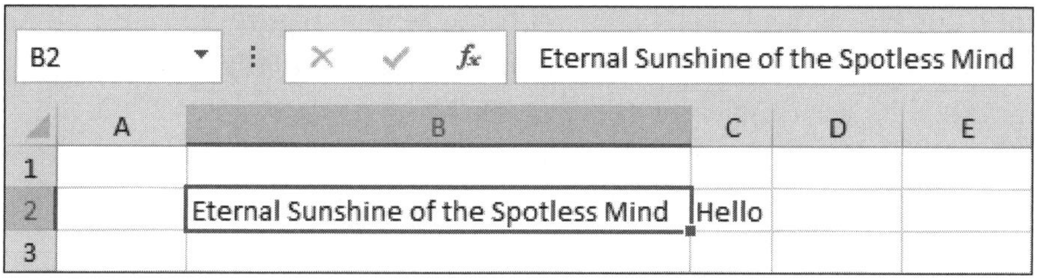

Figure 2.12

The AutoFit Column Width command.

Source: Microsoft® Corporation.

With this modification, we can now see all the text in columns B and C. The column widths have been adjusted to the data in their cells.

Also of interest under the Format command label are the Rename Sheet and Move or Copy Sheet commands. These allow you to organize your worksheets in your workbook in any desired order, and with meaningful names.

Another important set of commands under the Format label allow you to hide or unhide rows, columns, or worksheets, as follows:

- Hide Rows
- Hide Columns
- Hide Sheet
- Unhide Rows
- Unhide Columns

When a row, column, or worksheet is hidden, it is only temporarily removed from view. Similar Unhide commands make these elements visible again. All of these commands are also available as contextual commands by right-clicking on the desired row, column, or worksheet. Hiding rows or columns can be a handy way to reduce the amount of data displayed and reduce clutter. However, hidden rows or columns are still captured if you copy an area over hidden elements. When you do the subsequent paste, the hidden rows or columns will be displayed.

The commands in the Font section of the Home tab are standard font commands, similar to what's found in Microsoft Word. The one command unique to Excel is the Fill Color command. This allows you to change the background color of a cell from the default of white. This is a simple but effective way to highlight data.

The most significant command in the Alignment section is the Wrap Text command. This command is important, because it presents another solution to the problem of overlapping text seen in Figure 2.11. Let's start with the text in Figure 2.11 and make one quick adjustment, using the Column Width command to lengthen the width of column B to 15 pixels. The result is shown in Figure 2.13.

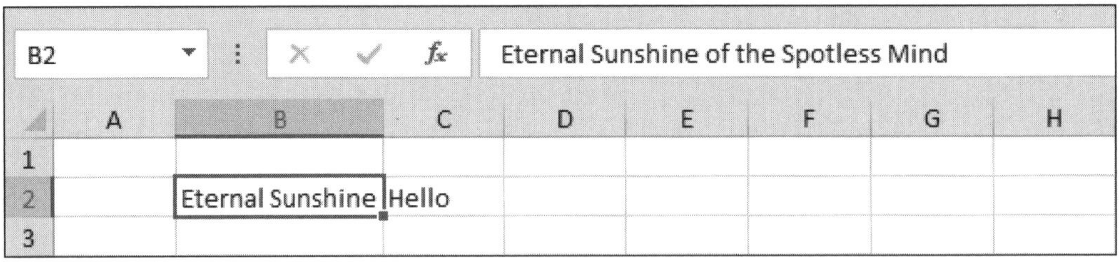

Figure 2.13
The Column Width command.
Source: Microsoft® Corporation.

Our next step will be to apply the Wrap Text command to cell B2. Figure 2.14 shows the result.

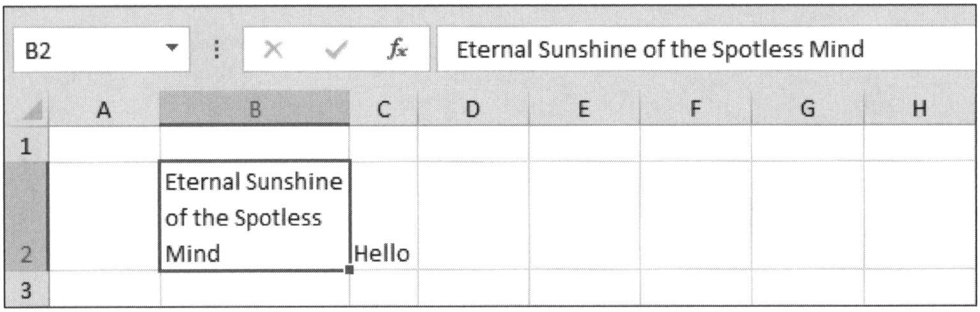

Figure 2.14
The Wrap Text command.
Source: Microsoft® Corporation.

Comparing Figure 2.12 to Figure 2.14, one can see the major advantage of using the Wrap Text command—namely, that it allows large amounts of text to be displayed in a more succinct fashion. With the Wrap Text command, column B isn't nearly as wide, allowing for the possibility of displaying more data on the screen.

Turning to the Clipboard group on the Home tab, these commands have to do with standard cut, copy, and paste operations. Of special significance in Excel are the various Paste commands, and in particular, the Paste Special command. When selected, the Paste label on the Ribbon displays the commands shown in Figure 2.15.

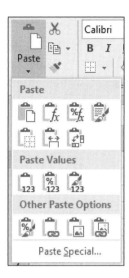

Figure 2.15
Paste commands.

Most of the Paste command icons are also available by selecting the Paste Special command. When selected, the Paste Special dialog box of Figure 2.16 appears.

Figure 2.16
The Paste Special dialog box.

Of particular interest in the Paste Special commands is the Values option. The Paste Values command allows you to copy and paste the value of a cell without including the underlying formula. This can be useful in several situations. You may want to start fresh with certain pieces of data without worrying about the formulas upon which they're based. The Paste Values option allows you to give someone the results of your calculations without sharing the formulas.

The Copy and Paste Special technique is particularly important when using pivot tables. As will be seen in Chapter 5, "Pivot Table Basics," the summarization in a pivot table can be based on thousands of rows of data. The underlying data might be in another Excel worksheet, or even in an external database. To share a pivot table with coworkers requires that they also have access to the underlying data upon which the pivot table is based. If you don't want to grant this access, the easiest solution is to simply do a Copy and Paste Special, pasting the values of the pivot table to an ordinary Excel worksheet. You can then share that new worksheet with your coworker without having to also share the underlying data.

Another interesting option in the Paste Special dialog box is the Transpose checkbox at the bottom. When this is option is selected, it allows you to transform the data shown in Figure 2.17 to that of Figure 2.18.

	A	B	C	D
1	Student	Carol	Joanna	Suresh
2	Grade	A	B	B+

Figure 2.17
Data before a Paste Special with a Transpose.
Source: Microsoft® Corporation.

	A	B
1	Student	Grade
2	Carol	A
3	Joanna	B
4	Suresh	B+

Figure 2.18
Data after a Paste Special with a Transpose.
Source: Microsoft® Corporation.

The method for creating the data in Figure 2.18 begins with highlighting the array of cells from A1 to D2 of Figure 2.17 and doing a copy. The next step is to highlight cell A1 of a different worksheet, and then select the Paste Special command with the

Transpose option. This procedure allows you to easily modify an arrangement of data in cells to a more suitable layout.

One final command to note is the Paste command icon labeled Keep Source Column Widths. This option isn't present in the Paste Special dialog box but is available among the icons displayed in Figure 2.15. This command lets you keep the original column widths when you copy entire columns from one location to another. This can be a nice convenience, as it eliminates the need for readjusting column widths after doing a copy and paste.

The commands in the Number section of the Ribbon under the Home tab affect how numbers are presented to the user. These formatting commands don't modify any actual values; they merely specify how they're displayed. The default format for numbers is the General format. This format displays numbers exactly as you type them, using as many decimal places as are needed. For example, if you enter the value 2.30 in a cell, it will display as 2.3. If you want to specify precisely how many decimal places to display, you can change the format of the cell or cells from General to Number. The default for the Number format is to display the number with two decimal places. With the Number format and two decimal places, the value 2.3 will be shown as 2.30. The value 5.238 will appear as 5.24. If using two decimal places doesn't suit you, you can utilize the Increase Decimal or Decrease Decimal commands to alter the number of decimal places. You can also use the Dialog Box Launcher at the bottom right of the Number group, and then use the Format Cells dialog box to more precisely specify the number of decimal places you'd like. The Format Cells dialog box allows you to choose from the following twelve formatting options:

- General
- Number
- Currency
- Accounting
- Date
- Time
- Percentage
- Fraction
- Scientific
- Text
- Special
- Custom

As mentioned, General is the default format. The Number format lets you specify any number of decimal places and choose whether to include comma separators. A few other formats are worth mentioning. The Currency format adds a dollar sign ($) to the left of the number. The Date and Time formats allow for a wide variety of formats for dates and times. The Percentage format converts numbers to a percentage by multiplying the value by 100 and adding a percent (%) sign. The Fraction format allows a number such as 3.75 to be displayed as 3 3/4. The Text format is significant in that it allows any value to be displayed exactly as it is typed. This allows you to override how Excel normally interprets and displays numbers, dates, and formulas. For example, you may want to enter a formula in a cell and display the actual formula rather than let Excel display the results of the formula. This can be accomplished by changing the format of the cell to Text.

The Styles group of commands consists of options that provide some advanced formatting techniques. Of special interest are the commands under the Conditional Formatting label. This set of commands is shown in Figure 2.19.

Figure 2.19
Conditional Formatting commands.
Source: Microsoft® Corporation.

These commands apply intuitive visual cues to values in individual cells, which quickly relate relative values to the viewer. Let's illustrate with the Data Bars command. Figure 2.20 has a column of values that we know fall in a range from 1 to 60.

	A
1	15
2	7
3	22
4	50
5	4
6	58
7	51
8	38
9	23
10	11

Figure 2.20

A column of numbers.

Source: Microsoft® Corporation.

At first glance, it's not immediately obvious how these numbers relate to each other. If one wanted to find the highest and lowest numbers, it might take a few seconds to peruse the numbers before making that determination. After applying the Data Bars command to these cells, the worksheet looks like Figure 2.21.

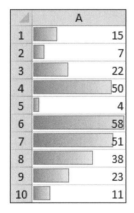

Figure 2.21

Numbers with Data Bars.

Source: Microsoft® Corporation.

With the visual cues that have been added to each cell, we can now easily pick out the highest and lowest values from this group of numbers. We can also observe the gradual decrease in values that takes place between cells A6 and A10. Of course, the Data Bars command has options that let you specify a variety of colors for the bars. In addition, a host of additional commands under the Conditional Formatting option utilize the same basic concept in a variety of ways. For example, the Color Scales command lets you apply differing colors to indicate low, medium, or high values. Similarly, the Icon Sets commands let you apply different shapes to indicate value levels and direction of change from the prior value. The Highlight Cells Rules has options that let you highlight values that are less than, greater than, or equal to a specified value. It also allows you to flag duplicates. The Top/Bottom Rules commands allow you to accomplish such things as indicating those values that are above average or in the top or bottom of the list. Figure 2.22 illustrates the same data in Figure 2.21, to which a Top/Bottom rule has been applied to mark those values that are above average.

	A
1	15
2	7
3	22
4	50
5	4
6	58
7	51
8	38
9	23
10	11

Figure 2.22

Numbers with Data Bars and an Above Average highlight.

Source: Microsoft® Corporation.

The data in Figure 2.22 now indicates not only the relative lengths of each value, but also whether the value is above the average of that group of numbers.

The final section of commands to be looked at under the Home tab is the Editing group, as seen in Figure 2.7. The AutoSum command provides a sum, count, average, min, or max of a selected series of numbers. It adds this value immediately below the list of numbers if they're in a column, or to the right, if they're in a row.

The Fill label has a number of commands that let you copy the value of a single cell in any direction from the original cell. One particularly useful option is the Series command. This lets you generate a series of numbers from a single specified value. To illustrate, let's say that you entered the number 1 in cell A1 and want to generate the values 2 through 9 in the nine cells below A1. To do this, you simply highlight cells A1 through A10 and select the Series command under the Fill label. The dialog box of Figure 2.23 then appears.

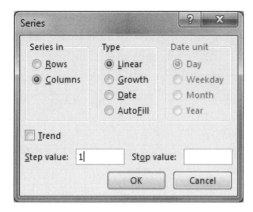

Figure 2.23
Series dialog box.
Source: Microsoft® Corporation.

This box indicates that we want to generate a linear series of numbers in a column, with a step value of 1. This means that each number would be one higher than the previous number. After clicking OK, the numbers 1 through 10 will appear in column A. As seen in the dialog box, this feature can also be used to generate dates in a sequence of days, weekdays, months, or years.

The final set of commands in the Editing group we'll discuss are those under the Find & Select label. The Find and Replace work as they do in Microsoft Word, letting you find or replace a specific value. Another useful option is the Formulas command. This finds and highlights any cells on your worksheet that contain formulas. Figure 2.24 shows the result of this command.

C2				f_x	=A2*B2	
	A	B	C	D	E	
1	Value 1	Value 2	Result			
2	2	3	6			
3	3	4	12			
4	5	6	30			
5	12	3	36			
6	8	4	32			

Figure 2.24
The Formulas command.
Source: Microsoft® Corporation.

The purpose of this command is to find all cells on your worksheet that contain formulas. As seen, it found four cells with formulas: C2, C3, C5, and C6. The focus is set on the first cell with a formula (C2) and the remaining three cells (C3, C5, and C6) are highlighted. The Formula Bar indicates that the formula in cell C2 is:

=A2*B2

This means that the value in cell C2 was derived by multiplying the value in A2 by the value in B2. The formulas in cells C3, C5, and C6 are similar. If our intention was to have formulas in cells C2 through C6, this command allowed us to discover that the value in cell C4 is missing the intended formula. Cell C4 merely contains the number 30. Although 30 is the correct number, it wasn't derived from a formula. As such, if we change the value in cell A4 or B4, C4 will still remain as 30. As noted in Chapter 1, Excel worksheets are really composed of three layers: data, formula, and presentation. The problem one often faces is that the formula layer is hidden. By identifying cells that contain formulas, the Formula command can alert you to cells that are missing this type of value.

View Commands

The commands under the View tab of the Ribbon have to do with different ways to view your worksheets. These commands have been divided into five groups: Workbook Views, Show, Zoom, Window, and Macros. Figures 2.25 and 2.26 show the left and right sides of the View tab portion of the Ribbon.

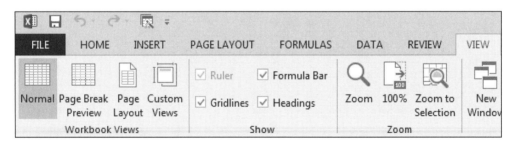

Figure 2.25
Left side of the Ribbon under the View tab.
Source: Microsoft® Corporation.

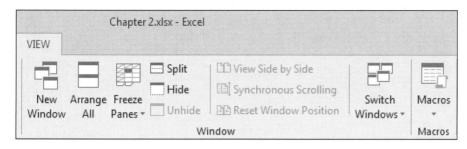

Figure 2.26

Right side of the Ribbon under the View tab.

Source: Microsoft® Corporation.

The commands in the Workbook Views group are fairly self-evident in their usage. In most situations, you'll want to stick with the default Normal view of your work-sheet. The Page Layout command changes the worksheet to display as it would when printed.

In the Show section on the Ribbon, there are checkboxes to turn on or off the display of the Gridlines, Formula Bar, Headings, and Ruler. Headings refers to the column and row headings. The Ruler checkbox can be used only when you are in the page layout.

The commands in the Zoom group let you view larger or smaller portions of the screen. The Zoom command in this section lets you select different magnification levels to zoom in to enlarge the cell portion of the screen, or zoom out to let more detail appear. The 100% command returns the zoom level to normal. The Zoom to Selection command zooms in at a 400% level and focuses on the cell you selected.

The commands in the Windows section of the Ribbon accomplish a number of tasks pertaining to how data in Excel windows is displayed on the screen. Clicking the New Window command displays a duplicate of all the worksheets contained within your current Excel file. It doesn't create a separate file but rather only a copy that can be viewed within the same file. This is usually used in conjunction with the Arrange All command, which lets you specify how the multiple windows you created are displayed on the screen: horizontally, vertically, tiled, or cascaded. To illustrate, let's click the New Window command, then select the Arrange All command, and then Vertical. This results in the screen shown in Figure 2.27.

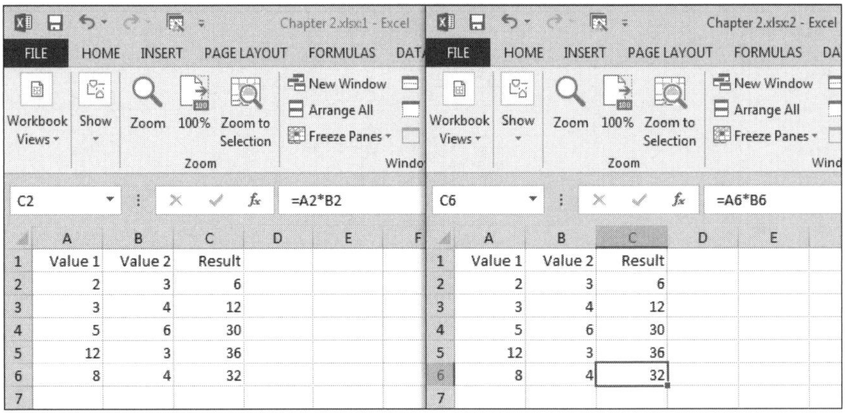

Figure 2.27

The New Window and Arrange All commands.

Source: Microsoft® Corporation.

The Excel window is now displaying two copies of the same workbook. The ability to see the same data twice is a convenience that allows you to easily switch to view multiple worksheets, or portions of the same worksheet, simultaneously.

After you've created multiple windows, you can use the Switch Windows command in the Windows group to select the specific window you'd like to work with. Besides the window copies you've created with the New Window command, the Switch Windows command also lets you select other Excel workbooks that you happen to have open.

The Split command is similar to the New Windows command, except that it pertains to only one worksheet. For example, if you select any column and then select the Split command, the window will divide into two vertical sections, both of which are views into the same worksheet.

Perhaps the most useful commands in the Windows group are those under the Freeze Panes label. There are three commands: Freeze Panes, Freeze Top Row, and Freeze First Column. To illustrate, let's apply the Freeze Top Row command to the worksheet seen in Figure 2.24. The result is shown in Figure 2.28.

	A	B	C	D	E
1	Value 1	Value 2	Result		
2	2	3	6		
3	3	4	12		
4	5	6	30		
5	12	3	36		
6	8	4	32		

Figure 2.28

The Freeze Top Row command.

Source: Microsoft® Corporation.

Notice the black line that now appears between rows 1 and 2. This line indicates that the data above the line will always remain on the screen, even if one scrolls down to lower rows on the window. Only the rows below the line will respond to vertical scrolling. As a practical matter, the ability to freeze rows or columns with header information is a useful technique for viewing large amounts of data in a worksheet. After a freeze is applied to any portion of the screen, an Unfreeze Panes command will appear, allowing you to undo the freeze.

The final group of commands under the View tab of the Ribbon is the Macros section. This section contains two commands that let you view or record macros. As mentioned in the Introduction, macros are beyond the scope of this book. In brief, however, macros are a device for recording all actions that you take while you are working with Excel. You can turn on the recording of these actions at any time, and stop the recording when you're done. You can then save this macro in order to execute the same actions at a later time.

As a simple example, let's say you want to create a macro that automates the execution of two commands together: the AutoFit Row Height and the AutoFit Column Width commands. The process is started by selecting the Record Macro command under the Macros label. The dialog box of Figure 2.29 then appears.

Figure 2.29
Record Macro dialog box.
Source: Microsoft® Corporation.

After entering an appropriate name for the macro, the OK button is clicked and the recording begins. Thereafter, any actions that you take are automatically recorded and captured in the macro. You can then select all cells on the worksheet and then execute both the AutoFit Row Height and AutoFit Column Width commands. After you've executed the commands you want to record for the macro, you would return to the Macros label and select the Stop Recording command. After stopping the recording, you can execute the macro by selecting the View Macros command. This causes a Macro dialog box to appear that lists all macros and allows you to run any desired macro. When doing so, all of the actions you previously recorded are immediately executed. After adding a macro, you won't be able to save the workbook with the normal .xlsx suffix. Workbooks with macros need to be saved as Macro-Enabled workbooks with an .xlsm suffix.

Page Layout Commands

The Page Layout tab of the Ribbon reveals commands that affect the layout of data on the printed page. These commands are divided into five groups: Themes, Page Setup, Scale to Fit, Sheet Options, and Arrange. The left and right sides of the Ribbon appear in Figures 2.30 and 2.31.

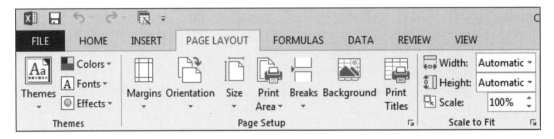

Figure 2.30
Left side of the Ribbon under the Page Layout tab.
Source: Microsoft® Corporation.

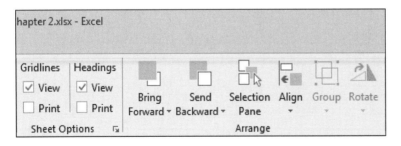

Figure 2.31
Right side of the Ribbon under the Page Layout tab.
Source: Microsoft® Corporation.

The twenty plus themes found in the Themes group of commands are the same themes found in other Office products. These affect the overall colors, fonts, and graphic effects that are shown in your spreadsheet. To experiment with the various themes, you can easily select a theme and see how it affects the overall look of your document.

The Page Setup group of commands allows you to handle the basics of the printed page. The options under the Margin command set the page margin. The Orientation commands let you set the page to print in portrait or landscape mode. The Breaks command permits you to create page breaks at any specific point in your document. The Print Titles command lets you specify rows that will appear at the top of every printed page.

The commands in the Scale to Fit group of commands are significant. These allow you to set the absolute maximum width or height of the printed page. The default value for the Width and Height is Automatic, which means that Excel will print large amounts of data in as many pages as it wants to. As a practical matter, however, it's convenient to specify that the data on your spreadsheet should be printed on a maximum of one page in width. In combination with changing the Orientation to Landscape, this is a handy technique.

The commands in the Sheet Options section specify whether gridlines and headings are visible, both when viewed on the screen and when printed. Note that the View checkboxes seen in Figure 2.31 under Gridlines and Headings are equivalent to the Gridlines and Headings checkboxes in the Show section under the View tab, previously seen in Figure 2.25.

The commands in the Arrange group of commands really have nothing to do with page layout. They deal with ways to arrange shapes that have been inserted on a worksheet—a topic that is beyond the scope of this book. If, for example, you were to insert overlapping rectangle and triangle shapes on your worksheet, you might want to specify which shape should appear on top of the other. The Arrange commands handle this situation. Note also that these Arrange commands are the same commands that appear under the Drawing Tools Format tab that appears when editing shapes.

Review Commands

The commands under the Review tab of the Ribbon, shown in Figures 2.32 and 2.33, pertain mainly to miscellaneous ways to proof and comment upon your Excel document.

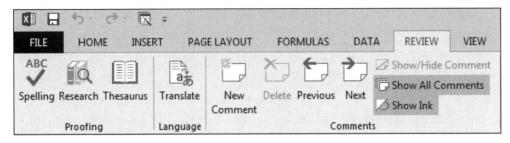

Figure 2.32

Left side of the Ribbon under the Review tab.

Source: Microsoft® Corporation.

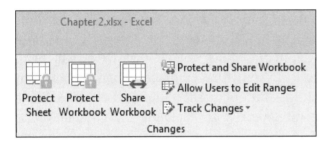

Figure 2.33

Right side of the Ribbon under the Review tab.

Source: Microsoft® Corporation.

We'll remark on only one of these: the New Comment command. This command lets you insert a floating sticky note that comments on one particular cell. Figure 2.34 shows a comment that was added to cell C4 of the worksheet previously seen in Figure 2.24.

▲	A	B	C	D	E	F	G
1	Value 1	Value 2	Result				
2	2	3	6				
3	3	4	12		**Larry Rockoff:**		
4	5	6	30		This cell is missing a formula.		
5	12	3	36				
6	8	4	32				

Figure 2.34

A comment.

Source: Microsoft® Corporation.

As such, comments are a useful device for sharing or saving thoughts regarding your data.

The Backstage View

Our final user interface topic is something called the Backstage View. This area is revealed by the File tab on the Ribbon, and allows you to utilize commands to manage files and specify setup options. Unlike the other tabs on the Ribbon, there are no Ribbon commands associated with the Backstage View. When the File tab is selected, your screen appears as in Figure 2.35.

Figure 2.35

The Backstage View.

Source: Microsoft® Corporation.

The default command in the Backstage View is the Info command. This command provides basic information about permissions of the Excel file. Of greater interest are four commands below the Info command: Save, Save As, Open, and Close. These perform basic save, open, and close operations. Additional file operation commands are New, Print, Share, and Export. New and Print allow you to create a new document or print the current workbook. The Share command lets you save and share your file on SkyDrive, Microsoft's cloud, or via email or fax. The export command allows you to export the document to a PDF or XPS format.

The account command lets you manage your Microsoft account and also alter the background and theme of all your Office products.

The majority of what you can do in the Backstage View is accessible after you click the Options command. You will then see a pane as shown in Figure 2.36.

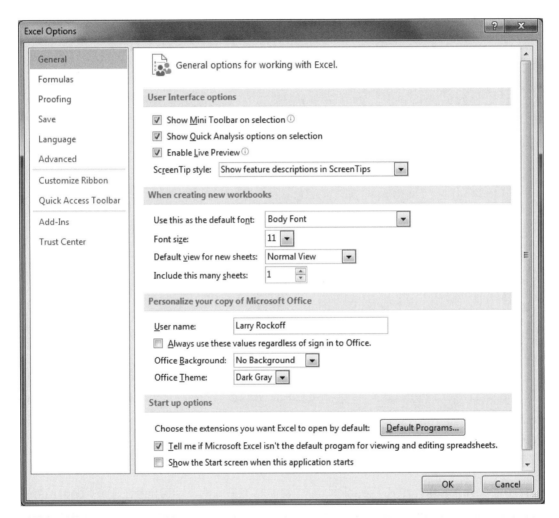

Figure 2.36
Excel Options.
Source: Microsoft® Corporation.

This Excel Options pane contains its own subset of tabs, each of which allows you to specify numerous settings. These options fall into these ten categories: General, Formulas, Proofing, Save, Language, Advanced, Customize Ribbon, Quick Access Toolbar, Add-Ins, and Trust Center. Of the dozens of available settings, a few are of particular interest.

First, under the General tab, there's an option to specify the number of worksheets to create when a new workbook is created. The default is 1. If you want to have more worksheets on new Excel workbooks, this is where you can do that. There are also options to specify the default font for new workbooks.

Under the Save tab, you'll find an option that lets you specify the default Excel file format. In most cases, you'll want to make sure to use the XLSX format, which has been the preferred file format since Excel 2007.

The Advanced tab contains numerous options for settings for the editing and display of data. For example, you can specify to insert two decimal places automatically in all your numbers. Another interesting option is the ability to disable AutoComplete. This feature, which is enabled by default, allows Excel to guess at your text entry as you type in letters, completing the word for you if you enter text that's immediately above or below a list of text that begins with the same letters. This feature, although well intended, can sometimes slow you down when entering text.

The Customize Ribbon tab lets you customize the placement of all commands on each tab of the Ribbon. You take any command and determine which tab you'd like it to appear in, or reorder how they appear. Not only can you create new tabs and groups within tabs, but you can also rename any of the tab or group names. You can also remove any commands you don't need. This means, for example, that if you have no need to ever use any commands under the Review tab, you can remove all of those commands and the Review tab itself.

Finally, the Quick Access Toolbar tab allows you to modify the icons on the top of the screen, just above the Ribbon. This toolbar, shown in Figure 2.37, allows you to assemble your most frequently used commands in one place.

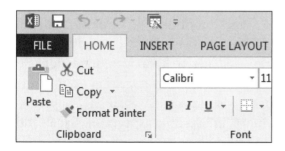

Figure 2.37
The Quick Access Toolbar.
Source: Microsoft® Corporation.

There are over a thousand commands that can be placed in the Quick Access Toolbar. In this example, the Quick Access Toolbar consists of the four icons immediately to the right of the Excel icon in the upper left corner of Figure 2.37. The four icons represent these commands: Save, Undo, Redo, and New Database Query. The Save command is particularly useful, since it allows you to do a quick save without having to click on the File tab and then the Save command in the Backstage View.

The Quick Access Toolbar is actually quite a useful device. Since the Ribbon is a dynamic structure that frequently changes appearance, it's sometimes difficult to locate specific commands, even when you think you know where they are. By placing a command in the Quick Access Toolbar, it will always be available.

Looking Ahead

We began this chapter with mention of the four key elements of its user interface: Worksheets, Cells, the Ribbon, and the Backstage View. We then proceeded to discuss the basics of how to enter data and formulas in cells, and view the various worksheets that can exist in an Excel workbook. Turning to the Ribbon, we distinguished between the eight tabs that are always visible, and contextual tabs that appear only when special elements, such as pivot tables, are referenced.

We then covered four of these tabs in detail: Home, View, Page Layout, and Review. Of these, the Home tab is the most significant and widely used. This tab provides much critically important functionality, such as commands to insert new columns or rows in your worksheet. There are also useful commands to wrap text and cut and copy text via the clipboard.

We concluded the chapter with a look at the Backstage View, a set of commands that are accessible via the File tab in the Ribbon. These commands allow you to do basic file operations and modify Excel settings that include configuration of the Ribbon and Quick Access Toolbar.

In the next chapter, we'll continue to provide some important background material by focusing on the problem of bringing external data into Excel. We'll begin by covering the basics of using the Excel Connection Manager to manage connections to external data. We'll also turn to Microsoft Query, a useful tool for getting your external data into an optimal structure for subsequent use in Excel. Then in Chapter 4, "Tables," we'll start to discuss some of the more interesting aspects of Excel and begin to demonstrate what can actually be accomplished with the software.

Chapter 3

Getting External Data

The first task of the business analyst is to obtain data to analyze. One might think that this would be a simple procedure, but this is often a far from trivial matter. In a sense, we've been spoiled by the ease of obtaining data on the Internet. These days, we can effortlessly use our smart phone to find all coffee shops located near the Empire State Building, or perhaps pull up a bunch of baseball scores and sports statistics. However, the ability to obtain data is generally not as easy when it's in your own business or organization. First, there are often organizational issues that can impede the ability to get to the data you want. The data may exist in several different departments. The data in one department may not match up with similar data in another department. Likewise, data may exist in operational databases, and thus be continually in flux. Even if an organization makes an effort to centralize its data in one big user-friendly data warehouse, there's still the problem of physically transferring that data to your Excel worksheet. There are also issues of volume, whereby a database may have millions of rows of data that you need to consolidate or summarize in some manner before you can begin your analysis. Perhaps in the future, we'll be able to simply speak to our computer and politely ask it to retrieve sales data from September and have it instantly appear in Excel in an appropriate format. However, this does not correspond to how things work in today's world.

In this chapter, we'll explore a number of ways to bring data into Excel from outside sources. The good news is that this can be a completely trivial task if your data source happens to be a software package that exports data into Excel as part of its core functionality. For example, if your data is coming from a package such as Quicken, the ability to export data to Excel is built into the software. You just need to use the commands of the package to create Excel spreadsheets from your data in Quicken. Similarly, virtually all reporting tools like Business Objects or Cognos let you export data directly into Excel. So in many cases, the ability to get data into Excel isn't an issue. However, there will undoubtedly be situations in which you will need to either manually bring data into Excel, or else transform data as it's being brought into Excel. The topics of this chapter address both of those situations.

The first few sections in this chapter deal with various ways to import data and manage connections to external data. While these may not seem to be terribly exciting subjects, be aware that this leads up to a very important topic covered towards the end of the chapter: how to use Microsoft Query. This tool allows you to import data from multiple tables in an external database in a single step and is therefore critical to the success of many analysis situations.

Data from Text Files

All of the commands in this chapter are found in the Get External Data and Connections groups under the Data tab. This area of the Ribbon is shown in Figure 3.1

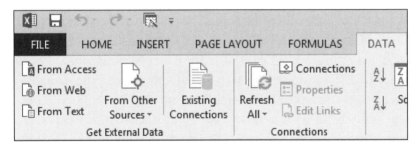

Figure 3.1

Left side of the Ribbon under the Data tab.

Source: Microsoft® Corporation.

Aside from situations where you can simply export data from an external software package, the simplest way to bring data into Excel is via a text file. Text files are a basic device for capturing and storing data in a format that is nearly free form. Data is stored as plain text, with each line corresponding to a row of data in a table. Text files appear in two basic formats: as a delimited file and as a fixed-width file. The two formats refer to the two ways in which the attributes in each row are separated out.

Let's illustrate with an example of a delimited text file. The text file shown in Figure 3.2 contains some basic information about five different books.

```
Book ID, Title, Author, Publication Date
1, Atonement, Ian McEwan, 2001
2, The Stranger, Albert Camus, 1942
3, Nineteen Eighty-Four, George Orwell, 1949
4, Glengarry Glen Ross, David Mamet, 1984
5, American Pastoral, Philip Roth, 1998
```

Figure 3.2

A comma delimited text file.

Source: Microsoft® Corporation.

The first line of the file has header information, and the subsequent five rows have the data. Each row, whether header or data, utilizes commas to separate the various attributes. The procedure to import this data into Excel is simple. One starts by selecting the From Text command in the Get External Data group under the Data tab of the Ribbon. One can then browse through files until the proper text file is located. After clicking on the Import button, one is presented with a Text Import Wizard dialog box such as shown in Figure 3.3.

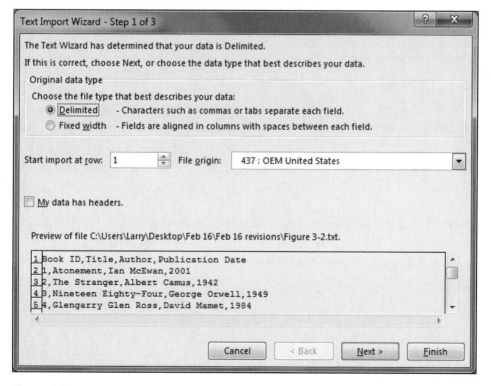

Figure 3.3

Step 1 of the Text Import Wizard.

Source: Microsoft® Corporation.

In this dialog box, we're merely asked to select whether the file is delimited or fixed width. We'll select Delimited, and then click the Next button. In the next pane, shown in Figure 3.4, we're asked to identify the type of delimiter that's employed.

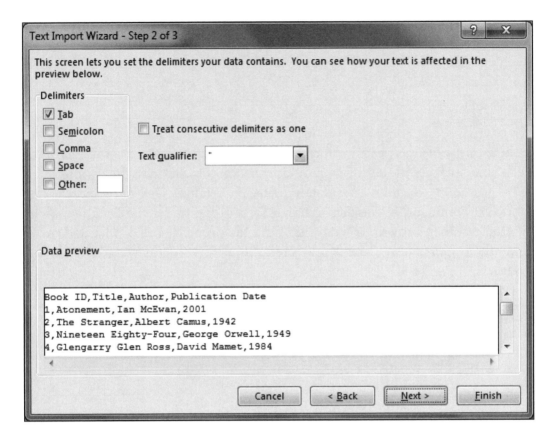

Figure 3.4
Step 2 of the Text Import Wizard.
Source: Microsoft® Corporation.

Figure 3.4 shows a selection of Tab as the delimiter. In this situation, we'll need to change the delimiter from Tab to Comma, and then click Next. The final Text Import Wizard dialog box is shown in Figure 3.5.

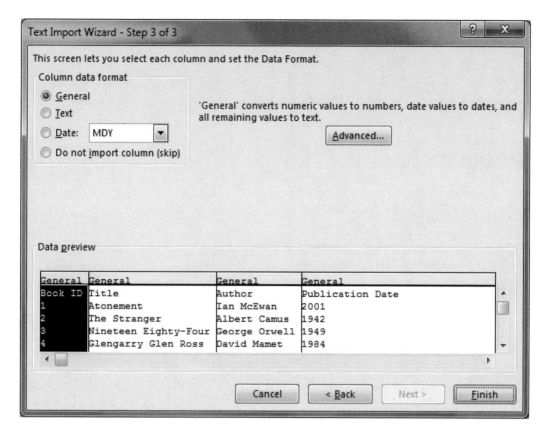

Figure 3.5
Step 3 of the Text Import Wizard.
Source: Microsoft® Corporation.

In this step, we have the ability to select each column of the text and modify the format. Since the data appears correct as is, we'll click the Finish button. A final Import Data dialog box, shown in Figure 3.6, appears asking where the data is to be placed. We'll respond that the data should begin in cell A1 of the existing worksheet, and then click OK. The data is then positioned on the Excel worksheet, as shown in Figure 3.7.

Figure 3.6
Import Data dialog box.
Source: Microsoft® Corporation.

◢	A	B	C	D
1	Book ID	Title	Author	Publication Date
2	1	Atonement	Ian McEwan	2001
3	2	The Stranger	Albert Camus	1942
4	3	Nineteen Eighty-Four	George Orwell	1949
5	4	Glengarry Glen Ross	David Mamet	1984
6	5	American Pastoral	Philip Roth	1998

Figure 3.7
An Excel worksheet from a delimited text file.
Source: Microsoft® Corporation.

We now see the comma delimited text file from Figure 3.2 clearly laid out in an Excel worksheet.

At this point, we need to return to the Import Data dialog box of Figure 3.6 for a moment to discuss some of the other available options. At the bottom of the box is a checkbox that allows the data to be added to a Data Model. Data models are a new feature of Excel 2013 that permits users to create relationships within Excel of two different sets of data. Each Excel workbook can contain only one Data Model, but each Data Model can include multiple relationships. Each relationship describes how two tables or ranges of data are connected.

In this example, you might have a second table that has sales data for each of these books. This second table would have the Book ID and other columns with sales information, such as the sale date, quantity sold, and unit price. The new Data Model feature would allow you to establish an explicit relationship between the two tables so that reporting can reference data in both tables simultaneously. If we had checked the Data Models option, we would then have been able to import the data into a table, pivot table, or pivot chart, rather than merely into cells on a worksheet. We're going to hold off on a discussion of Data Models until Chapter 5, when we'll talk about pivot tables. The reason for this is that the sole purpose of Data Models is for use in pivot tables or pivot charts. At that time, we'll go through an example of adding data to a Data Model, establishing the relationship, and then using that combined data in a pivot table.

Let's now turn to fixed-width text files. In contrast to the comma delimited text file of Figure 3.2, a fixed-width text file with the same data will look like Figure 3.8.

```
1    Atonement              Ian McEwan       2001
2    The Stranger           Albert Camus     1942
3    Nineteen Eighty-Four   George Orwell    1949
4    Glengarry Glen Ross    David Mamet      1984
5    American Pastoral      Philip Roth      1998
```

Figure 3.8
A fixed-width text file.
Source: Microsoft® Corporation.

Note that this file does not include a header line. This is typical of fixed-width files. Since field headers aren't necessarily the same size as the contents of their corresponding fields, header information is normally left out of fixed-width text files, since it might adversely affect the length of each field. The procedure for importing a fixed-width text file is nearly identical to that of importing a delimited file. It starts in the same way, by clicking the From Text command. The only difference is in Step 2 of the Text Import Wizard. Step 2 for importing fixed-width files looks like Figure 3.9.

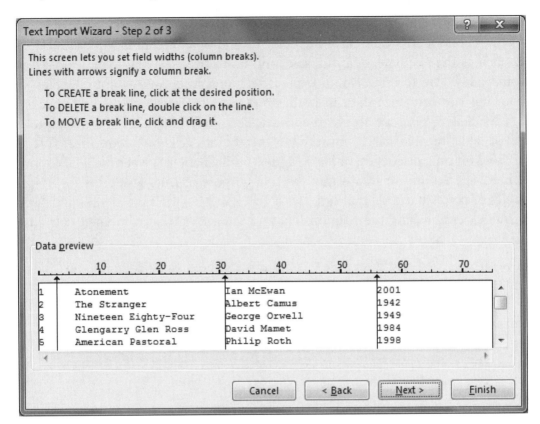

Figure 3.9

Step 2 of the Text Import Wizard for fixed-width files.

Source: Microsoft® Corporation.

In contrast to importing delimited files, step 2 of the wizard for fixed-width files doesn't need to ask which delimiter to use. Instead, it allows you to manipulate the way that fields are separated by clicking or dragging the separator lines. The result of importing this fixed-width file is identical to the worksheet shown in Figure 3.7, except that the header line isn't shown.

Data from Microsoft Access

As a fellow member of Office 2013, Microsoft provides special provisions in Excel for opening data that resides in Access. Let's say that we have an Access database that contains two tables and a query. The tables are the Books table with the data shown in Figure 3.7, and a Sales table that appears in Access as in Figure 3.10.

Sales			
Book ID ▾	Sales Date ▾	Quantity Sold ▾	Unit Price ▾
1	5/1/2013	2	12
1	5/4/2013	1	12
2	5/2/2013	1	8
4	5/2/2013	4	15
4	5/4/2013	2	15
5	5/3/2013	3	13

Figure 3.10

A Sales table in Microsoft Access.

Source: Microsoft® Corporation.

The Book ID column in the Sales table corresponds to the Book ID column in the Books table. In other words, the data in this table relates specific sales that took place for the books in the Books table. In addition to these two tables, this Access database also has a query, named Books Sold. The design and datasheet views of this query are shown in Figures 3.11 and 3.12.

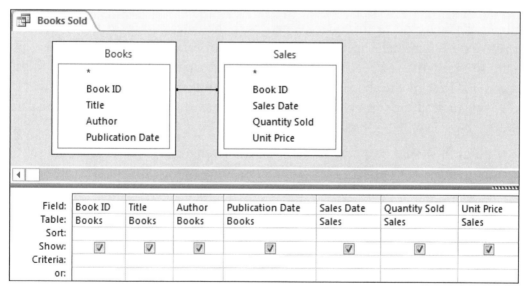

Figure 3.11

Design view of the Books Sold query in Access.

Source: Microsoft® Corporation.

Books Sold						
Book ID ▾	Title ▾	Author ▾	Publication Date ▾	Sales Date ▾	Quantity Sold ▾	Unit Price ▾
1	Atonement	Ian McEwan	2001	5/1/2013	2	12
1	Atonement	Ian McEwan	2001	5/4/2013	1	12
2	The Stranger	Albert Camus	1942	5/2/2013	1	8
4	Glengarry Glen Ross	David Mamet	1984	5/2/2013	4	15
4	Glengarry Glen Ross	David Mamet	1984	5/4/2013	2	15
5	American Pastoral	Philip Roth	1998	5/3/2013	3	13

Figure 3.12

Datasheet view of the Books Sold query in Access.

Source: Microsoft® Corporation.

Although this isn't a book about Microsoft Access, a few words of explanation are in order. The design view of the query shown in Figure 3.11 shows that the two tables in the query, Books and Sales, are joined together via the Book ID field. This means that values of the Book ID column in the Books table must equal values of the Book ID column in the Sales table. When rows from both tables with the same Book ID are found, those rows are joined together, combining the rows from the two separate tables into one. The grid of columns below this graphical depiction indicates the columns that will be available in the query. For example, the second column is the Title column, taken from the Books table. When this query is executed, the data appears as in Figure 3.12. This is referred to as the datasheet view. In its display of data in rows and columns, you might almost think that you're looking at an Excel worksheet. The only clue that this is Access and not Excel is the absence of row numbers and column letters, as one would find in Excel. Instead, one merely sees the column names, followed by rows of data values.

As a side point, it should be noted that one of the strengths of Access is its ability to easily create queries from tables. This allows you to easily manipulate data in one or more tables in a new view of the data. In fact, one can think of queries as a type of virtual table.

Let's say that we want to import some of this Access data into Excel. The procedure is simple. We first select the From Access command in the Get External Data group under the Data tab of the Ribbon. As we did with text files, we then browse through files until the Access database is located. After clicking the Open button, we're presented with the Select Table dialog box shown in Figure 3.13.

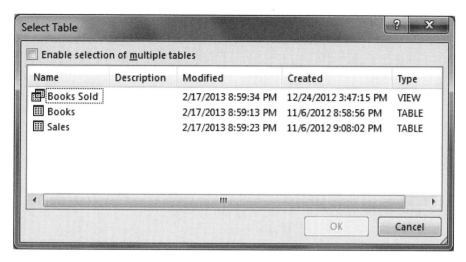

Figure 3.13
Select Table dialog box.
Source: Microsoft® Corporation.

We see listed the query and two tables in our Access database. Notice that the query is referred to as a "view" in this dialog box. This is in keeping with standard database nomenclature. To continue with the example, we'll select the Sales table, and then click the OK button. We're then presented with the Import Data dialog box of Figure 3.14.

Figure 3.14
Import Data dialog box.
Source: Microsoft® Corporation.

In this box, we can choose between three options: to import the selected data as an Excel table, as a pivot table, or as a pivot chart. We'll choose to import it as a table. Also, as before with the text files, we'll choose to not add this data to the worksheet's Data Model. After clicking OK, the data appears in Excel as in Figure 3.15.

	A	B	C	D
1	Book ID ▼	Sales Date ▼	Quantity Sold ▼	Unit Price ▼
2	1	5/1/2013	2	12
3	2	5/2/2013	1	8
4	4	5/2/2013	4	15
5	5	5/3/2013	3	13
6	4	5/4/2013	2	15
7	1	5/4/2013	1	12

Figure 3.15

Access data imported into an Excel table.

Source: Microsoft® Corporation.

The highlighted column names in row 1 tell you that this data is indeed stored in an Excel table. The drop-down indicators next to each column name allow for normal table functionality. The capabilities of Excel tables will be discussed in the following chapter, but for now, it's important to note that this data is in a table rather than just a range of data in an Excel worksheet. This movement of data into a table was done since the data being imported was in a database table. We would have had the same result even if we had imported the Access view, Book Sales, rather than one of the tables. Within the context of Access, queries don't contain any data. They're merely a view of data that reside in tables or in other queries. As mentioned, Access queries can be thought of as virtual tables. However, queries can be imported into Excel as if they were actual tables.

In this example, we imported data into a table. If we had chosen to import to a pivot table instead, the result would appear as in Figure 3.16.

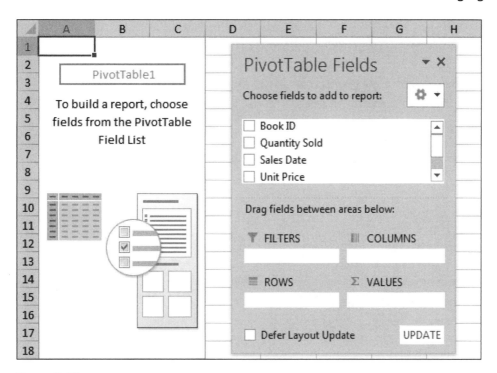

Figure 3.16
Access data imported into a pivot table.
Source: Microsoft® Corporation.

The subject of pivot tables will be covered in detail in Chapters 5 and 6. For now, it's only important to understand that pivot tables can be created directly from Access data. Likewise, we can also create pivot charts from Access data.

Managing Connections

Every time you connect to any external source, Excel automatically creates a special connection file. This file is given a suffix of ODC, which stands for Office Data Connection. Thus, connection files are often referred to as ODC files. There's nothing tremendously mysterious or complicated about these files, but it's helpful to know about their existence. As an example, in our last section we connected to a Microsoft Access database and imported a table from that database. As we selected a particular table in that database file, Excel created an ODC file to store information about the connection. This file would allow us to easily reconnect to the table without having to go through the entire procedure again.

Let's now look at the connection to see what it contains. This can be done in one of two ways. Referring back to Figure 3.1, there are two commands in this portion of the

Ribbon that pertain to connections: Existing Connections and Connections. When the Existing Connections command is selected, we see the dialog box shown in Figure 3.17.

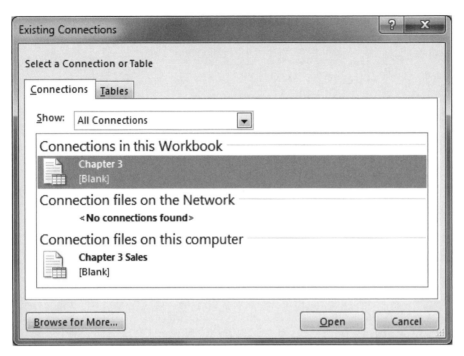

Figure 3.17
Existing Connections dialog box.
Source: Microsoft® Corporation.

This box displays three sets of connections files: those in the current workbook, files on the network, and connection files on your computer. The connection files on your computer or network are the ODC files we mentioned. These files are placed in a directory named "My Data Sources," which is located within My Documents. The connections in your workbook are embedded in your Excel file and contain the same information as the external files. The external files on your computer or network can be seen, no matter what you've done in your current Excel workbook. The connections in your workbook are only those that you've connected to from that particular workbook.

As seen, the connection to the Access database appears in the Existing Connections dialog box in both your workbook and on the computer. Even though they have slightly different names, they contain the same information. These connection files allow you to retrieve data that you viewed previously. By highlighting any row in the Existing Connections dialog box and clicking the Open button, that data is brought back in to your Excel file.

Let's now turn to the Connections command, found in the Connections group of the Ribbon. When selected, it displays the Workbook Connections dialog box of Figure 3.18.

Figure 3.18
Workbook Connections dialog box.
Source: Microsoft® Corporation.

This box displays only the connections that are present in this workbook. This is the same list seen in Figure 3.17. One additional feature of this dialog box is a Properties button that allows you to view the complete definition of the connection. When selected, a Connection Properties dialog box pops up that displays information such as the name and location of the Access database, and any passwords on the file. It also allows you to specify that you want to refresh data from that source on an automatic basis. Finally, the Connection Properties dialog box allows you to click an Export button that will save the connection ODC file in any location you choose. This means that you can save a connection file and share it with a co-worker, who would then be able to easily access the same data that you retrieved. Unlike the Existing Connections dialog box, the Workbook Connections pane doesn't allow you to open a file. It's merely there to organize files and view their properties.

Data from SQL Server

Connecting to a table in an Access database is a fairly trivial matter, but let's now take up a slightly more challenging task—that of connecting to a database that resides on an external server. In the following example, we'll demonstrate how to import data from Microsoft's SQL Server database. A very similar procedure would apply if you were connecting to other enterprise databases such as Oracle, MySQL, or DB2. To initiate the process of obtaining data from SQL Server, we'll start by clicking the From Other Sources label. We're then presented with the drop-down selection shown in Figure 3.19.

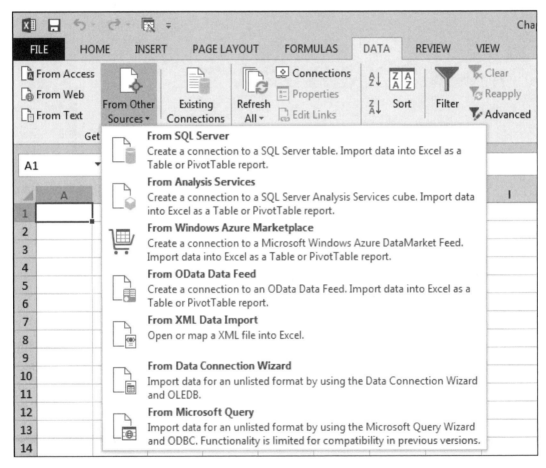

Figure 3.19

From Other Sources command.

Source: Microsoft® Corporation.

Since we're connecting to a SQL Server database, we'll select the From SQL Server option. If we wanted to connect to another database such as Oracle, we would select the From Data Connection Wizard option, and proceed similarly. After choosing the From SQL Server option, we see the Data Connection Wizard shown in Figure 3.20.

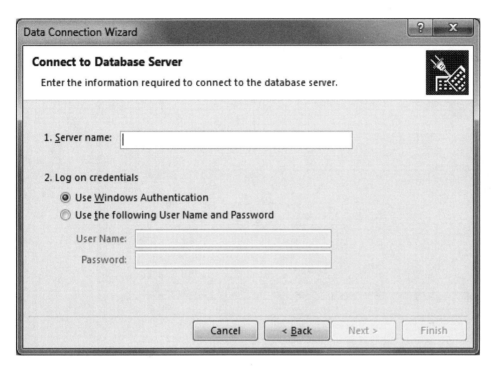

Figure 3.20

Data Connection Wizard: Connect to Database Server.

Source: Microsoft® Corporation.

At this point, we need to supply the name of the server we're connecting to and any credentials, such as a user name and password. After entering appropriate information, the next step of the wizard appears as in Figure 3.21.

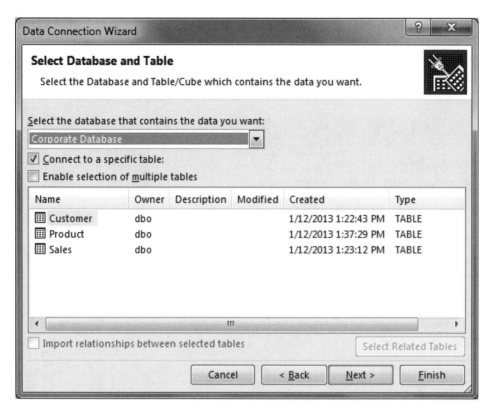

Figure 3.21

Data Connection Wizard: Select Database and Table.

Source: Microsoft® Corporation.

In this step, we're asked to select one of the databases that exist on that server, as well as a particular table to connect to. In this example, we'll select the database named Corporate Database, and then the Customer table.

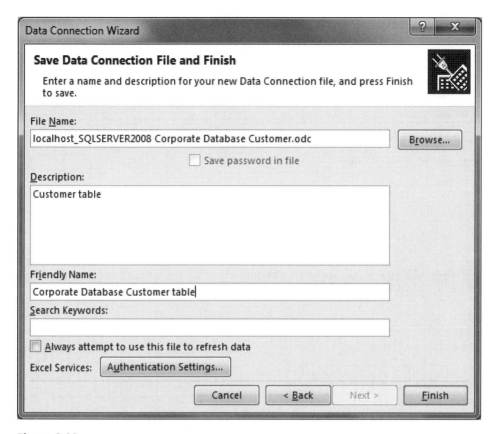

Figure 3.22

Data Connection Wizard: Save Data Connection File.

Source: Microsoft® Corporation.

Figure 3.22 shows the final step of the wizard. This step saves details about the ODC connection file that we're about to create. We must first specify a file name, or else simply use the name that's suggested for us. If we choose, we can browse to store this file anywhere we want. We then enter a Description and Friendly Name for the connection file. We'll see later on how these names appear in the connection list. After clicking the Finish button, we're presented with the same Import Data dialog box that was seen previously in Figure 3.14. This asks if we want to view the selected data as a Table, Pivot Table, or Pivot Chart. As before, we'll specify to place the data in a table. After completing these steps, our data from the SQL Server database appears in Excel, as in Figure 3.23.

	A	B	C	D	E
1	CustomerID ▼	CustomerName ▼	City ▼	State ▼	Zip ▼
2	1	Debra Smith	Chicago	IL	60641
3	2	Paul Jones	Peoria	IL	61601
4	3	Randy Davis	Nashville	TN	37205
5	4	Carla Crane	Pittsburgh	PA	15205

Figure 3.23

SQL Server data imported into an Excel table.

Source: Microsoft® Corporation.

To recap what was accomplished, let's look again at our Existing Connections, which now appears in Figure 3.24.

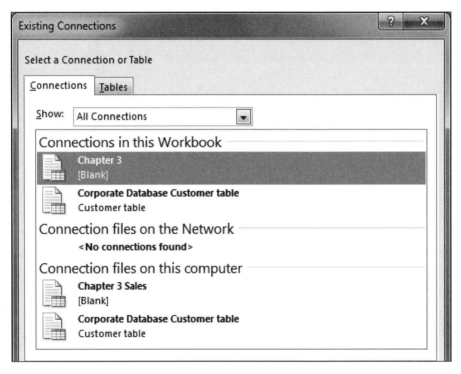

Figure 3.24

Existing Connections dialog box with a new connection.

Source: Microsoft® Corporation.

As expected, we now see a new connection that corresponds to the steps just taken. It appears both as a connection file on the computer and as a connection in this workbook. Comparing the entry to Figure 3.22, we see that the Friendly Name is displayed as the title for the connection, with the Description shown just under it.

Microsoft Query

In the prior section, we went through a somewhat laborious sequence of steps to import a table from an external database into Excel. The result of this effort is that we have data from only one table in the database. However, in analysis, the data we need often resides in more than one table in a database. It's very likely that related sets of data exist in multiple tables. Even with Excel's new Data Model feature that lets you establish relationships between multiple tables, there are some limitations, as will be seen in Chapter 5 when we cover pivot tables. As must be emphasized, Microsoft Excel is not a database and therefore can't join tables together with as much flexibility as can be done from within a database. The good news, however, is that Excel provides a useful component called Microsoft Query that allows you to utilize database functionality to import data from multiple tables into a single table in Excel. Let's examine how this works.

As a preliminary step, you first need to establish a connection to the database. This is different from creating an ODC file. A database connection is referred to as a DSN file, short for data source name. To accomplish this, you can begin by selecting the From Microsoft Query command, previously seen in Figure 3.19. After clicking this command, you'll see the Choose Data Source dialog box shown in Figure 3.25.

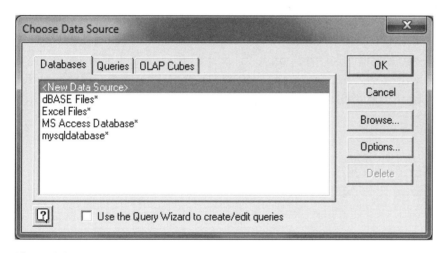

Figure 3.25

Choose Data Source dialog box.

Source: Microsoft® Corporation.

The next step is to select the New Data Source label and click OK. You'll then see the Create New Data Source dialog box shown in Figure 3.26.

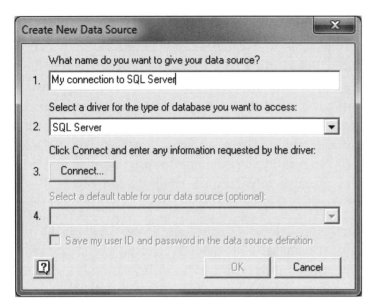

Figure 3.26
Create New Data Source dialog box.
Source: Microsoft® Corporation.

In this box, you'll specify a name for the connection, and then select a driver from a drop-down list. This will differ depending on the type of database you have. After clicking the Connect button, you'll be presented with a login screen, such as shown in Figure 3.27.

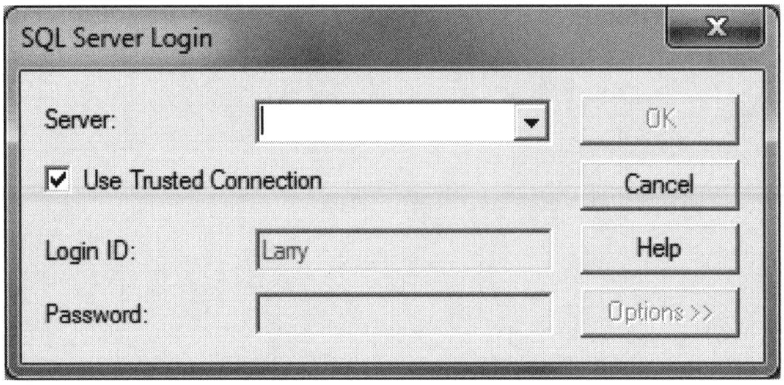

Figure 3.27
SQL Server Login dialog box.
Source: Microsoft® Corporation.

In this box, you'll need to first enter the server name, and then click the Options button. On the displayed options, select the specific database you want to work with. You'll then be returned to the Create New Data Source dialog box of Figure 3.26. The name of the database you've chosen will now appear to the right of the Connect button. After clicking OK, you'll be returned to the Choose Data Source dialog box of Figure 3.25, with your new data source appearing in the list. The data source just created is a permanent DSN file that will subsequently appear whenever you open a new Excel workbook. This is a one-time step that doesn't need to be repeated every time you want to access the database.

Now that the data source is available, we're ready to create our first query. To do this, we simply return to the Data Connection dialog box by again selecting the From Microsoft Query command. This appears as in Figure 3.28.

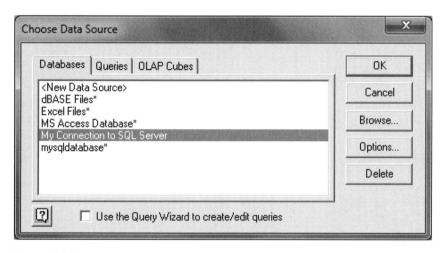

Figure 3.28
Choose Data Source dialog box.
Source: Microsoft® Corporation.

You'll want to make sure to uncheck the Use Query Wizard checkbox. This wizard is quite limited in its capabilities, in that it can only be used for queries that involve a single table. Since our purpose in using Microsoft Query is to join multiple tables together, we'll forgo the use of the wizard. After clicking OK, you'll be brought into the Microsoft Query application. This is a separate Windows application used in conjunction with Excel. When doing so, an Add Tables dialog box will pop up, asking you to select the tables to include in your query, as shown in Figure 3.29.

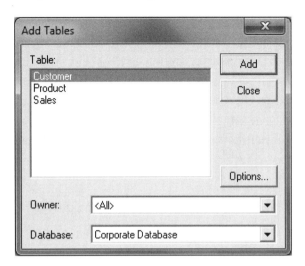

Figure 3.29

Add Tables dialog box.

Source: Microsoft® Corporation.

For our first query, we'll select both the Customer and Sales tables. This is done by selecting one table at a time, and then clicking the Add button. After adding these tables to the query, the Microsoft Query application appears as in Figure 3.30.

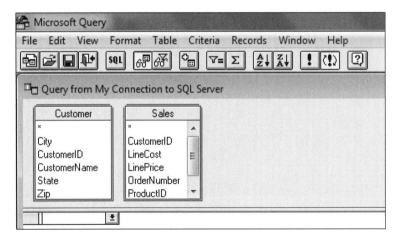

Figure 3.30

Microsoft Query tables pane.

Source: Microsoft® Corporation.

We now see all selected tables in the upper pane of the application. Each table is represented by a rectangle that contains a list of fields. To complete the query, two additional tasks are required. First, we need to specify how the two tables are related to

each other. In this situation, these tables are related by the CustomerID field. The CustomerID field is common to both tables and defines the relationship. This relationship,
referred to as a *join*, is specified by drawing a line between the CustomerID fields in
both tables. The second task is to specify those fields from both tables you want to see
when the query is run. This is accomplished by simply double-clicking on each desired
field. When doing so, each selected field is moved to the field grid pane, just below the
tables pane. There is no need to execute the query. Data results are shown immediately. The result of these two tasks is shown in Figure 3.31.

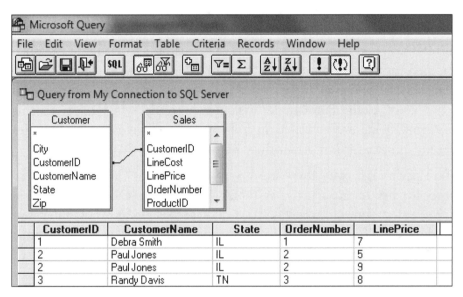

Figure 3.31
Microsoft Query field grid.
Source: Microsoft® Corporation.

Looking at Figure 3.31, we can see the line that joins the tables together, as well as the
data results in the field grid. Now that we have some data, there are two options for
proceeding. First, we can save the query so it can be referenced or rerun in the future.
This is done by selecting the Save or Save As commands under the File menu. This
saves the query as a separate file with a DQY suffix. If we want to run this query
later, we simply need to get into Microsoft Query again, and then select the Open command under the File menu. Secondly, we can return the results of the query to Excel.
This is done by selecting the Return Data to Microsoft Excel command under the File
menu. After this is done, we're presented with the same Import Data dialog box previously seen in Figure 3.13. This allows us to save the data as a table, pivot table, or pivot
chart. If we specify to import as a table, the data appears in Excel as in Figure 3.32.

	A	B	C	D	E
1	CustomerID ▼	CustomerName ▼	State ▼	OrderNumber ▼	LinePrice ▼
2	1	Debra Smith	IL	1	7
3	2	Paul Jones	IL	2	5
4	2	Paul Jones	IL	2	9
5	3	Randy Davis	TN	3	8

Figure 3.32

Microsoft Query data returned to an Excel table.

Source: Microsoft® Corporation.

In taking a closer look at this data, two questions might arise. First, one might wonder why there are two rows for Paul Jones when he had only one row in the Customer table. The answer is that there are two rows for this customer in the Sales table. When tables are joined together, the query finds all matches on the designated common field, which in this case is CustomerID. Since Paul Jones has one row in the Customer table and two rows in the Sales table, the query produces two rows for this customer. The customer fields are repeated in both rows. The fields from the Sales table contain different information, representing the two sales for this customer.

The second question pertains to why there are no rows shown for Carla Crane when we clearly see a row for her in the Customer table. The answer is that there are no matching rows in the Sales table. In other words, Carla was set up as a customer, but hasn't yet produced a sale. If we wish to include a row for Carla, even without a matching row in the Sales table, we need to alter the join property between the two tables. This is done by double-clicking the line that connects the two tables. This produces the Joins dialog box of Figure 3.33.

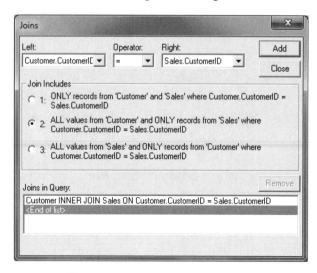

Figure 3.33

Joins dialog box.

Source: Microsoft® Corporation.

To alter the join property, we simply select option 2, which states that the query will include all rows from the Customer table and rows from the Sales table that match on CustomerID. When this is done, our data appears in Microsoft Query as in Figure 3.34.

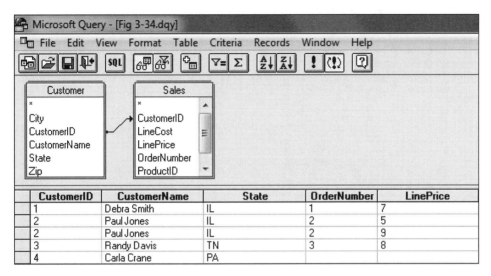

Figure 3.34

Microsoft Query with an outer join.

Source: Microsoft® Corporation.

Notice that we now see a fifth row for Carla. The fields from the Customer table contain data, but the fields from the Sales table are blank, because a matching row doesn't exist. Note that the line connecting the tables now appears as an arrow, indicating the direction of the join. This type of join, which takes all rows from one table and matching rows from a second table, is referred to as an outer join. This is in contrast to the inner join of Figure 3.31, in which data must match in both tables for a row to be selected.

At this point, we've seen how to use Microsoft Query to join multiple tables together using either an inner or an outer join. There is no limit to the number of tables that can be joined together in a single query. For example, we might very well want to extend this query by adding a join to the Product table. Although not shown, the Product table could be joined to the Sales table via the ProductID field. Fields from the Product table could then be displayed in the query, displaying attributes such as a product description.

Two remaining topics remain for Microsoft Query. First, we need to demonstrate how to add selection criteria to a query. This is simple. Starting with the query of Figure 3.34, let's say we want to see only data from Illinois. To accomplish this, we click on the Add

Criteria command under the Criteria menu. This causes the Add Criteria dialog box of Figure 3.35 to appear.

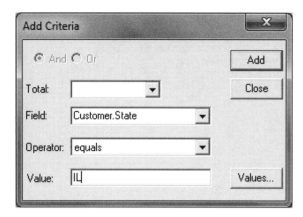

Figure 3.35

Add Criteria dialog box.

Source: Microsoft® Corporation.

In the Add Criteria box, we select the desired Field and Operator values from the supplied drop-down lists. After doing so, our query looks like Figure 3.36.

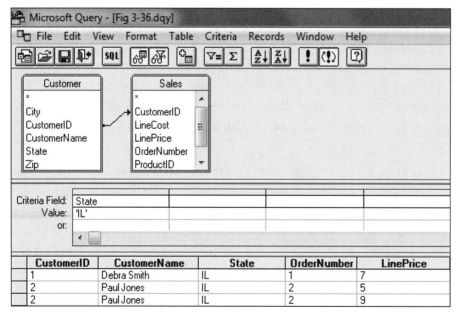

Figure 3.36

Microsoft Query with selection criteria.

Source: Microsoft® Corporation.

With this added criteria, we now see only three rows of data. A new criteria pane has been inserted between the tables pane and the data grid. If you're familiar with Microsoft Access, you might observe that the table and criteria panes in Microsoft Query correspond to the Design View of a query in Access. The data grid pane in Microsoft Query corresponds to the Datasheet View in Access. In other words, the upper two panes indicate the design of the query, and the lower pane displays the results.

Let's now discuss one final feature of Microsoft Query, which is its ability to group data and summarize quantitative values. To illustrate, let's start with a new query that contains just two fields: State from the Customer table, and LinePrice from the Sales table. This appears in Figure 3.37.

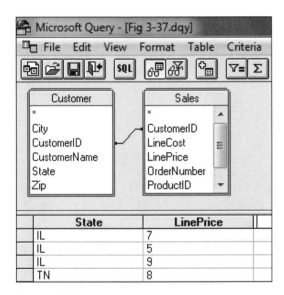

Figure 3.37

Microsoft Query with data to be summarized.

Source: Microsoft® Corporation.

Our objective in this example is to calculate the average LinePrice value for each state. To do this, we first select the Query Properties command under the View menu. This brings up a Query Properties dialog box that allows us to select whether we want to group records or see unique values only. We'll check the Group Records option. This has no immediate effect on the appearance of the query. However, if we highlight the LinePrice column in the data grid pane, and then click the Cycle Through Totals icon (which appears as a Greek summation symbol), we see a successive series of changes to the data grid that reflect different ways that the data can be grouped and summed. We can obtain sums, averages, counts, or minimum or maximum values. After we click the Summation symbols several times, we'll get to a view that displays averages, as seen in Figure 3.38.

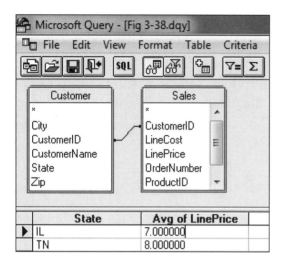

Figure 3.38

Microsoft Query with grouped data summarized by average.

Source: Microsoft® Corporation.

This tells us that the average sale price was 7 in Illinois and 8 in Tennessee. As always, remember that we can return any data in Microsoft Query to Excel at any time by selecting the Return Data to Microsoft Excel command under the File menu.

Let's step back for a minute and reflect on why the ability to group and summarize data in Microsoft Query is important. When taking the initial steps of importing data into Excel for analysis, one might be confronted with a relevant data set that consists of thousands, or even millions, of records. The sheer volume of data might overwhelm the resources of Excel. Furthermore, you may have no interest in certain data fields. You may want to group data on certain specific data elements and analyze only summarized information. Microsoft Query allows you to pre-summarize data before putting it through further analysis in Excel.

As we wrap up our discussion of Microsoft Query, another question that arises is what to do in situations where you want to relate data that exists in multiple databases, or perhaps in several spreadsheets. Microsoft Query allows you to join tables that exist in the same database. However, as is often the case, you may want to combine two sets of data that are in entirely different locations. One solution to that dilemma is to utilize Microsoft Access.

Although briefly mentioned in Chapter 1, it needs to be emphasized again that Microsoft Access is a fully functional relational database, and as such, complements the capabilities of Excel in many ways. The great strength of Access is that it allows you to separate data into tables, which can then be linked together via queries that join the common fields. The Books Sold query seen in Figures 3.11 and 3.12 earlier in this chapter is a perfect illustration of this feature. By themselves, the Books and Sales tables contain important information, but when joined together, the data in each table can be associated with the other, and thus provide greater value for the analyst.

As an example, let's say that the data in these two tables, Books and Sales, was not initially in Access. Let's assume that you were merely given this data as two separate spreadsheets. As mentioned, it's possible to use the Data Model feature of Excel to relate data in two separate tables into one logical entity. Additionally, in Chapter 13, we'll discuss lookup functions, which are another way to associate data in two separate tables entirely within Excel. However, if you're sufficiently fluent with Microsoft Access, this process is easily accomplished by exporting each set of data into a table in Access, and then creating a query in Access that joins the tables together. Just as in Microsoft Query, Access queries can utilize either an inner or an outer join to connect tables. Also, remember that a query doesn't require or produce any additional data. It's merely a virtual table that combines data logically. After the query is created, you can then import that data into Excel, as demonstrated earlier in this chapter. The process of moving data from Access to Excel can be accomplished either from Access or from Excel. The initial step of moving data into Access is more easily accomplished from within Access, as an import procedure.

Additionally, if you're sufficiently familiar with Access, you can forgo using Microsoft Query entirely and make use of Access for all situations where you need to relate separate data files or tables. Access has all the functionality of Microsoft Query, and much more. In general, the user interface of Access is decidedly more user friendly than that of Microsoft Query. The benefit of Microsoft Query is that it is integrated with Excel. However, the interface is somewhat clumsy in that it requires you to connect to Microsoft Query every time you want to work with a previously created query.

In the real world of business and organizational computing, nearly all data is stored in relational databases. The defining characteristic of a relational database, whether a desktop database such as Access or an enterprise database that resides on a server, such as SQL Server or Oracle, is in its ability to organize data into any number of interconnected entities. Through the process known as normalization, a savvy database architect will typically design tables so that each contains information about one and only one entity. For example, a Customer table would contain information strictly about the customer. If the organization was interested in analyzing the specific demographics of customer zip codes, that information would be stored in a separate table. Thus, the job of retrieving data about a customer would necessitate joining those two tables together to get a complete picture of the customer.

In short, both Microsoft Access and Microsoft Query offer the ability to join data together in a flexible manner, which is something not easily accomplished in Excel. In contrast, Excel's great strength is its capabilities for analysis on a single set of data.

Looking Ahead

This chapter demonstrated a number of ways to bring data into Excel for analysis. After covering both delimited and fixed-width text files, we proceeded to explain how to import data from Microsoft Access tables or queries. We then paused to discuss various methods of managing connections. In looking at the Existing Connections dialog box, we observed that connections can exist as separate ODC files on your computer or network, and are also embedded in your Excel workbook when referenced. We then moved on to the extraction of data from a SQL Server database. The limitation of this procedure, however, was that one can access only one table at a time. This brought us to Microsoft Query, a separate application that allows you to formulate queries that join multiple tables in the same database before bringing the data into Excel. Microsoft Query also allows you to aggregate data prior to its extraction. Finally, we discussed Microsoft Access as an alternative to Microsoft Query, in that it allows you to join sets of data together, even if they weren't originally in the same database. In Chapter 5, "Pivot Table Basics," we'll cover another way to bring together data from multiple tables via a Data Model.

In our next chapter, we'll begin some real analysis work by looking at the functionality of Excel tables. Tables provide some useful basic analysis capabilities involving the sorting and filtering of data.

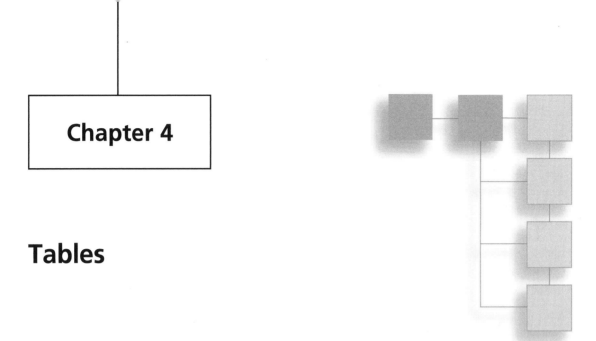

Chapter 4

Tables

In the prior chapter, we saw many examples of data being exported into Excel tables. When external data from a relational database is brought into Excel, the assumption is made that the data is in a standard tabular format, with the columns representing the various attributes of the entity, and rows representing instances of that entity. Rather than just dumping external data into a blank worksheet, Excel creates an object called a *table* for you. Just as external databases contain tables, Excel emulates the data structure by creating its own version of a table to hold the same data. Remember, however, that Excel tables are quite a bit different from true database tables. Unlike in databases, Excel tables do not contain primary keys or indexes. One can't retrieve data from tables in Excel as one could from tables in a relational database.

In functionality, tables occupy an interesting place above plain worksheets but below pivot tables. Tables extend the functionality of ordinary worksheets by adding a number of useful features often used by the analyst. This includes the ability to sort and filter data in an interactive way, without having to resort to formulas. The table takes a defined matrix of columns and rows and turns it into a distinct entity that can be explored in an interactive manner. While adding these features, tables still maintain the ability to insert formulas or functions in your data, just as you would do with the normal arrangement of cells in a worksheet.

Table Basics

In our brief survey of tables in Chapter 1, we noted that tables can be created from a matrix of cells in a worksheet. It's likewise true that tables can be converted back to ordinary cells at any point. Additionally, as seen in Chapter 3, external data in relational databases can be directly imported into Excel tables.

To illustrate some of the basic functionality of tables, let's begin with an array of data in a worksheet that has some information about a few movies. This is shown in Figure 4.1.

	A	B	C	D
1	Movie Title	Motion Picture Rating	Release Date	Average Rating
2	Love Actually	R	11/14/2003	3.6
3	Down with Love	PG-13	5/16/2003	3.5
4	The Social Network	PG-13	10/1/2010	3.4
5	Slumdog Millionaire	R	1/23/2009	3.3
6	Sideways	R	1/21/2005	2.9
7	Little Miss Sunshine	R	8/19/2006	2.8
8	The Wedding Singer	PG-13	2/16/1998	3.2
9	Midnight in Paris	PG-13	6/10/2011	2.6
10	The Hours	PG-13	1/24/2003	2.8
11	The Proposal	PG-13	6/19/2009	2.1

Figure 4.1

Movie data in a worksheet.

Source: Microsoft® Corporation.

In Excel terminology, this arrangement of data in a rectangular matrix is referred to as a *range*. Strictly speaking, a range is defined as any set of two more cells on an Excel worksheet. The cells do not necessarily have to be adjacent or in rectangular arrangement, but the layout of Figure 4.1 is typical. The range of data is presented in a standard tabular format, with column headers in row 1 that state the name of each attribute, and detailed data in rows 2 through 11. The font in row 1 is bold to emphasize the importance of that row. The attributes in our range are the movie title, the MPAA motion picture rating, the date released, and a rating for the movie, representing the presumed average number of "stars" the movie was rated by critics.

To turn this data into a table, we merely need to highlight any cell in the range of data and select the Table command under the Insert tab of the Ribbon, shown in Figure 4.2. After clicking the Table command, one is presented with the Create Table dialog box seen in Figure 4.3.

Figure 4.2

Table commands under the Insert tab of the Ribbon.

Source: Microsoft® Corporation.

Figure 4.3
Create Table dialog box.
Source: Microsoft® Corporation.

Figure 4.3 shows the range of cells in our matrix of values. The topic of cell references will be covered in depth in Chapter 9, "Formulas." For now, the important point to note is that Excel has automatically recognized the rectangular area that comprises the data we want to turn into a table. The noted cell reference, $A$1:$D$11, refers to the rectangle that extends from cell A1 on the upper left to D11 on the lower right. Furthermore, Excel has detected that the values in row 1 are different from the rest of the data, and therefore checked the "My table has headers" item. After clicking the OK button, we see the table of Figure 4.4.

	A	B	C	D
1	Movie Title	Motion Picture Rating	Release Date	Average Rating
2	Love Actually	R	11/14/2003	3.6
3	Down with Love	PG-13	5/16/2003	3.5
4	The Social Network	PG-13	10/1/2010	3.4
5	Slumdog Millionaire	R	1/23/2009	3.3
6	Sideways	R	1/21/2005	2.9
7	Little Miss Sunshine	R	8/19/2006	2.8
8	The Wedding Singer	PG-13	2/16/1998	3.2
9	Midnight in Paris	PG-13	6/10/2011	2.6
10	The Hours	PG-13	1/24/2003	2.8
11	The Proposal	PG-13	6/19/2009	2.1

Figure 4.4
Movie data in a table.
Source: Microsoft® Corporation.

Note that this table was placed in the same location as the original worksheet cells. Unlike pivot tables and charts, tables overlay existing data. In terms of functionality, the newly created table derives much of its ability from the filter button drop-downs that have been added to the header row, and from a new set of commands that appear in a new contextual Ribbon named Table Tools Design. This Ribbon, shown in Figures 4.5 and 4.6, appears whenever any cell in the table is selected.

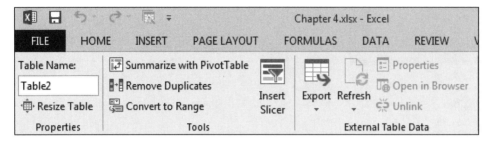

Figure 4.5
Left side of the Ribbon under the Table Tools Design tab.
Source: Microsoft® Corporation.

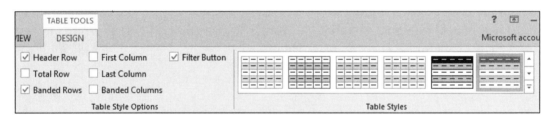

Figure 4.6
Right side of the Ribbon under the Table Tools Design tab.
Source: Microsoft® Corporation.

Note that the filter buttons in the header row of the table are identical to the functionality that is added to a range of cells when one selects the Filter command under the Data Ribbon. This command will be discussed in Chapter 8, "Data Commands." Most of the functionality of tables is found in the filter buttons in the header rows. These header row commands provide the means to sort and filter the data in tables.

There are a few ways to visually tell that we're looking at a table and not just a normal range of worksheet cells. The first is the appearance of the filter button drop-downs in the header, although as noted this functionality can also be applied via the Filter command. The second clue that this is a table is the alternating banded rows that Excel automatically applies to tables. This is a more definitive clue, since this stylistic design is one that's unique to tables. The third and most important clue that this is a table is the contextual Ribbon named Table Tools Design that appears when you click on any cell in a table. This Ribbon contains commands specific to tables. Finally, a fourth characteristic of tables is that they can be uniquely identified by a single name in the Name Manager. This feature will be discussed in Chapter 9.

Once a table is created, it can be resized at will. Additional rows or columns can be inserted or deleted without affecting the name or design of the table. As the size of the table changes, Excel keeps track of the current definition of the table. This is in keeping with how Excel works with rows and columns that aren't part of tables. As mentioned in Chapter 1, Excel always maintains the correctness of formulas and cell references as new rows or columns are added or deleted.

In addition to the table's ability to be resized, individual cells in tables can hold formulas and functions just like any normal cell in a worksheet. We're holding off on a discussion of formulas and functions until Chapter 9, but for now just remember that formulas can be utilized within tables. To illustrate the modification of a table size and the use of formulas, let's modify the table of Figure 4.4 by inserting a column between Release Date and Average Rating, and placing a formula in that column that takes the Average Rating in each row and multiplies it by .9. This is accomplished by first selecting any cell in column D and then selecting Insert Sheet Columns under the Insert command. The second step is to enter this formula in cell D2:

=E2 * .9

After this is done, Excel immediately propagates the formula to the remaining cells in column D. Since this is a table, Excel is smart enough to determine that you probably want the same formula in all cells in the column. If this had been a normal set of cells and not a table, you would have needed to copy the formula to the remaining cells in column D. The result of this procedure is shown in Figure 4.7.

	A	B	C	D	E
1	Movie Title	Motion Picture Rating	Release Date	Column1	Average Rating
2	Love Actually	R	11/14/2003	3.24	3.6
3	Down with Love	PG-13	5/16/2003	3.15	3.5
4	The Social Network	PG-13	10/1/2010	3.06	3.4
5	Slumdog Millionaire	R	1/23/2009	2.97	3.3
6	Sideways	R	1/21/2005	2.61	2.9
7	Little Miss Sunshine	R	8/19/2006	2.52	2.8
8	The Wedding Singer	PG-13	2/16/1998	2.88	3.2
9	Midnight in Paris	PG-13	6/10/2011	2.34	2.6
10	The Hours	PG-13	1/24/2003	2.52	2.8
11	The Proposal	PG-13	6/19/2009	1.89	2.1

Figure 4.7

A new column with formulas in a table.

Source: Microsoft® Corporation.

Notice that the new data in column D was given the header row value of Column1. Since this is a table, Excel assumes that you want each column to have a meaningful header. Column1 was used as a temporary placeholder, but you can type over it to provide a more expressive description.

A few more niceties of tables can be mentioned. Excel provides a number of colorful options on how tables can be displayed. The Table Style Options and Tables Styles groups under the Table Tools Design tab in the Ribbon, seen in Figure 4.6, offer a number of possibilities. Of note is the option that allows you to add a Total Row. This sums up all columns with numeric values that aren't calculated via a formula. In the case of the Table in Figure 4.7, it would sum the Average Ratings column, but not the values in column D. The Banded Rows option is what causes the alternating row colors to appear. The Header Row option allows you to show or hide the header row. The First Column and Last Column apply a bold font to either the first or the last columns. The Filter Button option lets you show or hide the filter button on the header row.

There's actually a second way to create tables, other than using the Table command under the Insert tab of the Ribbon. You can also create a table by selecting the Format as Table command under the Home tab of the Ribbon. In addition to creating a table, this command lets you select a desired Table Style at the same time.

Table Tools

After a table is created, it's usually a good idea to give it a name. Giving a table a name will be particularly important when we turn to the Data Model feature that will be discussed in Chapter 6, "Pivot Table Calculations." Giving a name to a table is as simple as typing over the generic Table Name shown in the Properties group in the Ribbon, seen in Figure 4.5. In Chapter 9, "Formulas," we'll discuss the Name Manager tool, which provides another way to explicitly manage the names of all objects in an Excel workbook.

The four commands in the Table Tools group under the Table Tools Design tab of the Ribbon offer some interesting possibilities for interacting with data in a table. These commands are also shown in Figure 4.5. The Summarize with Pivot Table command turns the table into a pivot table. This command will be illustrated in the following chapter on Pivot Tables.

The Convert to Range command turns the table back into a normal range of cells. If applied to the table of Figure 4.4, the result will appear as in Figure 4.8.

	A	B	C	D
1	Movie Title	Motion Picture Rating	Release Date	Average Rating
2	Love Actually	R	11/14/2003	3.6
3	Down with Love	PG-13	5/16/2003	3.5
4	The Social Network	PG-13	10/1/2010	3.4
5	Slumdog Millionaire	R	1/23/2009	3.3
6	Sideways	R	1/21/2005	2.9
7	Little Miss Sunshine	R	8/19/2006	2.8
8	The Wedding Singer	PG-13	2/16/1998	3.2
9	Midnight in Paris	PG-13	6/10/2011	2.6
10	The Hours	PG-13	1/24/2003	2.8
11	The Proposal	PG-13	6/19/2009	2.1

Figure 4.8

A table converted to a normal range of cells.

Source: Microsoft® Corporation.

The worksheet cells in Figure 4.8 retain the style characteristics of the old table but have lost all table functionality. The filter buttons in the header row have disappeared, as has the Table Tools Design tab in the Ribbon.

The Remove Duplicates command is significant for the business analyst, offering a straightforward way to remove duplicate rows. When this command is selected against the table in Figure 4.4, we see the Remove Duplicates dialog box of Figure 4.9.

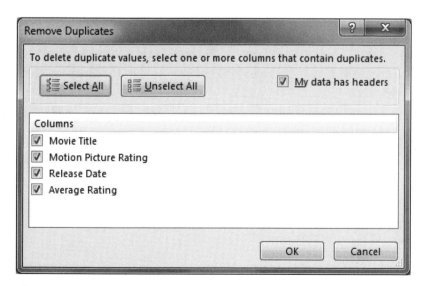

Figure 4.9

Remove Duplicates dialog box.

Source: Microsoft® Corporation.

This dialog box allows you to remove duplicates against a variety of criteria. If you leave all the displayed columns checked, then duplicate rows will be removed only if all columns in multiple rows have the same value. If you check only one column, Excel will remove duplicate rows based on that one column only. Consider the table in Figure 4.10.

Figure 4.10
Table with duplicate values.
Source: Microsoft® Corporation.

If you remove duplicates on this table and check both the City and State columns, no rows will be deleted. This is because all rows have a unique combination of city and state. However, if you check just the State column, Excel will search for duplicates only among the State values, and remove three rows, leaving one row for Arizona and one for Tennessee. The rows that remain will be the first occurrence of each of those states: Tucson Arizona and Nashville Tennessee. Excel also includes a command to remove duplicates outside of working with tables. This will be covered in Chapter 8.

The final command in the Table Tools group, Insert Slicer, is an improved feature of Excel 2013. When this command is applied to the table of Figure 4.4, the Insert Slicers dialog box of Figure 4.11 appears.

Figure 4.11
Insert Slicers dialog box.
Source: Microsoft® Corporation.

This dialog box allows you to select one or more columns in the table. For each selected column, a Slicer pane will appear. In this example, if we select the Motion Picture Rating column, the screen appears as in Figure 4.12.

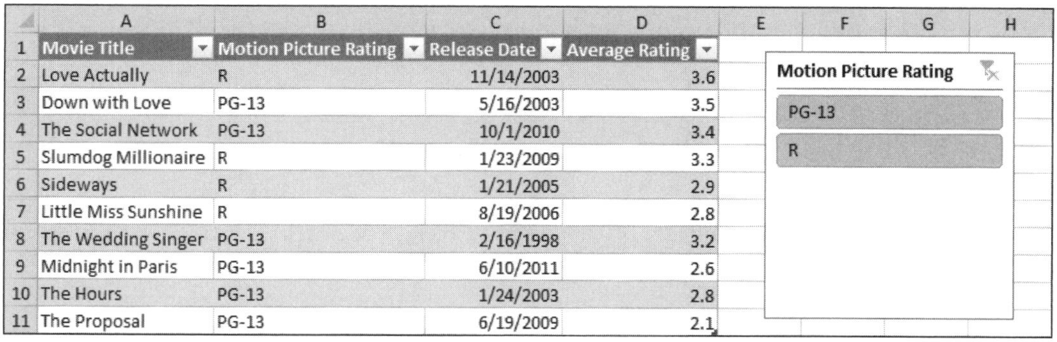

	A	B	C	D
1	Movie Title	Motion Picture Rating	Release Date	Average Rating
2	Love Actually	R	11/14/2003	3.6
3	Down with Love	PG-13	5/16/2003	3.5
4	The Social Network	PG-13	10/1/2010	3.4
5	Slumdog Millionaire	R	1/23/2009	3.3
6	Sideways	R	1/21/2005	2.9
7	Little Miss Sunshine	R	8/19/2006	2.8
8	The Wedding Singer	PG-13	2/16/1998	3.2
9	Midnight in Paris	PG-13	6/10/2011	2.6
10	The Hours	PG-13	1/24/2003	2.8
11	The Proposal	PG-13	6/19/2009	2.1

Figure 4.12

Table with a slicer.

Source: Microsoft® Corporation.

The Motion Picture Rating slicer pane allows the user to quickly and interactively select a value and immediately filter the table on that selection. For example, if we select the PG-13 value, the table is instantly transformed to that of Figure 4.13.

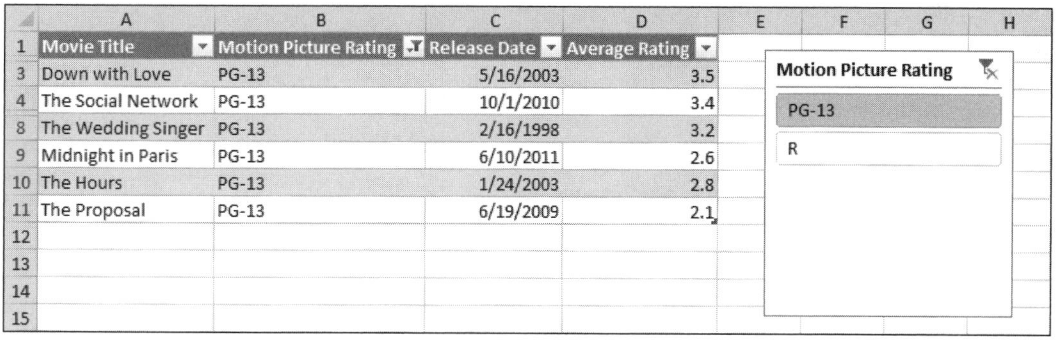

	A	B	C	D
1	Movie Title	Motion Picture Rating	Release Date	Average Rating
3	Down with Love	PG-13	5/16/2003	3.5
4	The Social Network	PG-13	10/1/2010	3.4
8	The Wedding Singer	PG-13	2/16/1998	3.2
9	Midnight in Paris	PG-13	6/10/2011	2.6
10	The Hours	PG-13	1/24/2003	2.8
11	The Proposal	PG-13	6/19/2009	2.1
12				
13				
14				
15				

Figure 4.13

Table with an applied slicer value.

Source: Microsoft® Corporation.

We now see only rows with a PG-13 rating. Later in this chapter, we'll discuss the filter options available via the filter button in the header row. Relative to slicers, filters offer more functionality but are also a bit more cumbersome to utilize. The convenience of slicers is that they are very interactive and require fewer keystrokes than comparable filters on the same columns. Slicers can filter on only one value for the column at a time, but that selection can be cleared by clicking the Clear Filter icon in the upper right corner of the slicer pane. Additionally, after a slicer pane has been added, it can be just as easily removed by highlighting the pane and pressing the Delete or Backspace key.

A number of commands apply specifically to slicers. When focus is on a slicer pane, a Slicer Tools Options tab appears on the Ribbon, as shown in Figures 4.14 and 4.15.

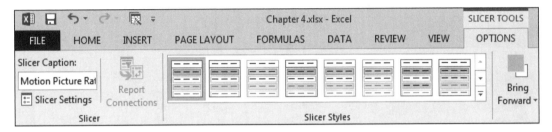

Figure 4.14
Left side of the Ribbon under the Slicer Tools Options tab.
Source: Microsoft® Corporation.

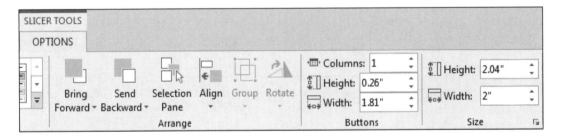

Figure 4.15
Right side of the Ribbon under the Slicer Tools Options tab.
Source: Microsoft® Corporation.

Most of these slicer commands are purely cosmetic in nature. The Slicer Styles options apply a color scheme to the slicer pane. The commands in the Arrange group specify how multiple slicer panes are arranged. The Selection Pane command in this group opens a special pane that lists all slicer panes in one location. The commands in the Buttons and Size groups specify the size of the various slicer pane elements. The only significant command in this Ribbon is Slicer Settings. This command opens a dialog box that lets you specify the sort order of items after a slicer is applied, and also contains an option that hides items with no data.

Sorting

We now turn to the commands and options that are available after clicking the filter button on each column in the header row of a table. When, for example, you click the filter button on the Movie Title column of Figure 4.4, you'll see the display shown in Figure 4.16.

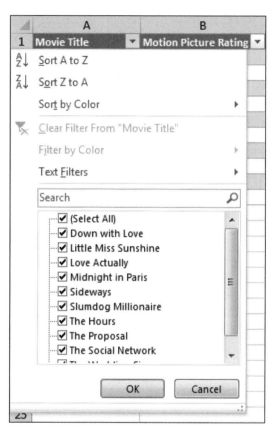

Figure 4.16

Filter button commands and options.

Source: Microsoft® Corporation.

We see four areas of commands and options in the drop-down list. At the top are sort commands, allowing you to sort in an ascending or descending sequence, or to sort by color. Since this column has text values, it states "A to Z" and "Z to A." If it were a numeric field, it would say "Smallest to Largest" and "Largest to Smallest." Date columns would say "Oldest to Newest" and "Newest to Oldest." Below the sort commands are text filters, which appear when the Text Filters label is selected. Numeric and Date columns would display "Number Filters" and "Date Filters." The next item is a Search box that allows for a search for any value of text in that column of the table.

Finally, below the Search box is a list of all the specific values that currently exist in that column. This list is dynamic in that it changes as values in the column are modified. This lets you select any or all specific values.

The sort commands are routine. By selecting the Sort A to Z option on the Movie Titles column, the rows in the table will be instantly arranged in an ascending alphabetic order. Once rows are sorted, they remain sorted until another sort is applied, although you can undo the sort by utilizing Excel's Undo command in the Quick Access Toolbar. You also have the ability to sort by color, whether it is the color of the cell or the color of the font. Note, however, that the colors that appear as a result of your table styles, such as the alternating rows seen in our examples, do not count as colors. They're merely decorative style elements.

The Sort by Color option is actually a bit of a misnomer. When this option is selected, the Sort dialog box displayed in Figure 4.17 appears.

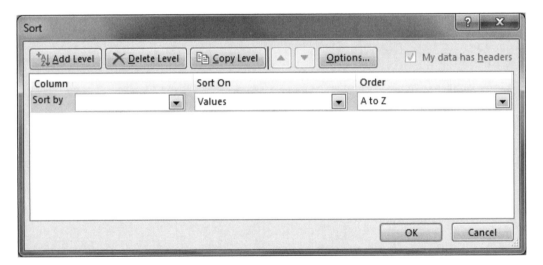

Figure 4.17
Sort dialog box.
Source: Microsoft® Corporation.

This dialog box offers a multitude of ways to modify the sort. The Column drop-down on the left lets you select the field to sort by. The Sort On drop-down in the middle has these options:

- Values
- Cell Color
- Font Color
- Cell Icon

When the Values option is selected, the Order drop-down on the right presents three options. The first two specify either ascending or descending order. The third option is called Custom Lists, and when selected, it brings up the dialog box shown in Figure 4.18.

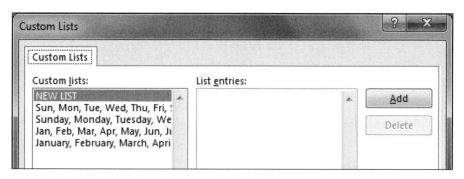

Figure 4.18
Custom Lists dialog box.
Source: Microsoft® Corporation.

The Custom Lists function is significant, as it allows an analyst to sort text fields with day or month names in the proper order. Without the use of custom lists, the value February would be sorted before January, since F is before J in the alphabet. Custom lists put month names in the proper order with January before February.

A second feature of the Sort dialog box is that it allows you to specify multiple levels in a sort. For example, if you want to sort the data by the Motion Picture Rating, and then the Movie title, you can use the Add Level button to add a second level to the sort. The Sort would then appear as in Figure 4.19.

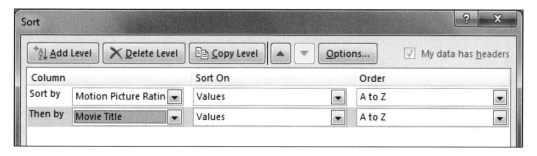

Figure 4.19
Sort dialog box with multiple levels.
Source: Microsoft® Corporation.

If this sort specification is applied, the data in Figure 4.4 will appear as in Figure 4.20.

	A	B	C	D
1	Movie Title	Motion Picture Rating	Release Date	Average Rating
2	Down with Love	PG-13	5/16/2003	3.5
3	Midnight in Paris	PG-13	6/10/2011	2.6
4	The Hours	PG-13	1/24/2003	2.8
5	The Proposal	PG-13	6/19/2009	2.1
6	The Social Network	PG-13	10/1/2010	3.4
7	The Wedding Singer	PG-13	2/16/1998	3.2
8	Little Miss Sunshine	R	8/19/2006	2.8
9	Love Actually	R	11/14/2003	3.6
10	Sideways	R	1/21/2005	2.9
11	Slumdog Millionaire	R	1/23/2009	3.3

Figure 4.20

Movie data with multiple levels in a sort.

Source: Microsoft® Corporation.

As seen, the sort causes the PG-13 movies to appear first. Within each group of PG-13 and R movies, the movies are displayed in alphabetic order by the Movie Title.

In a general sense, sorting serves two basic purposes for the analyst. First, it allows one to rearrange data so items of interest appear at the top of the list, making them easier to locate. This can be anything from the largest order amount to the most recent date. Second, sorting allows users to look at a long list of data and easily search for specific values, particularly if the sort item is a text item sorted alphabetically.

Filters

Filters are a mechanism by which Excel temporarily hides rows from view. The hidden rows are still present in the table but are not visible at the moment. This capability adds an interactive quality to tables, as filters can be easily modified without affecting the underlying data.

Filters have nothing to do with the hiding of rows that was briefly mentioned in Chapter 2. The Hide and Unhide commands under the Format label on the Home tab of the Ribbon can remove rows or columns from view. Filters apply only to rows. Rows that are hidden via a filter are generally easier to notice than rows hidden via the Hide command. Additionally, rows that are hidden via a filter are not included in the result if you copy and paste data in a table with filtered rows. In contrast, rows or columns that are hidden via the Hide command will show up if you copy that area of data to another location. For these reasons, we recommend using filtering rather than hiding rows when working with tables.

Excel provides several different ways to apply filters. The simplest method is to make use of the checkboxes that appear in the table header row commands. The bottom section of the filter commands seen in Figure 4.16 lists every value that currently exists in that column. The list is dynamically modified whenever a new value is added or removed. By default, the Select All item at the top of the list is checked, along with every item in the list. To select any number of individual rows to view, you simply need to uncheck the Select All item, and then check the desired values. In our example, if we select the movies *Down with Love* and *Midnight in Paris*, the result will appear as in Figure 4.21.

	A	B	C	D
1	Movie Title 🔽	Motion Picture Rating 🔽	Release Date 🔽	Average Rating 🔽
2	Down with Love	PG-13	5/16/2003	3.5
3	Midnight in Paris	PG-13	6/10/2011	2.6

Figure 4.21
Table filter results based on selected values.
Source: Microsoft® Corporation.

Notice that the filter button for the Movie Title column now displays an icon to indicate that a filter has been applied to that column. As seen, only the two selected movies are now visible. All others are filtered out. Of course, all rows of data are still in the table. The filter only means that certain rows are not currently visible. After a filter has been applied, it can be just as easily removed. Figure 4.22 shows the filter commands for the Movie Title column after the filter of Figure 4.21 has been applied.

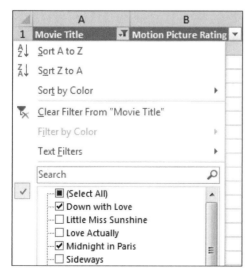

Figure 4.22
Filter commands after a filter has been applied.
Source: Microsoft® Corporation.

The filter can be removed either by selecting the Clear Filter option immediately below the sort commands or else by checking the Select All option just below the Search box. The list of values that appears in the header row commands is dependent on filters that may have already been applied in other columns. For example, if you first apply a filter to the Movie Picture Rating column to view only movies with an R rating, then when you subsequently look at the filter options for the Movie Title column, you will see only the values shown in Figure 4.23.

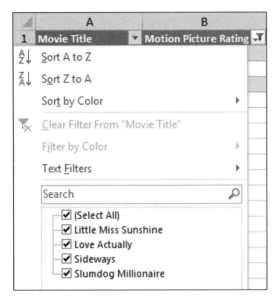

Figure 4.23

Filter commands after a filter in another column has been applied.

Source: Microsoft® Corporation.

As such, we now see only a list of R-rated movies, since we've already filtered out movies not having an R rating.

A second and more flexible way that filters can be applied is via a Search. When a value is entered in the Search box, shown in Figure 4.16, rows containing that value are made visible. All other rows are filtered out. For example, if we enter the word LOVE in the search box for our data in Figure 4.4, it will display the results seen in Figure 4.24.

	A	B	C	D
1	Movie Title	Motion Picture Rating	Release Date	Average Rating
2	Down with Love	PG-13	5/16/2003	3.5
9	Love Actually	R	11/14/2003	3.6

Figure 4.24

Table filter results based on a search.

Source: Microsoft® Corporation.

In our search for LOVE, the values can appear anywhere in the phrase. In this case, the word appears in the beginning of one movie and at the end of the other. Searches are not case sensitive, so a lowercase letter has the same effect as uppercase.

Additionally, searches can contain asterisk (*) or question mark (?) wildcards for additional search possibilities. The asterisk (*) is used to represent any series of characters. For example, if you specify a search value of S* for the movie title, this would return any movie that begins with the letter S. A search for *S would retrieve any movie that ends with the letter S. A search for S*S would find any movie that begins and ends with S. The question mark (?) wildcard is used to represent a single character, so this is of more limited value. As an example, a search for S??????S would retrieve all movies that begin and end with the letter S, and consist of exactly eight characters. In our example, this would find the movie *Sideways*.

The third and final method for applying filtering is to make use of special options that are dependent on the type of data in each column. In our example, the filter button commands for the Movie Title and Motion Picture Rating columns each have an option called Text Filters. The Release Date column presents a similar option called Date Filters. The Average Rating column has an option named Number Filters. When either of these options is selected, Excel presents a number of custom filters specific to that data type. For columns with text data, the available Text Filters are:

- Equals
- Does Not Equal
- Begins With
- Ends With
- Contains
- Does Not Contain

To illustrate, if the Does Not Contain option for the Movie Titles column is chosen, the dialog box of Figure 4.25 will be presented.

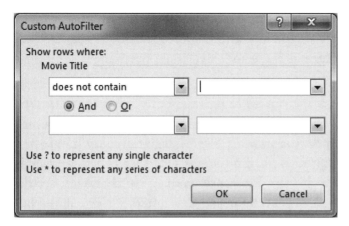

Figure 4.25
Custom AutoFilter dialog box.
Source: Microsoft® Corporation.

If you enter the word THE in the text box to the right of the Does Not Contain label, the table will appear as in Figure 4.26.

	A	B	C	D
1	Movie Title 🔽	Motion Picture Rating 🔽	Release Date 🔽	Average Rating 🔽
2	Love Actually	R	11/14/2003	3.6
3	Down with Love	PG-13	5/16/2003	3.5
5	Slumdog Millionaire	R	1/23/2009	3.3
6	Sideways	R	1/21/2005	2.9
7	Little Miss Sunshine	R	8/19/2006	2.8
9	Midnight in Paris	PG-13	6/10/2011	2.6

Figure 4.26
Table filter results based on Text Filter.
Source: Microsoft® Corporation.

We now see only movies that do not include the word THE. The meaning of the other text filters should be obvious. Equals and Does Not Equal require a match with the entire text value. Begins With and Ends With look at the beginning or end of the text value.

The options for Number Filters are:

■ Equals

■ Does Not Equal

■ Greater Than

- Greater Than or Equal To

- Less Than

- Less Than or Equal To

- Between

- Top 10

- Above Average

- Below Average

Of particular note is the Top 10 option. This allows you to list the top *x* rows in the table, where *x* is any specified number. You can select either the top *x* items or the top *x* percent. The top *x* selection is based only on values in that column. As an example, we'll select the top 3 items in the Average Rating column. The result is shown in Figure 4.27.

	A	B	C	D
1	Movie Title	Motion Picture Rating	Release Date	Average Rating
2	Love Actually	R	11/14/2003	3.6
3	Down with Love	PG-13	5/16/2003	3.5
4	The Social Network	PG-13	10/1/2010	3.4

Figure 4.27
Table filter results based on the Top 10 Number Filter.
Source: Microsoft® Corporation.

The results show the three movies with the highest ratings. If there had been two movies with a rating of 3.4, then both of those movies would have been shown. Note that the top *x* criteria isn't dependent on how the rows are sorted. This is unlike the way in which the top *x* feature works in Microsoft Access. The top *x* is dependent only on values in that column. This means that you can't use the top *x* option to show the three rows with the *lowest* scores.

The options for Date Filters are more numerous, and include:

- Equals

- Before

- After

- Between

- Tomorrow

- Today

- Yesterday

- Next Week

- This Week

- Last Week

- Year to Date

- All Dates in the Period

There are additional options for Month, Quarter, and Year similar to the Next Week, This Week, and Last Week options. The All Dates in the Period option has sub-options that include selections for each of the twelve calendar months and four calendar quarters.

Many but not all of the Text, Number, and Date filters make use of the Custom Auto-Filter dialog box that was seen in Figure 4.25. If you look closely at Figure 4.25, you'll see that it includes the ability to create a custom filter selection that involves two different criteria. Using Boolean Logic, Excel lets you create filters with two conditions, combined with an And or Or operator. To illustrate, let's specify that we want to see Movies that begin with either the letter L or the letter S. The filter dialog box that specifies this is shown in Figure 4.28, with the result in Figure 4.29.

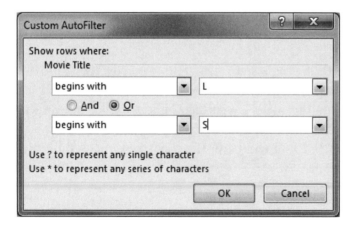

Figure 4.28

Custom AutoFilter dialog box with multiple criteria.

Source: Microsoft® Corporation.

⊿	A	B	C	D
1	Movie Title 🔽	Motion Picture Rating 🔽	Release Date 🔽	Average Rating 🔽
2	Love Actually	R	11/14/2003	3.6
5	Slumdog Millionaire	R	1/23/2009	3.3
6	Sideways	R	1/21/2005	2.9
7	Little Miss Sunshine	R	8/19/2006	2.8

Figure 4.29

Table filter results based on a Text Filter with multiple criteria.

Source: Microsoft® Corporation.

As seen, the text filter has removed any movies that don't begin with the letters L or S. Note that we needed to check the Or radio button in order to specify that *either* of these conditions can be true for the row to be displayed. If the And radio button is selected, then *both* conditions must be true. There's a limit of two conditions that can be specified in this dialog box. Another limitation is that the Or conditions can't span columns. This means, for example, that you can't specify logic to list movies that begin with the letter L or movies with a rating greater than 3.0.

Looking Ahead

The functionality provided by tables is fairly basic. In this chapter, we've seen how tables can remove duplicates, sort data, and apply a wide variety of filters to remove rows from consideration. The filtering feature is especially noteworthy because it adds a degree of interactivity to the exploration of data in Excel. However, it should be emphasized that it is not necessary to create a table in order to make use of sorting, filtering, or duplicate removal. All of these features are available for data in worksheet cells that have not been organized into a table. In fact, we'll mention these features again in Chapter 8, "Data Commands." That said, it's more convenient to apply this functionality when data is already part of a table, since the needed commands appear in either the Table Tools Design Ribbon or the header row filter button commands.

Although tables add some interesting features to worksheets, they don't come close to the full featured functionality of pivot tables, the topic of the next two chapters. While tables add a limited amount of interactivity to the process of data analysis, pivot tables extend the paradigm in a much more dynamic fashion, allowing you to summarize data, and also view data in a powerful crosstab format that promotes an understanding of relationships within data elements.

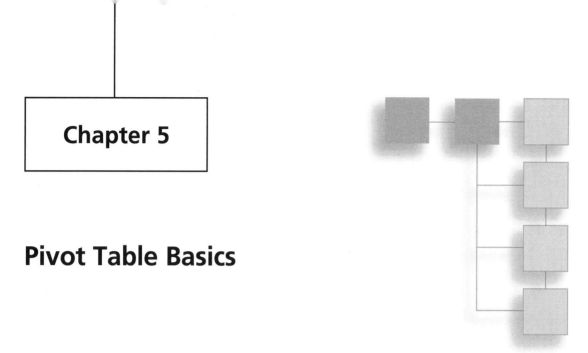

Chapter 5

Pivot Table Basics

The Excel tables described in the prior chapter provide some basic capabilities for data exploration. In addition to sorting and searching, table filters allow the analyst to hide rows of data that are irrelevant to the task at hand. However, even with these features, tables afford few opportunities for analysis. The problem is that no matter what you do, the data is essentially still the same data. There are no tools for summarization or for viewing data from a different perspective.

The pivot table, a tool that we consider the most powerful and significant feature of Excel, extends the marginally useful capabilities of tables to an entirely new level. Whereas tables can merely hide data, pivot tables allow you to rearrange, summarize, and present data in entirely new ways. A pivot table is a completely dynamic structure.

We cover pivot tables in this book prior to talking about formulas and functions. This is done for the simple reason that this sequence tends to follow the natural and normal way that data analysis is accomplished. When the business analyst is first presented with data, the first task is to get a handle on what it contains. One wants to see the big picture, summarize the data in any way that it can be summarized, and view the data from a few different perspectives to get a feel for what it holds. The pivot table is ideal for this task. One may also want to view the data graphically. Again, pivot charts, which are closely related to pivot tables in functionality, are perfect for this purpose. After the data has been sufficiently summarized, one may then want to explore the data in greater detail, and make use of Excel formulas to further view and manipulate that data.

It's important to understand that pivot tables exist apart from the underlying data upon which they're based. This is completely unlike table structures, in which the data and presentation layers overlap. When rows are filtered and hidden in a table, they are still on the same worksheet and in the same array of data. It's only that they're temporarily not visible. In contrast, the data behind pivot tables resides in a different place. The underlying data might be on another worksheet, in a different location on the same worksheet, or even in an external relational database. The pivot table is merely a device for manipulating data. The construct of pivot tables utilizes a special pane to list the data that it's connected to, thus making the data available for manipulation. This pane is called the Field List.

The Field List

Let's begin our journey into pivot tables with a specific set of data. We'll use the data shown in Figure 5.1 as the basis for the remainder of this chapter.

	A	B	C	D	E	F	G	H	I	J
1	Sales Date	Sales Month	Customer ID	Customer City	Customer State	Product	Product Category	Quantity	Unit Price	Total Sales
2	1/22/2013	2013-01	23	Nashville	TN	Breakfast Blend	Coffee	3	4	12
3	2/1/2013	2013-02	44	Seattle	WA	Vanilla	Spices	6	3	18
4	3/1/2013	2013-03	14	Knoxville	TN	Darjeeling	Tea	-3	4	-12
5	12/6/2012	2012-12	15	Atlanta	GA	Mustard	Spices	6	2	12
6	2/15/2013	2013-02	44	Seattle	WA	Cinnamon	Spices	8	3	24
7	3/16/2013	2013-03	23	Nashville	TN	Decaf	Coffee	9	4	36
8	2/18/2013	2013-02	18	Denver	CO	Earl Grey	Tea	4	5	20
9	3/31/2013	2013-03	19	Boulder	CO	Green Tea	Tea	-1	6	-6
10	2/6/2013	2013-02	20	Miami	FL	French Roast	Coffee	5	5	25
11	2/28/2013	2013-02	16	Chicago	IL	Hazelnut	Coffee	5	3	15
12	12/18/2012	2012-12	50	Peoria	IL	Curry	Spices	2	4	8
13	3/2/2013	2013-03	3	Portland	ME	Ginger	Spices	1	2	2
14	2/15/2013	2013-02	2	Minneapolis	MN	Oolong	Tea	8	3	24
15	1/11/2013	2013-01	11	Portsmouth	NH	Vanilla	Spices	4	3	12
16	12/27/2012	2012-12	44	Seattle	WA	Mustard	Spices	-2	2	-4
17	3/30/2013	2013-03	16	Chicago	IL	Vanilla	Coffee	4	4	16
18	1/17/2013	2013-01	49	Los Angeles	CA	Decaf	Coffee	6	4	24
19	2/17/2013	2013-02	22	Cleveland	OH	Green Tea	Tea	7	6	42
20	3/25/2013	2013-03	11	Portsmouth	NH	Oregano	Spices	10	5	50
21	2/18/2013	2013-02	45	Des Moines	IA	Curry	Spices	3	1	3

Figure 5.1

Underlying data for a pivot table.

Source: Microsoft® Corporation.

The data in Figure 5.1 describes sales of various coffee, tea, and spice products. Each row represents the sale of a specific item to a customer. Notice the rows with negative values for Quantity and Total Sales. These rows represent returns of a product. For example, row 4 is for a customer who returned $12 worth of Darjeeling Tea. Another unusual feature of this data is the Sales Month in column B. This type of data would not ordinarily be found in a database. However, we've added this column to illustrate an easy way to summarize our data by month.

Our first task is to create a pivot table from this data. We'll assume that the data already exists in a worksheet in Excel. We may have moved the data into Excel by any of the means discussed in Chapter 3, "Getting External Data," including the use of Microsoft Query to connect to an external database. At any rate, we now have this information sitting in Excel and would like to make use of it.

Creating a pivot table from data in an Excel worksheet is simple, and can be accomplished in two different ways. The first method, which we'll only briefly discuss, is via a feature that's new to Excel 2013: the Recommended PivotTables command. Referring back to Figure 4.2, this command is found under the Insert tab on the Ribbon. When this command is selected against any cell shown in Figure 5.1, the dialog box of Figure 5.2 appears.

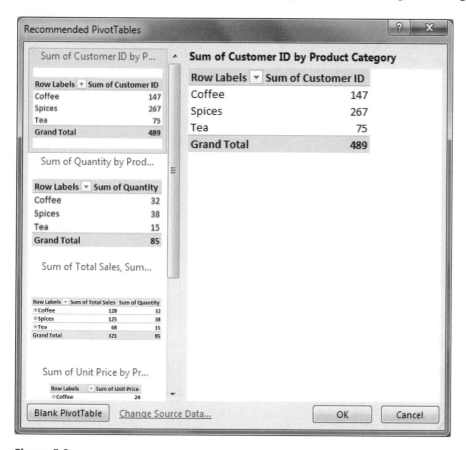

Figure 5.2

Recommended PivotTables dialog box.

Source: Microsoft® Corporation.

The left pane of this dialog box displays a number of recommended ways that a pivot table can be created from the specified data. When any of these options is highlighted, it appears in a larger display on the right pane. Clicking the OK button causes the pivot table to be created on a new worksheet. The Blank PivotTable button in the lower left ignores these recommendations and produces a blank pivot table from the data.

The second method of creating a pivot table, and the approach that we recommend, is as follows:

1. Click on any cell in the array of data.

2. Under the Insert tab on the Ribbon, select the PivotTable command.

3. On the Create PivotTable dialog box that appears, click OK.

The PivotTable command was previously seen in Figure 4.2 of the prior chapter. The Create PivotTable dialog box looks like Figure 5.3.

Figure 5.3
Create PivotTable dialog box.
Source: Microsoft® Corporation.

Three important options are seen in Figure 5.3. First, you have the ability to create a pivot table from either a selected table or range, or you can specify an external data source. If we had first created a table from the data in Figure 5.1, then the Create PivotTable dialog box would list the name of the table rather than the indicated range. Notice also that the range shown in Figure 5.3 is the fully qualified range name. Sheet1 is the name of our worksheet. The range of cells is given by $A$1:$J$21. If we had wanted to create the pivot table directly from an external data source, we could have selected that option and chosen a connection from those that we previously created.

Second, at the bottom of the dialog box is an option to add the data to a Data Model. This topic will be discussed in the following chapter. For now, we'll leave this option unchecked. Finally, we see that the Create PivotTable dialog box allows us to place the new pivot table either on a new worksheet or at a specified location in the current worksheet. In most cases, it's a good idea to place the pivot table on a separate worksheet to help reduce clutter in your Excel workbook. After the pivot table is created, the Excel window appears as in Figure 5.4.

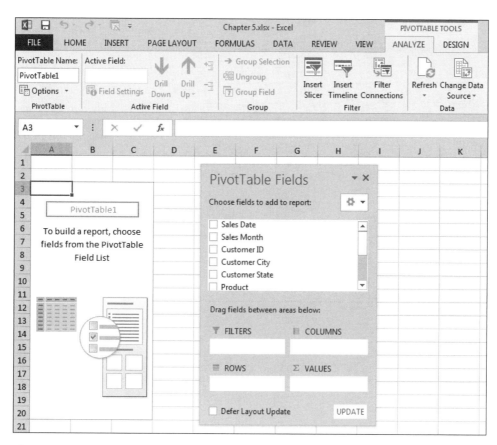

Figure 5.4

A pivot table with the PivotTable Field List.

Source: Microsoft® Corporation.

The depiction of the Field List in Figure 5.4 is not quite how it normally appears. In most situations, the Field List is at the far right of the screen, pinned to the edge. It can also be pinned to the left edge. For purposes of readability, however, we've chosen to detach it from the edge and drag it to the center of the screen. The Field List comprises two main sections: a Fields section and an Areas section. In our example, the Fields section is shown at the top of the Field List. This is a list of all the fields available for manipulation in the pivot table. The Areas section, shown in the bottom half of the Field List, consists of four different areas: the Filters, Columns, Rows, and Values. We'll talk shortly about what these four areas mean.

Before we proceed with that discussion, however, let's also mention that there are actually four different ways that the Field List can be displayed. The Tools icon in the upper right corner of the Field List is a drop-down that lets you select from among five options:

- Fields Section and Areas Section Stacked

- Fields Section and Areas Section Side-by-Side

- Fields Section Only

- Areas Section Only (2 by 2)

- Areas Section Only (1 by 4)

Figure 5.4 shows the Field List with the "Fields Section and Areas Section Stacked" option. If we select the "Fields Section and Areas Section Side-by-Side" option, it looks like Figure 5.5.

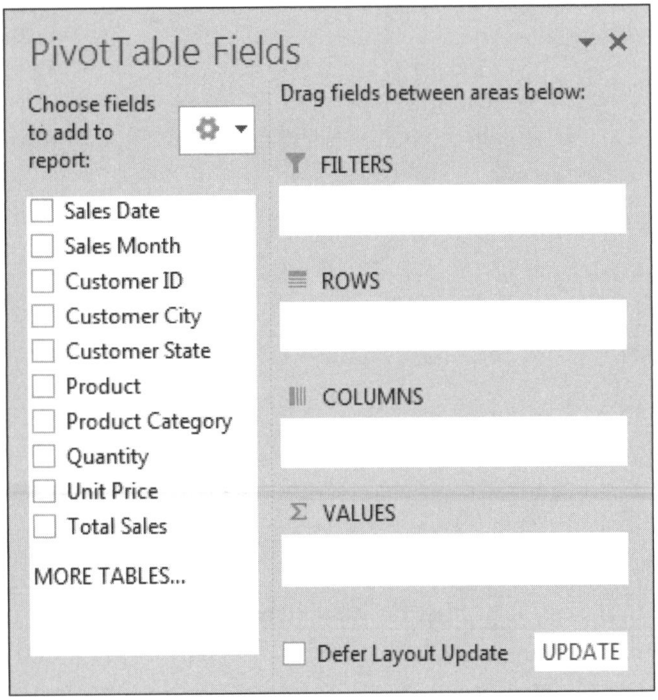

Figure 5.5

Field List with Fields Section and Areas Section Side-by-Side.

Source: Microsoft® Corporation.

With this arrangement, we can now see the entire list of fields, as well as the MORE TABLES label below the list. We'll discuss the meaning of that label in the next chapter when we talk about relationships and data models. We've briefly talked about the areas of the Field List, but the pivot table itself is completely empty at this point. In Figure 5.4, the Pivot Table can be in seen in the array of cells from A3 to C20. This is because we have not yet moved any data into the pivot table from the Field List.

It also needs to be noted that the Field List only appears on the screen when you've selected a cell in the pivot table. In Figure 5.4, we have selected cell A3, which is inside the pivot table, even if it currently contains no data. If we were to select a cell outside the pivot table, such as D3, the Field List would not be displayed.

In addition to the Field List, we can also see in Figure 5.4 that two new tabs appear in the Ribbon when the pivot table is selected. These two contextual tabs, named Analyze and Design, contain all of the commands specific to pivot tables. In Figure 5.4, the Analyze tab is selected, and the left side of that tab is displayed. Figure 5.6 shows the right side of the same Analyze tab.

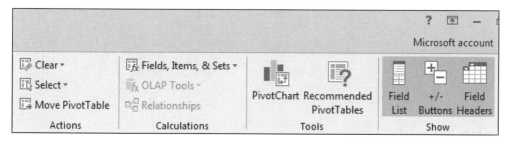

Figure 5.6

Right side of the PivotTable Analyze tab of the Ribbon.

Source: Microsoft® Corporation.

We mentioned that the Field List only appears when a cell in the pivot table is selected. In addition, the Field List command seen in Figure 5.6 allows you to toggle the Field List to be either hidden or visible.

With this background in place, we can now talk more specifically about the Field List. The key to the Field List are its four areas:

- Filters
- Rows
- Columns
- Values

The Field List is the key way in which data in pivot tables is manipulated. Fields are moved into any of the four desired areas from the Fields section of the Field List. This is done by either dragging the field, or by right-clicking on the field and selecting an option:

■ Add to Report Filter

■ Add to Row Labels

■ Add to Column Labels

■ Add to Values

Similarly, once a field is in one of the four areas, you can remove it or move it to any other area. To initiate our discussion of what the four areas represent, let's start with an example. We'll move the Customer State field to the filters area, the Sales Month to the rows area, the Product Category to the columns area, and Total Sales to the values area. The pivot table and Field List now appear as in Figure 5.7.

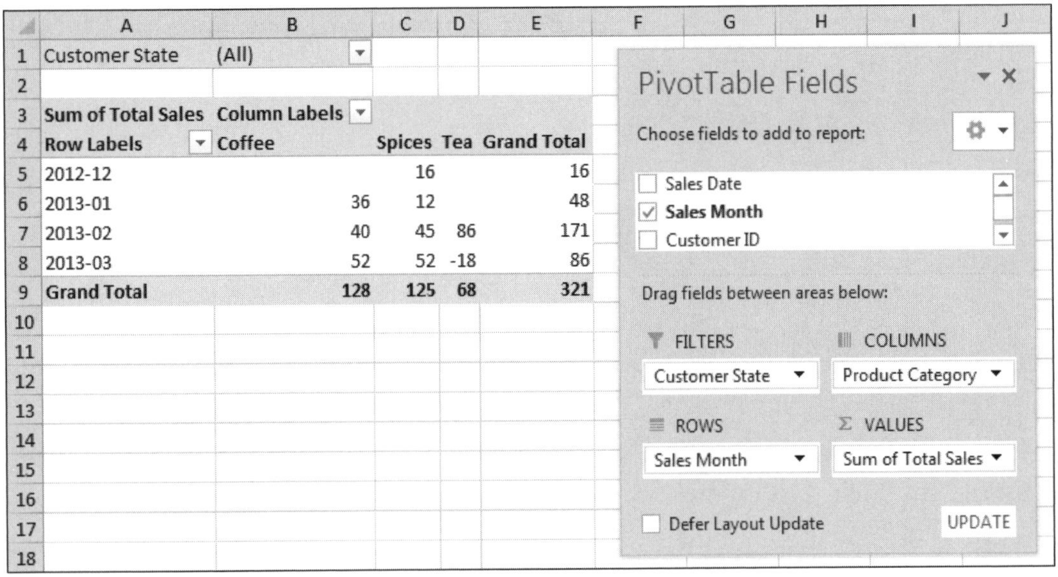

Figure 5.7
Pivot table with fields in all four areas.
Source: Microsoft® Corporation.

Let's examine what has happened to our data. The basic story with pivot tables is that they sum up all of the detailed data to which the pivot table is connected. The pivot table displays as many rows and columns as are necessary to display that data. The data is displayed in a crosstab-type format, with field values in the rows and columns.

The data that is actually summed up is placed in the values area. The report filter area is used to filter data that applies to everything else.

Once again, when fields are moved to any of the four areas, the pivot table is instantly updated with appropriate values corresponding to the new layout. The same is true when fields are removed from any of the areas, or moved from area to area. In other words, the pivot table is a highly interactive device that lets you manipulate data at will.

In this example, Sales Month is in the rows and Product Category is in the columns. Consequently, we see Sales Month values in cells A5 through A8. Product Category values appear in cells B4 to D4. The values in the rectangular array of cells from B5 to D8 contain the resulting summed amounts of each intersection of a Sales Month and a Product Category. For example, cell C7 indicates that 45 dollars worth of spices were sold during Feb 2013. This amount can be verified by looking again at Figure 5.1 and noticing that we had three separate purchases of spices during Feb 2013, shown on rows 3, 6, and 21. The Total Sales quantities shown on those three rows sum up to 45.

In addition to the report filter, rows, columns, and values areas, this pivot table also displays a Grand Total row and column, summing up all rows and columns. The Grand Total for the entire pivot table states that total sales for all data is $321.

In Figure 5.7, we moved the Customer State field to the filters area but didn't actually do any filtering. We'll discuss filtering later in this chapter.

Field Arrangement and Layout

In our example thus far, we moved one field to the rows area, one field to the columns area, one to the values area, and one to the filter. However, this is just a mere hint of what can be done. Not only can each area hold any number of fields, but it can also contain no fields at all. The only absolute requirement is that there is at least one field in the rows, columns, or values area.

There are two notable aspects to arranging fields. First, we can move any field in the Fields section of the Field List to any area. Thus, we can move a field to the filters, rows, columns, or values area. The ability to move fields at will is the primary means of manipulating the appearance of the pivot table. As fields are moved into different areas, the pivot table instantly and dynamically changes appearance, displaying the rows and columns of data that pertain to the specified layout.

A second aspect of field arrangements has to do with the selection made in a command named Report Layout. The Report Layout command appears under the PivotTable Tools Design tab. The Design tab, shown in Figures 5.8 and 5.9, is the second contextual tab that appears when a pivot table is selected.

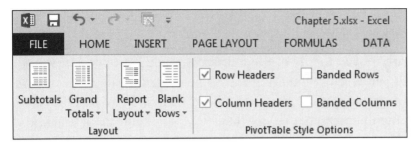

Figure 5.8
Left side of the Ribbon under the PivotTable Tools Design tab.
Source: Microsoft® Corporation.

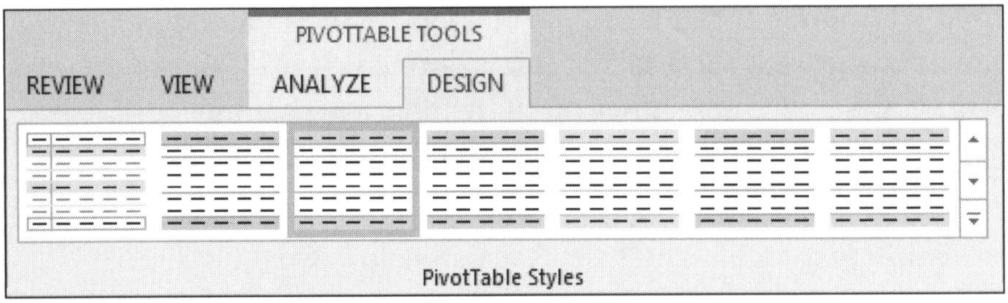

Figure 5.9
Right side of the Ribbon under the PivotTable Tools Design tab.
Source: Microsoft® Corporation.

The Report Layout command offers three options:

■ Show in Compact Form

■ Show in Outline Form

■ Show in Tabular Form

The selection of one of these three forms is secondary in importance to the arrangement of fields in the Field List, but nevertheless plays a significant role in the appearance of the pivot table.

Let's begin by rearranging the pivot table to place both the Product Category and Product fields in the rows area, and Total Sales in the values area. We'll put nothing in the columns or report filter areas. The resulting pivot table is shown in Figure 5.10.

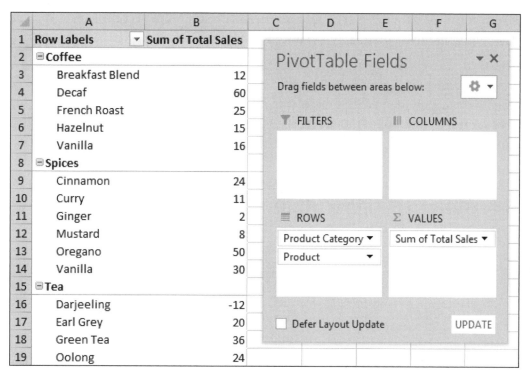

Figure 5.10

Pivot table with two fields in the rows area.

Source: Microsoft® Corporation.

For this figure, we modified the Field List to show only the areas section. We also turned off the display of subtotal and grand totals, features that will be discussed in the following chapter. Now that we're displaying two fields in the rows area, the pivot table automatically creates a hierarchy between the two fields. Thus, under each Product Category, we see the products that fall underneath it. There's nothing magical about this. As you might remember, each row in the original data seen in Figure 5.1 enumerates the Product Category and Product for each sale. The pivot table display is dynamic, in the sense that if we weren't displaying any products that were spices, then the Spices label would simply not appear. This might be the case if, for example, we had applied a filter to show only sales from a single state on a single day, and no one in the state purchased any spices on that day.

The displayed hierarchy reflects an underlying assumption that there is some relationship between the two fields. The order in which we list the fields in the Field List determines how the hierarchy is displayed. By placing Product below Product Category, we're saying that we want to see all products organized by category. We'll talk more extensively about hierarchies later, but let's first introduce the second aspect of field layout, which is the use of the Report Layout command.

As mentioned, there are three possibilities for report layouts: compact, outline, and tabular. The pivot table seen in Figure 5.9 is in the Compact Form. We didn't need to do anything to put the pivot table in this layout; the Compact Form is the default. New pivot tables always appear in Compact Form unless you specify a different layout. Let's now switch the pivot table to the Outline Form. This is shown in Figure 5.11.

	A	B	C	D	E	F	G	H
1	Product Category ▼	Product ▼	Sum of Total Sales					
2	Coffee							
3		Breakfast Blend	12		PivotTable Fields		▼ ✕	
4		Decaf	60					
5		French Roast	25		Drag fields between areas below:		⚙ ▼	
6		Hazelnut	15					
7		Vanilla	16		▼ FILTERS	III COLUMNS		
8	Spices							
9		Cinnamon	24					
10		Curry	11					
11		Ginger	2					
12		Mustard	8		≡ ROWS	Σ VALUES		
13		Oregano	50		Product Category ▼	Sum of Total Sales ▼		
14		Vanilla	30		Product ▼			
15	Tea							
16		Darjeeling	-12					
17		Earl Grey	20					
18		Green Tea	36		☐ Defer Layout Update		UPDATE	
19		Oolong	24					

Figure 5.11

Pivot table in Outline Form layout.

Source: Microsoft® Corporation.

In contrast to the Compact Form, a pivot table in the Outline Form layout places all fields in separate columns. If you look closely at Figure 5.10, you'll see that the Product Category and Product fields are both contained in column A. The Outline Form separates these two fields into two columns, A and B. One distinct advantage of this new layout is that the pivot table can now display field names. Whereas Figure 5.10 placed the name "Row Labels" in cell A1 as a reference to the fields in the rows area, the Outline Form of Figure 5.10 is able to use the labels "Product Category" and "Product" in cells A1 and B1. This gives the viewer more information about what the pivot table contains.

Let's now switch the pivot table of Figure 5.11 to the Tabular Form. The result is shown in Figure 5.12.

	A	B	C	D	E	F	G	H
1	Product Category ▾	Product ▾	Sum of Total Sales					
2	Coffee	Breakfast Blend	12					
3		Decaf	60					
4		French Roast	25					
5		Hazelnut	15					
6		Vanilla	16					
7	Spices	Cinnamon	24					
8		Curry	11					
9		Ginger	2					
10		Mustard	8					
11		Oregano	50					
12		Vanilla	30					
13	Tea	Darjeeling	-12					
14		Earl Grey	20					
15		Green Tea	36					
16		Oolong	24					

PivotTable Fields   ▾ ✕

Drag fields between areas below: ☼ ▾

▼ FILTERS   ▌▐ COLUMNS

☰ ROWS   Σ VALUES
Product Category ▾   Sum of Total Sales ▾
Product ▾

☐ Defer Layout Update   UPDATE

Figure 5.12

Pivot table in Tabular Form layout.

Source: Microsoft® Corporation.

This pivot table is almost identical to the Outline Form, except that it reduces the number of rows by eliminating unnecessary blank cells that are used to separate levels of the hierarchy in the rows area. For example, the blank cells B8 and C8 in Figure 5.11 have now been replaced with values from the next row. Whereas the Compact Form reduces the number of columns needed to display data, the Tabular Form reduces the number of rows.

In most situations, our preference is for the Tabular Form. This form has the advantage of always printing Row and Column field labels rather than the nondescript "Row Labels" and "Column Labels," plus it also reduces the number of rows in the pivot table. Additionally, the separation of all fields into individual cells assists in situations where you need to copy results from a pivot table into another worksheet and work further with that data. Therefore, most subsequent examples of pivot tables in this book will utilize the Tabular Form.

With this demonstration of the various Report Layout options behind us, let's now return to the task of rearranging fields in the Field List. We'll begin by rearranging the two fields in the rows area by placing the Product field above the Product Category field. The result is shown in Figure 5.13.

	A	B	C	D	E	F	G	H
1	Product ▾	Product Category ▾	Sum of Total Sales					
2	Breakfast Blend	Coffee	12					
3	Cinnamon	Spices	24					
4	Curry	Spices	11					
5	Darjeeling	Tea	-12					
6	Decaf	Coffee	60					
7	Earl Grey	Tea	20					
8	French Roast	Coffee	25					
9	Ginger	Spices	2					
10	Green Tea	Tea	36					
11	Hazelnut	Coffee	15					
12	Mustard	Spices	8					
13	Oolong	Tea	24					
14	Oregano	Spices	50					
15	Vanilla	Coffee	16					
16		Spices	30					

PivotTable Fields ▾ ✕

Drag fields between areas below: ⚙ ▾

FILTERS   COLUMNS

ROWS   Σ VALUES
Product ▾   Sum of Total Sales ▾
Product Category ▾

☐ Defer Layout Update   UPDATE

Figure 5.13

An inverted hierarchy.

Source: Microsoft® Corporation.

With the hierarchy of Product to Product Category inverted, we now have an arrangement of fields that is fairly meaningless. Whereas the pivot table of Figure 5.12 provides some useful information about how each Product in a Product Category sold, this presentation now merely tells us the Product Category to which a Product belongs. This is basically definitional. Most viewers would be able to determine that curry is a spice without having to be told specifically. The one anomaly that the pivot table of Figure 5.13 reveals is that Vanilla is both a coffee and a spice, but that's likely of little interest.

In our next example, in Figure 5.14, we'll place Product Category and Customer State in the rows area.

	A	B	C	D	E	F	G	H
1	Product Category ▾	Customer State ▾	Sum of Total Sales					
2	Coffee	CA	24					
3		FL	25					
4		IL	31					
5		TN	48					
6	Spices	GA	12					
7		IA	3					
8		IL	8					
9		ME	2					
10		NH	62					
11		WA	38					
12	Tea	CO	14					
13		MN	24					
14		OH	42					
15		TN	-12					

PivotTable Fields ▾ ✕

Drag fields between areas below: ⚙ ▾

FILTERS   COLUMNS

ROWS   Σ VALUES
Product Category ▾ Sum of Total Sales ▾
Customer State ▾

☐ Defer Layout Update   UPDATE

Figure 5.14

Two unrelated fields in the rows area.

Source: Microsoft® Corporation.

Since Product Category and Customer State are unrelated to each other, there is no natural hierarchy that exists between these fields. This means that it essentially doesn't matter which is listed first. Since Product Category is above Customer State, we see a breakdown of sales by states within category. If we had switched the order of these two fields, we would have seen a breakdown of categories within state. In either case, we have gained some useful information. The presentation of data makes sense.

In summary, if you have more than one field in the rows area of a pivot table, and if those fields are related, it's important to make sure that they are presented in the correct order, according to the natural hierarchy that exists between them. If the fields are unrelated, then the order isn't as critical.

Everything that we have said about fields in the rows area of the pivot table applies equally to the columns area. However, it must be said that, all things being equal, it is generally easier to read data when most fields are in the rows area. It's best to use the columns area only sparingly. As an example, let's refer back to the data in Figure 5.14. If we present this same data with the two fields in the columns area, rather than the rows area, the pivot table will look like Figure 5.15.

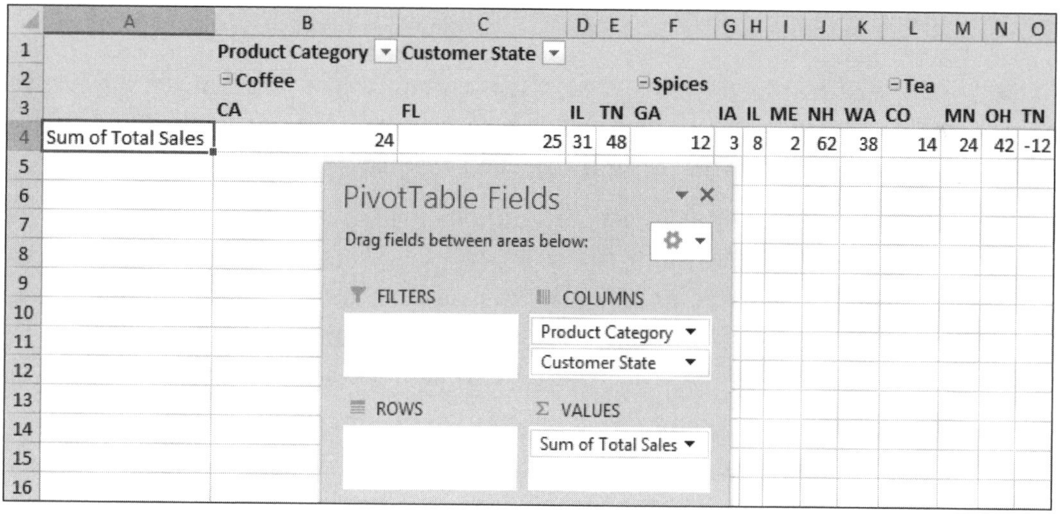

	A	B	C	D	E	F	G	H	I	J	K	L	M	N	O
1	Product Category ▾		Customer State ▾												
2	⊟ Coffee					⊟ Spices					⊟ Tea				
3	CA		FL	IL	TN	GA	IA	IL	ME	NH	WA	CO	MN	OH	TN
4	Sum of Total Sales	24		25	31	48	12	3	8	2	62	38	14	24	42 -12

PivotTable Fields ▾ ✕

Drag fields between areas below:

FILTERS

COLUMNS
Product Category ▾
Customer State ▾

ROWS

Σ VALUES
Sum of Total Sales ▾

Figure 5.15
Two fields in the columns area.
Source: Microsoft® Corporation.

The problem with this presentation is that it's difficult to decipher. Although the numbers are the same as before, the human eye can't as easily discern the pattern or individual values when they're laid out in columns. Layouts are particularly troublesome when nothing is in the rows area and everything is in the columns. However, despite this proviso, there are certainly situations when it's useful to make use of the columns area. Returning to Figure 5.14, let's alter this arrangement by adding the Sales Month to the columns. The result is shown in Figure 5.16.

	A	B	C	D	E	F	G	H	I	J	K
1	Sum of Total Sales		Sales Month ▼								
2	Product Category ▼	Customer State ▼	2012-12	2013-01	2013-02	2013-03					
3	Coffee	CA		24							
4		FL			25						
5		IL			15	16					
6		TN		12		36					
7	Spices	GA	12								
8		IA			3						
9		IL	8								
10		ME				2					
11		NH		12		50					
12		WA	-4		42						
13	Tea	CO			20	-6					
14		MN			24						
15		OH			42						
16		TN				-12					

PivotTable Fields ▼ ✕

Drag fields between areas below: ⚙ ▼

▼ FILTERS   ⬛ COLUMNS
                   Sales Month   ▼

⬛ ROWS   Σ VALUES
Product Category ▼ Sum of Total Sales ▼
Customer State   ▼

☐ Defer Layout Update   UPDATE

Figure 5.16

Fields in the rows and columns areas.

Source: Microsoft® Corporation.

With only one field in the columns area and the majority of fields in the rows area, this presentation is perfectly understandable. One can look at the pivot table and quickly comprehend the pattern, even if the Field List isn't visible.

Turning to the values area, this is where you can place fields that are meant to be summed up in some way. Fields in the rows and columns areas provide values for the attributes of interest. These are usually text values but can be numeric values on occasion. In our examples, the fields we've placed in the rows and columns area contain values such as "Coffee" or "Tea." These fields can also contain dates.

In contrast, fields that are placed in the values area are usually those that contain summable numeric values. In our example, the Total Sales field contains numbers that we would like to sum. As such, the fields in the values area are usually a key element of a pivot table. The summarization that pivot tables do so well is accomplished on these fields. Pivot tables can also perform other quantitative functions on the fields in the values area, such as averaging and counting, but we'll leave that topic for the next chapter.

All of our prior pivot table examples have used the Total Sales field in the values area. However, pivot tables can contain more than one field in the values area. It's also possible to have no fields in the values area. Let's illustrate the use of multiple fields in the values area by starting with the pivot table shown in Figure 5.12 and adding in the Quantity field. This is shown in Figure 5.17.

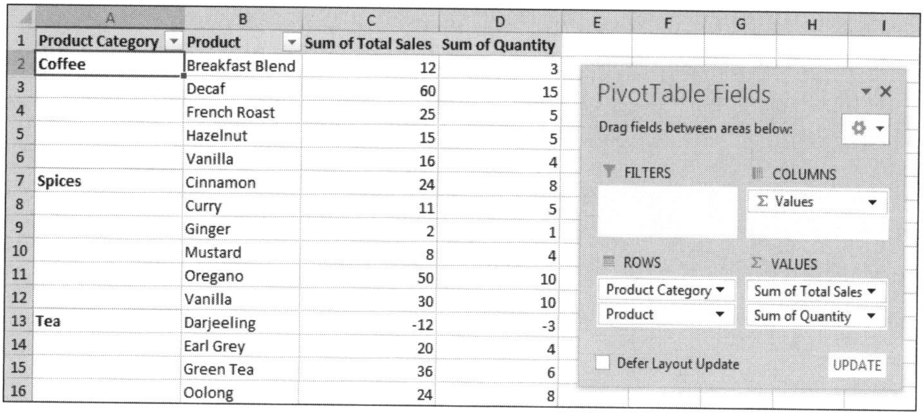

	A	B	C	D
1	Product Category	Product	Sum of Total Sales	Sum of Quantity
2	Coffee	Breakfast Blend	12	3
3		Decaf	60	15
4		French Roast	25	5
5		Hazelnut	15	5
6		Vanilla	16	4
7	Spices	Cinnamon	24	8
8		Curry	11	5
9		Ginger	2	1
10		Mustard	8	4
11		Oregano	50	10
12		Vanilla	30	10
13	Tea	Darjeeling	-12	-3
14		Earl Grey	20	4
15		Green Tea	36	6
16		Oolong	24	8

Figure 5.17

Two fields in the values area.

Source: Microsoft® Corporation.

The result of an additional field in the values area is readily apparent. We now see a new column with added information. Although the summation of item quantities isn't quite as useful as sales amounts, someone might be interested in the total of units that were sold.

Notice also that a "Σ Values" label has been placed in the columns area of the Field List. This indicates that the multiple fields from the values area have been placed in separate columns. This is normally the easiest arrangement for situations with multiple value fields. However, one does have the option to display multiple values in rows rather than in columns. This is accomplished by dragging the "Σ Values" label from the columns to the rows area. The result is shown in Figure 5.18.

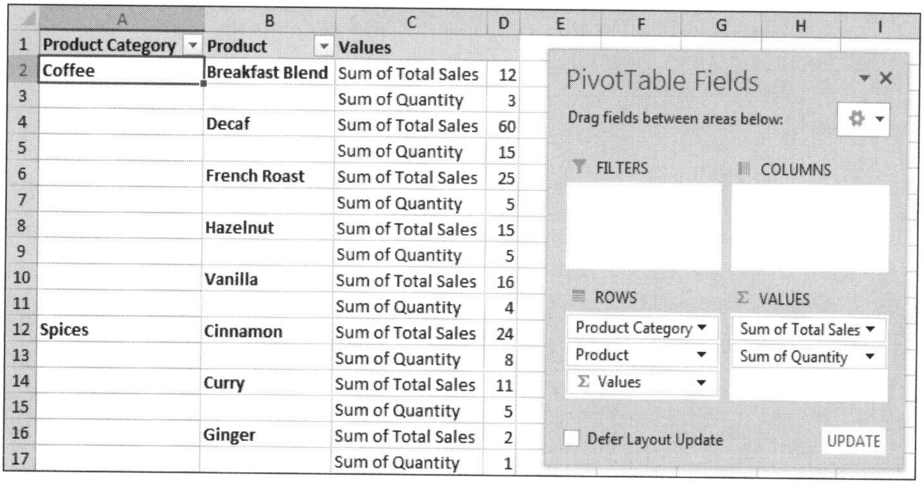

	A	B	C	D
1	Product Category	Product	Values	
2	Coffee	Breakfast Blend	Sum of Total Sales	12
3			Sum of Quantity	3
4		Decaf	Sum of Total Sales	60
5			Sum of Quantity	15
6		French Roast	Sum of Total Sales	25
7			Sum of Quantity	5
8		Hazelnut	Sum of Total Sales	15
9			Sum of Quantity	5
10		Vanilla	Sum of Total Sales	16
11			Sum of Quantity	4
12	Spices	Cinnamon	Sum of Total Sales	24
13			Sum of Quantity	8
14		Curry	Sum of Total Sales	11
15			Sum of Quantity	5
16		Ginger	Sum of Total Sales	2
17			Sum of Quantity	1

Figure 5.18

Multiple value fields in the rows area.

Source: Microsoft® Corporation.

Figure 5.18 shows only a partial view of the pivot table, but it's enough to indicate how the values are laid out. The awkward aspect of this display is that the pivot table needs to spell out "Sum of Total Sales" or "Sum of Quantity" on every row. For that reason, it's usually advisable to keep value fields in the columns area.

We mentioned that the values area does not necessarily require any fields. This is true in situations where you only need to view the value of the selected attributes, and don't care about any associated quantities. For example, one could certainly take the pivot table of Figure 5.17 and remove both fields in the values area. The result is shown in Figure 5.19.

	A	B	C	D	E	F	G
1	**Product Category** ▼	**Product** ▼					
2	Coffee	Breakfast Blend					
3		Decaf					
4		French Roast					
5		Hazelnut					
6		Vanilla					
7	Spices	Cinnamon					
8		Curry					
9		Ginger					
10		Mustard					
11		Oregano					
12		Vanilla					
13	Tea	Darjeeling					
14		Earl Grey					
15		Green Tea					
16		Oolong					

PivotTable Fields ▼ X

Drag fields between areas below: ⚙ ▼

▼ FILTERS   ▥ COLUMNS

≡ ROWS   Σ VALUES

Product Category ▼
Product   ▼

☐ Defer Layout Update   UPDATE

Figure 5.19

No fields in the values area.

Source: Microsoft® Corporation.

Even without the appearance of Sales Month and Quantity values, this display provides useful information if one simply wanted to see the hierarchy of available products by category. One could certainly imagine additional product attributes being added to the rows area of the pivot table, such as product ID's and item price.

In the following chapter, we'll delve into the use of the values area in more detail, particularly with reference to accomplishing other forms of summarization, such as counts and averages.

Expanding and Collapsing Fields

We now want to turn to a particularly important aspect of the interactivity provided by pivot tables. We've seen how two fields can be placed in the rows area. This is accomplished by dragging fields in the Field List to the rows area. However, there's another method for moving between fields that's much more interactive. Let's start with the pivot table shown in Figure 5.20, with only the Product Category field in the rows area and Total Sales as a value.

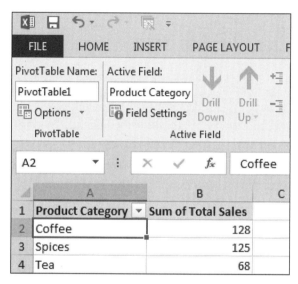

Figure 5.20

One field in the rows area.

Source: Microsoft® Corporation.

If we then want to add the Product field to the rows area, we can proceed as before by dragging the field in the Field List. However, this time we'll initiate a new procedure by first selecting any of the Product Category cells in the pivot table, and then selecting the Expand Field command in the PivotTable Analyze tab in the Ribbon. This command, which appears as an icon with a plus sign (+), appears to the right of the Drill Down and Drill Up labels shown in Figure 5.20. We're then presented with the Show Detail dialog box of Figure 5.21.

Figure 5.21
Show Detail dialog box.
Source: Microsoft® Corporation.

This pane is asking us to select a field for which we want to see more detail. In common usage, this is referred to as *drilling down* into a field. We'll proceed by selecting the Product field, indicating that we want to drill down from the Product Category to the Product. Behind the scenes, this will add the Product field to the rows area, producing the pivot table of Figure 5.22.

	A	B	C	D	E	F	G	H
1	Product Category ▾	Product ▾	Sum of Total Sales					
2	Coffee	Breakfast Blend	12					
3		Decaf	60					
4		French Roast	25					
5		Hazelnut	15					
6		Vanilla	16					
7	Spices	Cinnamon	24					
8		Curry	11					
9		Ginger	2					
10		Mustard	8					
11		Oregano	50					
12		Vanilla	30					
13	Tea	Darjeeling	-12					
14		Earl Grey	20					
15		Green Tea	36					

PivotTable Fields ▾ ✕

Drag fields between areas below: ✿ ▾

▼ FILTERS   ‖‖ COLUMNS

☰ ROWS   Σ VALUES
Product Category ▾ | Sum of Total Sales ▾
Product ▾

☐ Defer Layout Update   UPDATE

Figure 5.22
Pivot table after expanding a field.
Source: Microsoft® Corporation.

So far, we haven't accomplished anything particularly new, relative to just moving fields around in the Field List. However, there is additional functionality that can now be demonstrated. We can now select any cell in column A under the Product Category label, and select the Collapse Entire Field (–) command from the PivotTable Analyze tab in the Ribbon. After this is done, the pivot table appears as in Figure 5.23.

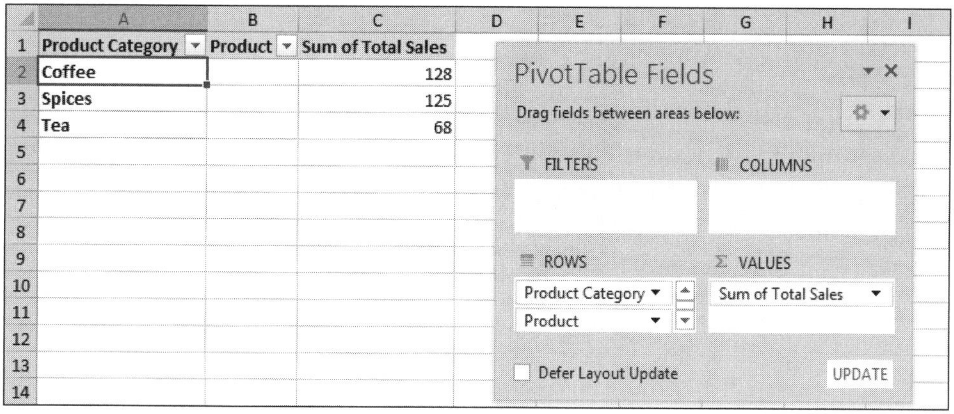

Figure 5.23

Pivot table after collapsing a field.

Source: Microsoft® Corporation.

Notice that, after this operation, the Product field remains in the pivot table. We can see it as a blank column and also in the Field List. What we've done is to temporarily hide the Product field values. This is the equivalent of what's normally referred to as *drilling up*. We've drilled up from the Product field back to the Product Category field and are now seeing values summarized by Product Category.

Now that we have brought two fields in the rows area, we can also perform the expand or collapse operations on a single Product Category cell. For example, if we were to double-click the Spices label in cell A3 of Figure 5.23, the new pivot table would then appear as in Figure 5.24.

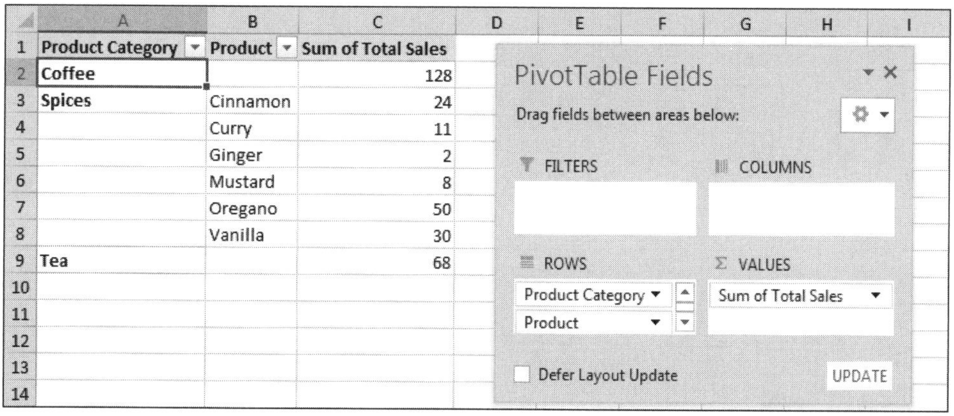

Figure 5.24

Pivot table after expanding a single cell.

Source: Microsoft® Corporation.

The ability to expand or collapse a single cell can also be accomplished by right-clicking on the cell and selecting Expand or Collapse.

In Chapter 1, we mentioned that Excel can be connected to OLAP databases, which are also referred to as cubes. One of the key features of cube structures is that they allow the designer to predefine hierarchical structures that may exist in the data. If the data that we've been looking at had been in a cube, a designer could design a product dimension with a hierarchy consisting of the Product Category and Product fields. With this definition stored in the cube, a pivot table connected to this cube could drill down from Product Category to Product without having to specify the relationship between these two fields. One could click on the Product Category cell and immediately be taken to the Product level. In our prior examples of drilling down, we don't have the benefit of a predefined cube. However, we can accomplish equivalent drill-down and drill-up operations, just as is done with cubes. In fact, since our data is not related to a predefined cube, we actually have more flexibility in terms of how we can drill into our data. In essence, the drill-down operation we've witnessed creates hierarchies in the data on the fly, in any manner we choose.

Showing Details

Just as cells in the rows or columns area of a pivot table can be expanded or collapsed, we can also view details for cells in the values area of a pivot table. Looking at Figure 5.24, we can see that the total sales for coffee is $128. We might want to see the original detail rows that contributed to the value of 128 that's being shown. The detail rows that this pivot table is based on were originally seen on the worksheet of Figure 5.1. When we double-click on cell C2 of Figure 5.24, a new worksheet that looks like Figure 5.25 opens up in our Excel file.

	A	B	C	D	E	F	G	H	I	J
1	Sales Date	Sales Month	Customer ID	Customer City	Customer State	Product	Product Category	Quantity	Unit Price	Total Sales
2	1/22/2013	2013-01	23	Nashville	TN	Breakfast Blend	Coffee	3	4	12
3	1/17/2013	2013-01	49	Los Angeles	CA	Decaf	Coffee	6	4	24
4	3/16/2013	2013-03	23	Nashville	TN	Decaf	Coffee	9	4	36
5	2/6/2013	2013-02	20	Miami	FL	French Roast	Coffee	5	5	25
6	2/28/2013	2013-02	16	Chicago	IL	Hazelnut	Coffee	5	3	15
7	3/30/2013	2013-03	16	Chicago	IL	Vanilla	Coffee	4	4	16

Figure 5.25

Showing details on a pivot table.

Source: Microsoft® Corporation.

In addition to double-clicking on a cell in the values area, the same result can be accomplished by right-clicking on the cell and selecting the Show Details contextual command. The Show Details command is not available on the Ribbon.

The data in Figure 5.25 is presented as an Excel table. This displays all the original data that's associated with the value of 128 in cell C3 of Figure 5.22. In common usage, the Show Details procedure is referred to as a *drillthrough*. In essence, we have drilled through from the summary information in the pivot table back to our original data. This can be a valuable tool when doing analysis. For example, the drillthrough technique can be used to validate data. By summing up the numbers in column J of Figure 5.25, we can verify that they really do add up to 128.

Another benefit of the drillthrough is that it allows the analyst to see values for important fields that may otherwise be irrelevant for a pivot table. In this example, we can now see the Customer IDs for all customers who purchased coffee. Of course, we can always move the Customer ID field to the pivot table, but that tends to clutter things up. It can be useful to keep the pivot table as a summarization device, and use the drillthrough operation to view details. In short, the drillthrough is a way to view detailed data for values of interest in the pivot table.

Filters

Data in pivot tables can be filtered in four basic ways:

- Report Filters
- Field Filters
- Slicers
- Timelines

Report filters refer to fields placed in the filters area of the Field List. Filters can be applied to fields placed in this area, to include or exclude various values. Field filters refer to commands on fields that have already been placed in the rows or columns area of the pivot table. For example, in Figure 5.24, the filter buttons next to the Product Category and Product labels in cells A1 and B1 allow for a number of field filter commands. Clicking on these buttons brings up a variety of filter options. Slicers and Timelines refer to two completely different forms of filtering, and will be illustrated later in this chapter.

Report filters are the simplest of the four options. By placing a field in the filters area of the Field List, you can select values to include or exclude for the entire pivot table report. Fields placed in the filters area have no visual effect on the presentation of data, comparable to fields in the rows, columns, or values areas. To illustrate this type of filter, let's place the Sales Month field in the filters area and Product Category in the rows area. We'll specify Total Sales as the value. This pivot table looks like Figure 5.26.

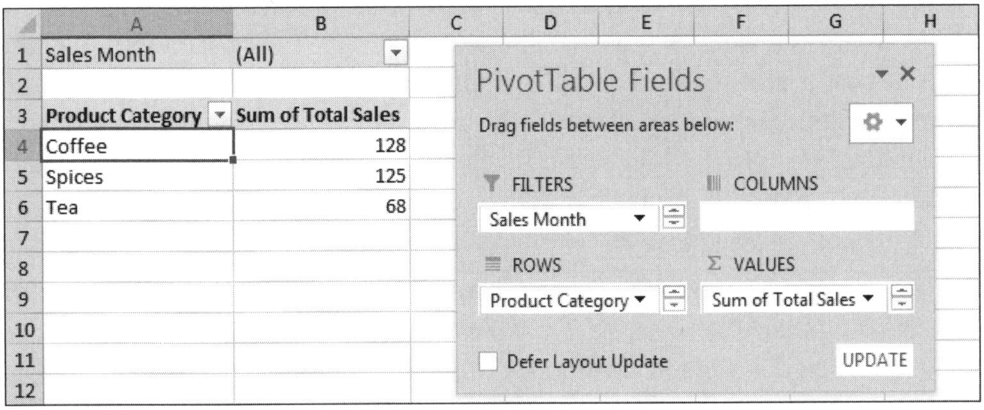

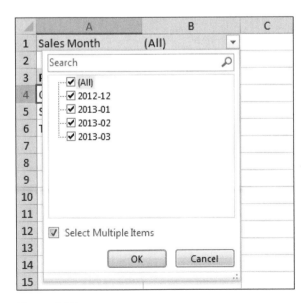

Figure 5.26
A field in the report filter area.
Source: Microsoft® Corporation.

Since we haven't yet modified the filter values for the Sales Month field, it appears as "(All)," indicating that all values are allowed. After selecting the report filter drop-down next to the Sales Month field, we see the list shown in Figure 5.27.

Figure 5.27
The report filter drop-down.
Source: Microsoft® Corporation.

In Figure 5.27, we've already checked the Select Multiple Items box, which causes checkboxes to appear next to every item. Without this, only one item can be selected. The "(All)" item at the top of the list can be used to check or uncheck all items. After selecting item 2013-01 and clicking OK, the pivot table changes appearance to that of Figure 5.28.

	A	B
1	Sales Month	2013-01
2		
3	Product Category	Sum of Total Sales
4	Coffee	36
5	Spices	12

Figure 5.28

Selecting one item in a field in the report filter.

Source: Microsoft® Corporation.

Now that a filter has been applied to view only data from January 2013, we see only sales from that month. The label in cell B1 displays the one value that has been selected in the filter. Note that we don't see any sales for tea, since no one purchased tea during January of 2013. If we modify the filter to select both 2013-01 and 2013-02, the pivot table changes to that of Figure 5.29.

	A	B
1	Sales Month	(Multiple Items)
2		
3	Product Category	Sum of Total Sales
4	Coffee	76
5	Spices	57
6	Tea	86

Figure 5.29

Selecting multiple items in a field in the report filter.

Source: Microsoft® Corporation.

The label in cell B1 now states "(Multiple Items)," indicating that more than one item has been selected in the report filter. One needs to click the filter button to see what has actually been selected. With more data selected in the filter, we now see some sales for tea.

Just as the rows and columns areas can contain multiple fields, so can the report filter. If we add Customer State to the report filter and select only sales from California, we see the pivot table shown in Figure 5.30.

◢	A	B
1	Sales Month	(Multiple Items) ⊤
2	Customer State	CA ⊤
3		
4	**Product Category** ▼	**Sum of Total Sales**
5	Coffee	24

Figure 5.30

Placing multiple fields in the report filter.

Source: Microsoft® Corporation.

With two fields in the report filter, data must satisfy the filters in both fields in order to be displayed. We therefore see only $24 of coffee sales, from California in January or February of 2013.

Whereas report filters provide relatively simplistic options, the possibilities for filtering in the fields placed in the rows or columns area of the pivot table are much more extensive. We'll begin by returning to the pivot table of Figure 5.22 and selecting the filter button next to the Product field label in cell B2. This reveals the filtering options shown in Figure 5.31.

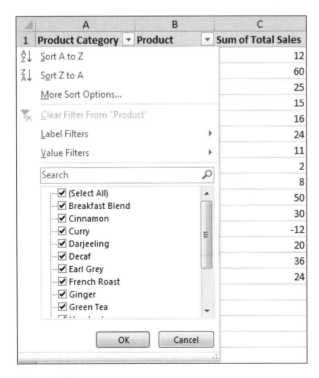

Figure 5.31

Field filter options.

Source: Microsoft® Corporation.

Filtering can be applied to individual fields in four ways. First, you can check or uncheck individual values, in a similar manner as was done for fields in the report filter. Second, you can enter a value in the Search box to find a specific value. For example, you might want to search for all products containing the word "Decaf."

The next two options, Label Filters and Value Filters, are much more powerful. The options under Label Filters are similar to the filters provided in Excel tables:

- Equals
- Does not equal
- Begins with
- Does not begin with
- Ends with
- Does not end with
- Contains
- Does not contain
- Greater than
- Greater than or equal to
- Less than
- Less than or equal to
- Between
- Not Between

After selecting one of these options, one provides the associated value and then the filter is applied. For example, if one specifies "Begins with G" as the Label Filter, one sees the pivot table shown in Figure 5.32.

	A	B	C
1	Product Category ▾	Product ▾	Sum of Total Sales
2	Spices	Ginger	2
3	Tea	Green Tea	36

Figure 5.32
Field with a Label Filter.
Source: Microsoft® Corporation.

The result is that we see only products that begin with the letter G. These products happen to fall under the Spices and Tea product categories.

The Value Filters option is a bit trickier. Whereas the Labels Filter applies to values for the field that's being filtered, the Values Filter operates on what's in the values area. The available options after selecting Value Filters are:

- Equals
- Does not equal
- Greater than
- Greater than or equal to
- Less than
- Less than or equal to
- Between
- Not Between
- Top 10

Let's say that one selects the "Greater than or equal to" option. This causes a Value Filter dialog box to pop up, as shown in Figure 5.33.

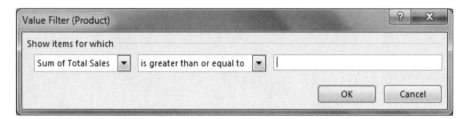

Figure 5.33
Value Filter dialog box.
Source: Microsoft® Corporation.

If we then enter a value of 25, the filter will be applied to select products where total sales for that product are greater than or equal to 25. The result is shown in Figure 5.34.

	A	B	C
1	Product Category ▼	Product ▼	Sum of Total Sales
2	Coffee	Decaf	60
3		French Roast	25
4	Spices	Oregano	50
5		Vanilla	30
6	Tea	Green Tea	36

Figure 5.34
Field with a Value Filter.
Source: Microsoft® Corporation.

We now see total sales for items for which total sales of the product is at least $25. It should be noted that we're not filtering on individual sales rows. We're only considering the total sales for the product in the values cell. Unlike Label Filters, Value Filters require that there be at least one field in the values area of the pivot table. The filter is applied via a combination of the field in the rows or columns area, and a field in the values area.

Slicers

Slicers are a type of filter that's functionally equivalent to the report filters just seen. Like report filters, slicers are a way to filter data at the report level, outside of the rows, columns, and values that are visible in the pivot table. This is in contrast to field filters, which apply directly to fields in the rows or columns areas.

The main difference between report filters and slicers is that slicers are more interactive. Report filters work very nicely when you want to create a filter on the entire report and leave it that way during your analysis. In our example, if you want to view only the sales of coffee products, you can simply place the Product Category field in the report filter area and then select Coffee as the value for that filter. However, if you should later want to change the filter from Coffee to Tea, that involves selecting the filter button in the report filter, unselecting the checkbox next to Coffee, selecting the checkbox next to Tea, and then clicking the OK button. That's four separate clicks. In contrast, slicers allow the switch from Coffee to Tea to be accomplished with a single click. Let's demonstrate how that works.

To set up a slicer, we simply select the Insert Slicer command under the PivotTable tools Analyze tab on the Ribbon. We're then presented with a list of available fields, such as seen in Figure 5.35.

Figure 5.35
Insert Slicers dialog box.
Source: Microsoft® Corporation.

One can then select any number of fields for which slicers are desired. We'll proceed with checking the Product Category field. A slicer pane such as the one shown in Figure 5.36 will be created for every field selected.

Figure 5.36
Slicer pane.
Source: Microsoft® Corporation.

This slicer pane floats anywhere on the screen, in a similar manner to the Field List pane. After a slicer pane is created, it can be removed with the Del key. After the slicer is created, it acts like an instant filter on everything in the pivot table. Let's say that our pivot table currently contains only the Sales Month in the rows area and Total Sales as a value, as in Figure 5.37.

	A	B	C	D	E	F
1	Sales Month ▾	Sum of Total Sales		Product Category		
2	2012-12	16		Coffee		
3	2013-01	48				
4	2013-02	171		Spices		
5	2013-03	86				
6				Tea		
7						
8						

Figure 5.37
Pivot table before a slicer is applied.
Source: Microsoft® Corporation.

After clicking on the Coffee label on the slicer of Figure 5.37, the pivot table instantly changes to that of Figure 5.38.

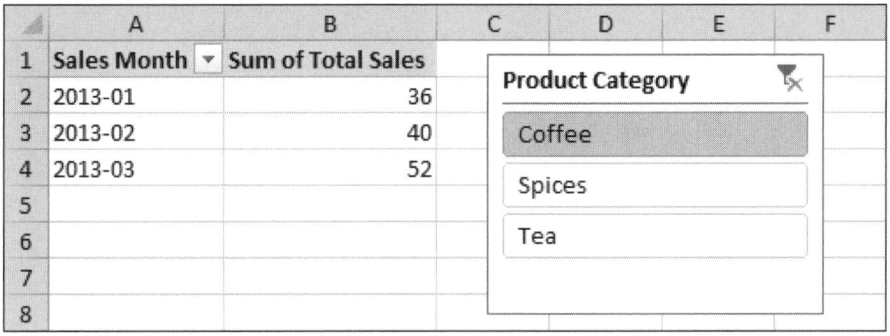

Figure 5.38
Pivot table after a slicer is applied.
Source: Microsoft® Corporation.

This single click on the Coffee label in the slicer pane causes the filter to be applied. The amounts are reduced to show only sales of coffee. As seen, slicers have functionality identical to report filters, but with more interactivity.

It should also be noted that one is not limited to selecting only a single item in the slicer pane. By using the Ctrl key, you can select multiple items. Additionally, you can create any number of slicers. Each slicer associated with a pivot table appears in a separate pane.

Timelines

Timelines, a new feature of Excel 2013, are similar to Slicers in that they provide a quick way to apply filters with a minimum number of clicks. However, whereas slicers can be created for any field in the Field List, timelines apply only to date fields. To illustrate, let's first rearrange the data we've been looking at to place the Sales Month and Sales Date fields in the rows area and Total Sales in the values area. The data appears as in Figure 5.39.

	A	B	C	D	E	F	G	H
1	Sales Month ▾	Sales Date ▾	Sum of Total Sales					
2	2012-12	12/6/2012	12					
3		12/18/2012	8					
4		12/27/2012	-4					
5	2013-01	1/11/2013	12					
6		1/17/2013	24					
7		1/22/2013	12					
8	2013-02	2/1/2013	18					
9		2/6/2013	25					
10		2/15/2013	48					
11		2/17/2013	42					
12		2/18/2013	23					
13		2/28/2013	15					
14	2013-03	3/1/2013	-12					
15		3/2/2013	2					
16		3/16/2013	36					
17		3/25/2013	50					
18		3/30/2013	16					
19		3/31/2013	-6					

PivotTable Fields   ▾ ✕

Drag fields between areas below: ✿ ▾

▼ FILTERS   ▥ COLUMNS

≡ ROWS   Σ VALUES

Sales Month ▾   Sum of Total Sales ▾
Sales Date ▾

☐ Defer Layout Update   UPDATE

Figure 5.39
Pivot table before a timeline is applied.
Source: Microsoft® Corporation.

As seen, the dates run from 12/6/2012 to 3/31/2013. To create the timeline, we select the Insert Timeline command under the PivotTable tools Analyze tab on the Ribbon. This command is shown in Figure 5.4. The result is a dialog box that lists the date fields in the data set, as seen in Figure 5.40.

Insert Timelines   ? ✕

☐ Sales Date

OK   Cancel

Figure 5.40
Insert Timelines dialog box.
Source: Microsoft® Corporation.

Since there is only one date field, only one timeline can be created. After checking the Sales Date field in this dialog box, the timeline pane of Figure 5.41 appears.

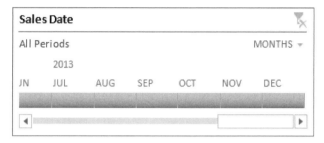

Figure 5.41
Timeline pane.
Source: Microsoft® Corporation.

This pane displays a horizontal timeline of dates. The Months drop-down in the upper right corner can be changed to Years, Quarters, or Days. Sticking with Months, we can click on the timeline to select a range of months. Figure 5.42 shows the result after selecting Jan and Feb.

	A	B	C	D	E	F	G	H	I
1	Sales Month ▼	Sales Date ▼	Sum of Total Sales						
2	2013-01	1/11/2013	12						
3		1/17/2013	24						
4		1/22/2013	12						
5	2013-02	2/1/2013	18						
6		2/6/2013	25						
7		2/15/2013	48						
8		2/17/2013	42						
9		2/18/2013	23						
10		2/28/2013	15						

Figure 5.42
Pivot table after a Timeline has been applied.
Source: Microsoft® Corporation.

If we switch the Timeline from Months to Days, and select a range of Feb 15 to 18, the pivot table appears as in Figure 5.43.

	A	B	C	D	E	F	G	H	I
1	Sales Month ▼	Sales Date ▾	Sum of Total Sales	Sales Date					▼ₓ
2	2013-02	2/15/2013	48	Feb 15 - 18 2013				DAYS ▾	
3		2/17/2013	42	FEB 2013					
4		2/18/2013	23	13 14 15 16 17 18 19 20 21 22 23					
5									
6									
7				◄			□		►
8									

Figure 5.43
A timeline that selects by days.
Source: Microsoft® Corporation.

As seen, timelines are a quick and easy way to select a range of dates with just a few clicks. The only limitation of timelines is that only one date range can be selected at a time.

Sorting

Sorting data in pivot tables is a relatively routine operation. By default, fields in the row or column areas are sorted in alphabetical order by the value of the label. For example, look at the data in Figure 5.44.

	A	B
1	Sales Month ▼	Sum of Total Sales
2	2012-12	16
3	2013-01	48
4	2013-02	171
5	2013-03	86

Figure 5.44
Pivot table before sorting.
Source: Microsoft® Corporation.

Data is arranged in ascending order by the value of the Sales Month. Sorts can be applied to fields in the rows or columns area by either selecting the filter button on the field label, or else by right-clicking any cell associated with the desired field. As previously seen in Figure 5.31, the sort options that appear are for an ascending sort, a descending sort, or more options. Figure 5.31 shows the ascending options as A to Z because Product Category is a text field. Numeric fields will show the ascending sort as

Smallest to Largest, and Date fields will show it as Oldest to Newest. If the More Sort Options choice is selected, an additional dialog box will appear that allows you to apply a custom sort by manually rearranging the desired items. When we select a descending sort (Z to A) on the Sales Month field, the pivot table appears as in Figure 5.45.

	A	B
1	Sales Month ↓	Sum of Total Sales
2	2013-03	86
3	2013-02	171
4	2013-01	48
5	2012-12	16

Figure 5.45

A descending sort.

Source: Microsoft® Corporation.

Sorts can also be applied to fields in the values area of a pivot table. By right-clicking any cell in the values area, and then selecting a descending sort, the pivot table is transformed to the display of Figure 5.46.

	A	B
1	Sales Month ▾	Sum of Total Sales
2	2013-02	171
3	2013-03	86
4	2013-01	48
5	2012-12	16

Figure 5.46

A descending sort applied to the values area.

Source: Microsoft® Corporation.

This layout shows the months with the highest total sales first. Depending on your analysis goals, this might be a useful way to organize this data. If you'd like to remove a sort after it has been applied, you'll need to go into any field in the rows or columns areas, and first change the sort to the default, which is ascending. After doing that, selecting the Manual option totally removes the sort.

Looking Ahead

This chapter has covered a lot of ground. We began with an explanation of how to create pivot tables and the basics of the Field List. Pivot tables are all about layout, and the Field List is a guide to that layout. By placing fields in any of the four areas of the Field List, you can instantly change the content and design of your data. We then proceeded to discuss various ways that data can be arranged, such as placing multiple fields in the rows section. In doing so, we stressed the importance of the Report Layout command. Although our preference is for the Tabular Form, there are certainly times when the Compact Form or Outline Form makes perfect sense. We discussed reasons for choosing to place fields in the rows area over the columns area. An important consideration with placing multiple fields in the rows or columns area is whether a natural hierarchy exists among the fields. If this is the case, you need to make sure that fields are listed in the proper order.

The topic of expanding and collapsing fields adds to the pure pleasure of using pivot tables. By being aware of the ability to drill down into data, and then back up again, we can experience the power of being able to explore data with ease. As such, pivot tables offer much of the functionality of full-blown OLAP cubes, but without the overhead of having to design and create cubes in advance. An operation related to expanding fields is the ability to view details by double-clicking on cells in the values area. This drill-through technique allows you to move instantly from the summary capabilities of pivot tables back to your raw data.

Finally, we looked at various ways to filter data via report filters, field filters, slicers, and timelines. Of these, field filters offer the most features. The ability to filter data on either label filters or value filters provides quite a bit of flexibility. Slicers and timelines are relatively recent innovations for pivot tables that substantially add to their ease of use.

As a simplistic way to summarize data, the topic of sorting provides a bridge to our next chapter, "Pivot Table Calculations." In this next chapter, we'll discuss some more advanced ways to summarize data. After dealing with subtotals and totals, a focus of the next chapter will be on alternative ways to summarize fields in the values area. Up until now, we only summed up numbers. However, pivot tables also allow for many other arithmetic operations, such as counting and averaging. From that, we'll move on to percentages and the ranking of data. We'll also discuss calculated fields that can be added into your pivot tables. Finally, the chapter will conclude with an important new feature of Excel, which is the ability to establish relationships between multiple tables with a Data Model. This allows you to view more than one table at a time in a pivot table.

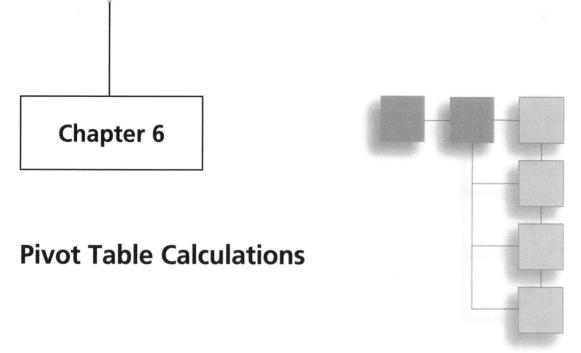

Chapter 6

Pivot Table Calculations

With the basics of pivot table functionality behind us, we now want to consider some more creative and advanced ways that pivot tables can be employed. From an analysis perspective, pivot tables allow you to both summarize and explore relationships in your data. By placing one column in the rows area and another in the columns, you can view the various intersections of values between the two fields. Alternatively, by placing multiple related fields in the rows area, you can view the natural hierarchy that exists between those attributes and drill down into subcategories that allow you to view greater detail for categories of interest. In this chapter, we'll explore different ways to extend this paradigm. Of primary interest will be the ability to do something other than simply sum numeric values. Excel provides other aggregate functions that can be utilized in the values area of the pivot table, such as counts and averages. Additionally, such numbers can be translated into percentages and ranks that give a clearer picture of the relationships between numbers.

To conclude this chapter, we'll discuss a powerful new feature of Excel 2013 that permits the user to create relationships between multiple tables to form what's called a *data model*. With a defined data model, pivot tables can access and join data from more than one data source, allowing the user to view a larger and more comprehensive set of data.

Subtotals and Totals

We've seen in the prior chapter that pivot tables exceed at summarizing data. In our previous examples, this has consisted of summing up data in the values area. To that end, Excel provides two commands in the Layout group of the Pivot Tools Design tab of the Ribbon that add extra layers of summarization, subtotals, and grand totals. The Layout group of the Ribbon is shown in Figure 6.1.

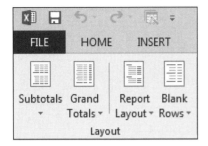

Figure 6.1
Layout group of the Ribbon under the Pivot Tools Design tab.
Source: Microsoft® Corporation.

When the Grand Totals command is selected, these four options are presented in a drop-down:

- Off for Rows and Columns
- On for Rows and Columns
- On for Rows Only
- On for Columns Only

In Figure 6.2, we started with a pivot table derived from the same data discussed in the prior chapter originally seen in Figure 5.1. We then added the On for Rows and Columns option in the Grand Totals command. To reduce the amount of data shown, we've also added a number of filters to the fields in the rows and columns areas.

	A	B	C	D	E	F
1	Sum of Total Sales		Sales Month 🔽			
2	Product Category 🔽	Product 🔽	2013-01	2013-02	2013-03	Grand Total
3	Coffee	French Roast		25		25
4		Hazelnut		15		15
5		Vanilla			16	16
6	Spices	Ginger			2	2
7		Oregano			50	50
8		Vanilla	12	18		30
9	Grand Total		12	58	68	138

Figure 6.2
Pivot table with grand totals on for rows and columns.
Source: Microsoft® Corporation.

As seen, Grand Total rows and columns have been inserted that sum up the values across and down the matrix of numbers. Subtotals provide similar capabilities. When selecting the Subtotals command, these options are available:

- Do Not Show Subtotals
- Show all Subtotals at Bottom of Group
- Show all Subtotals at Top of Group

After choosing the option to show subtotals at the bottom of the group, we see the pivot table of Figure 6.3.

	A	B	C	D	E	F
1	Sum of Total Sales		Sales Month ▼			
2	Product Category ▼	Product ▼	2013-01	2013-02	2013-03	Grand Total
3	Coffee	French Roast		25		25
4		Hazelnut		15		15
5		Vanilla			16	16
6	Coffee Total			40	16	56
7	Spices	Ginger			2	2
8		Oregano			50	50
9		Vanilla	12	18		30
10	Spices Total		12	18	52	82
11	Grand Total		12	58	68	138

Figure 6.3

Pivot table with subtotals at the bottom of the group.

Source: Microsoft® Corporation.

As seen, extra rows have now been inserted that provide subtotals for each of the groups in the rows. Even though the option states that the subtotals are at the *bottom* of the group, subtotals can also be applied when the groups are in the columns area. To illustrate, if we rearrange the data in Figure 6.3 so Product Category and Product are in the columns, and Sales Month is in the rows, then the pivot table, with subtotals, will look like Figure 6.4.

	A	B	C	D	E	F	G	H	I	J
1	Sum of Total Sales	Product Category ▼	Product ▼							
2		Coffee			Coffee Total	Spices			Spices Total	Grand Total
3	Sales Month ▼	French Roast	Hazelnut	Vanilla		Ginger	Oregano	Vanilla		
4	2013-01							12	12	12
5	2013-02	25	15		40			18	18	58
6	2013-03			16	16	2	50		52	68
7	Grand Total	25	15	16	56	2	50	30	82	138

Figure 6.4

Pivot table with subtotals in columns.

Source: Microsoft® Corporation.

We now see the subtotals added as columns. The difficulty in comprehending the data in the pivot table in Figure 6.4, as compared to that in Figure 6.3, illustrates the point made in the prior chapter that it is generally best not to put more than one field in the columns area. The human eye can more easily perceive and comprehend multiple fields in the rows area.

Returning to the pivot table of Figure 6.3, if we attempt to change the design to show the subtotals at the top rather than the bottom, we'd find that there is no difference in appearance. This is because we've been using the report layout in the Tabular Form. We need to switch to either Compact or Outline Form to see subtotals at the top of a group. Figure 6.5 shows the same data in Compact Form with subtotals at the top.

	A	B	C	D	E
1	Sum of Total Sales	Column Labels ⊓			
2	Row Labels ⊓	2013-01	2013-02	2013-03	Grand Total
3	⊟Coffee		40	16	56
4	French Roast		25		25
5	Hazelnut		15		15
6	Vanilla			16	16
7	⊟Spices	12	18	52	82
8	Ginger			2	2
9	Oregano			50	50
10	Vanilla	12	18		30
11	Grand Total	12	58	68	138

Figure 6.5
Pivot table in Compact Form with subtotals at the top of the group.
Source: Microsoft® Corporation.

Grouping

Related to subtotals is the notion of grouping data. Just as subtotals provide an additional summary level of a group of data, Excel allows you to create additional groups interactively. Subtotals can then be viewed for these additional groups, if desired. To illustrate, let's return to the data shown in Figure 6.2, but add in the Product Category of Tea that was seen in the prior chapter. Our pivot table now looks like Figure 6.6.

	A	B	C	D	E
1	Sum of Total Sales		Sales Month 🔽		
2	Product Category 🔽	Product 🔽	2013-01	2013-02	2013-03
3	Coffee	French Roast		25	
4		Hazelnut		15	
5		Vanilla			16
6	Spices	Ginger			2
7		Oregano			50
8		Vanilla	12	18	
9	Tea	Darjeeling			-12
10		Earl Grey		20	
11		Green Tea		42	-6

Figure 6.6

Pivot table with three product categories.

Source: Microsoft® Corporation.

Let's say that we want to look at the combined sales of Coffee and Tea. To accomplish this, we turn to the commands in the Group Selection command in the Ribbon, shown in Figure 6.7.

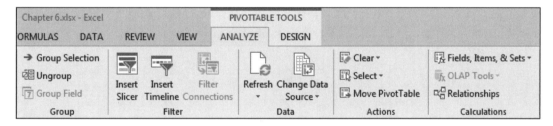

Figure 6.7

Commands under the PivotTable Tools Analyze tab in the Ribbon.

Source: Microsoft® Corporation.

To create the desired grouping, we need to first use the Ctrl key to highlight both the Coffee and Tea labels in column A of the pivot table in Figure 6.6. We then click the Group Selection command. After doing so, our pivot table appears as in Figure 6.8.

▲	A	B	C	D	E	F
1	Sum of Total Sales			Sales Month ⊤		
2	Product Category2 ▼	Product Category ▼	Product ⊤	2013-01	2013-02	2013-03
3	Group1	Coffee	French Roast		25	
4			Hazelnut		15	
5			Vanilla			16
6		Tea	Darjeeling			-12
7			Earl Grey		20	
8			Green Tea		42	-6
9	Spices	Spices	Ginger			2
10			Oregano			50
11			Vanilla	12	18	

Figure 6.8

Pivot table with a new group.

Source: Microsoft® Corporation.

We now see a new group, named Group1, that combines Coffee and Tea. The name of the field associated with this new group is Product Category2, and this field now appears in the Field List. To make this a little nicer to look at, we'd like to change the field name to Super Category, and change the group name to Coffee/Tea. To do this, you merely highlight the Product Category2 and Group1 labels and type in the new names. Finally, after typing in those new labels, we also want to add subtotals and grand totals to the pivot table. The result is shown in Figure 6.9.

▲	A	B	C	D	E	F	G
1	Sum of Total Sales			Sales Month ⊤			
2	Super Category ▼	Product Category ▼	Product ⊤	2013-01	2013-02	2013-03	Grand Total
3	Coffee/Tea	Coffee	French Roast		25		25
4			Hazelnut		15		15
5			Vanilla			16	16
6		Coffee Total			40	16	56
7		Tea	Darjeeling			-12	-12
8			Earl Grey		20		20
9			Green Tea		42	-6	36
10		Tea Total			62	-18	44
11	Coffee/Tea Total				102	-2	100
12	Spices	Spices	Ginger			2	2
13			Oregano			50	50
14			Vanilla	12	18		30
15		Spices Total		12	18	52	82
16	Spices Total			12	18	52	82
17	Grand Total			12	120	50	182

Figure 6.9

Pivot table with grouping, subtotals, and grand totals.

Source: Microsoft® Corporation.

We now have two levels of subtotals—on the new Super Category level and on the Product Category level. The grand totals sum up everything. If you wish to remove any groups that you've created in your pivot table, you merely highlight the group, and then click the Ungroup command in the Ribbon.

You may have also noticed a Group Field command in the Ribbon, just below the Ungroup command. This command applies to groups that are numeric or dates. To illustrate with dates, we'll place the Sales Date in the rows area and Product Category in the columns. Our pivot table appears as in Figure 6.10.

	A	B	C	D
1	Sum of Total Sales	Product Category ▼		
2	Sales Date ⊺	Coffee	Spices	Tea
3	1/11/2013		12	
4	1/17/2013	24		
5	1/22/2013	12		
6	2/1/2013		18	
7	2/6/2013	25		
8	2/15/2013		24	24
9	2/17/2013			42
10	2/18/2013		3	20
11	2/28/2013	15		

Figure 6.10
Pivot table with dates in the rows area.
Source: Microsoft® Corporation.

In this example, we filtered out dates not in January or February. If we now click on any date and select the Group Field command, the dialog box shown in Figure 6.11 will appear.

Figure 6.11
Group dialog box.
Source: Microsoft® Corporation.

This box allows you to group individual dates by a variety of levels. We'll opt to group by month, and specify a date range of 1/1/2013 to 2/28/2013. The result is shown in Figure 6.12.

	A	B	C	D
1	Sum of Total Sales	Product Category ▼		
2	Sales Date ▼	Coffee	Spices	Tea
3	<1/1/2013		16	
4	Jan	36	12	
5	Feb	40	45	86
6	>2/28/2013	52	52	-18

Figure 6.12
Pivot table with grouped dates.
Source: Microsoft® Corporation.

Conveniently, Excel has not only created groups for each month, but has also added items to indicate data that exists prior to and after the indicated date range. Unlike the Group Selection command discussed previously, the Group Field command doesn't create a new field. It merely consolidates existing data. If you want to create a separate field for the month, you would need to utilize the Group Selection command on each monthly set of dates, selecting each date range separately. In either case, this ability to create groups on dates can be useful if you'd like to summarize data at a broader level.

Calculated Items and Fields

Another variant on the theme of forming groups presents a slightly different alternative to what we've already done. To illustrate, let's begin with the data in Figure 6.13, which has Product Category in the rows and Sales Month in the columns.

	A	B	C	D	E
1	Sum of Total Sales	Sales Month ▼			
2	Product Category ▼	2012-12	2013-01	2013-02	2013-03
3	Coffee		36	40	52
4	Spices	16	12	45	52
5	Tea			86	-18

Figure 6.13

Pivot table before a calculated item is added.

Source: Microsoft® Corporation.

Let's say that we want to combine coffee and tea together, but honestly don't care if the product is a coffee or tea product. We simply want to list all coffee and tea sales under one category. In our prior example of doing a Group Selection on coffee and tea, we created a group named Coffee/Tea that was, in effect, a level above the Product Category. But what if we want to create a Coffee/Tea product category that exists on the same level as coffee and tea? The way to accomplish this is via something called a calculated item.

To create a calculated item, we select one of the Product Category cells on the pivot table and select the Fields, Items, & Sets command displayed in Figure 6.7. When this command is selected, we see the options shown in Figure 6.14.

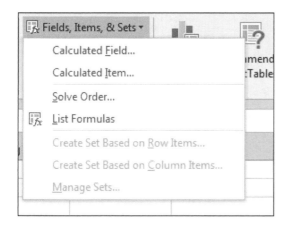

Figure 6.14

Fields, Items, & Sets command under the PivotTable Tools Analyze tab.

Source: Microsoft® Corporation.

After selecting the Calculated Item option, we are presented with the Insert Calculated Item dialog box of Figure 6.15.

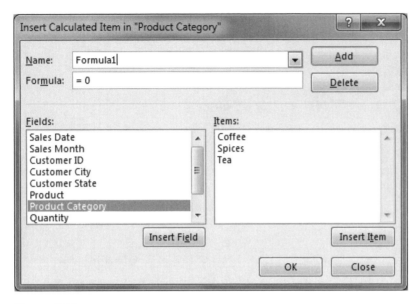

Figure 6.15

Insert Calculated Item dialog box.

Source: Microsoft® Corporation.

The Product Category field is already selected. We then select the Coffee and Tea items in the Items panel, and add the plus (+) sign to create this formula in the Formula box:

=Coffee+Tea

We'll also type over the name, calling it Coffee & Tea, click the Add button, and then OK. After doing so, our pivot table appears as in Figure 6.16.

	A	B	C	D	E
1	Sum of Total Sales	Sales Month			
2	Product Category	2012-12	2013-01	2013-02	2013-03
3	Coffee		36	40	52
4	Spices	16	12	45	52
5	Tea			86	-18
6	Coffee & Tea	0	36	126	34

Figure 6.16

Pivot table with a Calculated Item.

Source: Microsoft® Corporation.

As seen, a new Coffee & Tea product category has appeared that combines coffee and tea. Of course, we now have a duplication of sales, with coffee and tea sales listed twice. However, that's easily corrected by going into the Product Category filter and removing the individual Coffee and Tea product categories from view, leaving only Spices and the new Coffee & Tea category.

Note that calculated items exist only at the level at which they are created. They have no effect on other fields. For example, if we alter the pivot table of Figure 6.16 to filter the Product Category field to show only the new Coffee & Tea calculated item, and then add the Product field to the rows area, the pivot table would appear as in Figure 6.17.

	A	B	C	D	E	F
1	Sum of Total Sales		Sales Month ▼			
2	Product Category ⫪	Product ▼	2012-12	2013-01	2013-02	2013-03
3	⊟ Coffee & Tea	Breakfast Blend	0	12	0	0
4		Cinnamon	0	0	0	0
5		Curry	0	0	0	0
6		Darjeeling	0	0	0	-12
7		Decaf	0	24	0	36
8		Earl Grey	0	0	20	0
9		French Roast	0	0	25	0
10		Ginger	0	0	0	0
11		Green Tea	0	0	42	-6
12		Hazelnut	0	0	15	0
13		Mustard	0	0	0	0
14		Oolong	0	0	24	0
15		Oregano	0	0	0	0
16		Vanilla	0	0	0	16

Figure 6.17
Pivot Table with a Calculated Item and another field.
Source: Microsoft® Corporation.

The Product field shows products from all categories, including spices. In other words, the Coffee & Tea calculated item has no effect on the Product. There is no extra intelligence provided that allows the calculation at the Product Category level to extend to the Product level. Despite this shortcoming, the ability to create new categories grants the analyst an opportunity to reorganize existing data as business conditions change. The combination of coffee and tea may seem trivial, but consider a situation such as changing sales territories. If you previously had separate territories for Arizona and Nevada that now need to be combined together for reporting, you can utilize calculated items to accomplish that purpose without having to modify the underlying data.

Calculated fields are a close cousin to calculated items. Whereas calculated items apply to items that are typically placed in rows or columns, calculated fields generally apply to fields in the values area of a pivot table. In this case, the term "calculated" refers to an adjustment of a numeric value. Let's say, for example, that your organization pays its salespeople a commission of 15% of sales. In our example, we can calculate the commission by applying a formula to the existing Total Sales field. To initiate this process, we select the Calculated Field option under the Fields, Items & Sets command. This brings up the dialog box shown in Figure 6.18.

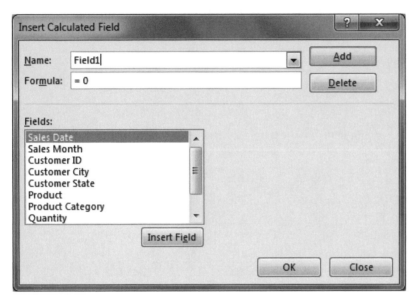

Figure 6.18
Insert Calculated Field dialog box.
Source: Microsoft® Corporation.

To create the calculated field, we simply provide a name, such as Commission, and the following formula:

    = 'Total Sales' * .15

After creating this formula, we'll return to the pivot table of Figure 6.6 and replace the Total Sales in the values area with the new Commission field. With the Product Category and Product in the rows area, the pivot table then appears as in Figure 6.19.

	A	B	C	D	E
1	**Sum of Commission**		**Sales Month** ▼		
2	**Product Category** ▼	**Product** 🔽	**2013-01**	**2013-02**	**2013-03**
3	Coffee	French Roast	0	3.75	0
4		Hazelnut	0	2.25	0
5		Vanilla	0	0	2.4
6	Spices	Ginger	0	0	0.3
7		Oregano	0	0	7.5
8		Vanilla	1.8	2.7	0
9	Tea	Darjeeling	0	0	-1.8
10		Earl Grey	0	3	0
11		Green Tea	0	6.3	-0.9

Figure 6.19

Pivot table with a Calculated Field.

Source: Microsoft® Corporation.

One further adjustment we'd like to make is to not display any negative numbers as the commission. To do this, we'll modify the formula, altering it to:

=IF('Total Sales'> 0,'Total Sales'* 0.15, 0)

This new formula follows the syntax of the Excel IF function that will be covered in Chapter 13. It specifies that if Total Sales is greater than 0, then multiply Total Sales by .15. Otherwise, the result should be 0.

After entering a number of calculated items or fields, you may want to view all of these custom calculations in a single location. Fortunately, Excel lets you do this via the List Formulas option under the Fields, Items, & Sets command. When this option is selected, Excel creates a separate worksheet with formula information such as that shown in Figure 6.20.

	A	B	C
1	*Calculated Field*		
2	**Solve Order**	**Field**	**Formula**
3		1 Commission	=IF('Total Sales'> 0,'Total Sales'* 0.15, 0)
4			
5	*Calculated Item*		
6	**Solve Order**	**Item**	**Formula**
7		1 'Coffee & Tea'	=Coffee+Tea

Figure 6.20

Formula list worksheet.

Source: Microsoft® Corporation.

The "solve order" displayed in the formula list refers to the order in which calculations are made. This is significant only if there is any overlap or potential conflict between different calculations. This solve order can be modified via the Solve Order option under the Fields, Items, & Sets command. After calculated items or fields are created, they can be just as easily removed by going back to the Insert Calculated Item or Insert Calculated Field dialog boxes, selecting the formula, then clicking the Delete button.

Percentages and Ranks

Up until now, all the values that we've displayed in the values area of the pivot table have consisted of sums of raw data. The potential problem with this approach is that, when looking at a bunch of numbers, the significance of those numbers may not be entirely obvious. This is where percentages and ranks can be of immense value. To illustrate, let's return to a display of a few coffee and spice products, as shown in Figure 6.21.

	A	B	C
1	Product Category ⏷	Product ⏷	Sum of Total Sales
2	Coffee	French Roast	25
3		Hazelnut	15
4		Vanilla	16
5	Spices	Ginger	2
6		Oregano	50
7		Vanilla	30
8	Grand Total		138

Figure 6.21
Pivot table with no calculations.
Source: Microsoft® Corporation.

Percentages are applied by right-clicking on any cell in the values area and selecting the Show Values As command from the contextual menu. More than 15 options are presented, including:

■ No Calculation

■ % of Grand Total

■ % of Column Total

■ % of Row Total

■ % of Parent Row Total

■ % of Parent Column Total

- % Running Total In…
- Rank Smallest to Largest
- Rank Largest to Smallest

The default value for this list is the No Calculation option. This means that no percentages or ranks are calculated. Let's now illustrate a few of the possibilities. To initiate this command, we need to first select a cell in the measures area of the pivot table. If we then select the % of Grand Total option under the Show Values As command, Excel will list the values as a percentage of the grand total, and display the pivot table of Figure 6.22.

	A	B	C
1	Product Category ⫟	Product ⫟	Sum of Total Sales
2	Coffee	French Roast	18.12%
3		Hazelnut	10.87%
4		Vanilla	11.59%
5	Spices	Ginger	1.45%
6		Oregano	36.23%
7		Vanilla	21.74%
8	Grand Total		100.00%

Figure 6.22

Pivot table with Percent of Grand Total calculation.

Source: Microsoft® Corporation.

The grand total, previously seen as 138, now appears as 100%, and all other values display as an appropriate percentage of 138. All percentages add up to 100. Note the simplicity and power of converting this data to a percentage. We can now easily comprehend that Oregano comprises exactly 36.23% of all sales. When we initially looked at this data in Figure 6.19, we might have guessed that Oregano, with sales of 50 out of a total of 138, was a little over a third of all sales, but this calculation would have been far from obvious.

With this data, the % of Column Total calculation would display the same values, since there is only one column in this pivot table. If there had been more than one field in the values area, then you could display separate percentages for each column. Likewise, the % of Row Total calculation would merely display 100% for each row, since there is only one value in each row. Let's now change the Total Sales field to the % of Parent Row Total calculation. The result is in Figure 6.23.

⬜	A	B	C
1	Product Category 🔽	Product 🔽	Sum of Total Sales
2	Coffee	French Roast	44.64%
3		Hazelnut	26.79%
4		Vanilla	28.57%
5	Spices	Ginger	2.44%
6		Oregano	60.98%
7		Vanilla	36.59%
8	Grand Total		100.00%

Figure 6.23

Pivot table with Percent of Parent Row calculation.

Source: Microsoft® Corporation.

Since this calculation refers to parent rows, it creates separate calculations for each group of parents. Thus, the three products in the Coffee category have percentages that add up to 100, as do the three products in the Spices category.

Another useful calculation is the % Running Total In. However, this calculation makes sense only when the data is in some sort of useful order, such as by date. When we rearrange the pivot table to put Sales Month in the rows area and apply this calculation, we see the pivot table of Figure 6.24.

⬜	A	B
1	Sales Month 🔽	Sum of Total Sales
2	2012-12	4.98%
3	2013-01	19.94%
4	2013-02	73.21%
5	2013-03	100.00%
6	Grand Total	

Figure 6.24

Pivot table with Percent Running Total calculation.

Source: Microsoft® Corporation.

This tells us that, of the four months of data we're looking at, only 4.98% of sales occurred in the first month. The first two months provided a total of 19.94% of the total.

Finally, looking at the two ranking functions, we'll apply the Rank Largest to Smallest calculation to our list of sales in these four months. The result is shown in Figure 6.25.

	A	B
1	Sales Month ▼	Sum of Total Sales
2	2012-12	4
3	2013-01	3
4	2013-02	1
5	2013-03	2
6	Grand Total	

Figure 6.25

Pivot table with Rank Largest to Smallest calculation.

Source: Microsoft® Corporation.

This informs us that the month with the highest sales was February, followed by March, January, and then December.

Summarization

Percentages and ranks provide an opportunity to present the data in the values area of a pivot table in a variety of ways. Rather than simply summing up numeric values, percentages and ranks transform those numbers to a different scale. However, we've been skirting around the possibility of aggregating data in ways other than by adding their values. The Summarize Values command can be used to provide a number of alternative ways to summarize data. This command is found in the contextual menu when right-clicking on any cell in the values area, right below the Show Values As command. The Summarize Values command provides these options:

- Sum
- Count
- Average
- Max
- Min
- Product
- More Options

The More Options choice offers these additional possibilities:

- Count Numbers
- StDev
- StDevp

- Var

- Varp

Up until now, everything we've done has made use of the Sum option, which is the default. Of the remaining choices, the most significant is the Count function. But first, let's briefly mention the other possibilities. Average is a straightforward way to provide an average of the detailed data that lay behind this summary statistic. For example, to see the average sales for each of the three product categories, we can arrange the pivot table as shown in Figure 6.26 and select Average on the Summarize Values By command.

	A	B
1	Product Category ▼	Average of Total Sales
2	Coffee	21.33333333
3	Spices	13.88888889
4	Tea	13.6
5	Grand Total	16.05

Figure 6.26
Pivot table with summarization by average.
Source: Microsoft® Corporation.

The meaning of this data should be obvious. The value of 13.6 for Tea means that all of the rows that have sales of Tea have an average value of 13.6. If desired, we can prove that 13.6 really is the average by double-clicking on the cell with 13.6 to do a drillthrough. That brings up the data seen in Figure 6.27.

	A	B	C	D	E	F	G	H	I	J
		Sales	Customer	Customer	Customer		Product		Unit	Total
1	Sales Date ▼	Month ▼	ID ▼	City ▼	State ▼	Product ▼	Category ▼	Quantity ▼	Price ▼	Sales ▼
2	2/17/2013	2013-02	22	Cleveland	OH	Green Tea	Tea	7	6	42
3	2/15/2013	2013-02	2	Minneapoli	MN	Oolong	Tea	8	3	24
4	3/1/2013	2013-03	14	Knoxville	TN	Darjeeling	Tea	-3	4	-12
5	3/31/2013	2013-03	19	Boulder	CO	Green Tea	Tea	-1	6	-6
6	2/18/2013	2013-02	18	Denver	CO	Earl Grey	Tea	4	5	20

Figure 6.27
Drillthrough on a cell with an average.
Source: Microsoft® Corporation.

The detailed data that appears in Figure 6.27 clearly shows that we have five rows with total sales of 68. The average for these rows is 13.6. Remember that the numbers in the values area of a pivot table are always a summarization of some kind. Doing the drillthrough allows you to view the detailed data being summarized. In addition to doing a drillthrough, there is actually an easier way to understand how the average was computed, and thus ascertain its validity. Remembering that more than one field can be placed in the values area of a pivot table, we'll drag the same Total Sales field to the values area two more times, and then modify the summarization on these two additional instances of the field so that one sums and one counts. The resulting pivot table appears as in Figure 6.28.

	A	B	C	D
1	Product Category ▾	Average of Total Sales	Sum of Total Sales	Count of Total Sales2
2	Coffee	21.33333333	128	6
3	Spices	13.88888889	125	9
4	Tea	13.6	68	5
5	Grand Total	16.05	321	20

Figure 6.28
Pivot table with multiple summarizations for the same field.
Source: Microsoft® Corporation.

This shows the Total Sales field summarized in three different ways, by average, sum, and count. As before, this tells us that there are five detail rows for tea with total sales of 68. This produces an average of 13.6. Of course, the grand total average is computed from all the detail data and not from the displayed averages for coffee, spices, and tea. Thus, the average grand total of 16.05 is computed by dividing 321 by 20.

Other than the Count option, the other possibilities for summarization are fairly routine. Min and Max provide the minimum and maximum values for the data in that cell. Product, an option that is seldom used, calculates the product of all values. StdDev and StdDevp calculate the standard deviation for a sample and for a population. Var and Varp calculate the sample and population variance.

At this point, it needs to be emphasized that the summarization possibilities for the values area of a pivot table all involve numeric computations. Excel does not allow non-numeric values to be displayed in the values area of a pivot table. The most that you can do with fields with non-numeric values is to count the rows. To illustrate, if we attempt to place the Customer ID in the rows area, the State in the columns area, and the City in the values area, the result is a pivot table such as the one shown in Figure 6.29. In this example, we've filtered out a number of customers to reduce the amount of data displayed.

	A	B	C	D	E	F
1	**Count of Customer City**	**Customer State** ▼				
2	**Customer ID**	◢ **CA**	**CO**	**FL**	**NH**	**TN**
3		11			2	
4		14				1
5		18	1			
6		19	1			
7		20		1		
8		23				2
9		49	1			

Figure 6.29

Pivot table with text values in the values area.

Source: Microsoft® Corporation.

We may have optimistically hoped to see the names of the cities under each state. However, Excel can only display quantitative data in the values area of a pivot table. As such, when fields with text values are placed in the values area, they can only be counted. Their values can't be displayed. Interestingly, readers familiar with Microsoft Access might remember that Access *does* allow non-numeric values to be used in the values area of a crosstab query, a construct that is similar to Excel pivot tables. This is accomplished in Access by applying an aggregation function named *First* to the text values in the values area of a crosstab. Excel, however, does not provide the First function.

The ability to summarize by count is in some ways more complex, and perhaps less intuitive, than summarizing by sum. Consider the pivot table shown in Figure 6.30.

	A	B	C	D
1	**Sales Month** ▼	**Count of Total Sales**	**Count of Customer State**	**Count of Customer City**
2	2012-12	3	3	3
3	2013-01	3	3	3
4	2013-02	8	8	8
5	2013-03	6	6	6
6	**Grand Total**	20	20	20

Figure 6.30

Pivot table with counts of three fields.

Source: Microsoft® Corporation.

In this pivot table, we've placed the Sales Month in the rows area and three different fields in the values area: Total Sales, Customer State, and Customer City. Since Total

Sales is a numeric field, its default method of summarization is to sum. We subsequently changed it from Sum to Count. For Customer State and Customer City, being text fields, their default method of summarization is to count. We left those fields as is. The result is that we see counts of three different fields, all with the same data. The moral of this story is that it doesn't really matter what field is being counted. The values in the underlying data for the field are ignored. The count function simply counts rows, and it doesn't matter what values are in the fields of whatever fields you choose to count. The field to use for the counting of rows is an arbitrary choice.

For this reason, we sometimes recommend adding a special field to your underlying data table that has a value of 1 in all rows. For example, if we were to add a field named Sales Count to the table upon which the pivot table is based, we could sum up that field rather than count it. With this added field, the first few rows of our data now look like Figure 6.31, and the resulting pivot table appears as Figure 6.32.

	A	B	C	D	E	F	G	H	I	J	K
1	Sales Date	Sales Month	Customer ID	Customer City	Customer State	Product	Product Category	Quantity	Unit Price	Total Sales	Sales Count
2	1/22/2013	2013-01	23	Nashville	TN	Breakfast Blend	Coffee	3	4	12	1
3	2/1/2013	2013-02	44	Seattle	WA	Vanilla	Spices	6	3	18	1
4	3/1/2013	2013-03	14	Knoxville	TN	Darjeeling	Tea	-3	4	-12	1
5	12/6/2012	2012-12	15	Atlanta	GA	Mustard	Spices	6	2	12	1

Figure 6.31

Revised data with a Sales Count column.

Source: Microsoft® Corporation.

	A	B
1	Sales Month ▾	Sum of Sales Count
2	2012-12	3
3	2013-01	3
4	2013-02	8
5	2013-03	6
6	Grand Total	20

Figure 6.32

Pivot table that sums a field with values of 1.

Source: Microsoft® Corporation.

If we double-click on cell B2 of this pivot table, the drillthrough displays the underlying data shown in Figure 6.33.

	A	B	C	D	E	F	G	H	I	J	K
		Sales	Customer	Customer	Customer		Product		Unit	Total	Sales
1	Sales Date	Month	ID	City	State	Product	Category	Quantity	Price	Sales	Count
2	12/27/2012	2012-12	44	Seattle	WA	Mustard	Spices	-2	2	-4	1
3	12/18/2012	2012-12	50	Peoria	IL	Curry	Spices	2	4	8	1
4	12/6/2012	2012-12	15	Atlanta	GA	Mustard	Spices	6	2	12	1

Figure 6.33
Drillthrough showing the Sales Count field.
Source: Microsoft® Corporation.

As seen, the Sales Count field has been added to the table for the sole purpose of counting rows. To some extent, this lessens confusion for the user as to which field to count. With a field designated for counting, the user knows to select that field if a count is desired. In actuality, however, this field, since it's numeric, will then be *summed* rather than counted. The value of using this type of field is strictly a matter of personal preference. If one understands the quirks of the Count function, then it really isn't needed at all.

Incidentally, if at any time you add columns to the data that underlies a pivot table, you don't need to rebuild the pivot table from scratch. You merely need to click the Refresh command, seen in Figure 6.7, to refresh the list of fields in the pivot table Field List from the data source.

Let's now look at some layout and design possibilities for counting data. We'll start with a new set of data, shown in Figure 6.34.

	A	B	C
1	Patient Name	Question	Response
2	Sandra	Are you happy	Yes
3	Kim	Are you happy	No
4	Paul	Are you happy	No
5	Paul	How is health	Excellent
6	Sandra	How is health	Poor
7	Kim	How is health	Average
8	Bethany	Are you happy	No
9	Lauren	How is health	Average
10	Lauren	Are you happy	Whatever

Figure 6.34
Table with survey data.
Source: Microsoft® Corporation.

This Excel table shows the responses to some questions that were asked of some patients. Let's say that we want to count how many of each response was given to each question. We want to see a total count for each question and response combination, as well as detail on what each patient responded. One way to lay out the data is via the pivot table displayed in Figure 6.35.

	A	B	C	D	E	F	G
1	Count of Response	Question ▼	Response ▼				
2		Are you happy			How is health		
3	Patient Name ▼	No	Whatever	Yes	Average	Excellent	Poor
4	Bethany	1					
5	Kim	1			1		
6	Lauren		1		1		
7	Paul	1				1	
8	Sandra			1			1
9	Grand Total	3	1	1	2	1	1

Figure 6.35
Pivot table with survey data.
Source: Microsoft® Corporation.

In this pivot table, we placed the Patient Name in the rows area, and both the Question and Response in the columns area. The Response is also in the values area, with a summarization of count applied to the field. As explained, it really doesn't matter which field is counted in the values area. From this, we see that there were three responses of No to the question "Are you happy." Because the Patient Name is in the rows area, the pivot table groups all the data by patient. Besides illustrating how pivot tables can count data, this example also nicely illustrates the fact that the data displayed in a pivot table is quite dynamic, and is based on the actual data present. If the underlying data table had hundreds of rows, there would be no easy way to determine in advance how many columns would be displayed in the pivot table. In this example, we happen to see the column with a response of "Whatever" under the "Are you happy" question only because one patient happened to give that response. One of the virtues of pivot tables is that they can turn a general data structure into a useful display. Without the use of pivot tables, one would need to have a table such as shown in Figure 6.36 to represent the "How is Health" question.

◢	A	B	C	D
1	Patient Name ▼	Excellent ▼	Average ▼	Poor ▼
2	Paul	1		
3	Sandra			1
4	Kim		1	
5	Lauren		1	

Figure 6.36

Table with data in a less flexible structure.

Source: Microsoft® Corporation.

In this table, we hard-coded three columns with the possible responses to the question, indicating the responses of each patient under the appropriate column. With this data design, we would need separate tables for each question, and we would need to spell out each possible response in a column. This makes reporting less flexible. By making use of the more general data structure in Figure 6.34, and by using a pivot table to turn responses into columns, we can achieve our goals with much less pain, both for the data designer and for the analyst doing the reporting.

Before leaving this example, let's present the data in Figure 6.35 in one additional way. The pivot table of Figure 6.37 displays responses in the rows area and dispenses with counts entirely.

◢	A	B	C
1	Patient Name ▼	Question ▼	Response ▼
2	Bethany	Are you happy	No
3	Kim	Are you happy	No
4		How is health	Average
5	Lauren	Are you happy	Whatever
6		How is health	Average
7	Paul	Are you happy	No
8		How is health	Excellent
9	Sandra	Are you happy	Yes
10		How is health	Poor

Figure 6.37

Pivot table with no fields in the columns or values area.

Source: Microsoft® Corporation.

The layout for this pivot table has the Patient Name, Question, and Response fields in the rows area. Nothing has been placed in the columns or values area. There are no counts or summarization of any kind. However, this layout nicely accomplishes the objective of displaying the responses that patients gave to questions in an easy-to-read format. We can see that Kim responded No to the "Are you happy" question and Average to the "How is health" question. By placing all three fields in the rows area, and utilizing the natural order of the hierarchy, we can easily make sense of this data. Even though pivot tables excel at summing quantitative data, nothing says that you can't use them merely to display textual data. You can even use pivot tables if you only want to group text data. Let's say, for example, that you have a table of customer information and merely want to see all the cities in which your customers reside. You could simply place both the State and City fields in the rows area of a pivot table to produce a display as in Figure 6.38.

Figure 6.38
Pivot table with grouped data in the rows area.
Source: Microsoft® Corporation.

In this example, the grouping ability of pivot tables has eliminated all duplicate cities, so we see only unique city/state combinations.

To complete our discussion of summarization, we will now turn to a more comprehensive example that encompasses a number of features we've discussed before, but combines them together in a more realistic scenario. We'll also introduce another creative way to sum data, via the use of indicator fields. Sometimes called 0/1 fields, indicator fields assign yes or no values to attributes. As shown in Figure 6.39, the data set for this example is customer data for a bank that includes a customer ID, state, and balances in savings or checking accounts the customer may have.

	A	B	C	D
1	Customer ID	State	Savings Balance	Checking Balance
2	1	Vermont	500	500
3	2	Vermont	250	0
4	3	Vermont		550
5	4	New Hampshire	420	772
6	5	New Hampshire	40	0
7	6	New Hampshire	15	905

Figure 6.39

Bank data with customer information.

Source: Microsoft® Corporation.

In this example, our analysis objective is to determine, by state, what percentage of customers have only a checking account, only a savings account, checking and savings accounts, or neither checking nor savings accounts (assuming that they have some other type of account with the bank). Our first problem is that, while the data states the dollar amount of the accounts, this doesn't translate into a variable that simply states whether the customer has a savings or checking account. This is where indicator fields come in. Even before creating a pivot table from this data, we need to create some additional columns for this purpose, calculated from existing data. To do this, we'll create three new columns, shown in Figure 6.40.

	A	B	C	D	E	F	G
1	Customer ID	State	Savings Balance	Checking Balance	Savings Account	Checking Account	Customer Count
2	1	Vermont	500	500	yes	yes	1
3	2	Vermont	250	0	yes	no	1
4	3	Vermont		550	no	yes	1
5	4	New Hampshire	420	772	yes	yes	1
6	5	New Hampshire	40	0	yes	no	1
7	6	New Hampshire	15	905	yes	yes	1

Figure 6.40

Bank data with customer information and additional calculated columns.

Source: Microsoft® Corporation.

Columns E and F have been added to translate the amount of the savings and checking balances into indicator fields with yes/no values. To accomplish this, we needed to enter formulas in those cells. The topic of formulas will be discussed in Chapter 9, and the specific function used is covered in Chapter 13. We present this information to emphasize the importance of the topics to come. As in this situation, very often data must be transformed in some manner before a pivot table can be employed. In this example, the formula entered in cell E2 is:

=IF(C2>0,"yes","no")

This formula evaluates the value of cell C2. If it is greater than zero, a value of "yes" is placed in cell E2. If it's less than 0 then "no" is put in cell E2. The assumption is that a value of 0 means that the customer doesn't have a savings account. The same formula is propagated to the other cells in columns E and F, with appropriate relative references. For example, the formula in cell F5 reads:

=IF(D5>0,"yes","no")

In addition to the calculations in rows E and F, we also added a literal value of 1 in each cell in column G, to indicate a count of 1 for each customer.

At this point, we're ready to translate our data into a pivot table format, but to make the problem slightly more realistic, we'll first consider an additional step. Let's say that we're a large multi-national bank, and instead of having a few thousand customers in Vermont and New Hampshire, we actually have a few million customers in numerous states. With this volume of data, we might very well want to consolidate our data even before we create the pivot table. After all, we really don't need Customer ID for our analysis. In other words, we can group our data by unique combinations of the state and the indicator fields, along with a count of how many customers are in each group.

To accomplish this grouping, we'll turn to Microsoft Query. In our previous examples of Microsoft Query in Chapter 3, we explained how to import data from external sources. However, nothing says that we can't formulate a query from another worksheet in the current Excel workbook. With that in mind, we'll open up a new worksheet in Excel, select the From Other Sources command on the Data tab of the Ribbon, and then select the Microsoft Query option. We'll then browse until we find our current workbook, and select the worksheet that contains the data in Figure 6.39. One slight trick in this endeavor is that you need to make sure that your worksheets are available for selection. If your worksheets don't appear after the Excel file is selected, then select the Options button in the Add Tables pane and check that you want to view both Tables and System Tables. You can then find and select the appropriate worksheet. Figure 6.41 shows the Microsoft Query that would be created to group the data.

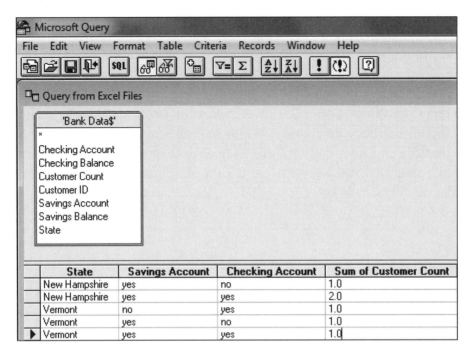

Figure 6.41

Microsoft Query that groups bank data.

Source: Microsoft® Corporation.

In this query, we highlighted the Customer Count row and then selected the group option via the Greek summation sign until it sums the data. Notice that the query shows a value of 2 for New Hampshire customers with both savings and checking accounts. That is because our data has two customers with this characteristic. After creating this query, we can select the Return Data to Microsoft Excel command under the File menu. Our Excel worksheet then appears as in Figure 6.42.

	A	B	C	D
1	State	Savings Account	Checking Account	'Sum of Customer Count'
2	New Hampshire	yes	no	1
3	New Hampshire	yes	yes	2
4	Vermont	no	yes	1
5	Vermont	yes	no	1
6	Vermont	yes	yes	1

Figure 6.42

Microsoft Query results returned to Excel.

Source: Microsoft® Corporation.

Of course, we could have used Microsoft Access in place of Microsoft Query to accomplish the same result shown in Figure 6.42. The choice of software is a matter of preference. This process of using Microsoft Query doesn't yet show the millions of rows of data that were mentioned. If we had many more customers and went through the same process, our data might look something like Figure 6.43.

	A	B	C	D
1	State	Savings Account	Checking Account	Customer Count
2	Vermont	yes	yes	23500
3	Vermont	yes	no	13500
4	Vermont	no	yes	14000
5	Vermont	no	no	7500
6	New Hampshire	yes	yes	9500
7	New Hampshire	yes	no	2500
8	New Hampshire	no	yes	3500
9	New Hampshire	no	no	1000

Figure 6.43
Grouped bank data for a larger group of customers.
Source: Microsoft® Corporation.

The data in this figure shows how the data of interest for 75,000 customers can be condensed into only nine rows. This table shows, for example, that there are 13,500 customers in the state of Vermont who have a savings account but no checking account.

With our preliminary tasks accomplished, we are now ready to create a pivot table to produce the results we desire. To do this, we'll take the normal steps to create a pivot table, and place the two indicator fields in the rows area, the State field in the columns, and the Customer Count field in the values area, as shown in Figure 6.44.

	A	B	C	D
1	Sum of Customer Count		State ▾	
2	Savings Account ▾	Checking Account ▾	New Hampshire	Vermont
3	no	no	1000	7500
4		yes	3500	14000
5	yes	no	2500	13500
6		yes	9500	23500

Figure 6.44
Pivot table with indicator fields and customer counts.
Source: Microsoft® Corporation.

Note that it really didn't matter which field was listed first in the rows area. If we had placed the Checking Account field to the left of the Savings Account field, we'd have the same data, displayed in a slightly different arrangement. In other words, since there isn't a natural hierarchy to the two indicator fields, the order they're listed in doesn't matter. Also, note that this pivot table has summation by sum, not count. Even though our quantitative field is named Customer Count, it has values that need to be summed, not counted. If we had applied a summation type of count to this field, we'd see all 1's in the values area, since our grouped data has only one row per state/indicator combination.

To extend the analysis a little further, this pivot table shows us raw customer counts, but we really would like to see our data in percentages. To do this, we select the % of Column Total option under the Show Values As command. The result is in Figure 6.45.

	A	B	C	D
1	Sum of Customer Count		State ▾	
2	Savings Account ▾	Checking Account ▾	New Hampshire	Vermont
3	no	no	6.06%	12.82%
4		yes	21.21%	23.93%
5	yes	no	15.15%	23.08%
6		yes	57.58%	40.17%

Figure 6.45

Pivot table with indicator fields and percentages.

Source: Microsoft® Corporation.

The raw data of Figure 6.44 has now been transformed into percentages that show each combination's relative standing within each column. We can now see, for example, that whereas 57.58% of Vermont's customers have both savings and checking accounts, only 40.17% of Vermont's customers share that characteristic.

Relationships and Data Models

Excel 2013 provides an exciting new feature that allows users to combine data from multiple tables or data sources into one logical entity that can be analyzed via pivot tables or pivot charts. This ability was previously available in the PowerPivot add-in for Excel 2010, but has now been migrated to the base version of Excel.

To illustrate, we'll begin with the three tables shown in Figures 6.46, 6.47, and 6.48.

	A	B	C
1	Customer ID	Customer Name	State Abbreviation
2	1	Rafael Mendez	SD
3	2	Louis Gordon	ND
4	3	Susan Winkler	MN
5	4	Penelope Brown	MN
6	5	Inidira Kapur	SD

Figure 6.46

Customer table.

Source: Microsoft® Corporation.

	A	B	C
1	Customer ID	Date	Sales
2	1	5/1/2013	50
3	2	5/1/2013	65
4	1	5/2/2013	45
5	3	5/2/2013	30
6	4	5/3/2013	25
7	5	5/3/2013	75
8	3	5/3/2013	40

Figure 6.47

Sales table.

Source: Microsoft® Corporation.

	A	B
1	State Abbreviation	State Name
2	MN	Minnesota
3	ND	North Dakota
4	SD	South Dakota

Figure 6.48

States table.

Source: Microsoft® Corporation.

All three of these tables are Excel tables, and have been given the indicated names. The Customer table of Figure 6.46 lists customers with their ID, name, and state. The Sales table in Figure 6.47 lists individual sales from these customers. The States table of Figure 6.48 provides the full name for the state abbreviations in the Customer table.

Without the Data Model capabilities of Excel, we would have needed to utilize Microsoft Query or Microsoft Access to join the data in the three tables together before the data could be analyzed in a pivot table. If this had been done, the data would appear as in Figure 6.49.

	A	B	C	D	E	F
1	Customer ID	Customer Name	State Abbreviation	State Name	Date	Sales
2	1	Rafael Mendez	SD	South Dakota	5/1/2013	50
3	1	Rafael Mendez	SD	South Dakota	5/2/2013	45
4	2	Louis Gordon	ND	North Dakota	5/1/2013	65
5	3	Susan Winkler	MN	Minnesota	5/2/2013	30
6	3	Susan Winkler	MN	Minnesota	5/3/2013	40
7	4	Penelope Brown	MN	Minnesota	5/3/2013	25
8	5	Inidira Kapur	SD	South Dakota	5/3/2013	75

Figure 6.49

Table with joined data from Customer, Sales, and States tables.

Source: Microsoft® Corporation.

This table combines data from all three tables. The table has eight rows due to the eight rows in the Sales table, which is the table with the highest level of detail. For each row in the Sales table, the Customer ID was joined to the Customer table to obtain the Customer Name. Likewise, the State Abbreviation of the Customer table was used to get the State Name from the States table.

We'll now demonstrate how the Data Model capabilities of Excel can be utilized to combine these three tables together. There are actually several ways to establish the relationships. The simplest is to start with any of the three tables and select the Pivot-Table command on the Insert tab of the Ribbon. Doing so brings up the Create Pivot-Table dialog box shown in Figure 6.50.

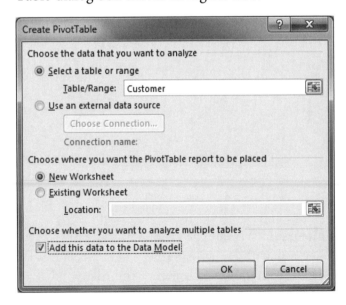

Figure 6.50

Create PivotTable dialog box.

Source: Microsoft® Corporation.

In this case, we started with the Customer table. The important aspect of this procedure is to check the "Add this data to the Data Model" item at the bottom. This tells Excel that you're building a Data Model. After doing so, and clicking OK, an empty pivot table is created in a new worksheet. For the pivot table, the Fields section of the Field List appears as in Figure 6.51.

Figure 6.51

Fields section of Field List showing active tables.

Source: Microsoft® Corporation.

Notice that the Active label at the top is highlighted. This means that we are only looking at the currently active table, which is the Customer table that was just added to the pivot table. However, if we click on the All label, we see the Fields section shown in Figure 6.52.

Figure 6.52

Fields section of Field List showing all tables.

Source: Microsoft® Corporation.

When we added the Customer table to the Data Model, Excel was smart enough to add all tables in the current workbook. We therefore see all three tables available in the pivot table. However, we have not yet specified the relationships between the tables. This process is initiated by selecting the Relationships command under the Analyze tab of the Ribbon. This command was previously seen in Figure 6.7. After doing so, a blank Manage Relationships dialog box appears. To add a relationship, we click the New button, after which the Create Relationship dialog box of Figure 6.53 is shown.

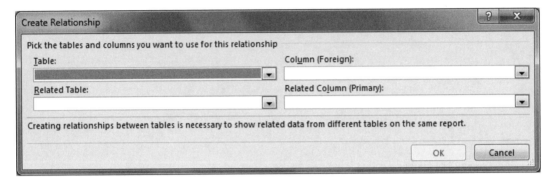

Figure 6.53
Create Relationship dialog box.
Source: Microsoft® Corporation.

Since all tables are already in the Data Model, we merely need to select each drop-down item to select the proper table and column. We'll start by creating the relationship between the Customer and the Sales tables. After making our selections, the Create Relationship dialog box looks like Figure 6.54.

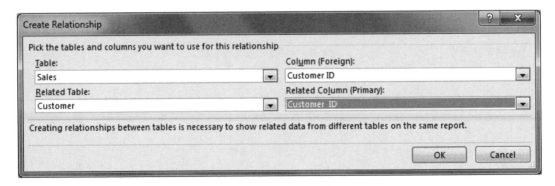

Figure 6.54
Create Relationship dialog box with specifications.
Source: Microsoft® Corporation.

There are two elements to the relationship being specified. First, we're relating which two tables are involved. One table is called the Related Table. Every row in the primary table needs to point to exactly one row in the related table. In this example, the Sales table is primary since it has more detail than the Customer table. Every row in the Sales points to exactly one row in the Customer table. The reverse is not true. In fact, if we had specified the Sales table as the related table, Excel would come back with a message saying that the relationship cannot be created in that direction. Excel then offers to reverse the direction for you automatically when the OK button is clicked. In other words, Excel actually examines the data in each table to verify the direction of the relationship. The second element of the specification is the columns specified. The columns tell Excel precisely how the tables are related to each other. In this example, the Customer ID of the Sales table has the same data as the Customer ID of the Customer table. After clicking OK, the relationship is added to the Data Model.

We'll proceed do to the same for the other relationship in our data, which is the relationship between the Customer and States tables. This is shown in Figure 6.55.

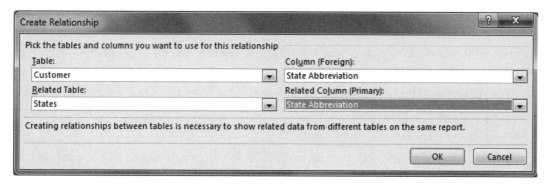

Figure 6.55
A second Create Relationship dialog box with specifications.
Source: Microsoft® Corporation.

This relationship states that the State Abbreviation column establishes a relationship between the Customer table and the related States table. After adding this second relationship to the data model, the Manage Relationships dialog box is no longer blank, and appears as in Figure 6.56.

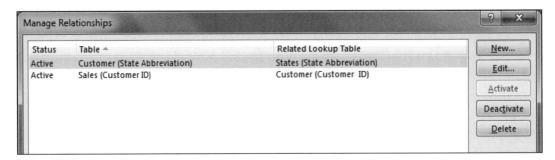

Figure 6.56

Manage Relationships dialog box.

Source: Microsoft® Corporation.

The Manage Relationships dialog box shows the two relationships that have been created. From this pane, one can modify or delete the relationships already established. Note that this dialog box can be accessed directly from the Relationships command on the Data tab of the Ribbon. This allows the user to create relationships prior to the creation of a pivot table.

There are also alternate methods of adding a table to the Data Model. Referring back to Figure 5.5 of the prior chapter, you'll notice a MORE TABLES label at the bottom of the Fields Section of the Field List. This allows the user to create another pivot table based on a different table, which in effect adds the table to the Data Model. Also, one can directly add any connection to the Data Model after invoking the Connections command under the Data tab of the Ribbon.

Now that the proper relationships are established, we can proceed with adding any desired fields from any table to the pivot table areas. We'll start by adding the Customer ID, Customer Name, and State Name to the rows area, and the Sales field to the values area. This is shown in Figure 6.57.

	A	B	C	D
1	Customer ID ▾	Customer Name ▾	State Name ▾	Sum of Sales
2		1 Rafael Mendez	South Dakota	95
3		2 Louis Gordon	North Dakota	65
4		3 Susan Winkler	Minnesota	70
5		4 Penelope Brown	Minnesota	25
6		5 Indira Kapur	South Dakota	75

Figure 6.57

Pivot table with data from three tables.

Source: Microsoft® Corporation.

The power of what has just been accomplished should be emphasized. We've taken data from three different tables, established relationships, and presented the data in a single pivot table. The Customer ID and Customer Name are from the Customer table, the State Name is from the States table, and Sales is from the Sales table. Without relationships present, we would have needed to create a table such as the one in Figure 6.49 to accomplish the same result.

When a Data Model is utilized, there is one noteworthy new feature of pivot table functionality aside from the ability to reference fields from multiple tables. In addition to the summarization methods discussed earlier in this chapter, one now also has the ability to do distinct counts. This is slightly different from a normal count. For example, if we do a Distinct Count of dates, with the State in the rows area, the resulting pivot table is in Figure 6.58.

	A	B
1	State Name ▼	Distinct Count of Date
2	Minnesota	2
3	North Dakota	1
4	South Dakota	3

Figure 6.58

Pivot table with a Distinct Count.

Source: Microsoft® Corporation.

This data is telling us that the state of Minnesota had two dates with sales. If we had used a normal Count rather than the Distinct Count, we'd see the value of 3 for Minnesota, since there are three rows of sales for Minnesota. Whereas the Count function merely counts rows, the Distinct Count looks for the number of unique values. Note that this Distinct Count function is available only when using Data Models, even if there is only one table in the Data Model. When Data Models are employed in a pivot table, Excel uses an entirely different technology to process the pivot table. This is something called the xVelocity analytics engine, which was previously available only with the PowerPivot add-in.

Since Data Models utilize this different engine, there are also some limitations to using Data Models. For example, when Data Models are employed, you can't utilize grouping or the calculated items and fields discussed earlier in this chapter. Another quirk of Data Models is that they require that there be at least one field in the values area of the pivot table for the specified relationships to work correctly. For example, if we attempt to create a pivot table with only the Customer Name and State Name in the rows area, we see the data in Figure 6.59.

◢	A	B
1	Customer Name ▼	State Name ▼
2	Indira Kapur	Minnesota
3		North Dakota
4		South Dakota
5	Louis Gordon	Minnesota
6		North Dakota
7		South Dakota
8	Penelope Brown	Minnesota
9		North Dakota
10		South Dakota
11	Rafael Mendez	Minnesota
12		North Dakota
13		South Dakota
14	Susan Winkler	Minnesota
15		North Dakota
16		South Dakota

Figure 6.59

Pivot table with invalid relationships.

Source: Microsoft® Corporation.

In this situation, the relationships are being ignored. Each of the available states is being repeated for every customer. To correct this situation, we need to add any field to the values area. After adding the Customer name to the values area, we see the pivot table of Figure 6.60.

◢	A	B	C
1	Customer Name ▼	State Name ▼	Count of Customer Name
2	Indira Kapur	South Dakota	1
3	Louis Gordon	North Dakota	1
4	Penelope Brown	Minnesota	1
5	Rafael Mendez	South Dakota	1
6	Susan Winkler	Minnesota	1

Figure 6.60

Pivot table with valid relationships.

Source: Microsoft® Corporation.

We now see the data in its correct format and with relationships intact, displaying the indicated state for each customer.

As mentioned at the start of this section, the functionality associated with Data Models and relationships was previously available in the PowerPivot add-in for Excel 2010. For Office 2013, Microsoft has migrated much of this functionality to what's now called a Data Model, but they have also decided to retain other functionality strictly for the PowerPivot add-in. Microsoft has also chosen to restrict the availability of the PowerPivot add-in to the Professional Plus and Office 365 ProPlus versions of Excel. Although we don't cover PowerPivot in this book, please note these additional capabilities provided by that add-in:

- Modify relationships in a diagram view
- Create Key Performance Indicators (KPIs)
- Create hierarchies to enable drill-down functionality
- Utilize advanced data analysis functions (DAX)

Looking Ahead

The topics in this chapter extended our knowledge of pivot tables beyond the basics to include such sophisticated topics as calculated fields and items, and ways to make use of various grouping and summation properties. We began this chapter with an explanation of how to utilize subtotals and grand totals to add an additional layer of summation to pivot table values. We then delved into groupings as a way to expand the concept of subtotals even further. Calculated items and fields provided a means to add additional data to a pivot table beyond what is present in the underlying data. Our discussion of percentages and ranks focused on important methods of presenting raw numbers in a more understandable way. It's much easier to comprehend the relationships in a pivot table when it states that a certain cell is 30% of the total, rather than relying on the user to view a value of 600 and try to guess how it relates to a total of 2000.

Our next topic in this chapter, summation, went through a number of examples covering counts, averages, and the use of indicator fields. In our final example, we looked back to the use of Microsoft Query as a way to summarize data, and ahead to the use of formulas and functions to transform our data into more useful values prior to analysis. We rounded out the chapter with a discussion of Data Models and relationships, a new feature that allows the analyst to combine data from multiple tables. This is a much easier solution than using Microsoft Query. It's also considerably simpler than using the VLOOKUP function to relate data from multiple tables—a topic that will be covered later in this book.

Our next chapter on charts and pivot charts will allow us to translate the grouping and summarization properties of pivot tables into a visual representation. In the words of the somewhat trite adage, a picture is sometimes worth a thousand words. The ability to encapsulate the results of an analysis in a single graphic can have an impact far beyond the display of a bunch of numbers. Charts can be used not only to present summary findings, but also as a means of data exploration to help uncover data patterns that may not otherwise be obvious or visible.

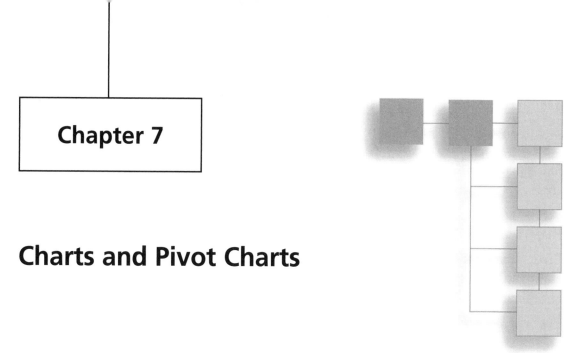

Chapter 7

Charts and Pivot Charts

In broad terms, charts serve two purposes for the analyst. First, they permit one to present key findings in a simple graphic that encapsulates and emphasizes key results. Just as pivot tables are an effective tool to summarize raw data, charts can further summarize an assemblage of numbers into a visual image of shapes and lines. Second, charts also allow the analyst to explore data via a more visual means to help uncover patterns that may not have been otherwise obvious. No matter how clear the layout of data in a spreadsheet or pivot table may be, there is always a certain challenge in making the leap from viewing data to achieving an understanding of what it means. In that regard, the visual representation of data can have immense value.

Excel provides two basic mechanisms for creating graphical representations of data: charts and pivot charts. Pivot charts are created from and associated with pivot tables. In contrast, standard charts are created directly from data on an Excel worksheet. The emphasis in this chapter will be on pivot charts, so we'll begin by discussing how to create and use pivot charts, and then turn to standard charts toward the end of the chapter. Most of the functionality of charts can be accomplished by either pivot charts or standard charts, but as will be seen, pivot charts are decidedly easier to use.

Not only are pivot charts more user friendly than standard charts, but they are also more flexible. For standard charts to be created from data on a worksheet, the data must be arranged in a crosstab type of layout. In contrast, a pivot table, with its arrangement of data in rows, columns, and values, already has data in the required crosstab layout. Thus, arranging data in pivot charts is relatively easy, since the associated data in pivot tables is already in the proper layout for creating charts.

Furthermore, since pivot tables have the ability to summarize data into the crosstab type of layout, you can work from raw data and immediately transform that data in a pivot chart without having to first perform any summarization.

The main limitation of using pivot charts, as compared to standard charts, is that there are a small number of chart types that only apply when they reference detailed data. Since pivot tables and pivot charts automatically summarize data for you, these few chart types can be implemented only via standard charts.

Pivot Chart Basics

Pivot charts can be created in three different ways. First, one can utilize the PivotChart command found in the Charts group under the Insert tab of the Ribbon. When this command is selected, two options appear:

- PivotChart
- PivotChart & PivotTable

In either case, both a pivot table and pivot chart will be created. The second way to create a pivot chart is from an existing pivot table. The PivotChart command, found in the Tools group under the PivotTable Tools Options tab of the Ribbon, causes a pivot chart to be created from the selected pivot table. No matter which of these procedures is followed, the pivot chart will have the same underlying data source as the associated pivot table.

New with Excel 2013, a third option is available for creating pivot charts. The Recommended Charts command, found in the Charts group under the Insert tab of the Ribbon causes Excel to analyze your data and display a set of recommended charts. This feature will be presented shortly.

After a pivot chart is created, a set of contextual tabs appear under a PivotChart Tools label, analogous to the tabs that appear under the PivotTable Tools label. Whereas pivot tables have two contextual tabs in the Ribbon, Options and Design, pivot charts have three contextual tabs:

- Analyze
- Design
- Format

The most significant command under the Design tab allows you to select from more than 40 types of charts in eight categories, such as column, bar, and pie. The Design tab also has commands to adjust the various components of a chart, such as its title, axis labels, legend location, and gridlines. The Format commands pertain to the fine-tuning of a chart's appearance via various shape and Word art options. Finally, the commands under the Analyze tab are related to the pivoting aspects of the pivot chart, such as Slicer and Timeline options, viewing the associated pivot table Field List, as well as filtering options on the pivot chart itself.

To begin our exploration into pivot charts, we'll start with some data that is similar in structure to the coffee, tea, and spices sales data of the prior two chapters.

The data in Figure 7.1 has one row per sale to any individual customer. The sales date is indicated, as well as the customer ID and state, the channel, and amount of sale. Of course, real-life data would likely include many more fields, but these fields are suffi-cient for our purpose. Since pivot charts require a fair amount of data to provide a realistic image, we'll pretend that our data source contains many more rows of data. We'll use the table in Figure 7.2, which presumes to summarize the detailed data, as a basis for the subsequent charts.

	A	B	C	D	E
1	Sales Date ▼	Customer ID ▼	Customer State ▼	Channel ▼	Sales Amount ▼
2	4/1/2013	101 NY		Internet	50
3	4/1/2013	108 NY		Phone	40
4	4/1/2013	102 NY		Retail	30
5	4/1/2013	103 VT		Internet	120
6	4/1/2013	105 VT		Phone	80
7	4/1/2013	145 VT		Retail	90
8	4/1/2013	182 NY		Internet	520
9	4/1/2013	101 NY		Phone	350
10	4/1/2013	180 NY		Retail	300
11	4/1/2013	181 VT		Internet	130

Figure 7.1

Table with channel sales data.

Source: Microsoft® Corporation.

	A	B	C	D
1	Sales Month ▾	Customer State ▾	Channel ▾	Sales Amount ▾
2	2013-04	NY	Internet	4800
3	2013-04	NY	Phone	3200
4	2013-04	NY	Retail	2000
5	2013-04	VT	Internet	1200
6	2013-04	VT	Phone	800
7	2013-04	VT	Retail	900
8	2013-05	NY	Internet	5200
9	2013-05	NY	Phone	3500
10	2013-05	NY	Retail	3000
11	2013-05	VT	Internet	1300
12	2013-05	VT	Phone	700
13	2013-05	VT	Retail	1400
14	2013-06	NY	Internet	7200
15	2013-06	NY	Phone	4000
16	2013-06	NY	Retail	2500
17	2013-06	VT	Internet	1300
18	2013-06	VT	Phone	900
19	2013-06	VT	Retail	800

Figure 7.2

Table with summarized sales data.

Source: Microsoft® Corporation.

In this table with summarized data, we've grouped data by month, state, and channel. Since we have data covering three months, two states (Vermont and New York), and three channels (Internet, Phone, and Retail), there are a total of 18 combinations, and thus 18 rows in the table. The sales amount shown is the total sales for that month/state/channel combination. For example, the first row of data indicates that there was a total of $4800 in sales on the Internet to customers in New York in April. The data in this table could have been created by using Microsoft Query to group data, as demonstrated in the prior chapter. The only field present in the data in Figure 7.2 not in Figure 7.1 is Sales Month, which might have been calculated in Microsoft Query, or else added to the underlying Excel worksheet.

As a convenience to allow us to trace back chart values to actual data, the following example will use the data in Figure 7.2 as a data source. In the real world, it would not be necessary to first summarize the data of Figure 7.1 to the summarization in Figure 7.2. We can easily rely on the ability of pivot charts to summarize the data for us.

To initiate creation of the pivot chart, we'll start by selecting the Recommended Charts command in the Charts group under the Insert tab of the Ribbon. This produces the Insert Chart dialog box shown in Figure 7.3.

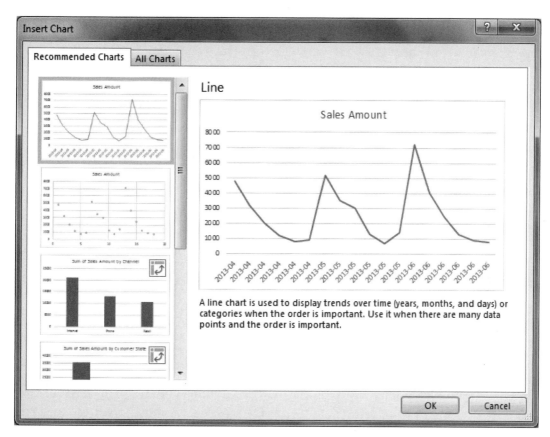

Figure 7.3

Insert Chart dialog box.

Source: Microsoft® Corporation.

Similar to the Recommended PivotTables dialog box seen in Figure 5.2, this feature shows a number of recommended charts. The chart options shown are typically a mixture of both standard charts and pivot charts. The pivot charts are designated with an icon in the upper right corner of the charts shown in the left pane. In Figure 7.3, the top two charts are standard charts, and the bottom two are pivot charts.

For purposes of understanding the various charts, we'll ignore the recommendations offered by Excel and proceed by exploring the different chart types individually, and in a more manual fashion. To do this, we'll select the Pivot Chart option under the Pivot Chart command under the Insert tab of the Ribbon. This causes the dialog box of Figure 7.4 to appear.

Figure 7.4
Create PivotChart dialog box.
Source: Microsoft® Corporation.

This dialog box is identical to what would have appeared if we were just creating a pivot table. In this example, the table is named ChannelSalesSummary. As before, we'll ignore the option to add the data to the Data Model. As with pivot tables, Data Models allow you to join multiple tables together for analysis in a single pivot chart. After clicking the OK button, a new worksheet appears that looks like Figure 7.5.

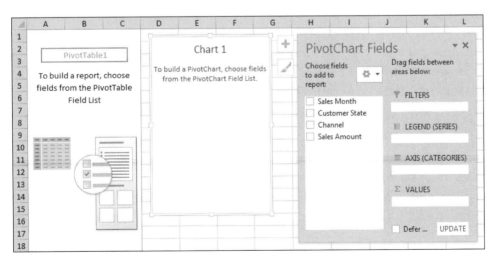

Figure 7.5
Excel worksheet with an empty pivot table and pivot chart.
Source: Microsoft® Corporation.

As with the creation of pivot tables, the worksheet shows a blank pivot table area, plus a Field List to allow one to build and manipulate the pivot chart. The addition to this scenario is a pane with a blank pivot chart. The pivot table and pivot chart are tied to each other. As fields are moved to any of the four areas at the bottom of the Field List, both the pivot table and pivot chart immediately reflect the change.

Since we're focused on the pivot chart, the Field List has a title of PivotChart Fields rather than PivotTable Fields. Notice also that four areas at the bottom of the Field List have labels that are slightly different from what appears for pivot tables. As may be recalled, the four areas of a pivot table are:

- Filters
- Columns
- Rows
- Values

The same four areas in a pivot chart are called:

- Filters
- Legend (Series)
- Axis (Categories)
- Values

Thus, while we refer to the areas of a pivot table as filters, columns, rows, and values, we'll call the corresponding areas of a pivot chart filters, series, categories, and values. The important thing to remember is that pivot table rows are like pivot chart categories, and columns are like a pivot chart series. To actually create a pivot chart, the next step is to drag fields in the Field List to the appropriate area. It doesn't matter if the pivot table or pivot chart is selected. Both will be modified as fields are moved.

Our initial objective is to view sales by month. Therefore, we'll drag the Sales Amount field to the values area and the Sales Month field to the categories area (or rows area of the pivot table). The resulting pivot chart is displayed in Figure 7.6.

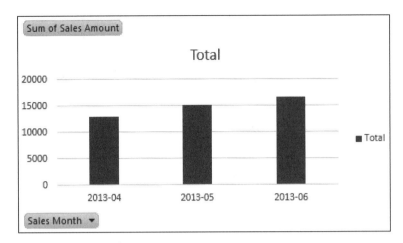

Figure 7.6

Pivot chart with one field in the categories area.

Source: Microsoft® Corporation.

As a first step, Excel has created a column chart for us. More specifically, it created a clustered column chart. This is the default chart type. Next, note that the vertical axis has been automatically populated with appropriate labels to indicate the value of each column. Since we have only one field in the categories (or rows) area, we see only one column per category. We'll soon see what happens when a field is added to the series (or columns) area. Finally, unlike pivot tables, pivot charts require a field in the values area. If nothing is in the values area, the pivot chart will be completely blank. Incidentally, as we modified the Field List, the pivot table also changed, reflecting the same arrangement. The pivot table that corresponds to Figure 7.6 is shown in Figure 7.7.

	A	B
1	Row Labels ▼	Sum of Sales Amount
2	2013-04	12900
3	2013-05	15100
4	2013-06	16700
5	**Grand Total**	**44700**

Figure 7.7

Corresponding pivot table.

Source: Microsoft® Corporation.

Let's now add the Channel field to the series area and see how the pivot chart changes, as shown in Figure 7.8.

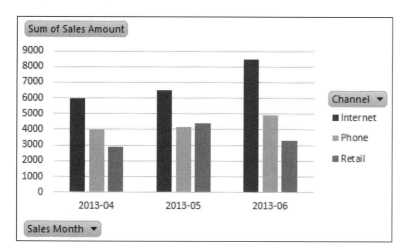

Figure 7.8

Pivot chart with fields in the categories and series areas.

Source: Microsoft® Corporation.

With fields in both the categories and series areas, we see a more typical chart. The sales in each month are now broken down by channel. The Sales Month field in the categories area corresponds to rows in a pivot table. Labels for this category field appear below the horizontal axis. The Channels field, placed in the series area, corresponds to columns in a pivot table. In this example, labels for series appear to the right of the values grid. Just as rows are somewhat primary in importance relative to columns in a pivot table, categories are primary to series. As with pivot table columns, one would not typically place more than one field in the series area of a pivot chart.

Taking a closer look at the chart, we also see three buttons that have been added: Sum of Sales Amount, Sales Month, and Channel. The Sales Month and Channel buttons display drop-down icons indicating that these fields can be filtered interactively in the pivot chart, just like filtering in a pivot table. If we click the drop-down for the Sales Month button, the filter shown in Figure 7.9 appears.

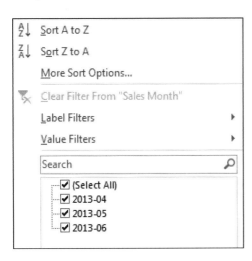

Figure 7.9
Filter drop-down in a pivot chart.
Source: Microsoft® Corporation.

The capabilities of the commands in the filter drop-down are identical to the filtering functionality of pivot tables discussed in Chapter 5. Note that these buttons can be hidden from the chart if you should want to copy the chart for a presentation to others. This is accomplished via the Field Buttons command under the Analyze tab of the Ribbon, shown in Figure 7.10.

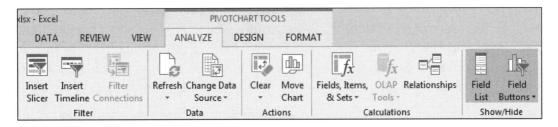

Figure 7.10
Right side of the PivotChart Analyze tab of the Ribbon.
Source: Microsoft® Corporation.

Clicking the Field Buttons command toggles the display of these buttons. Additionally, this tab has Field List, Refresh, Insert Slicer, and Insert Timeline commands with functionality identical to the same commands on the pivot table Options tab on the Ribbon.

Layout Options

Before discussing various chart options, let's first explore the layout options for the chart just created. The pivot chart in Figure 7.8 has the default layout, but there are many opportunities to adjust its appearance. The commands that we'll examine are those under the Add Chart Element label, which is found in the Chart Layouts group under the Design tab of the Ribbon. These commands are shown in Figure 7.11.

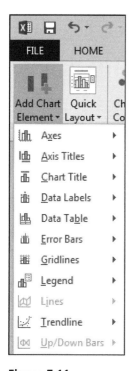

Figure 7.11
Add Chart Element commands in the Design tab of the Ribbon.
Source: Microsoft® Corporation.

The options for the Chart Title command are:

- None
- Above Chart
- Centered Overlay

The Axis Titles command has these options, allowing you to specify titles on the horizontal or vertical axes:

- Primary Horizontal
- Primary Vertical

The chart in Figure 7.8 has no title or axis titles. After we apply the Chart Title and Axis Titles commands to supply the chart title, horizontal axis title, and vertical axis title, the chart appears as in Figure 7.12. We'll also opt to use the Field Buttons command under the Analyze tab to hide the field buttons on the chart. This allows the chart itself to take up more space, and thus display more detail.

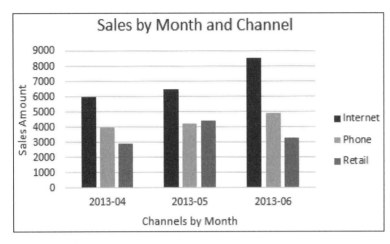

Figure 7.12
Pivot chart with a chart title and axis titles.
Source: Microsoft® Corporation.

In this chart, the title and axis titles can have any desired wording. The chart title is employing the Above Chart option.

The Legend command holds several options that specify where the legend can be located. The legend is the area on the far right of the chart that specifies the values for Channel. This lists the values in the series area of the pivot chart. The options for this command are to display the legend at the top, bottom, left, or right. The default, shown in Figure 7.12, is to place the legend on the right.

The Data Labels command serves the purpose of displaying numbers on the chart so the viewer can discern the exact quantity for each value element. The options for this command are:

- None
- Center
- Inside End
- Inside Base
- Outside End
- Data Callout

Utilizing the Outside End option, the chart appears as in Figure 7.13.

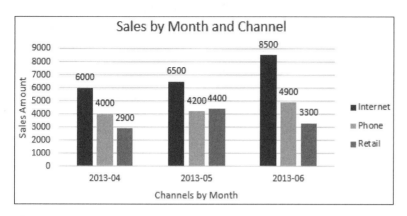

Figure 7.13

Pivot chart with data labels.

Source: Microsoft® Corporation.

In order for the numbers to not overlap, we needed to stretch the size of the pivot chart pane horizontally. The Data Table command provides an interesting alternative to the Data Labels command. The data table is a listing of the values in a tabular format, below the chart. The three options for this command are:

- None
- With Legend Keys
- No Legend Keys

After choosing the With Legend Keys option and removing the Data Labels, the chart now looks like Figure 7.14.

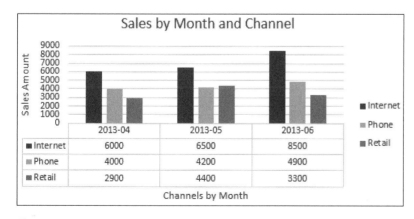

Figure 7.14

Pivot chart with a data table.

Source: Microsoft® Corporation.

Notice that a table with column values now appears below each set of columns. The data table aligns perfectly with the columns, and avoids the clutter of data labels.

The Gridlines command lets you specify the following options for both the horizontal and vertical gridlines:

- Primary Major Horizontal
- Primary Major Vertical
- Primary Minor Horizontal
- Primary Minor Vertical

The default for this type of chart, seen in Figure 7.12, is to show major gridlines horizontally and no gridlines vertically. In this example, there would be little point in changing the horizontal gridline option, but for vertical gridlines, let's make a modification to display major gridlines. The result is displayed in Figure 7.15.

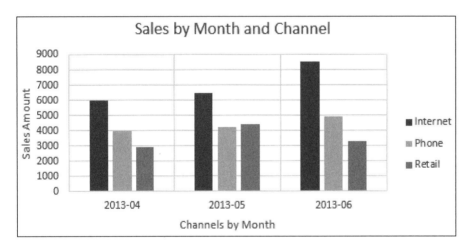

Figure 7.15
Pivot chart with vertical gridlines.
Source: Microsoft® Corporation.

As seen, the vertical gridlines for this type of chart consist of lines that separate the three major sets of columns.

One final layout option for pivot charts that we'll mention is the ability to resize or move the chart itself. Pivot charts typically exist as objects on an Excel worksheet. One can resize the chart object at any time by dragging any of the horizontal or vertical edges of the chart pane. In addition, one can move the chart to another existing worksheet or to its own worksheet. Moving the chart is accomplished via the Move Chart command in the Location group under the Design tab of the Ribbon, shown in

Figure 7.16. When this command is selected, you'll see the Move Chart dialog box shown in Figure 7.17.

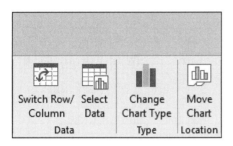

Figure 7.16
Right side of the PivotChart Design tab of the Ribbon.
Source: Microsoft® Corporation.

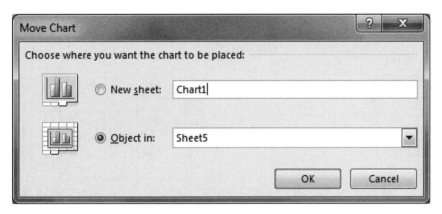

Figure 7.17
Move Chart dialog box.
Source: Microsoft® Corporation.

When the Object In option of this dialog box is selected, the pivot chart is moved to another worksheet. When the New Sheet option is selected, the pivot chart is moved to a special type of worksheet, referred to as a *chart sheet*. The new chart sheet will not have any cells as does a normal worksheet. It consists only of the chart itself, filling the entire area of the worksheet.

Column and Bar Charts

Now that the basics of pivot chart creation and layout have been covered, we can turn our attention to the real purpose of charts, which is to present data in a way that clarifies and highlights the patterns contained within. For this to occur, one must select the most appropriate chart type for the data at hand. We will focus initially on two additional commands seen in Figure 7.16. Our primary concern will be on the Change Chart Type command, but let's first look at the Switch Row/Column command. Unlike pivot tables, pivot charts provide the user with a command that switches the fields in the rows and columns (or categories and series) areas. Starting with the pivot chart in Figure 7.15, clicking the Switch Row/Column command produces the pivot chart shown in Figure 7.18.

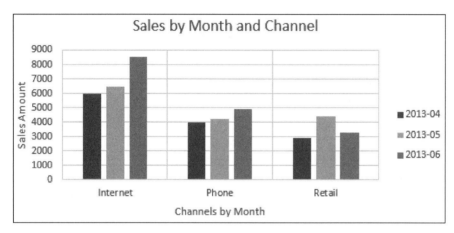

Figure 7.18
The Switch Row/Column command.
Source: Microsoft® Corporation.

The effect of this command is to move the Sales Month field from the category to the series area, and the Channel field from the series to the category. Rather than seeing a breakdown of month by channel, the chart now has a breakdown of channel by month. Notice that the axis titles didn't change. That has to be done manually.

Turning to the Change Chart Type command, one sees the dialog box in Figure 7.19 when this command is selected.

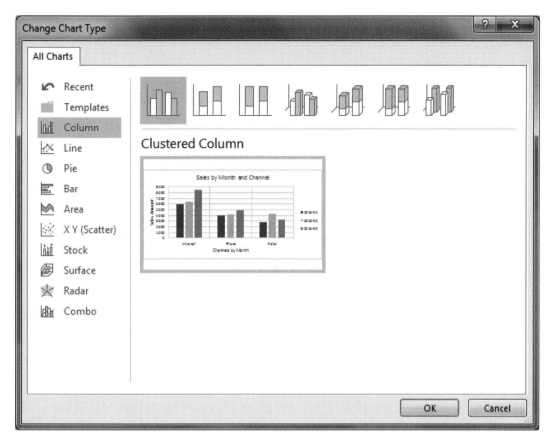

Figure 7.19

Change Chart Type dialog box.

Source: Microsoft® Corporation.

The categories in the left pane indicate the general type of chart. The specific variation of the category is selected in the right pane. Although the left pane lists ten chart types, only eight are available as pivot charts. Scatter charts and stock charts are available only as standard charts. There are over 40 variations for these eight chart types.

Our initial focus will be on column and bar charts. It must first be emphasized that the only difference between column and bar charts is in their orientation. Whereas column charts have vertical columns, bar charts have horizontal bars. Otherwise, their functionality is identical. For that reason, we'll discuss only column charts, as they tend to be more common. To illustrate, if we use the Change Chart Type command to switch the column chart of Figure 7.15 to a bar chart, it appears as in Figure 7.20.

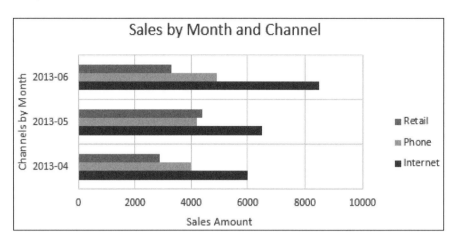

Figure 7.20
A bar pivot chart.
Source: Microsoft® Corporation.

As a bar chart, the Sales Amount field remains in the categories area as before, and the Channel field is in the series area. The only difference in design is that the chart has been rotated 90 degrees to the right, so the bars go toward the right, rather than toward the top. The axis labels are automatically moved to the correct position.

To be more specific about this chart type, the pivot charts in both Figure 7.15 and 7.20 are referred to as *clustered* charts. Figure 7.15 is a clustered column chart, and Figure 7.20 is a clustered bar chart. Focusing on column charts, there are seven types of column charts available. Of these, there are really only three basic types of column (or bar) charts:

■ Clustered Column

■ Stacked Column

■ 100% Stacked Column

The other chart types are 3-D variants of these same types. To illustrate, Figure 7.21 converts Figure 7.15 to a 3-D clustered column chart.

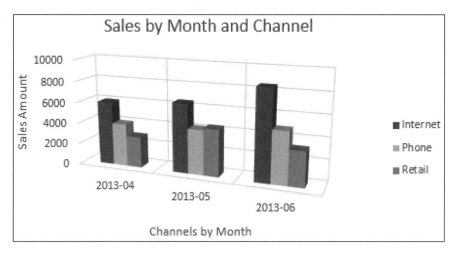

Figure 7.21

A 3-D clustered column pivot chart.

Source: Microsoft® Corporation.

The main problem with three-dimensional column charts is that it is more difficult to accurately perceive and interpret the lengths of each column. Whereas one can fairly easily determine the heights of the various columns in Figure 7.15, that is a much more challenging exercise for the chart in Figure 7.21. Thus, our general recommendation is to avoid 3-D graphs if possible.

As originally stated, the two-dimensional column charts are clustered, stacked, and 100% stacked. Let's turn to a stacked column chart of the same data, shown in Figure 7.22. Again, all that's needed to create this chart is to turn to the Change Chart Type command, and select the Stacked Column option in the right pane.

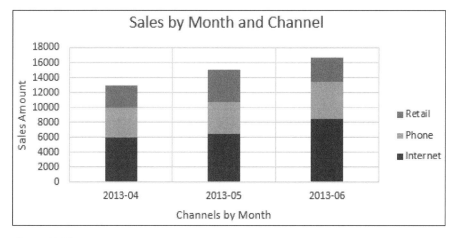

Figure 7.22

A stacked column pivot chart.

Source: Microsoft® Corporation.

Comparing this chart to Figure 7.15, the three separate columns for each channel have now been combined into one column that stacks the three channel elements on top of each other. Notice also that the vertical scale has changed to accommodate the larger values required by combining the three channels together. In contrast to the clustered chart, the stacked chart emphasizes the combined volume of each month. We can clearly see the rise in sales from April to June. This fact was not obvious from looking at Figure 7.15. However, the clustered chart does a better job of emphasizing the individual contributions of each of the channels in each month.

The third basic column chart type is the 100% stacked chart. This is shown in Figure 7.23.

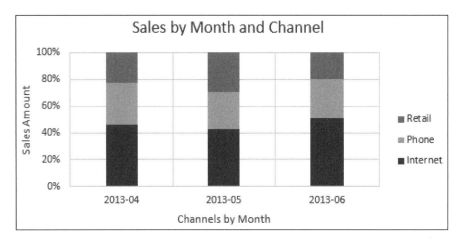

Figure 7.23

A 100% stacked column pivot chart.

Source: Microsoft® Corporation.

In this version of the stacked chart, units are expressed as percentages. The total value of each of the months has the same height and a value of 100%. The virtue of this chart type is that it emphasizes the relative contributions of each of the channels to the month's sales. For example, when you look at Figure 7.22, you can't really tell much about the relative contributions of Internet sales to each month. You can see that Internet sales increased from May to June, but so did overall sales. In contrast, Figure 7.23 clearly shows that the relative importance of Internet sales increased from May to June. It must be said, though, that even in a 100% stacked chart, it's not easy to tell how values in the *middle* of each column changes. The relative contributions of phone sales, being in the middle of each column, are more difficult to determine than Internet or retail sales.

The clustered column type tends to provide better information for the viewer in the most succinct manner. By separating out each element in the series into its own column, one can more readily compare how the values of the individual elements fared.

Pie Charts

Pie charts are perhaps the most overused and underpowered of all chart types. Popular in newspaper graphics, pie charts are designed to present a simple, even simplistic, image. As such, the pie chart often has limited value for the analyst. One significant limitation of pie charts is that all fields must be in the categories area of the pivot chart. Any fields placed in the series area are ignored. Figure 7.24 is a pie chart of our prior data, with the Sales Month field placed in the categories area.

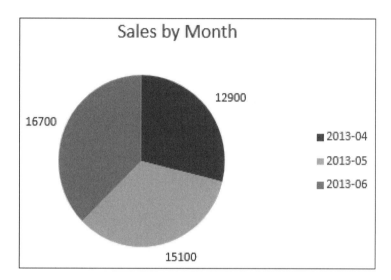

Figure 7.24
A pie pivot chart.
Source: Microsoft® Corporation.

One of the difficulties with pie charts is that the relative areas of the slices of the pie are difficult to evaluate. In this example, it may not be obvious to the casual viewer that June sales are slightly larger than those for May. For that reason, we've chosen to utilize the Data Labels command to add numeric values outside each area of the pie. Although all fields in a pie chart must be in the categories area, it is possible to place more than one field in that area. Figure 7.25 shows a pie chart with both the Sales Month and Channel fields in the categories area.

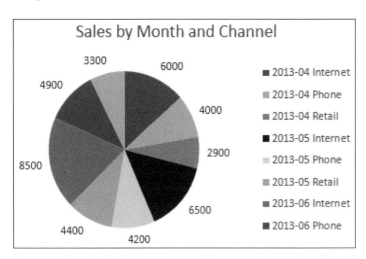

Figure 7.25
A pie pivot chart with two fields in the categories area.
Source: Microsoft® Corporation.

Unlike column charts, which can provide a breakdown of channel within month, or month within channel, this pie chart simply takes every combination of Sales Month and Channel and indicates an appropriate portion of the pie for that combination.

There are actually five variants of the pie chart, but none offer much beyond the basic pie chart. One variant worth mentioning is the doughnut chart. Figure 7.26 shows the same data in Figure 7.24, presented as a doughnut chart.

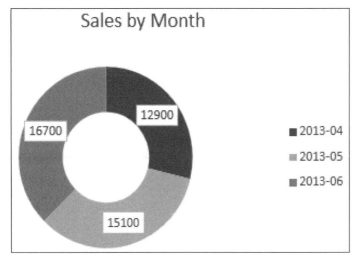

Figure 7.26
A doughnut pivot chart.
Source: Microsoft® Corporation.

The doughnut chart is kind of a cross between a pie chart and column chart. By removing the center of the circle, the areas of the pie appear more like curved columns or bars. As such, the lengths of these areas are somewhat easier to perceive. Still, we have opted to place data labels in each of the areas to clarify the associated value. One important difference from the pie chart is that doughnut charts permit you to place fields in the series area. If we add the Channel field to the series area, the doughnut chart is transformed to the image in Figure 7.27.

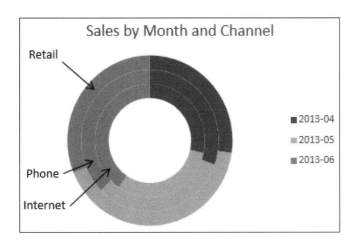

Figure 7.27
A doughnut pivot chart with a series field.
Source: Microsoft® Corporation.

In this chart, the channels appear as concentric rings in the circle. The rings are organized in alphabetic or numeric order, with the first element in the sort sequence appearing in the inner ring. Unfortunately, it is incumbent on the designer to label these rings. As such, we've added text boxes and arrows to the chart to label each of the rings. These elements are found under the Layout tab of the Ribbon. The additional concentric rings add variety to the chart but are not easy to decipher. The effort involved to interpret the meaning of the various areas tends to negate the value of having multiple rings in a doughnut chart.

The main difficulty of both pie and doughnut charts is that they tend to be simplistic and somewhat difficult to interpret. They're nice for making a basic point with limited data elements, but in most cases, you're better off with a column or bar chart in its place.

Line and Radar Charts

Next to column charts, line charts are probably the next most important mainstay in an analyst's charting toolkit, and offer distinct value for certain types of data situations. To examine the usefulness of line charts, we'll switch to a different data set. Figure 7.28 displays an array of data with the gross receipts of several movies that played during December 2012 and January 2013.

▲	A	B	C
1	Week Ending	Movie	Gross Receipts
2	12/27/2012	Django Unchained	33.3
3	12/27/2012	Les Miserables	39.4
4	12/27/2012	Silver Linings Playbook	5.1
5	12/27/2012	This is 40	23.9
6	12/27/2012	Zero Dark Thirty	0.8
7	1/3/2013	Django Unchained	52.9
8	1/3/2013	Les Miserables	48
9	1/3/2013	Silver Linings Playbook	7.8
10	1/3/2013	This is 40	22
11	1/3/2013	Zero Dark Thirty	0.7

Figure 7.28

Movie receipts data.

Source: Microsoft® Corporation.

This data set, which has weekly movie receipts in millions, has five weeks of data on five movies. Figure 7.28 shows only two of those weeks. The remaining rows have the receipts for the same five movies for three additional weeks. In a first attempt to display this data in visual form, we'll create a clustered column chart, placing the Week Ending field in the categories area, the Movie in the series area, and the Gross Receipts in the values. This chart appears in Figure 7.29.

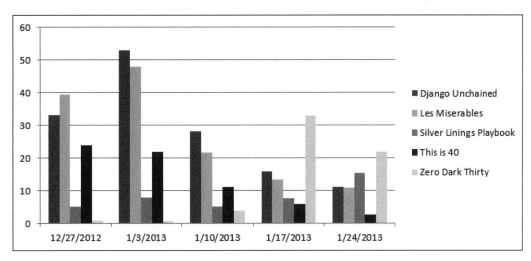

Figure 7.29

A clustered column pivot chart with movie receipt data.

Source: Microsoft® Corporation.

This chart presents a lot of information but is somewhat cluttered. Since this data has a time element, it makes sense to put the Sales Month in the categories area, so the passage of time can be observed from left to right. The breakdown showing the movies within each month is informative, but it's difficult to discern any patterns in the data. With this limitation in mind, let's now present the same data as a line chart, shown in Figure 7.30.

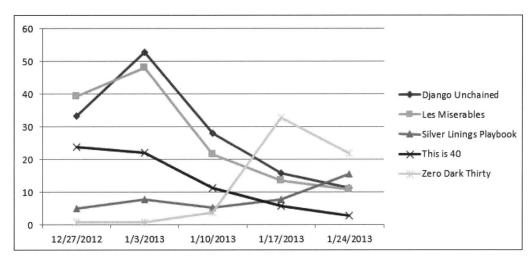

Figure 7.30

A line pivot chart.

Source: Microsoft® Corporation.

In this vastly improved presentation, each movie appears as a separate line, rather than as multiple columns. Again, the switch from a clustered column chart to a line chart is accomplished by invoking the Change Chart Type command. The element of time is preserved, as the data proceeds from left to right. However, in contrast to the clustered column chart, this line chart clearly reveals the patterns present in the data. For example, we can see that *Django Unchained* and *Les Miserables* both followed a similar sales history throughout these five weeks. We can see that, whereas the movie *This is 40* is on the descent during this period, *Silver Linings Playbook*'s receipts are rising. We can observe the sharp spike in receipts for *Zero Dark Thirty* during the week of January 17. As such, line charts are ideal for describing values that occur over the passage of time. This explains why stock charts are typically presented as line charts. Whereas column and bar charts excel at showing total volume and relative values, line charts are a better tool to delineate changes and the rate of change of data, especially when time is an element in the analysis.

Line charts have seven different variants, but there are only three basic types: line, stacked line, and 100% stacked line. Each of these three types comes in an additional variation that displays markers. Markers are the small shapes (seen in Figure 7.30) that, along with color, help to identify the series value associated with the line. For example, the movie *Les Miserables* in Figure 7.28 uses small squares as data points to reinforce the fact that the line is for that movie. The same markers are displayed in the series legend. The stacked line and 100% stacked line options actually have very limited value. The entire notion of stacked elements applies nicely to column or bar charts, but makes little sense for line charts. There is also one 3-D version of line charts.

Radar charts are another interesting chart type that's similar to line charts in many ways. To illustrate, we'll turn to a new data set with the average high temperatures for three cities. Figure 7.31 shows the first six rows of this data. The full data set consists of 36 rows, with values for each of the 12 months.

	A	B	C
1	**Month**	**City**	**Average High Temperature**
2	January	Chicago	29
3	January	Miami	76
4	January	Nashville	46
5	February	Chicago	34
6	February	Miami	77
7	February	Nashville	52

Figure 7.31
Weather data.
Source: Microsoft® Corporation.

Figure 7.32 shows the radar chart that results from this data. In this chart, we've placed the Month field in the categories area, City in the series area, and Average High Temperature in the values.

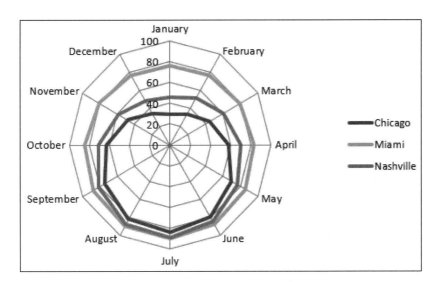

Figure 7.32
A radar pivot chart.
Source: Microsoft® Corporation.

Radar charts convert each element in the category, in this case the month, into an outward pointing line in a spider web-type of graphic. The web has as many slices as there are values for the category field. In this case, since there are 12 months, we see 12 triangular areas, as if there were 12 slices of pizza whose circumference was not quite circular. The series fields, which in this example are the three cities, are represented as lines that move around the circular web. Thus, we see that the average high temperature for Miami in January is just less than 80 degrees.

As a side note, you might be wondering how we managed to arrange months in the proper order around the perimeter of the chart. Even though labels would normally be sorted in alphabetic order, we were able to list the months as they appear in the calendar. The solution was to sort the original data list with one of Excel's custom lists with calendar months, as was discussed in Chapter 4.

Radar charts are ideal for the display of cyclical or seasonal data. Whereas line charts typically display the element of time along a horizontal axis, radar charts can display time in a circle, thus complementing the seasonal nature of the months. The lines in the radar chart of Figure 7.31 are easily interpreted, clearly showing that Miami has consistently higher temperatures than Chicago does, year round. The contours of the lines also indicate the larger variances in temperature between the cities that occur during the winter months.

In our survey of pivot table charts, we've now covered all chart types except for area, surface, and combo charts. Area charts are a variant of line charts that fill in areas under each of the lines with color. As such, these are quite a bit more difficult to interpret. Surface charts are a chart type that serves as a visualization tool to represent data as a three-dimensional surface. Surface charts are like a three-dimensional scatter chart—a topic that will be discussed later in this chapter. In surface charts, the height of the surface is derived from the field in the values area. The fields in the category and series areas are used for the other coordinates in the three-dimensional structure. Combo charts combine elements of other chart types—for example, a combination of a clustered column chart and a line chart.

Standard Charts

With our survey of pivot charts complete, we now turn to charts based on arrays of data in worksheets. Prior to the appearance of pivot charts, introduced with Excel 2000, all charts were based on worksheet data, and this original chart type remains a viable option. Everything that can be done with pivot charts can also be accomplished with standard worksheet charts, but with slightly more difficulty. We'll illustrate the process by returning to the data shown at the beginning of this chapter in Figure 7.2. Let's say that we want to convert this data into a chart like the one shown in Figure 7.8, a clustered column chart with the Sales Month field in the categories area and Channel in the series area. As before, the quantitative value is in the Sales Amount field.

Standard charts are created by using one of the commands in the Charts group under the Insert tab of the Ribbon. These commands are displayed in Figure 7.33.

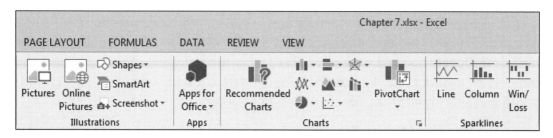

Figure 7.33
Chart commands under the Insert tab of the Ribbon.
Source: Microsoft® Corporation.

When you click on any of these commands, you'll see a drop-down pane showing options for that chart type. To create a chart from the table shown in Figure 7.2, we'll select any cell in that table, and then choose the Insert Column Chart command. After choosing the Clustered Column icon from the drop-down, we see the chart displayed in Figure 7.34.

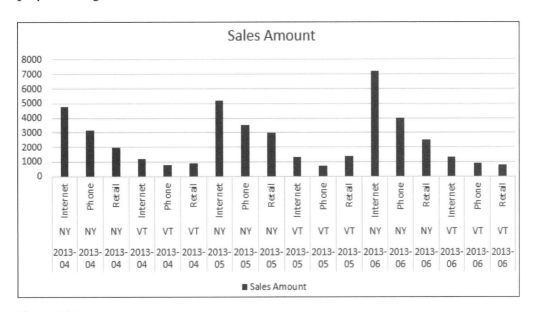

Figure 7.34
A clustered column chart.
Source: Microsoft® Corporation.

As seen, the result is not even close to what was intended. To understand what went wrong, let's look at a key command that's used to configure standard charts. When a new chart is created, two new tabs appear on the Ribbon under a Chart Tools label. These tabs are Design and Format. Under the Design tab is a command named Select Data. In fact, the key commands for charts appear on the Ribbon in an identical layout as that shown in Figure 7.16, which shows the same commands for pivot charts. The key difference is that the Select Data command has much more functionality for standard charts than it does for pivot charts. When we click on this command for the chart of Figure 7.34, we see the dialog box displayed in Figure 7.35.

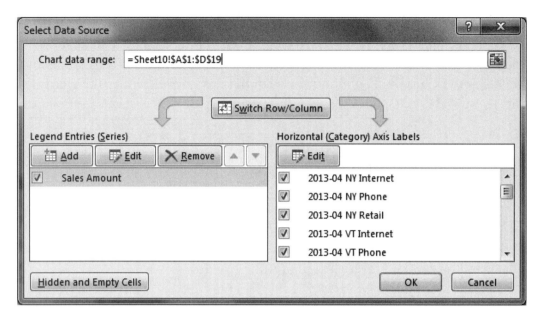

Figure 7.35

Select Data Source dialog box.

Source: Microsoft® Corporation.

Unlike pivot tables, where the Field List is used to organize fields into category and series areas, standard charts rely on this dialog box to organize data into what are called legend entries and horizontal labels. Legend entries are the equivalent of series labels, and appear on the vertical axis. Horizontal labels are the equivalent of category fields and are on the horizontal axis. The problem with our data is that Excel has interpreted each combination found on each row as a distinct item to display in the chart. This is indicated by the list of fields in the horizontal axis pane.

The issue is that standard tables can't quite handle data in the format that it currently exists. The data in Figure 7.2 has one row per occurrence, but Excel needs us to first summarize the data in some manner before it can convert it into a table. The easiest solution is to create a pivot table from the tabular data, and then rearrange the fields in a desired manner. After doing this, our data appears as in Figure 7.36.

	A	B	C	D
1	Sales Month	Internet	Phone	Retail
2	2013-04	6000	4000	2900
3	2013-05	6500	4200	4400
4	2013-06	8500	4900	3300

Figure 7.36

Original data transformed to a crosstab format.

Source: Microsoft® Corporation.

In Figure 7.36, we've actually copied the results of the pivot table to another worksheet, using the Paste Special command to copy values only. We now have data that's in a format from which we can easily create a chart. After doing so, the chart appears as in Figure 7.37.

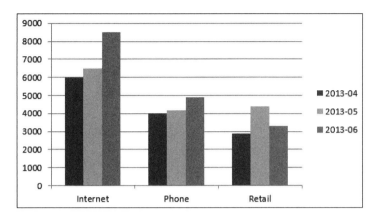

Figure 7.37

Clustered column chart.

Source: Microsoft® Corporation.

We're much closer, but not quite there. Although we wanted the months to appear on the horizontal axis, and the channels to be the individual series elements, these are reversed. The problem can be addressed by using Data Source command, which now displays the dialog box shown in Figure 7.38.

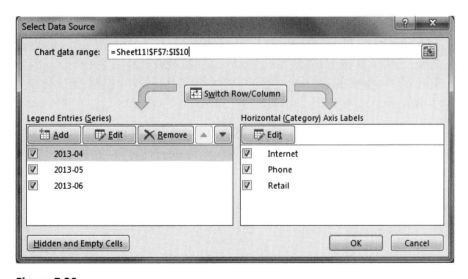

Figure 7.38

Data Source dialog box.

Source: Microsoft® Corporation.

Unlike before, the Data Source dialog box now shows the correct data elements in the legend and horizontal axis panes. The only problem is that they are reversed. To rectify this, we merely click the Switch Row/Column button. After doing so, the chart of Figure 7.39 is displayed.

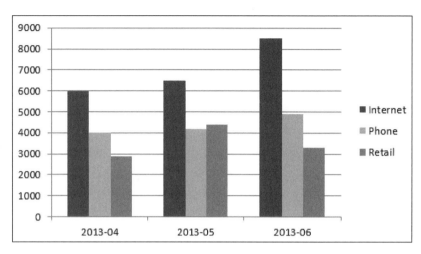

Figure 7.39
Clustered column chart.
Source: Microsoft® Corporation.

Comparing Figure 7.39 to Figure 7.8, you can see that we've now created a standard chart equivalent to what we previously accomplished via pivot charts. As with pivot charts, all of the same layout niceties can be applied to standard charts via the commands under the Add Chart Element label and other options. The main difficulty in working with standard charts is the increased manual effort required to manipulate data on the Data Source dialog box. In contrast, pivot tables allow you to use the Field List to arrange data elements interactively.

Despite the limitations of standard charts, two chart types can be created only via standard charts: scatter charts and stock charts. Scatter charts can't be handled by pivot charts, because this chart type depends on the display of detailed data. The summarization that's inherent to pivot charts and tables doesn't apply. To illustrate, consider some data that states the sales that resulted from a number of advertising campaigns. Figure 7.40 shows the data, and Figure 7.41 has the resulting scatter chart.

	A	B
1	**Advertising**	**Sales**
2	500	2200
3	650	2900
4	900	3000
5	400	2050
6	800	2900
7	100	700
8	150	1200
9	50	300
10	300	1400

Figure 7.40

Sales and Advertising data.

Source: Microsoft® Corporation.

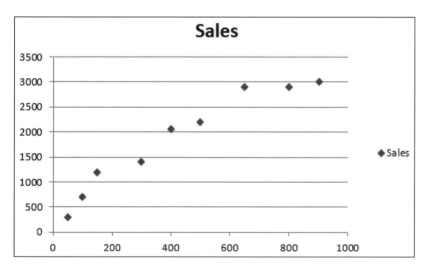

Figure 7.41

Scatter chart.

Source: Microsoft® Corporation.

Scatter charts are all about relationships. Each point represents a specific occurrence, tied to values on the horizontal and vertical axes. In this case, the horizontal axis measures advertising dollars spent, and the vertical axis has resulting sales. By considering the various data points, one can observe a general trend. Additionally, Excel provides a Trendline command under the Add Chart Element label of the Ribbon that inserts a linear regression trend line that plots the trend more precisely. This is shown in Figure 7.42.

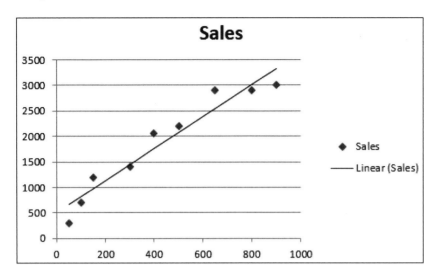

Figure 7.42

Scatter chart with a trend line.

Source: Microsoft® Corporation.

The second chart type that can be created only via standard charts is the stock chart. Stock charts can represent data for a single stock, showing its performance over time. There are four variants of the stock chart, all of which require data to be laid out in a very specific format. To illustrate, the High-Low-Close stock chart can transform the data shown in Figure 7.43 to the chart in Figure 7.44.

⊿	A	B	C	D	E	F
1		Jan	Feb	Mar	Apr	May
2	HIGH	100	110	115	125	115
3	LOW	92	102	100	95	95
4	CLOSE	94	98	112	115	100

Figure 7.43

Stock data.

Source: Microsoft® Corporation.

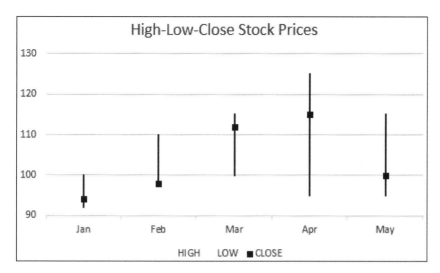

Figure 7.44

High-Low-Close stock chart.

Source: Microsoft® Corporation.

As seen, the data in Figure 7.43 shows the high, low, and closing prices for a stock over several periods of time. The corresponding chart in Figure 7.44 lays out the data with the vertical columns indicating the range of prices of the stock in the period, from low to high, and the small square marking the closing price. The other three variants for stock charts include the ability to include volume and the opening price. As with scatter charts, stock charts can be created only as a standard chart, due to their use of detailed data.

Sparklines

Introduced with Excel 2010, sparklines are like miniature charts that are contained within a single cell in a worksheet. This feature can be very handy when an analyst wants to quickly convey the gist of a bunch of numbers on a worksheet, without having to resort to full-scale charts. To illustrate, we'll look at a new set of stock data displayed in Figure 7.45.

	A	B	C	D
1	Stock	Open	Midday	Close
2	IBM	202.12	203.83	205.24
3	AAPL	480.11	475.28	453.62
4	MCD	95.41	95.52	95.95
5	JNJ	73.98	74.51	74.18
6	MMM	100.57	101.38	101.56

Figure 7.45

Stock data.

Source: Microsoft® Corporation.

Our objective is to provide a graphic indication of how each stock performed during the day. This could be accomplished by creating a line chart with lines for each stock, but we prefer to keep this within the worksheet. To accomplish this, we'll add sparkline charts to column E. The result appears in Figure 7.46.

	A	B	C	D	E
1	Stock	Open	Midday	Close	Trend
2	IBM	202.12	203.83	205.24	
3	AAPL	480.11	475.28	453.62	
4	MCD	95.41	95.52	95.95	
5	JNJ	73.98	74.51	74.18	
6	MMM	100.57	101.38	101.56	

Figure 7.46

Sparklines.

Source: Microsoft® Corporation.

The sparklines in column E were created by highlighting cell E2 and selecting the Line command in the Sparklines group under the Insert tab of the Ribbon. This command is shown in Figure 7.33. The dialog box shown in Figure 7.47 then appears.

Figure 7.47

Create Sparklines dialog box.

Source: Microsoft® Corporation.

The Location Range, $E$2, refers to the current cell. The Data Range that needs to be supplied is B2:D2. This represents the range of cells from B2 to D2, which contains the data that the sparkline is to be based on. Incidentally, these values can be inserted automatically by clicking the data selector icon to the right of the Data Range text box, and then selecting those cells. After this is done, the sparkline for cell E2 is created. That cell can then be copied down to cells E3 to E6 to create the other four sparklines. Once a sparkline is created, a Design tab appears on the Ribbon under a Sparkline Tools label when a cell with a sparkline is selected. This appears in Figures 7.48 and 7.49.

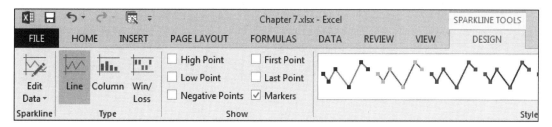

Figure 7.48

Left side of the Sparkline Tools Design tab of the Ribbon.

Source: Microsoft® Corporation.

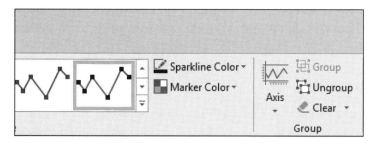

Figure 7.49

Right side of the Sparkline Tools Design tab of the Ribbon.

Source: Microsoft® Corporation.

The options for modifying sparklines are fairly obvious. For the sparklines in Figure 7.46, we've chosen to check the Markers box in the Ribbon to cause the three small circles to appear in each sparkline. The main option for sparklines is the type. The sparklines in Figure 7.46 are the Line type. The two other options are Column and Win/Loss. Note that sparklines lack the scale of standard and pivot charts. The scale of each individual sparkline is unique for that chart. Whether the percent change in stock price was small or large, the sparkline chart will fill the area of the cell it's in.

Just as with charts, the sparkline type can be changed at any time. The appearance of Column sparklines is obvious, as is indicated by the icon in Figure 7.48. Win/Loss sparklines show small rectangles in either the upper or lower portion of the cell, depending on whether the value it's based on is positive or negative. To illustrate, we'll add two new columns, E and F, to the worksheet in Figure 7.46 with a calculation of the changes from Open to Midday, and Midday to Close. We can then insert meaningful Win/Loss sparklines based on those two additional columns. The result is shown in Figure 7.50.

	A	B	C	D	E	F	G	H
1	Stock	Open	Midday	Close	Open to Midday	Midday to Close	Trend	Changes
2	IBM	202.12	203.83	205.24	1.71	1.41		
3	AAPL	480.11	475.28	453.62	-4.83	-21.66		
4	MCD	95.41	95.52	95.95	0.11	0.43		
5	JNJ	73.98	74.51	74.18	0.53	-0.33		
6	MMM	100.57	101.38	101.56	0.81	0.18		

Figure 7.50

Win/Loss sparklines.

Source: Microsoft® Corporation.

The Win/Loss sparklines appear in column H, and are based on the values in columns E and F. Columns E and F are the newly added columns that calculate the change between columns B and C, and C and D. For example, the Win/Loss sparkline for JNJ portrays the fact that the stock went up between Open and Midday, but moved down between Midday and Close.

Looking Ahead

In this chapter, we've surveyed a wide variety of charts, with an emphasis on pivot charts. The exemplary feature of pivot charts is that they are tied to pivot table functionality, and work in much the same way. Just as pivot tables comprise filters, rows, columns, and values, pivot tables consist of filters, categories, series, and values. All of the filtering and summarization capabilities of pivot tables apply equally to pivot charts. The layout options of charts and pivot charts are numerous, from titles to gridlines to data tables. We then looked at the numerous variants of the column chart, which is probably the most prevalent and useful of all the chart types. We discussed the differences between clustered, stacked, and 100% stacked column charts. We then turned to the sometimes-overused pie chart, and its cousin, the doughnut chart. In contrast, line charts are an extremely effective tool in the visualization of time series data and in detecting patterns amongst multiple series in a set of data. The radar chart is similarly useful, particularly when it comes to seasonal data. We then turned to standard charts that are based on an array of cells in a worksheet. While more difficult to manipulate, standard charts include a few chart types, such as scatter charts, that allow you to view detailed data in a manner that can't be accomplished with pivot charts. We finished off the chapter by looking at sparklines, a unique way to encapsulate a simple line or column chart within the confines of an individual worksheet cell.

In our next chapter, we'll move on from pivot tables and pivot charts and begin to explore the capabilities of standard Excel worksheets. Our first point of emphasis will be on learning different ways to sort, filter, and group data in a worksheet without the use of a pivot table.

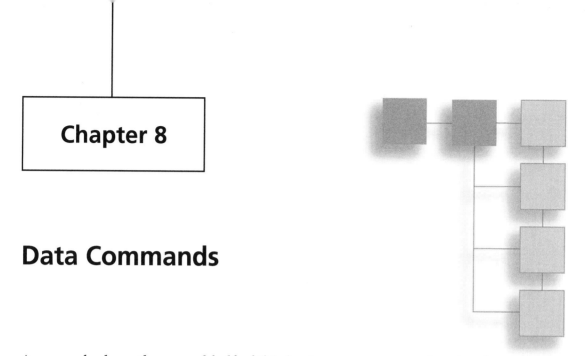

Chapter 8

Data Commands

As we embark on the second half of this book, we move toward topics that are more focused on what can be done with worksheets. Looking back to the Excel components that were initially discussed in Chapter 1, we've already talked about tables, pivot tables, pivot charts, and charts. The major remaining component yet to be discussed is cells. Identifying this component by the term *cells* is actually a bit awkward and limiting. The term *cells* in this context really refers to the entire worksheet that cells reside in. Of course, tables also exist in cells on a worksheet. Pivot tables reside in a worksheet, and also make use of cells, and charts and pivot charts reside as separate objects in a worksheet. We use the term *cells* merely to refer to the arrangement of cells in a worksheet, and the arrangement of data in blocks of cells.

As a business analyst, tables, pivot tables, and charts are useful devices for quickly summarizing and getting a handle on what a set of data contains. As a beneficial first step in any analysis situation, a good practice is to create a pivot table and play with the data to see what it contains. However, as one delves into data more deeply, there will come a time when pivot charts must be discarded and the specific capabilities of cells and worksheets utilized to further analyze and manipulate data. Pivot tables are great at summarizing, manipulating, and interacting with data, but business analysis often requires details beyond those functions.

The tools discussed in this chapter serve as a bridge from the summarization capabilities of pivot tables to the specifics of worksheet design. Excel provides a number of tools under the Data tab of the Ribbon that are similar in spirit to the capabilities of pivot tables and charts, but which firmly reside in the world of worksheets and cells.

The section of the Data tab of the Ribbon that will be addressed in this chapter is shown in Figure 8.1.

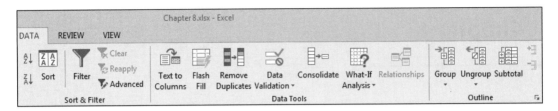

Figure 8.1
Data tab of the Ribbon.
Source: Microsoft® Corporation.

This portion of the Data tab features commands in three groups: Sort & Filter, Data Tools, and Outline. To the left of this portion of the Ribbon are the Get External Data and Connections groups of commands previously discussed in Chapter 3. To the right of this section of the Ribbon is the Analysis group of commands that will be discussed in Chapter 14, "Analysis Tools." Likewise, the commands under the What-If Analysis label will also be discussed in Chapter 14.

Sorting and Filtering

Starting with the Sorting & Filtering commands, the good news is that functionality of most of these commands was already covered when tables were discussed in Chapter 4, "Tables." When the Filter command is selected while a cell in a rectangular array of data is selected, the top row in the rectangle is assumed to be a header row with column headings, and filter drop-downs are added to every header row cell, as if a table had been inserted. Even though adding a filter doesn't create a table, the effect is the same, with regard to filters. Let's say that any cell in the data shown in Figure 8.2 is highlighted, and then the Filter command is selected. The result is as shown in Figure 8.3.

	A	B
1	Animal	Name
2	Dog	Buddy
3	Cat	Felix
4	Monkey	Coco

Figure 8.2
Data before the Filter command is applied.
Source: Microsoft® Corporation.

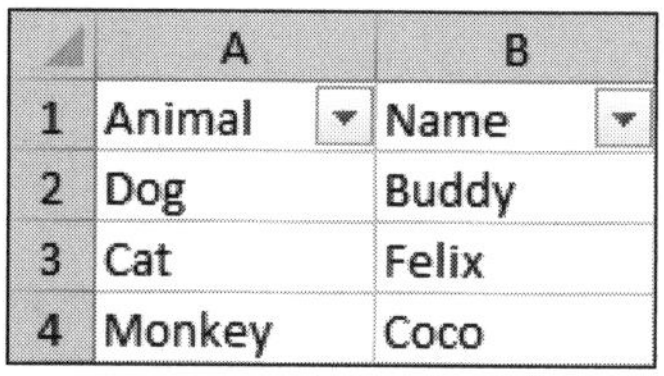

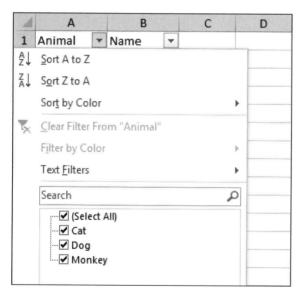

Figure 8.3

Data after the Filter command is applied.

Source: Microsoft® Corporation.

The drop-down icons in Figure 8.3 display commands identical to those available in tables. For example, if we select the drop-down in the Animal column header, we see the commands in Figure 8.4.

Figure 8.4

Filter commands.

Source: Microsoft® Corporation.

As with the filters available in tables, one can select specific values from the enumerated list, search for values, or use the provided text, number, or date filters. The one caveat that must be remembered regarding filters is that there is an assumption that a header row exists on the block of data selected. If, for example, row 1 of Figure 8.2 didn't exist, then a filter would be created on the first available row of data, and the filter would appear as in Figure 8.5.

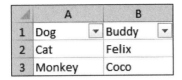

Figure 8.5
A filter on a row of data.
Source: Microsoft® Corporation.

In this instance, the filter that has been created in row 1 is meaningless. The value Dog in cell A1 has been incorrectly interpreted as a column header. The filter in this cell allows the user to select between Cat and Monkey, but we've lost the ability to select Dog. Similarly, cell B1 has interpreted the value Buddy as a column header, when it's really just a value.

As with filters, the Sort command under the Data tab of the Ribbon is similarly identical to the sorting capabilities in tables. When one selects the Sort command on any cell in the data of Figure 8.2, the Sort dialog box shown in Figure 8.6 is displayed.

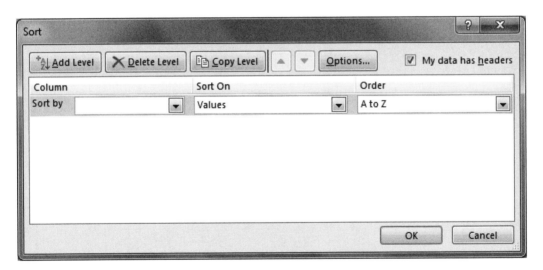

Figure 8.6
Sort dialog box.
Source: Microsoft® Corporation.

Note that this is identical to the Sort dialog box that appears when working with tables, when one selects the Sort by Color option. Referring back to Chapter 4, Figure 8.6 is the same as Figure 4.17. All the sorting capabilities discussed with reference to tables are thus available with this command, such as the ability to add levels, and sort on values, cell color, or font color. As with tables, custom lists can be invoked to sort calendar day or month names in proper date order.

There is, however, one command in the Sort & Filter group in the Data Ribbon that offers some functionality that's not found in tables. The Advanced command, seen in Figure 8.1, offers the ability to add complex Boolean logic to your filter specifications. The term *Boolean logic* refers to the ability to specify selection criteria that groups multiple criteria, connected with AND or OR conditions. For example, you may want to select rows where the state is Illinois or Indiana, and the customer has sales of over 500. We've already encountered similar functionality with custom filters that can be applied to data in tables. If you look back to Figure 4.25, you'll see the Custom Auto-Filter dialog box that allows you to apply Boolean logic to a single column in a table.

The added functionality of advanced filters over custom filters in tables is that advanced filters can be specified for multiple columns at the same time. To illustrate, we'll look at the data shown in Figure 8.7.

	A	B	C
1	Customer ID	Customer State	Monthly Sales
2		VT	> 100
3			
4	Customer ID	Customer State	Monthly Sales
5	1	NY	550
6	2	NY	230
7	3	VT	320
8	4	NH	35
9	5	VT	80
10	6	VT	90
11	7	VT	680
12	8	NY	60

Figure 8.7
Customer sales data with an advanced filter.
Source: Microsoft® Corporation.

The use of advanced filters requires a separate range of column headers and detail rows that indicate the desired logic. The block of data from cell A4 down to C12 is referred to as the *data range*. The array of data from A1 to C2 is called the *criteria range*. The criteria range can be placed anywhere on the worksheet. It doesn't necessarily need to be above the data, as in Figure 8.7. To invoke the advanced filter from the data in Figure 8.7, we begin by selecting any cell in the data range, and selecting the Advanced filter command. This produces the dialog box shown in Figure 8.8.

Figure 8.8

Advanced Filter dialog box.

Source: Microsoft® Corporation.

Note that we've entered the range A4:C12 for the list range and A1:C2 for the criteria range. In the next chapter, we'll discuss in detail the use of absolute cell references, indicated by dollar signs ($), but for now, just know that these references specify a location that doesn't change if new rows or columns are added to a worksheet.

Row 2 of the criteria range states that we want to apply a filter so we see rows only where the state equals VT, and the monthly sales are greater than 100. When multiple criteria appear on the same row, as in this example, there is an implied AND condition between the two elements of the criteria. After clicking the OK button in the Advanced Filter dialog box, the data changes to that seen in Figure 8.9.

	A	B	C
1	Customer ID	Customer State	Monthly Sales
2		VT	> 100
3			
4	Customer ID	Customer State	Monthly Sales
7	3	VT	320
11	7	VT	680

Figure 8.9

Data after an advanced filter has been applied.

Source: Microsoft® Corporation.

As seen, the filter has removed all rows except two. These rows are both from Vermont and have sales over 100. We can tell that a filter has been applied by noticing that only rows 7 and 11 are visible. The logic in this example can actually have been applied with the use of normal filters, by first applying a filter on the Customer State column, specifying Vermont, and then applying another filter on the Monthly Sales column, selecting values greater than 100. However, this next example in Figure 8.10 can't be accomplished with normal filters.

	A	B	C
1	Customer ID	Customer State	Monthly Sales
2		VT	> 100
3		NH	
4			
5	Customer ID	Customer State	Monthly Sales
8	3	VT	320
9	4	NH	35
12	7	VT	680

Figure 8.10
An advanced filter with two rows in the criteria range.
Source: Microsoft® Corporation.

In this example, the criteria range specifies that we want rows where the state is Vermont and sales are greater than 100, or rows where the state is New Hampshire. When there is more than one row in the criteria range, there is an implied OR condition between each row. Rows are displayed when the logic in any of the rows in the criteria range are satisfied. The logic in this example can't be implemented via normal filters, since normal filters can be applied to only one column at a time.

We've seen that sorting and filtering in worksheet ranges is similar to functionality previously seen with tables. One additional command that's basically identical is the Remove Duplicates command, shown in Figure 8.1. As seen previously in Chapter 4, this command provides a Remove Duplicates dialog box that allows duplicate rows to be removed against a variety of criteria.

Subtotals and Grouping

Referring to Figure 8.1, the Grouping, Ungroup, and Subtotal commands are related commands that allow you to create meaningful groups of rows or columns, and also apply subtotals to grouped elements. We'll first address the Subtotal command, as it is the most significant of the three. To illustrate, we'll begin with the range of data displayed in Figure 8.11.

	A	B	C	D	E
1	Sales Date	State	Customer ID	Revenue	Cost
2	5/1/2013	NY	101	50	30
3	5/1/2013	NY	108	40	34
4	5/1/2013	VT	102	30	26
5	5/2/2013	NY	101	350	290
6	5/2/2013	VT	182	520	440
7	5/2/2013	VT	180	300	225
8	5/2/2013	VT	103	120	95

Figure 8.11

Data prior to applying subtotals.

Source: Microsoft® Corporation.

This data shows sales for three dates from a number of customers, indicating the date, customer ID, state, revenue, and cost. In this example, we'll want to obtain subtotals for revenue and cost for each sales date. An important requirement that must be in place before any subtotals are applied is that the data must be sorted by the field on which the subtotal will be calculated. In this case, the data needs to be sorted by sales date. As seen in Figure 8.11, this has already been done. To add subtotals, we begin by clicking the Subtotal command shown in Figure 8.1. This brings up the Subtotal dialog box of Figure 8.12.

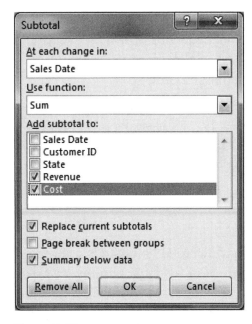

Figure 8.12

Subtotal dialog box.

Source: Microsoft® Corporation.

As seen, several items need to be specified. First, we need to specify which column the subtotals are to be calculated on. In this case, we've stated to calculate subtotals on Sales Date. Second, we need to specify the function to apply. We've indicated to calculate the subtotal as a sum, but the drop-down allows for all of these function types:

- Sum
- Count
- Average
- Max
- Min
- Product
- Count Numbers
- StdDev
- StdDevp
- Var
- Varp

Next, we check the column or columns for which the subtotal function is to be applied. In this example, we're selecting Revenue and Cost. After selecting these options and clicking the OK button, the worksheet changes to that of Figure 8.13.

	A	B	C	D	E
1	Sales Date	State	Customer ID	Revenue	Cost
2	5/1/2013	NY	101	50	30
3	5/1/2013	NY	108	40	34
4	5/1/2013	VT	102	30	26
5	5/1/2013 Total			120	90
6	5/2/2013	NY	101	350	290
7	5/2/2013	VT	182	520	440
8	5/2/2013	VT	180	300	225
9	5/2/2013	VT	103	120	95
10	5/2/2013 Total			1290	1050
11	Grand Total			1410	1140

Figure 8.13
Data with subtotals.
Source: Microsoft® Corporation.

As seen, subtotals have been added as new rows. For example, row 5 now indicates that the total revenue for 5/1/2013 is 120, and the total cost is 90. In addition to these new values, we now also see outline controls to the left of the row numbers that group the data into three levels. As indicated by the level controls in the upper left, there are three levels: 1, 2, and 3. We're currently viewing level 3. If we click the number 2 control, the display changes to that of Figure 8.14.

	A	B	C	D	E
1	Sales Date	State	Customer ID	Revenue	Cost
5	5/1/2013 Total			120	90
10	5/2/2013 Total			1290	1050
11	Grand Total			1410	1140

Figure 8.14
Data with subtotals on level 2.
Source: Microsoft® Corporation.

On level 2, we see only the header, subtotal, and grand total rows. If we were to select level 1, we'd only see rows 1 and 11, the header and grand total rows. In addition to clicking the level controls, we can also click the plus (+) or minus (–) controls to interactively expand or collapse the groups of rows that have been created. For example, if we click on the first plus sign in Figure 8.14, the display changes to that of Figure 8.15.

	A	B	C	D	E
1	Sales Date	State	Customer ID	Revenue	Cost
2	5/1/2013	NY	101	50	30
3	5/1/2013	NY	108	40	34
4	5/1/2013	VT	102	30	26
5	5/1/2013 Total			120	90
10	5/2/2013 Total			1290	1050
11	Grand Total			1410	1140

Figure 8.15
Data with two different levels of detail.
Source: Microsoft® Corporation.

We now see data at two different levels of detail. For data on 5/1/2013, we see rows at level 3 with all detail rows displaying, but 5/2/2013 is at level 2 with only the subtotal showing. Thus, in addition to adding subtotal values, the Subtotal command also adds some useful interactivity to your data, allowing you to drill up and down within data as desired.

It is also possible to apply more than one subtotal break on your data. Returning to Figure 8.13, we can apply a second subtotal grouping on the State column. Notice that the data is already sorted by State within Sales Date. This was accomplished by specifying a two-level sort on the data, sorting it by Sales, then by State. To add another subtotal by State, we select the Subtotal command again and make the specifications shown in Figure 8.16.

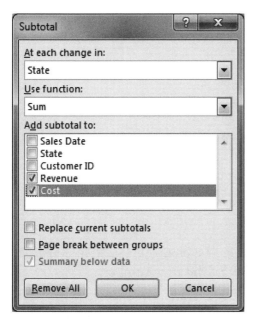

Figure 8.16
Subtotal dialog box.
Source: Microsoft® Corporation.

In this dialog box, we specified to calculate subtotals based on the State column. Notice that we unchecked the Replace Current Subtotals option. This has the effect of adding a second set of subtotals in addition to the original subtotals on Sales Date. The result is shown in Figure 8.17.

1 2 3 4		A	B	C	D	E
	1	Sales Date	State	Customer ID	Revenue	Cost
	2	5/1/2013	NY	101	50	30
	3	5/1/2013	NY	108	40	34
	4		NY Total		90	64
	5	5/1/2013	VT	102	30	26
	6		VT Total		30	26
	7	5/1/2013 Total			120	90
	8	5/2/2013	NY	101	350	290
	9		NY Total		350	290
	10	5/2/2013	VT	182	520	440
	11	5/2/2013	VT	180	300	225
	12	5/2/2013	VT	103	120	95
	13		VT Total		940	760
	14	5/2/2013 Total			1290	1050
	15	Grand Total			1410	1140

Figure 8.17

Data with two sets of subtotals.

Source: Microsoft® Corporation.

We now see additional subtotal rows every time there's a change in state. We also see one additional level in the group controls to the left of the row numbers.

The commands under the Group and Ungroup labels, seen in Figure 8.1, provide a subset of the functionality of the Subtotal command. When selecting the Group label, the two available commands are Group and Auto Outline. Returning to the data in Figure 8.11, if we highlight rows 2 through 4 and select the Group command, we see the worksheet of Figure 8.18.

1 2		A	B	C	D	E
	1	Sales Date	State	Customer ID	Revenue	Cost
	2	5/1/2013	NY	101	50	30
	3	5/1/2013	NY	108	40	34
	4	5/1/2013	VT	102	30	26
	5	5/2/2013	NY	101	350	290
	6	5/2/2013	VT	182	520	440
	7	5/2/2013	VT	180	300	225
	8	5/2/2013	VT	103	120	95

Figure 8.18

Grouped rows.

Source: Microsoft® Corporation.

The Group command applies an outline control to rows 2 through 4, allowing you to interactively hide or show those rows. There is no additional functionality. The Group command can also be applied to columns. If you then highlight columns B and C and click the Group command, the worksheet turns into that of Figure 8.19.

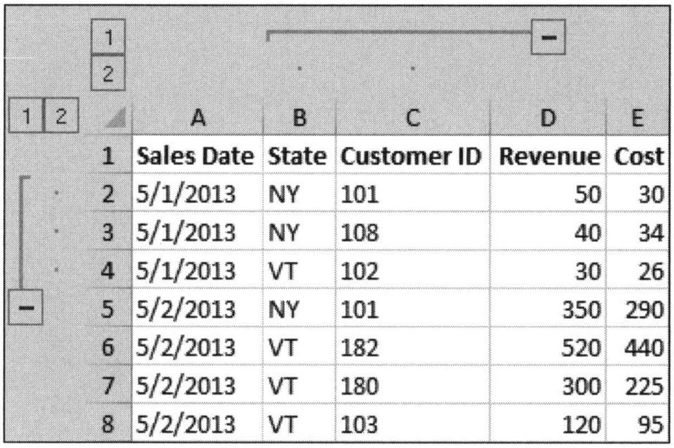

	A	B	C	D	E
1	Sales Date	State	Customer ID	Revenue	Cost
2	5/1/2013	NY	101	50	30
3	5/1/2013	NY	108	40	34
4	5/1/2013	VT	102	30	26
5	5/2/2013	NY	101	350	290
6	5/2/2013	VT	182	520	440
7	5/2/2013	VT	180	300	225
8	5/2/2013	VT	103	120	95

Figure 8.19
Grouped rows and columns.
Source: Microsoft® Corporation.

If we click both of the minus (–) controls, the worksheet then appears as in Figure 8.20.

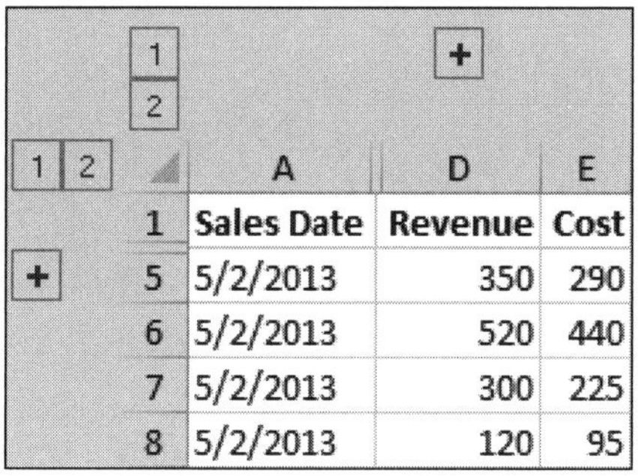

	A	D	E
1	Sales Date	Revenue	Cost
5	5/2/2013	350	290
6	5/2/2013	520	440
7	5/2/2013	300	225
8	5/2/2013	120	95

Figure 8.20
Collapsed groups of rows and columns.
Source: Microsoft® Corporation.

We no longer see rows 2 through 4, or columns B to C. In short, the ability to group rows and columns is a way to hide rows or columns, but with much greater interactivity. The provided controls allow you to quickly expand or contract selected rows or columns as needed.

Text to Columns and Flash Fill

The next set of commands we'll examine provides ways to break out or combine text. The Text to Columns command, seen in Figure 8.1, allows you to break text in a single column into multiple columns. To illustrate, we'll begin with the data in Figure 8.21.

Figure 8.21

Text data in a single column.

Source: Microsoft® Corporation.

The Text to Columns command allows us to separate the city and state values in this column into separate columns. To initiate the process, we highlight all cells and select the Text to Columns command. This causes the dialog box of Figure 8.22 to appear.

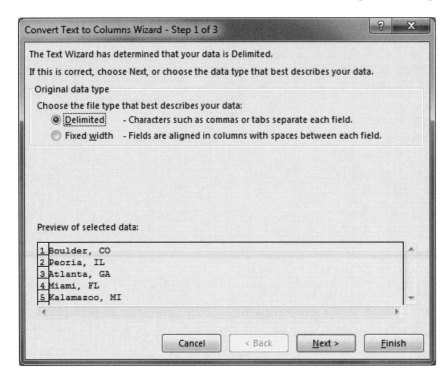

Figure 8.22

Step 1 of the Convert Text to Columns Wizard.

Source: Microsoft® Corporation.

In this first step, we specify whether the data is delimited or fixed width. In this case, the data is delimited. The next step of the wizard is shown in Figure 8.23.

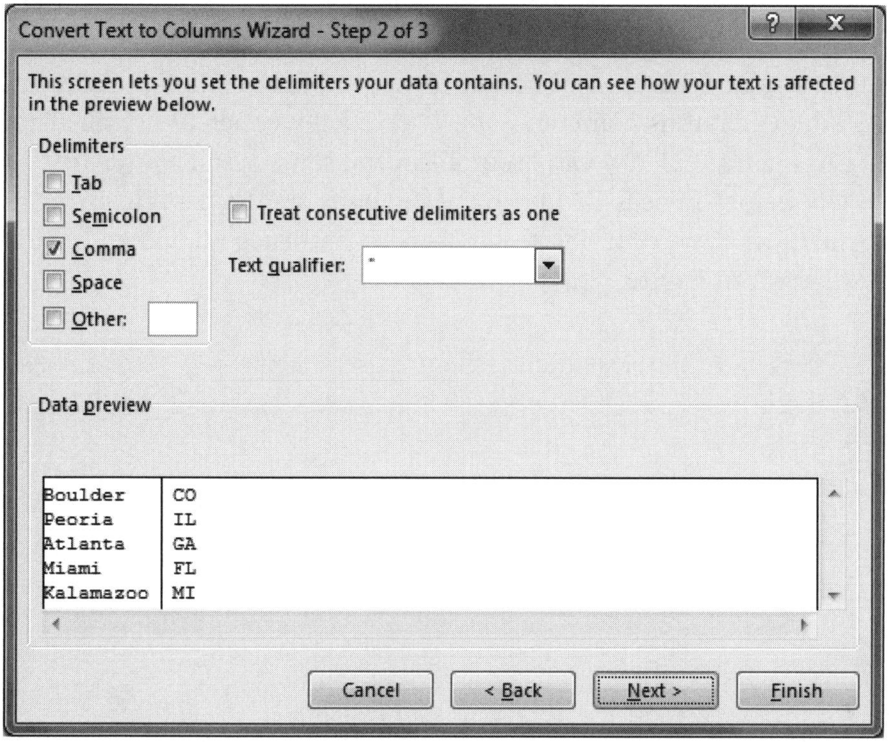

Figure 8.23
Step 2 of the Convert Text to Columns Wizard.
Source: Microsoft® Corporation.

The second step is used to specify the delimiter value. In this example, the delimiter is a comma. The third step, not shown, allows you to fine-tune the delimited columns by specifying the data type for the column. After the wizard completes, the data of Figure 8.24 is displayed.

	A	B
1	Boulder	CO
2	Peoria	IL
3	Atlanta	GA
4	Miami	FL
5	Kalamazoo	MI

Figure 8.24
Result of Text to Column command.
Source: Microsoft® Corporation.

As seen, city and state are now separated into two columns. The only flaw in this result is that there is an extra space before each state in column B. This occurred because there is a space after the comma in the original data. This extra space can be removed by using the TRIM function, which will be explained in Chapter 10, "Text Functions."

The Flash Fill command, a new feature of Excel 2013, accomplishes much of what can be done with the Text to Columns command and is decidedly easier to use. Starting again with the data in Figure 8.21, we can accomplish the same result by starting to type in the desired city names in cells B1 and B2. After entering the first character in cell B2, Excel recognizes what we're trying to accomplish and suggests values for the rest of column B, as shown in Figure 8.25.

	A	B
1	Boulder, CO	Boulder
2	Peoria, IL	Peoria
3	Atlanta, GA	Atlanta
4	Miami, FL	Miami
5	Kalamazoo, MI	Kalamazoo

Figure 8.25
Flash Fill suggestion.
Source: Microsoft® Corporation.

After hitting Enter, these suggested values populate the column. We can repeat the same procedure to place the state abbreviations in column C. The result is shown in Figure 8.26.

	A	B	C
1	Boulder, CO	Boulder	CO
2	Peoria, IL	Peoria	IL
3	Atlanta, GA	Atlanta	GA
4	Miami, FL	Miami	FL
5	Kalamazoo, MI	Kalamazoo	MI

Figure 8.26
Flash Fill result.
Source: Microsoft® Corporation.

Notice that, unlike with the Text to Columns command, the Flash Fill procedure doesn't create a space before the state. Even more significantly, the Flash Fill procedure can also be used in the opposite direction. Figure 8.27 shows the values suggested by Flash Fill if we reverse the procedure and use city and state values to obtain city/state combinations.

⧫	A	B	C
1	Boulder	CO	Boulder, CO
2	Peoria	IL	Peoria, IL
3	Atlanta	GA	Atlanta, GA
4	Miami	FL	Miami, FL
5	Kalamazoo	MI	Kalamazoo, MI

Figure 8.27

Flash Fill in reverse direction.

Source: Microsoft® Corporation.

After hitting Enter, all the suggested values will populate column C. Note that the column to be filled can also be to the left of the other columns. The Flash Fill command can be used in many different situations, for example to separate a full phone number into its area code and phone number.

Data Validation

Excel provides some useful tools to allow you to prevent invalid data from being entered in specific worksheet cells. This is accomplished via three commands under the Data Validation label shown in Figure 8.1: Data Validation, Circle Invalid Data, and Clear Validation Circles. When selected, the Data Validation command produces a dialog box such as the one in Figure 8.28.

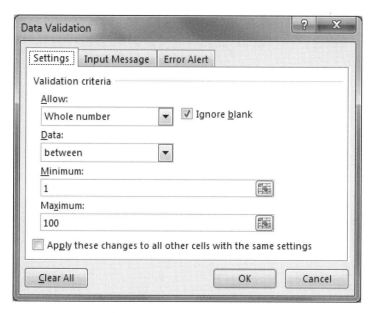

Figure 8.28

Settings tab of the Data Validation dialog box.

Source: Microsoft® Corporation.

The Settings tab of this dialog box allows you to specify a formula for the types of allowable values. In Figure 8.27, we've already changed the Allow drop-down to Whole Number, and specified that the number must be between 1 and 100. Possible values for the Allow drop-down are:

- Whole Number
- Decimal
- List
- Date
- Time
- Text Length
- Custom

Aside from when List or Custom is specified, the Data drop-down provides further refinement, with these options:

- between
- not between
- equal to
- not equal to
- greater than
- less than
- greater than or equal to
- less than or equal to

After selecting any of these options, you can then enter specific values in the Minimum and/or Maximum boxes that appear. The List option allows you to select a range of cells with allowable values. The Custom option prompts you to enter a formula.

The Input Message tab of the Data Validation dialog box lets you specify a message associated with the validation. This appears in Figure 8.29.

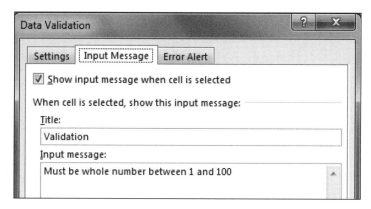

Figure 8.29

Input Message tab of the Data Validation dialog box.

Source: Microsoft® Corporation.

In this example, we entered a title for the message box that appears when one selects the cell being validated, as well as additional text as an input message. If we had entered the information in Figures 8.28 and 8.29 for cell A1, and then highlighted that cell, the worksheet would appear as in Figure 8.30.

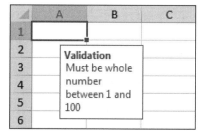

Figure 8.30

Data validation message.

Source: Microsoft® Corporation.

The Error Alert tab of the Data Validation dialog box lets you specify a message if an invalid entry was made. You can choose whether to stop if an invalid entry was made, issue a warning, or simply post an informative message. With a warning, the user has the option to allow the invalid value or prevent it from being accepted.

Finally, the Circle Invalid Data command, found below the Data Validation command, creates circles around any invalid data that was entered. This situation might arise if the user ignores warnings or informative messages that were issued regarding the entry of invalid data. For example, if the user entered the value 400 in cell 1 and this was set up as a warning that was ignored, the Circle Invalid Data command would produce the result seen in Figure 8.31.

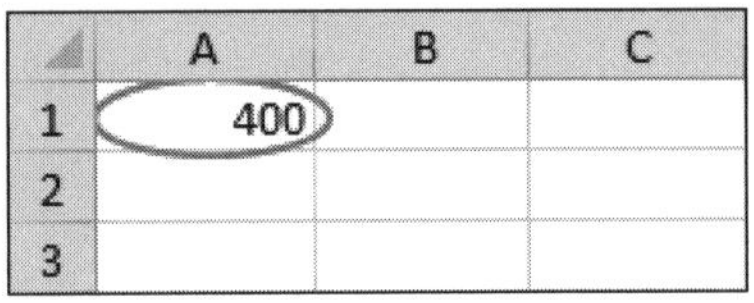

Figure 8.31
Circled invalid data.
Source: Microsoft® Corporation.

The Clear Validation Circles command, found just below the Circle Invalid Data command, clears any circled data.

Looking Ahead

This chapter has begun our foray into the world of worksheet cells. The commands we covered are all under the Data tab of the Ribbon. The one set of significant tabs under the Data tab that will be saved for later are those under the What-If Analysis label. These commands—Scenario Manager, Goal Seek, and Data Table—will be discussed in the final chapter.

Most of the functionality provided by the sorting and filtering commands is identical to what was seen previously with Excel tables. The one exception is with the Advanced command, which adds the ability to use Boolean logic in your filtering, allowing for more complex selection of data. Subtotals and Grouping commands move beyond what's available in tables and apply solely to worksheet cells. Of particular note is the Subtotals command that adds subtotals at any desired level in your data. As with subtotals in pivot tables, worksheet subtotals can be calculated with different functions, such as sum, count, and average. The Group command offers the ability to group rows or columns of data, but without the subtotals appearing.

The Text to Columns and Flash Fill commands offer different ways to transpose single columns of text into multiple columns, and also the reverse. The Flash Fill feature is a particularly exciting new feature of Excel 2013 that adds a great deal of intelligence to Excel, in terms of how it is able to interpret your intent and turn it into meaningful data. Finally, we looked at some data validation options, which are a useful way to ensure that inputs made to a spreadsheet are consistent and meaningful.

In our next chapter, we'll turn to the core functionality of worksheets and explore the ins and outs of cell references and the Name Manager. We'll also begin to discuss the all-important topic of functions. After introducing functions in the next chapter, we'll then cover the details of the more significant functions in most of the remainder of the book.

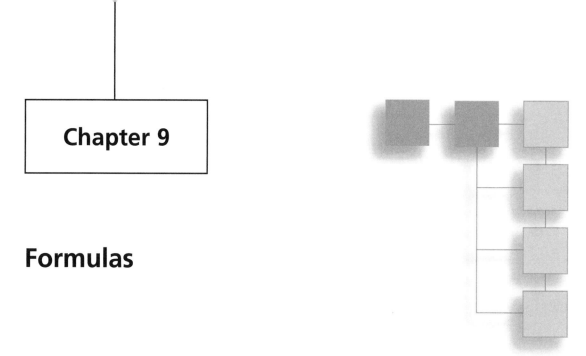

Chapter 9

Formulas

In the prior chapter, we changed our focus from pivot tables and charts to worksheet cells, and discussed a number of tools that allow you to sort, filter, group, and subtotal data within those cells. In this chapter, we want to address the core functionality of worksheets and cells, and talk about how formulas can be utilized to interact with and transform data in other cells. To accomplish this, we'll need a firm understanding of how cells can be referenced and how formulas are created. In doing so, we'll learn how functions can be employed to unleash the built-in power of Excel.

We'll also cover a number of related topics. The Name Manager is a tool within Excel that lets you substitute user-friendly names for cell references that may be more difficult to discern and decipher. For example, rather than referring to cell D3, we might want to use the Name Manager to refer to D3 as *July Revenue*. This makes it easier to comprehend the meaning of formulas when such cells are referenced. We'll also look at a number of Formula Auditing commands that Excel provides to allow you to view dependencies among your formulas.

The commands that we'll look at in this chapter are all contained within the Formulas tab of the Ribbon, shown in Figures 9.1 and 9.2.

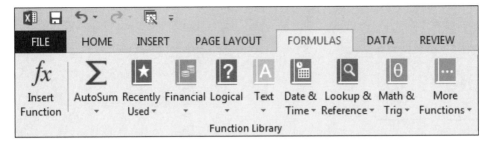

Figure 9.1
Left side of the Formulas tab of the Ribbon.
Source: Microsoft® Corporation.

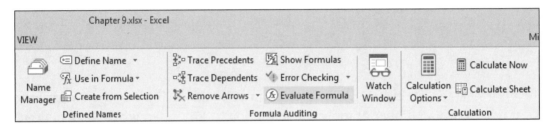

Figure 9.2
Right side of the Formulas tab of the Ribbon.
Source: Microsoft® Corporation.

We'll introduce some of the functions shown in Figure 9.1 but will save details for the subsequent four chapters. The emphasis in this chapter is on the commands shown in Figure 9.2.

Formula Basics

A worksheet cell can contain either a value or a formula. A value can be any type of numeric or alphabetic text. For example, if you type the word CHIP in cell B5, that word will be displayed in the cell. Similarly, if you type the number 13 in cell B6, that number becomes visible.

The power of Excel is derived from its ability to create formulas. Formulas always begin with an equals sign (=). For example, the following are all valid formulas:

=3 + 5

=B5 + 6

=C8/C9

=LEFT(A8, 3)

=SUM(A1:A5)

The first formula says to add the numbers 3 and 5. The displayed result is 8. The second formula specifies to add the contents of cell B5 and the number 6. The cell B5 might contain a value or another formula. If B5 contains either the value 14 or a formula that evaluates to 14, the result shown will be 20. The third formula says to divide the value of cell C8 by the value of cell C9. The fourth formula utilizes the LEFT function. The two arguments in the function, A8 and 3, specify to evaluate the value in cell A8, and display only the first three characters on the left side of the expression. If cell A8 happens to contain the value CAPTIVATE, the displayed result will be CAP. The fifth formula uses the SUM function, indicating to sum the values in the range of cells from A1 to A5.

These examples illustrate the fact that all formulas consist of some or all of these four components:

- Constants
- Operators
- Functions
- References

In the above examples, the 3 and 5 in the first formula are constants. The plus sign (+) in the first formula and the division sign (/) in the third formula are operators. The colon (:) in the fifth formula is a special kind of operator called a *reference* operator. The LEFT and SUM functions in the fourth and fifth formulas are examples of functions. The values contained within the sets of parentheses that follow the function name are the *arguments* of the function. The values B5 in the second formula and C8 and C9 in the third formula are examples of references. References refer to values in other cells. For example, B5 in the second formula refers to the value contained in cell B5.

The meaning of constants is obvious, but there is more complexity with operators. There are four types of operators:

- Arithmetic
- Comparison
- Concatenation
- Reference

Arithmetic operators are those that perform a numeric calculation. This includes the plus sign (+) for addition, the minus sign (–) for subtraction, an asterisk (∗) for multiplication, the slash (/) for division, the percent sign (%) for a percentage, and a caret (^) for exponentiation. For example, the expression 4^2 yields the value 16, since 4 squared is 16.

Comparison operators compare two values and yield a value of either TRUE or FALSE, depending on whether the expression evaluates to true or false. These operators are:

- Equal to (=)
- Greater than (>)
- Less than (<)
- Greater than or equal to (>=)
- Less than or equal to (<=)
- Not equal to (<>)

Here are some examples of formulas with comparison operators:

```
=B1 > 5
=D1 = D2
=IF(B4 >= 70, "PASS", "FAIL")
```

The first formula evaluates the expression B1 > 5. If the value in cell B1 is greater than 5, the result is TRUE and the value TRUE is displayed in the cell. Otherwise, the result is FALSE and FALSE is displayed. In the second formula, the first equal sign (=) indicates that this is a formula, and the second equal sign is a comparison operator. If the values of cells D1 and D2 are equal, then the value TRUE is displayed in the cell. The third formula makes use of a comparison operator within a function. The IF function (discussed in detail in Chapter 13, "Logical and Lookup Functions") has three arguments. The first argument evaluates an expression and determines whether the value is TRUE or FALSE. In this case, the expression is B4 >= 70. If it's true that the value of cell B4 is greater than or equal to 70, then the value of the second argument, PASS, is displayed in the cell. If false, the value of the third argument, FAIL, is displayed.

There is only one concatenation operator, and that is the ampersand (&) sign. When placed between two text values, this indicates that the two values should be joined together. For example, the formula:

```
="HOG" & "WASH"
```

evaluates to the value HOGWASH. Reference operators are sometimes used as part of a cell reference. C5 is a reference that indicates the value of cell C5. Sometimes, though, it is desirable to indicate a range of cells rather than a single cell. That is where reference operators come in. There are three possibilities:

- Colon (:)
- Comma (,)
- Space

The colon is a *range operator*. This is used to denote the array of cells between two cell references. Referring to Figure 9.3, the reference B2:B5 refers to the four cells that are in column B between and including cells B2 and B5, with the values 1, 2, 3, and 4. The reference B4:F4 indicates the five cells that are in row 4 between and including cells B4 and F4, with the values 3, 13, 40, 42, and 100. It's also possible to use the colon reference operator to specify a rectangular array of cells. The reference B2:F5 refers to all twenty numbers on the worksheet.

	A	B	C	D	E	F	G
1							
2		1	11	20	40	98	
3		2	12	30	41	99	
4		3	13	40	42	100	
5		4	14	50	43	105	
6							

Figure 9.3
A range of cells.
Source: Microsoft® Corporation.

The comma is a *union operator*. This is used to combine more than one range of cells into one. Referring to Figure 9.4, the reference (B2:C5, E3:F4) refers to all twelve numbers on the worksheet.

	A	B	C	D	E	F	G
1							
2		1	11				
3		2	12		41	99	
4		3	13		42	100	
5		4	14				
6							

Figure 9.4
Two ranges of cells.
Source: Microsoft® Corporation.

A space can be used as an *intersection operator*. This operator is seldom used with the cell references we've shown in the prior examples but has more viability when names are assigned to cell ranges with the Name Manager—a topic that will be explained later in this chapter. To illustrate, let's refer to the sales data in Figure 9.5.

◢	A	B	C	D
1		Jan	Feb	March
2	North	55	15	18
3	South	22	19	42
4	East	30	35	10
5	West	40	45	33

Figure 9.5

A range of cells.

Source: Microsoft® Corporation.

Let's say we would like to identify the sales for the East region during February. The answer, 35, is found in cell C4. However, let's say that we have adopted the use of the Name Manager, and we assigned names to our cell ranges. Using the Name Manager, we can assign the name EAST to the cell range B4:D4. Similarly, we can assign the name FEB to the cell range C2:C5. Now that names have been assigned to these cell ranges, we can identify February sales for the East region by this formula:

=FEB EAST

The space between the FEB and EAST names tells Excel that the intersection operator is to be applied to find the cell where these two ranges intersect. That is the value of the cell C4, so the value that this formula yields is 35. To apply the same concept without the use of names, we can also identify the February sales for the East region by this formula:

=B4:D4 C2:C5

Relative and Absolute Cell References

Up until now, most of the cell references we've seen have been *relative* cell references. This is the default. In fact, much of the power of Excel formulas derives from the fact that cell references can be relative. To illustrate, let's examine the data in Figure 9.6.

	A	B	C	D
1	Category	January	February	
2	Paper	500	800	
3	Pencils	150	350	
4	Pens	200	450	
5	Total	850	1600	
6				

Figure 9.6

A range of cells with formulas.

Source: Microsoft® Corporation.

This data displays sales data for three product categories. To see where these numbers are coming from, let's first make use of the Show Formulas command seen in Figure 9.2. When this command is invoked, the worksheet appears as in Figure 9.7.

	A	B	C
1	Category	January	February
2	Paper	500	800
3	Pencils	150	350
4	Pens	200	450
5	Total	=SUM(B2:B4)	=SUM(C2:C4)

Figure 9.7

Result of Show Formulas command.

Source: Microsoft® Corporation.

This command transforms the worksheet to show any formulas that may exist. This shows us, for example, that the total in cell B5 contains a formula that makes use of the SUM function to add up the cell range B2:B4. Now, let's insert a row above row 2. The result is shown in Figure 9.8.

	A	B	C
1	Category	January	February
2			
3	Paper	500	800
4	Pencils	150	350
5	Pens	200	450
6	Total	=SUM(B3:B5)	=SUM(C3:C5)

Figure 9.8

Adding a row above cells with formulas.

Source: Microsoft® Corporation.

Notice that the cell references in the formulas have adjusted automatically for the row numbers that have changed. The formula in B6 now refers to cells B3 to B5, rather than the original B2 to B4 of Figure 9.7. The same would be true if we had inserted a column to the left of the formulas, or even if we had deleted any rows or columns that affected the formulas. Since all cell references are relative, the values automatically adjust to reflect inserted or deleted rows or columns in the worksheet.

Let's now carry the example further by adding totals in column D that add the values of January and February for each category. Figure 9.9 illustrates how we would begin this task.

	A	B	C	D
1	Category	January	February	Total
2				
3	Paper	500	800	=SUM(B3:C3)
4	Pencils	150	350	
5	Pens	200	450	
6	Total	=SUM(B3:B5)	=SUM(C3:C5)	

Figure 9.9

Adding a total column.

Source: Microsoft® Corporation.

The formula added in cell D3 adds the cells from B3 to C3, producing a value of 1300. The next step is to copy that formula to cells D4 through D6. This can be done by copying the cell and pasting it into those cells or by utilizing the fill handle in the lower right corner of cell D3 to drag that cell down to cells D4 through D6. In either case, the result is shown in Figure 9.10 with the Show Formulas command on, and in Figure 9.11 with the Show Formulas command off.

	A	B	C	D
1	Category	January	February	Total
2				
3	Paper	500	800	=SUM(B3:C3)
4	Pencils	150	350	=SUM(B4:C4)
5	Pens	200	450	=SUM(B5:C5)
6	Total	=SUM(B3:B5)	=SUM(C3:C5)	=SUM(B6:C6)

Figure 9.10

Copying a formula down a column, showing formulas.

Source: Microsoft® Corporation.

◢	A	B	C	D
1	Category	January	February	Total
2				
3	Paper	500	800	1300
4	Pencils	150	350	500
5	Pens	200	450	650
6	Total	850	1600	2450

Figure 9.11

Adding a total column, not showing formulas.

Source: Microsoft® Corporation.

The main point to observe is that, since the cell references in D3 are relative, when that formula was copied to D4 to D6, the cell references for the copied formulas remained valid. For example, the formula in D4 properly refers to cells B4 to C4. There are, however, situations where relative cell references prevent a formula from being copied correctly to other cells. To illustrate, consider the scenario in Figure 9.12, in which we are attempting to multiply the Total values in column D by a multiplier value in cell B6, to derive an adjusted total.

◢	A	B	C	D	E
1	Category	January	February	Total	Revised Total
2					
3	Paper	500	800	=SUM(B3:C3)	=D3 * B8
4	Pencils	150	350	=SUM(B4:C4)	
5	Pens	200	450	=SUM(B5:C5)	
6	Total	=SUM(B3:B5)	=SUM(C3:C5)	=SUM(B6:C6)	
7					
8	Multiplier:	1.5			

Figure 9.12

Adding another formula that uses a value in a single cell.

Source: Microsoft® Corporation.

We've begun by entering the desired formula in cell E3 that multiplies the value in D3 by the multiplier constant in B8. This is a routine formula that presents no difficulties. The problem, however, comes when we attempt to copy this formula to cells E4 to E6, as shown in Figure 9.13.

◢	A	B	C	D	E
1	Category	January	February	Total	Revised Total
2					
3	Paper	500	800	=SUM(B3:C3)	=D3 * B8
4	Pencils	150	350	=SUM(B4:C4)	=D4 * B9
5	Pens	200	450	=SUM(B5:C5)	=D5 * B10
6	Total	=SUM(B3:B5)	=SUM(C3:C5)	=SUM(B6:C6)	=D6 * B11
7					
8	Multiplier: 1.5				

Figure 9.13

Result of copying another formula that uses a value in a single cell.

Source: Microsoft® Corporation.

Even without seeing the resulting values, we can tell that the formulas are incorrect. For example, the formula in E4 says to multiply D4 by B9. Since this formula was copied from a formula one cell above, it incorrectly adjusted the B8 to a B9. Our intent, however, is always to use the value in cell B8, regardless of where the formula is copied. The solution to this dilemma is to specify an absolute cell reference in the original formula. This is done by adding dollar signs ($) in the cell reference for cell B8. Figure 9.14 shows the new formula in cell E3, and the result of copying that formula to cells E4 to E6. Figure 9.15 shows the resulting values, without the Show Formulas command.

◢	A	B	C	D	E
1	Category	January	February	Total	Revised Total
2					
3	Paper	500	800	=SUM(B3:C3)	=D3 * $B$8
4	Pencils	150	350	=SUM(B4:C4)	=D4 * $B$8
5	Pens	200	450	=SUM(B5:C5)	=D5 * $B$8
6	Total	=SUM(B3:B5)	=SUM(C3:C5)	=SUM(B6:C6)	=D6 * $B$8
7					
8	Multiplier: 1.5				

Figure 9.14

Formulas with absolute cell references, showing formulas.

Source: Microsoft® Corporation.

	A	B	C	D	E
1	Category	January	February	Total	Revised Total
2					
3	Paper	500	800	1300	1950
4	Pencils	150	350	500	750
5	Pens	200	450	650	975
6	Total	850	1600	2450	3675
7					
8	Multiplier:	1.5			

Figure 9.15

Formulas with absolute cell references, not showing formulas.

Source: Microsoft® Corporation.

The absolute cell reference was accomplished by inserting a dollar sign ($) before each element of the cell name. In this example, the relative cell reference B8 was renamed with an absolute cell reference of $B$8. The dollar sign before the B indicates that the column should never change, and the dollar sign before the 8 says that the row shouldn't change. In truth, though, we really needed only to specify that the row not change. This means that we could have used a cell reference of B$8 with the same effect.

The Name Manager

As may be surmised, the usage of cell references, whether relative or absolute, is pervasive in Excel formulas. Excel has almost unlimited flexibility in terms of creating formulas. Formulas can contain numerous cell references to other cells, which in turn can also consist of formulas with cell references to other cells. These cell references can be on the same worksheet or in other worksheets in the workbook. However, as worksheets and the formulas they contain increase in complexity, there comes a point where it becomes an inordinate challenge to understand the formulas being used. Assigning names to individual cells or ranges of cells can help with one's ability to quickly comprehend what formulas mean. If you have a cell that computes gross profit as revenues minus cost of goods sold, it's more understandable if the formula is written as:

=Revenue − Cost

rather than as:

=B9 − B5

The ability to create and maintain names is done via a tool called the Name Manager. We've actually seen an example of the Name Manager in Chapter 4 on tables. Every time a table is created, Excel automatically adds an entry to the Name Manager with the name of the table. For example, looking at the table shown in Figure 9.16, we can see on the Table Tools Design tab of the Ribbon that the table has been given the name of Portfolio.

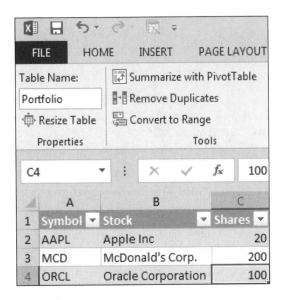

Figure 9.16

Table with a name.

Source: Microsoft® Corporation.

If we then select the Name Manager command, seen in Figure 9.2, we're shown the Name Manager dialog box of Figure 9.17.

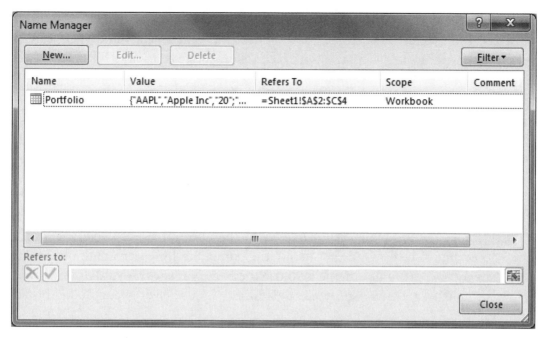

Figure 9.17
Name Manager dialog box.
Source: Microsoft® Corporation.

The Name Manager dialog box allows you to edit any table or cell names. To illustrate, let's begin with the data in Figure 9.18.

	A	B
1	**Stocks**	**Current Value**
2	AAPL	7800
3	IBM	2300
4	WAG	4500
5	Total Stocks	
6		
7	**Bonds**	
8	Bank of America	5500
9	US Treasury 6%	6600
10	Total Bonds	
11		
12	**Total Assets**	

Figure 9.18
A worksheet prior to adding formulas.
Source: Microsoft® Corporation.

Our immediate objective is to add formulas to cells B5, B10, and B12 that sum up, respectively, total stock value, total bond value, and total assets value. This can be accomplished with formulas that utilize cell references, as in the following three formulas:

=SUM(B2:B4)

=SUM(B8:B9)

=B5 + B10

The first formula totals the individual stocks, the second totals the bonds, and the third adds up stocks and bonds for a grand total. Alternatively, one can create formulas that reference names, which in turn refer to the appropriate cell references. The best way to accomplish this is to first define the names, and then create the formulas. The easiest way to create a new name is to use the New Name command, found under the New Name label seen in Figure 9.2. This brings up the New Name dialog box of Figure 9.19.

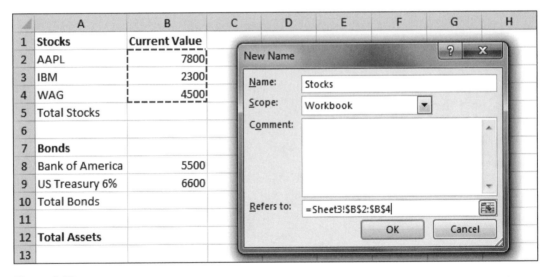

Figure 9.19

New Name dialog box.

Source: Microsoft® Corporation.

In this dialog box, we've already entered the desired name, and we've used the Refers To control to select the desired range of cells. We specified that the Scope should be the entire workbook, as opposed to just the current sheet. After clicking OK, the name is created and added to the Name Manager. Notice that the cell reference utilizes an absolute reference rather than a relative reference. You might think that this would reduce the subsequent flexibility of this name, but Excel does adjust the absolute reference value if rows are subsequently added to or deleted from the defined cell range.

In order to create the necessary names for our formulas, we'll add a similar name for Bonds, defined as the cell range B8 to B9. Finally, we'll need to add a name for the Total Stocks calculation that will be in cell B5, and the Total Bonds calculation of B10. We'll use the names Total_Stocks and Total_Bonds. After adding all of these names, the Name Manager appears as in Figure 9.20.

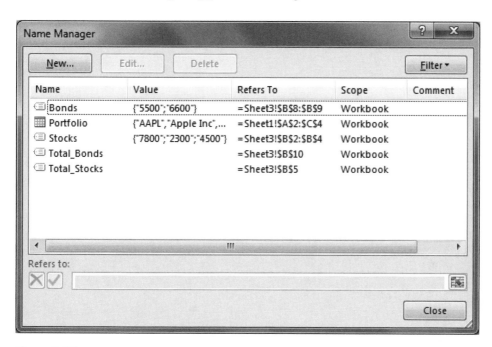

Figure 9.20
Name Manager dialog box with table and cell names.
Source: Microsoft® Corporation.

Notice that no value appears for the Total_Bonds and Total_Stocks names. This is because we haven't yet entered a formula for those cells. Now that all the required names have been created, all that remains is to add the formulas to cells B5, B10, and B12 of Figure 9.18. The result is displayed in Figures 9.21 and 9.22, showing and not showing formulas.

	A	B
1	Stocks	Current Value
2	AAPL	7800
3	IBM	2300
4	WAG	4500
5	Total Stocks	=SUM(Stocks)
6		
7	Bonds	
8	Bank of America	5500
9	US Treasury 6%	6600
10	Total Bonds	=SUM(Bonds)
11		
12	Total Assets	=Total_Stocks + Total_Bonds

Figure 9.21
A worksheet with defined names, showing formulas.
Source: Microsoft® Corporation.

	A	B
1	Stocks	Current Value
2	AAPL	7800
3	IBM	2300
4	WAG	4500
5	Total Stocks	14600
6		
7	Bonds	
8	Bank of America	5500
9	US Treasury 6%	6600
10	Total Bonds	12100
11		
12	Total Assets	26700

Figure 9.22
A worksheet with defined names, not showing formulas.
Source: Microsoft® Corporation.

The defined names in the Name Manager do not necessarily need to refer to cells in your workbook. It's also possible to create a name that exists only to hold a constant value. For example, let's say that you have a worksheet that utilizes a sales tax calculation in numerous cells. One option is to hard-code the sales tax amount in every formula. Another option is to place the sales tax multiplier in a specific cell on a worksheet and reference that cell via an absolute cell reference in every formula that has a sales tax component. A third option is to create a defined name in the Name Manager that holds that constant value. The New Name dialog box for such an effort would appear as in Figure 9.23.

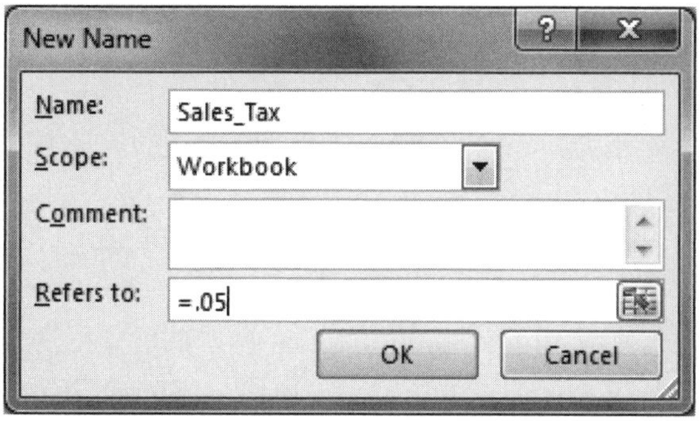

Figure 9.23
Creating a defined name with a constant value.
Source: Microsoft® Corporation.

In this example, the Refers To entry is merely a constant value, entered as a formula. Then, whenever the Sales_Tax name is referenced in a formula, the value .05 is used in its place.

At a certain level, substituting names for cell references aids in the understanding of the formulas. It's certainly easier to comprehend the meaning of SUM(Stocks) as opposed to SUM(B2:B4). Cell references in formulas force you to inspect the worksheet to see what values are in those particular cells being referenced. On the other hand, though, the use of defined names requires an extra step, and may still require you to view the Name Manager to see what cells the names refer to. In other words, the value of the Name Manager is up for debate in many situations, and is definitely a matter of personal preference.

Formula Auditing

Excel provides a number of formula auditing commands that, like the use of defined names, allow the analyst to more readily understand the relationships between formulas in a worksheet. Let's begin with the data shown in Figure 9.24.

	A	B	C	D	E	F
1	Stocks	Jan Value	Feb Value	Change	Subtotal	Total
2	AAPL	7800	6800	-1000		
3	IBM	2300	2400	100		
4	WAG	4500	5600	1100	200	
5						
6	Bonds					
7	Bank of America	5500	5550	50		
8	US Treasury 6%	6600	6595	-5	45	245

Figure 9.24

Worksheet prior to a formula audit.

Source: Microsoft® Corporation.

This worksheet computes the change in values for a number of stocks and bonds. Columns B and C show the value of each asset in January and February. Column D computes the change in values, with formulas such as C2 – B2. Column E computes the subtotals for the changes in values for both stocks and bonds. Cell E4, for example, contains the formula SUM(D2:D4). Finally, column F computes the total change in asset value, adding the values in cells E4 and E8.

Of course, most of these computations are fairly intuitive. However, let's imagine for the moment that this worksheet was much more complex with many more rows, columns, and formulas. The question is how to determine the values that contribute to the final total. To address this issue, Excel provides a Trace Precedents command, seen in Figure 9.2. To invoke this command, we select cell F8, and then click this command. The worksheet then appears as in Figure 9.25.

	A	B	C	D	E	F
1	Stocks	Jan Value	Feb Value	Change	Subtotal	Total
2	AAPL	7800	6800	-1000		
3	IBM	2300	2400	100		
4	WAG	4500	5600	1100	200	
5						
6	Bonds					
7	Bank of America	5500	5550	50		
8	US Treasury 6%	6600	6595	-5	45	245

Figure 9.25

Worksheet after a Trace Precedents command.

Source: Microsoft® Corporation.

As seen, two new arrows appear that indicate that the value of F8 is derived from values in cells E4 and E8. So far, so good. But this isn't the end of the story. To trace the data back further, we click the Trace Precedents command again. We then see what appears in Figure 9.26.

	A	B	C	D	E	F
1	Stocks	Jan Value	Feb Value	Change	Subtotal	Total
2	AAPL	7800	6800	-1000		
3	IBM	2300	2400	100		
4	WAG	4500	5600	1100	200	
5						
6	Bonds					
7	Bank of America	5500	5550	50		
8	US Treasury 6%	6600	6595	-5	45	245

Figure 9.26

Worksheet after two Trace Precedents commands.

Source: Microsoft® Corporation.

The trace now indicates one prior level, showing that the data in E4 comes from the data in the cell range D2:D4. Likewise, the data in E8 comes from D7:D8. This doesn't tell us the exact formula so that we can determine precisely how the data was derived, but it does gives us useful information about the source. Taking it one more level, we can click the Trace Precedents one more time to see the information in Figure 9.27.

	A	B	C	D	E	F
1	Stocks	Jan Value	Feb Value	Change	Subtotal	Total
2	AAPL	7800	6800	-1000		
3	IBM	2300	2400	100		
4	WAG	4500	5600	1100	200	
5						
6	Bonds					
7	Bank of America	5500	5550	50		
8	US Treasury 6%	6600	6595	-5	45	245

Figure 9.27

Worksheet after three Trace Precedents commands.

Source: Microsoft® Corporation.

We now see that each cell in column D is derived from the cells in the same row in columns B and C. Again, we're not shown the formula itself, but we can easily deduce the nature of the computation. If we want to see all the formulas involved, we can simply utilize the Show Formulas command and go through the same exercise. The equivalent of Figure 9.27 with formulas showing is shown in Figure 9.28.

◢	A	B	C	D	E	F
1	Stocks	Jan Value	Feb Value	Change	Subtotal	Total
2	AAPL	7800	6800	=C2-B2		
3	IBM	2300	2400	=C3-B3		
4	WAG	4900	5000	=C4-B4	=SUM(D2:D4)	
5						
6	Bonds					
7	Bank of America	5900	5950	=C7-B7		
8	US Treasury 6%	6800	6995	=C8-B8	=SUM(D7:D8)	=E4+E8

Figure 9.28

Worksheet with Trace Precedents showing formulas.

Source: Microsoft® Corporation.

A few limitations of using the Trace Precedents command may not be obvious. If, for example, all of the relevant cells are in the same column, it may be difficult to decipher the beginning and ends of each arrow. Also, if the source for a formula is on a different worksheet, you'll simply see an icon that indicates a different worksheet. You'll have to click on the arrow to see where the source is. In addition to the Trace Precedents command, there is a similar Trace Dependents command that lets you trace the flow from a source cell to any cells that utilize that cell in a formula. After displaying either Trace Precedents or Trace Dependents, the Remove Arrows command can be used to remove the added arrows.

Functions

As mentioned at the beginning of this chapter, all formulas consist of one or more of these components: constants, operators, functions, and references. We've talked at some length about constants, operators, and references but now want to focus on functions. Without the availability of functions, the ability to create complex formulas would be extremely limited. It is through the more than 450 functions that Excel provides that the analyst can invoke and apply sophisticated formulas and computations to the data at hand.

By definition, functions are a device that transforms any number of input parameters, called *arguments*, into a single output. Likewise, a single formula can contain any number of functions, along with operators, constants, and cell references, to produce a single value, which is then displayed in the cell that holds the formula. In general, a function has this format:

FUNCTION_NAME(argument1, argument2, argument3, …)

The FUNCTION_NAME is a name that identifies the function. Arguments for the functions are always enclosed in parentheses, with all arguments separated by commas. The left parenthesis must immediately follow the name of the function, without an intervening space. The number of arguments in a function depends on the specific function. For example, the LEFT function has two arguments, one of which is optional. Functions can have any number of arguments. Whereas the LEFT function has two arguments, some functions have more arguments, and some have none. For example, the TODAY function has no arguments. It simply returns the current date. Even with no arguments, however, the parentheses are always required. The parentheses are necessary to tell Excel that it is a function and not merely a text value. Additionally, some functions have arguments that can be repeated. For example, the SUM function has only one argument, but it can be repeated up to 255 times. Thus, it can sum up to 255 numbers, or ranges of numbers.

Let's look at a few typical examples of functions:

LEFT("DOGMA", 3)
PI( )
POWER(3, 2)
AVERAGE(10, 20)
DATE(2014, 7, 10)

The LEFT function above has two arguments. The first is a text value, and the second is the number of characters to capture. The function returns the value DOG, being the first three characters of DOGMA. The PI function has no arguments. It simply returns the irrational number 3.14159, to any number of decimal places. The POWER function has two arguments: a number and the power to raise that number to. This example returns the value 9, since 3 to the second power is 9. The AVERAGE function can have up to 255 instances of a number. It calculates the average of those numbers. In this example, the average of 10 and 20 would be returned as 15. The DATE function has three arguments: year, month, and day. The values in this example return the date 7/10/2014.

In many situations, functions provide a shorthand way to describe a complex calculation. For example, the function AVERAGE(10, 20) is a short way of expressing the calculation (10 + 20) / 2. The power of functions is further extended by the fact that cell references can be used in place of specific values. For example, the function AVERAGE(D1:D10) will take an average of the values of all cells between D1 and D10.

When invoking any specific function, it's important to determine what arguments are involved. There are several ways to figure that out. One method is to utilize Excel IntelliSense. When entering a function, IntelliSense will recognize the function and display something like that shown in Figure 9.29.

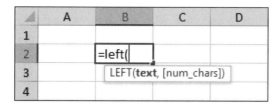

Figure 9.29

IntelliSense on a function.

Source: Microsoft® Corporation.

The IntelliSense that's displayed indicates that there are two arguments, *text* and *num_chars*. The *text* argument is required, but the brackets signify that the *num_chars* argument is optional.

Another option for entering a function and learning about its arguments is to select it from the Function Library group of commands on the Ribbon, as shown in Figure 9.1. To locate the LEFT function, one would select the Text label on the Ribbon, and then the LEFT function from the drop-down. This appears in Figure 9.30.

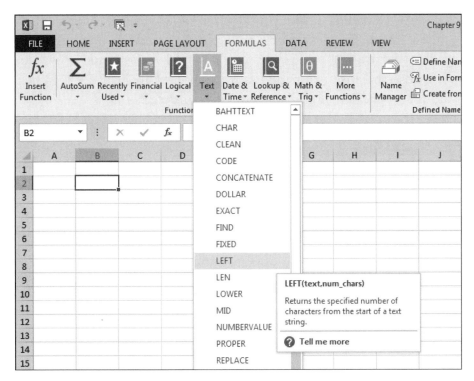

Figure 9.30

Selecting a function from the Ribbon.

Source: Microsoft® Corporation.

In selecting the LEFT function, we see the IntelliSense with the required and optional parameters, and a brief description. After selecting the function, a Function Arguments dialog box appears, as shown in Figure 9.31.

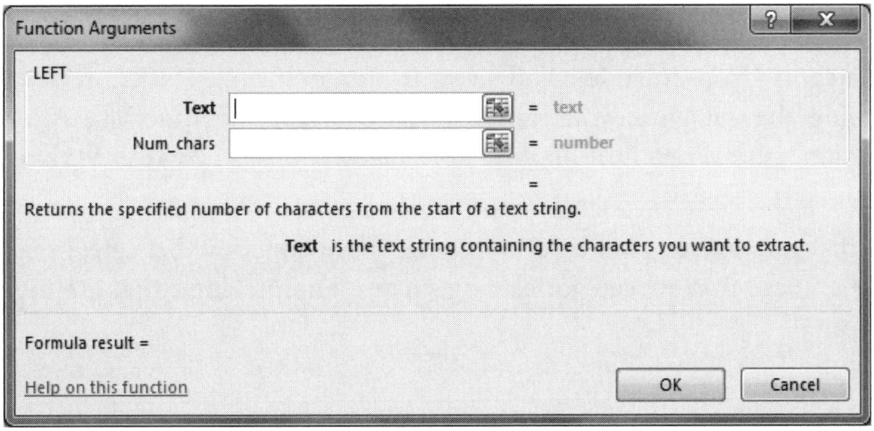

Figure 9.31

Function Arguments dialog box.

Source: Microsoft® Corporation.

The Function Arguments dialog box allows you to enter values for each argument or select values using the control. This dialog box can also be viewed when entering the function manually, as in Figure 9.29, simply by pressing Ctrl-A. Yet another way to select a function is to use the Insert Function command seen in Figure 9.1. When selected, it brings up the Insert Function dialog box of Figure 9.32.

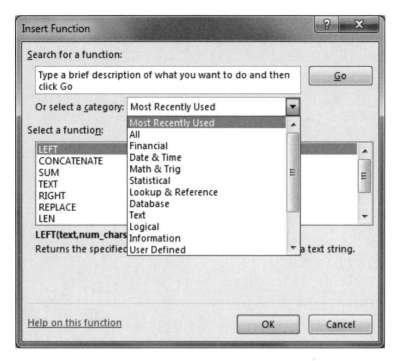

Figure 9.32
Insert Function dialog box.
Source: Microsoft® Corporation.

As seen, a Select Category drop-down lets you select from a number of function categories. After choosing the category, you can then select a specific function. After selecting the function, the Function Arguments dialog box of Figure 9.31 is displayed.

The Insert Function command of Figure 9.32 organizes functions into 14 categories. As seen in Figure 9.1, these first six categories have corresponding labels that are displayed on the Ribbon:

- Date & Time
- Financial
- Logical

- Lookup & Reference
- Math & Trig
- Text

We'll discuss functions in all of the above categories in the subsequent four chapters. Functions in the following six categories can be found under the More Functions label on the Ribbon, seen in Figure 9.1.

- Compatibility
- Cube
- Engineering
- Information
- Statistical
- Web

Of the above categories, we'll discuss functions in the Information and Statistical categories but not the other four. These final two categories of functions aren't available from the Function Library labels on the Ribbon but can be obtained from the Insert Function command:

- Database
- User Defined

At this point, we'll offer a few comments on some of the function categories that we will not be discussing in this book. Compatibility functions are included solely to maintain compatibility with earlier versions of Excel. Cube functions are used to manipulate data in OLAP cubes to which Excel can connect. Database functions are an older class of functions that allow users to select data in a way that simulates database functionality. These functions require data to be laid out in a spreadsheet in a very specific layout. However, the purpose of these functions can be accomplished by other functions in a more direct manner.

Nested Functions

By themselves, functions add a great deal of computational strength to formulas. As mentioned, a formula in a cell can contain any number of functions, along with operators, constants, and cell references. What's even more remarkable is that functions can be contained within other functions. Since a function always returns a single value, an entire function can exist as an argument within another function. When one function resides within another function, it is referred to as a *nested function*. Let's illustrate with a simple example that combines two text functions:

LEFT(TRIM("   CATALOG"), 3)

In this expression, there are five spaces before the word CATALOG. Whenever functions are nested, the innermost function is evaluated first. In this example, this is the function:

TRIM("   CATALOG")

The TRIM function removes all spaces from a text string, except for spaces between words. Since the text value includes spaces before the word CATALOG, the result of the TRIM function is the value "CATALOG" with spaces removed. After the inner function is evaluated, the outer function, LEFT, is examined. The LEFT function looks at "CATALOG" and returns the first three characters, which is CAT. Thus, the result of the entire expression is the value CAT.

In many cases, the order of nested functions is significant. If we had attempted to evaluate this function:

TRIM(LEFT("   CATALOG", 3)

the result would be spaces rather than CAT. If we apply the LEFT function first and take the first three characters of "   CATALOG", we would get spaces. Applying a TRIM to that value would still result in spaces. Thus, it's important to do the TRIM first, and then apply the LEFT function.

It is, however, certainly possible to have a nested function where the order of the functions doesn't matter. For example, both of the following expressions produce the same result.

UCASE(TRIM("   chicken")
TRIM(UCASE("   chicken")

The TRIM function removes spaces surrounding a text value. The UCASE function converts any lowercase text value to all uppercase. Both of these expressions will evaluate to the value CHICKEN. It doesn't matter if you trim the spaces first, and then convert to uppercase, or convert to uppercase first, and then trim the spaces.

In short, the ability to combine functions allows the analyst to create complex expressions with an enhanced degree of power. Nested functions will be seen as particularly important when we examine logical functions in Chapter 13. Logical functions, such as AND, OR, and NOT, are often used in combination with each other in nested functions.

Looking Ahead

The intent of this chapter was to provide a foundation for an understanding of Excel formulas. We began with the observation that formulas can consist of any of four elements—namely constants, operators, functions, and references. We then delved into the nature of cell references, both relative and absolute. We saw that relative cell references are a key element of Excel's flexibility. Cells can be inserted or deleted at will without affecting formulas in other cells. However, there are times when absolute cell references are necessary, particularly when a formula that includes a reference to a single cell is copied to other cells. In this situation, an absolute cell reference allows the single cell to remain the same in all copied formulas. We then turned to the Name Manager, a useful device for simplifying formulas. Naming allows formulas to be more immediately understood. However, on the downside, it also adds an extra layer of complexity to a worksheet.

As an aside, we made use of the Show Formulas command in many of our examples. This very useful command allows you to instantly view the formulas in any cell. Another device for tracing the elements that contribute to a formula is the Trace Precedents command, one of the commands in the Formula Auditing group of commands on the Formulas tab of the Ribbon.

We then turned our attention to functions, discussing their general structure. We looked at examples of functions with different types and numbers of arguments, and also at various ways to enter and learn about the requirements of specific functions. We ended our general discussion of functions with a look at nested functions—a way to combine more than one function to enhance their overall power and flexibility.

In the next four chapters, we'll explore different classes of functions in detail, beginning with Chapter 10, "Text Functions." Chapter 11 will cover numeric and date functions, and includes a discussion of financial functions. Chapter 12 deals with a number of important aggregate and statistical functions. Finally, Chapter 13 looks at logical and lookup functions. Taken together, these four chapters will introduce you to the most widely used and powerful functions in Excel.

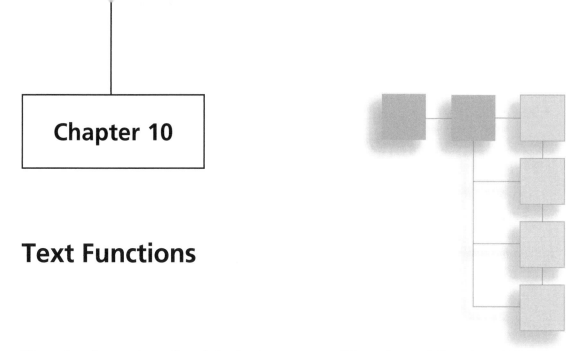

Chapter 10

Text Functions

The prior chapter introduced the basic concepts of formulas and functions. With that foundation in place, we now turn in the next four chapters to a detailed look at the most useful of the more than 450 functions that Excel provides. We begin this chapter with the most basic category of functions, the text functions. This set of functions deals with various ways to transform and manipulate text. In most cases, the primary activity of the business analyst involves working with numeric values. One thinks of critical numeric transformations such as counting, adding, summing, averaging, counting, or simply applying a quantitative formula. However, before that analysis can take place, text functions often play a role in the categorization of data. In the real world, the data one sees is often messy and not in a format that allows data to be properly grouped and organized. For example, one might encounter a field that has both city and state combined together. One would like to separate this into two separate data elements. Or one might be faced with an anomaly such as a four-digit zip code that's missing a leading zero. As such, text functions can play an important role in cleaning up data so that further analysis can take place. Furthermore, text functions can often prove useful for their own sake. For example, one might want to combine first and last name fields into a single field for a better presentation of data.

Case Conversion

The simplest text functions are those that convert lowercase to uppercase, or vice versa. The three functions we'll examine first are:

- UPPER
- LOWER
- PROPER

The UPPER function converts specified text to all uppercase. The syntax of the function is:

UPPER(text)

This indicates that the UPPER function has only one argument, named *text*. As an aside, please note that in this book we maintain the convention of displaying functions in all caps, so that functions can be clearly identified as such. However, there is no requirement that functions be typed in capital letters. We'll also show argument names in italics when referenced. Two examples of the UPPER function might be:

=UPPER("Dog")

=UPPER(A3)

The first example converts the text string "Dog" to "DOG". The second example converts the value of cell A3 to all uppercase. If A3 happens to contain the value "apple", then it will return the value "APPLE". Similarly, the LOWER function converts text to all lowercase. The syntax of the LOWER function is:

LOWER(text)

This function has the reverse effect. For example, it can be used to transform "BOTTLE" to "bottle". Finally, the PROPER function can be used to capitalize the first letter of every word in the provided text. For example, it can convert the text string "SAN FRANCISCO" to "San Francisco". Its syntax is:

PROPER(text)

To illustrate all three functions at once, consider the worksheet of Figure 10.1.

	A	B
1	Value	Formula
2	president	=UPPER(A2)
3	JEFFerson	=UPPER(A3)
4	KENNEDY	=LOWER(A4)
5	Eisenhower	=LOWER(A5)
6	THEODORE ROOSEVELT	=PROPER(A6)
7	abraham lincoln	=PROPER(A7)
8	IBM CORPORATION	=PROPER(A8)

Figure 10.1

Case conversion text functions, showing formulas.

Source: Microsoft® Corporation.

In this worksheet, we've utilized the Show Formulas command on the Formulas tab of the Ribbon to show the formulas in column B. The first two rows illustrate the UPPER function, the next two rows show the LOWER function, and the final three rows the PROPER function. After unselecting the Show Formulas command, the worksheet appears as in Figure 10.2.

	A	B
1	Value	Formula
2	president	PRESIDENT
3	JEFFerson	JEFFERSON
4	KENNEDY	kennedy
5	Eisenhower	eisenhower
6	THEODORE ROOSEVELT	Theodore Roosevelt
7	abraham lincoln	Abraham Lincoln
8	IBM CORPORATION	Ibm Corporation

Figure 10.2

Case conversion text functions, not showing formulas.

Source: Microsoft® Corporation.

We now see the results of the formulas in column B. As expected, the values in rows 2 and 3 are in all uppercase, and rows 4 and 5 are in all lowercase. Utilizing the PROPER function, the values in rows 6 through 8 capitalize the first letter of each word. Note that the PROPER function is not smart enough to capitalize all three letters of IBM.

Joining Text

The next text functions to be discussed are those that combine or join text in some manner. The CONCATENATE function is the most widely used of these functions, and has this syntax:

    CONCATENATE(text1, [text2], …)

The brackets surrounding the *text2* argument indicate that this is optional, and the three-dot ellipsis indicates that any number of text items can be included as arguments in the function. In practice, the CONCATENATE function will contain at least two text arguments. As before, the text arguments can be literal values or references to values in other cells. Examples might include:

    =CONCATENATE("SOME", "WHAT")
    =CONCATENATE(A3, B3)
    =CONCATENATE(A3, " ", B3)

In the first example, the function combines the words SOME and WHAT to create SOMEWHAT. The second example combines the values in cells A3 and B3. The third example combines the values in cells A3 and B3, while adding a space between the two values.

As mentioned in the previous chapter, Excel also provides an ampersand (&) concatenation operator. This operator can accomplish the same result as the CONCATENATE function. The following three formulas will produce the identical results as the above three formulas:

="SOME" & "WHAT"

=A3 & B3

=A3 & " " & B3

It's strictly a matter of personal preference as to whether one uses the CONCATENATE function or the ampersand to join text. To illustrate these types of formulas within a worksheet, let's look at the examples in Figure 10.3.

	A	B	C	D
1	Value 1	Value 2	Formula	Formula Result
2	Jefferson	Smith	=CONCATENATE(A2, " ", B2)	Jefferson Smith
3	Jefferson	Smith	=A2 & " " & B2	Jefferson Smith
4	Chicago	IL	=CONCATENATE(A4, ", ", B4)	Chicago, IL

Figure 10.3
Concatenation functions and formulas.
Source: Microsoft® Corporation.

In Figure 10.3, we are showing both the formula in column C and the result of that formula in column D. This was done by entering the data in columns A and B, and the formula in column D. We changed the format of the cells in column C from General to Text, and then copied the formulas in column D to column C. This is done by copying the formula in the Formula Bar. Note that it was necessary to change the cells in column C to Text to prevent the formulas from being interpreted as formulas and immediately executed.

In Figure 10.3, we've joined the words Jefferson and Smith in rows 2 and 3. Row 2 uses the CONCATENATE function, while row 3 employs the ampersand operator. In both cases, a literal space was inserted between the first and last names to separate the names. Row 4 joins a city and state name, while inserting a comma and space between the two values.

A somewhat similar function, named REPT, repeats a single character, or set of characters, a specified number of times. The syntax for this function is:

REPT(text, number_times)

This function, for example, can specify that an asterisk (*) should be repeated 10 times to form the text string **********. In essence, this function is similar to the CONCATENATE function in that it joins data together. The difference is that it combines only a single value, but it can specify how many times that value is to be repeated. One interesting use of this function is to create the equivalent of a bar chart that's contained entirely within a series of cells. Figure 10.4 illustrates how this is accomplished.

	A	B	C
1	Value	Formula	Formula Result
2	29	=REPT("*", ((A2-1)/10)+1)	***
3	30	=REPT("*", ((A3-1)/10)+1)	***
4	31	=REPT("*", ((A4-1)/10)+1)	****
5	85	=REPT("*", ((A5-1)/10)+1)	*********

Figure 10.4
The REPT function.
Source: Microsoft® Corporation.

In this example, the numbers in column A contain values ranging from 1 to 100. The objective is to produce a series of 1 to 10 asterisks to represent that value. Anything from 1 to 10 is to be displayed as one asterisk. A value between 11 and 20 gets two asterisks, and so on. It may take a bit of thought to understand how the formula works, but it basically subtracts one from the value, divides by 10, and then adds 1 to the result. Looking at the formula in cell B2, the nested sets of parentheses ensure that 1 is subtracted from A2 before the result is divided by 10, and also that all of this occurs before 1 is added to the result. When there are nested parentheses, all calculations in the innermost parentheses occur first. If you want to get really fancy with the display of data in column C, you can utilize the Wingdings font in cells C2 through C5. In this font, which has graphical "dingbat" characters, the letter "n" appears as a black square. Figure 10.5 illustrates the effect.

▲	A	B	C
1	Value	Formula	Formula Result
2	29	=REPT("n", ((A2-1)/10)+1)	■■■
3	30	=REPT("n", ((A3-1)/10)+1)	■■■
4	31	=REPT("n", ((A4-1)/10)+1)	■■■■
5	85	=REPT("n", ((A5-1)/10)+1)	■■■■■■■■■

Figure 10.5

The REPT function with the Wingdings font.

Source: Microsoft® Corporation.

As seen, we now have what appears as a miniature bar graph in column C. Of course, outside of this book, it would be unnecessary to copy formulas to text cells as we do. This is done only to display the formulas and results in separate columns. A more succinct view of this data is shown in Figure 10.6.

▲	A	B
1	Value	Result
2	29	■■■
3	30	■■■
4	31	■■■■
5	85	■■■■■■■■■

Figure 10.6

The REPT function without showing formulas.

Source: Microsoft® Corporation.

Text Substrings

We now move to a class of text functions that serve the purpose of extracting a substring of text from a larger text value. Four functions will be discussed:

- LEFT
- RIGHT
- TRIM
- MID

The LEFT and RIGHT functions select a specified number of characters from the left or right side of some text. The syntax of these two functions is:

LEFT(text, [num_chars])

RIGHT(text, [num_chars])

In both cases, the first argument specifies a text value. As before, this can be a hard-coded value enclosed in quotes or a reference to a value in another cell. The second argument, *num_chars*, is an optional argument that specifies how many characters to select from the left or right. If the argument is not present, the default value is 1. The worksheet in Figure 10.7 illustrates a few examples of the LEFT and RIGHT functions.

	A	B	C
1	Value	Formula	Formula Result
2	HOTEL	=LEFT(A2, 3)	HOT
3	MAURICE	=LEFT(A3)	M
4	SUNLIGHT	=RIGHT(A4, 5)	LIGHT
5	PITTSBURGH, PA	=RIGHT(A5, 2)	PA

Figure 10.7

The LEFT and RIGHT functions.

Source: Microsoft® Corporation.

The LEFT function in row 2 takes the left three characters of HOTEL, returning HOT. The LEFT function in the next row takes the first character of the name MAURICE, returning the initial M. Since the *num_chars* argument isn't specified, it's presumed to have a value of 1. The next row selects the last five characters from SUNLIGHT, producing the value LIGHT. The last row selects the last two characters from the city and state in cell A5, returning the state abbreviation PA.

When working with data that has been imported from a database, text values will often have trailing spaces at the end of the field. For example, if a text value is taken from a database where that field is defined as having a length of 20, you will receive all 20 characters when the data is moved to Excel. This can cause complications when using the RIGHT function in conjunction with such a value. In these situations, the TRIM function can be used to remove extra spaces from the right (or left) side of a text value. The syntax of the TRIM function is:

TRIM(text)

As an example, the function:

=TRIM("   GEORGE WASHINGTON   ")

will return the value "GEORGE WASHINGTON" without any leading or trailing spaces.

The syntax of the MID function is:

  MID(text, start_num, num_chars)

The first argument, *text*, is a literal text value or a reference to a value in another cell. The *start_num* argument specifies the starting position of the desired substring. The *num_chars* argument determines how many characters to extract, starting with the *start_num* character. For example, the function

  =MID("PLUTONIC",4,3)

says to take three characters from PLUTONIC, starting with the fourth character. This returns the value TON. Figure 10.8 shows a few more examples, as they would appear in a worksheet.

	A	B	C
1	Value	Formula	Formula Result
2	800-243-1111	=MID(A2, 5, 3)	243
3	Atlanta, GA 30301	=MID(A3, 10, 2)	GA
4	NEVERTHELESS	=MID(A4, 6, 3)	THE

Figure 10.8
The MID function.
Source: Microsoft® Corporation.

The MID function in row 2 returns the three characters of text, starting with the fifth character, bringing back 243. Similarly, the MID function in row 3 returns the two-character state, and the function in row 4 brings back the letters THE, as those are the three characters of text that start in position 6.

We'll now proceed with another example of concatenation that involves using two functions in a single formula. As discussed in the prior chapter, functions can be nested within each other to produce a cumulative effect that makes use of more than one function. Our objective is to take a series of numbers and pad those numbers with leading zeros. If, for example, there's a requirement that a set of numbers be 10 digits long with padded zeros on the left, we would want the number 23 to appear as 0000000023. The trick to accomplishing this is to first concatenate a text string of ten zeros and the value. This can be accomplished with the CONCATENATE function. Such a formula might be:

  =CONCATENATE("0000000000", A2)

The two arguments in this CONCATENATE function are "0000000000" as *text1* and the value of cell A2 as *text2*. The second step is to use the RIGHT function to take only the 10 digits on the right side of the result. Thus, the entire result of the above function is nested within a RIGHT function, as in:

   =RIGHT(CONCATENATE("0000000000", A2), 10)

The arguments in this RIGHT function are the entire CONCATENATE function as the *text* argument, and the value 10 as the *num_chars* argument. Figure 10.9 shows how this formula with nested functions might appear in a worksheet.

	A	B	C
1	Value	Formula	Formula Result
2	23	=RIGHT(CONCATENATE("0000000000", A2), 10)	0000000023
3	555	=RIGHT(CONCATENATE("0000000000", A3), 10)	0000000555
4	222333444	=RIGHT(CONCATENATE("0000000000", A4), 10)	0222333444

Figure 10.9

Nested RIGHT and CONCATENATE functions.

Source: Microsoft® Corporation.

As explained, the innermost function, CONCATENATE, combines a string of ten zeros with the number in column A. The RIGHT function then returns the ten rightmost digits from that expression. The result is shown in column C.

Let's now take this example a step further by saying that we want to create a twenty-digit number with leading zeros. To accomplish this, we could simply replace the string of ten zeros in the formula with twenty zeros. However, a more concise formulation would involve using the REPT function to produce the string of twenty zeros. The solution is illustrated in Figure 10.10.

	A	B	C
1	Value	Formula	Formula Result
2	23	=RIGHT(CONCATENATE(REPT("0", 20), A2), 20)	00000000000000000023
3	555	=RIGHT(CONCATENATE(REPT("0", 20), A3), 20)	00000000000000000555
4	222333444	=RIGHT(CONCATENATE(REPT("0", 20), A4), 20)	00000000000222333444

Figure 10.10

Nested RIGHT, CONCATENATE, and REPT functions.

Source: Microsoft® Corporation.

In this revised formula, we replaced the "0000000000" of Figure 10.9 with REPT("0", 20). We also adjusted the RIGHT function to display the 20 rightmost digits rather than just 10.

Finding and Replacing Text

Another useful set of text functions are those that involve finding and replacing text. The functions we'll cover are:

- SEARCH
- FIND
- SUBSTITUTE
- REPLACE

The SEARCH and FIND functions are very similar. They both return the starting position of a specified character or string of characters within another text string. The syntax of these functions is:

SEARCH(find_text, within_text, [start_num])

FIND(find_text, within_text, [start_num])

Both functions will find a specified text string within a larger text string, and they both have identical arguments. The third argument, *start_num*, is optional and lets you specify the character position to start the search. The main difference between the two functions is that the FIND function is case sensitive, whereas the SEARCH function isn't. A second difference is that the SEARCH function permits you to use question mark (?) and asterisk (∗) wildcards in the *find_text* argument. The question mark wildcard can be used to represent any single character, and the asterisk can stand for any sequence of characters. Essentially, the SEARCH function can be used in all situations unless you need to do a case-sensitive search. Let's illustrate with a few examples, seen in Figure 10.11.

	A	B	C
1	Value	Formula	Formula Result
2	100 Main Street	=SEARCH("MAIN", A2)	5
3	100 Main Street	=SEARCH("MAIN", A3, 10)	#VALUE!
4	100 Main Street	=FIND("MAIN", A4)	#VALUE!
5	100 Main Street	=SEARCH("100*ST", A5)	1

Figure 10.11

SEARCH and FIND functions.

Source: Microsoft® Corporation.

The SEARCH function in row 2 looks for the value MAIN in the address of cell A2. Since this text string begins in position 5 of the address, the function returns the value 5. When we discuss the REPLACE function shortly, we'll explain what can be done with this piece of information. The SEARCH function in row 3 specifies a value of 10 for the optional *start_num* argument. This means that the search begins in position 10 of the address. Since the word MAIN occurs before position 10, it ends up finding nothing, and therefore returns the #VALUE! identifier. This means that an error occurred, in that the function was unable to return a value. In Chapter 13, "Logical and Lookup Functions," we'll explain how to use the IFERROR function to return a meaningful value rather than #VALUE! in this type of situation. The FIND function in row 3 also produces an error. This is because the FIND function is case sensitive, and the specified value of MAIN does not exactly match the word "Main" in the address. Finally, the SEARCH function in row 5 makes use of the asterisk wildcard to look for any value that begins with 100 and ends with the text string ST. It finds this string within the value in cell A5 and returns the value 1, since that's the position of the first character of what was found.

Just as the SEARCH and FIND functions are similar, so are SUBSTITUTE and REPLACE. Of the two, the SUBSTITUTE function is decidedly easier to use. Its syntax is:

SUBSTITUTE(text, old_text, new_text, [instance_num])

The first argument, *text*, specifies the text string to be analyzed. The *old_text* argument states the text string to search for, and *new_text* specifies its replacement. The optional *instance_num* argument says which instance of *old_text* to replace. If nothing is specified for *instance_num*, the function will substitute all occurrences that it finds. If a number is specified, it will only perform the substitution for that occurrence. For example, an *instance_num* of 2 means to substitute *new_text* for *old_text* in the second occurrence of *old_text* that it finds.

The syntax of the REPLACE function is:

REPLACE(old_text, start_num, num_chars, new_text)

For the REPLACE function, the *old_text* argument specifies the text string to be analyzed. The function will replace the string starting in the position of the *start_num* argument, for *num_chars* characters, replacing those characters with the value of the *new_text* argument. The examples in Figure 10.12 illustrate both the SUBSTITUTE and REPLACE functions.

	A	B	C
1	Value	Formula	Formula Result
2	100 Main Street	=SUBSTITUTE(A2, "Street", "St")	100 Main St
3	100 North North Street	=SUBSTITUTE(A3, "North", "N")	100 N N Street
4	100 North North Street	=SUBSTITUTE(A4, "North", "N", 1)	100 N North Street
5	100 Main Street	=REPLACE(A5, 10, 6, "St")	100 Main St
6	100 Main Street	=REPLACE(A6, SEARCH("STREET", A6), 6, "St")	100 Main St

Figure 10.12

SUBSTITUTE and REPLACE functions.

Source: Microsoft® Corporation.

The SUBSTITUTE function in row 2 does a simple substitution of the value "St" for "Street" on the text in cell A2. The example in row 3 examines an address that has two occurrences of the word North. Since the optional *instance_num* argument is not specified, both occurrences of the word are replaced. However, this is not the intended result. Row 4 shows the correct solution, which utilizes the *instance_num* argument to specify that we want to substitute only the first occurrence of "North" with "N".

Row 5 of Figure 10.12 illustrates the REPLACE function. This function requires that you specify the starting position and the number of characters to replace. This example states to replace six characters, beginning with position 10, with the text string "St". The example in row 6 explains how to use the SEARCH function in conjunction with REPLACE. As the inner function, the SEARCH function returns the value 10, which is then used as the *start_num* argument of the REPLACE function.

In summary, if you need to find text, it's generally easier to use the SEARCH function rather than FIND. Likewise, for replacing text, SUBSTITUTE is simpler than REPLACE.

Splitting Text

We now turn to a common problem when dealing with text—namely, the need to split text into separate substrings. For example, one may have a part number that consists of two sets of numbers, separated by a dash. In this scenario, our sample part numbers might be 122-44444 or 33-5566. If the values on either side of the dash have some particular meaning, we might want to split the 122-44444 value into two separate columns, 122 and 44444. If the values have variable lengths, we can't simply use the LEFT or RIGHT functions to obtain the numbers on the left or right of the dash. The solution is to utilize several different functions in combination. However, one needed function hasn't yet been introduced: the LEN function. The LEN function, short for "length," returns the number of characters in a specified text string. This includes any spaces within the string. Its syntax is:

LEN(text)

As an example, the formula LEN("SAN DIEGO") will return the value 9, since there are nine characters in the text string, including the space between the words. Turning now to the splitting problem, we will use the SEARCH, LEN, LEFT, and RIGHT functions to split our part numbers into two separate fields. The solution is shown in Figures 10.13 and 10.14, where Figure 10.13 uses the Show Formulas command to display all formulas, and Figure 10.14 shows the result, without displaying formulas.

	A	B	C	D	E
1	Value	Location of dash	Length of field	Field ONE	Field TWO
2	23-456	=SEARCH("-", A2)	=LEN(A2)	=LEFT(A2, B2 - 1)	=RIGHT(A2, C2 - B2)
3	5551-1222	=SEARCH("-", A3)	=LEN(A3)	=LEFT(A3, B3 - 1)	=RIGHT(A3, C3 - B3)
4	123-858522	=SEARCH("-", A4)	=LEN(A4)	=LEFT(A4, B4 - 1)	=RIGHT(A4, C4 - B4)

Figure 10.13

Splitting text, showing formulas.

Source: Microsoft® Corporation.

	A	B	C	D	E
1	Value	Location of dash	Length of field	Field ONE	Field TWO
2	23-456	3	6	23	456
3	5551-1222	5	9	5551	1222
4	123-858522	4	10	123	858522

Figure 10.14

Splitting text, not showing formulas.

Source: Microsoft® Corporation.

Let's examine the formulas one at a time. The formula in column B uses the SEARCH function to locate the position of the dash of the part numbers in column A. In row 2, for example, this formula determined that the dash is in position 3. Column C uses the LEN function to calculate the total length of the text string. For row 2, the length is 6. The formulas in column D use the LEFT function in conjunction with the values in columns B and C to return the substring of text to the left of the dash. As you may recall, the LEFT function has two arguments: *text* and *num_chars*. The value of column A is used for the *text* argument, and the value of column B minus 1 is used for the *num_chars* argument. Similarly, the formulas in column E use the RIGHT function in conjunction with the values in columns A, B, and C to return the substring to the right of the dash. This is slightly trickier, since it needs to use the difference of columns C and B as the *num_chars* argument. As seen in Figure 10.14, the result of these formulas is the splitting of the text in column A into two separate values in columns D and E.

In this example, we've placed intermediate formulas in columns B and C to break down the final calculations in columns D and E into smaller steps. If we should want to be more concise, we can utilize nested functions to combine all the functions into one larger formula. This is shown in Figure 10.15. In this figure, we've returned to our earlier practice of showing the formula and formula result in separate columns.

	A	B	C	D	E
				Field ONE Formula Result	Field TWO Formula Result
1	Value	Field ONE Formula	Field TWO Formula		
2	23-456	=LEFT(A2, SEARCH("-", A2) - 1)	=RIGHT(A2, LEN(A2) - SEARCH("-", A2))	23	456
3	5551-1222	=LEFT(A3, SEARCH("-", A3) - 1)	=RIGHT(A3, LEN(A3) - SEARCH("-", A3))	5551	1222
4	123-858522	=LEFT(A4, SEARCH("-", A4) - 1)	=RIGHT(A4, LEN(A4) - SEARCH("-", A4))	123	858522

Figure 10.15
Splitting text with nested LEN, SEARCH, LEFT, and RIGHT functions.
Source: Microsoft® Corporation.

The functions shown in Figure 10.15 are identical to those shown in Figure 10.13, except that they've been nested for compactness. This eliminates the need for columns B and C that were used in Figures 10.13 and 10.14. For example, the formula in cell B2 uses the SEARCH function as an inner function to return the location of the dash. The value 1 is subtracted from this result to calculate the *num_chars* argument of the LEFT function. As before, columns D and E of Figure 10.15 aren't strictly needed. They're included only to display both the formula and result in a single worksheet, for purposes of illustration.

Converting to and from Text

As mentioned in Chapter 2, Excel provides a number of formatting options for worksheet cells. These include General, Number, Currency, Date, Percentage, and Text. These formats allow you to alter the appearance of numbers or text in a worksheet. Similarly, Excel also provides a number of functions that convert numbers to text, or text to numbers, in a variety of specified formats. In such situations, it's largely a matter of personal preference as to whether to utilize functions or cell formatting to accomplish your objective. We'll discuss the following functions, which all pertain to converting numbers to or from text:

- DOLLAR
- FIXED
- TEXT
- VALUE

The DOLLAR function converts a number to text, in a currency format. The syntax of this function is:

DOLLAR(number, [decimals])

The optional *decimal* argument lets you specify the number of decimals to display. The default is 2. If the number has a value of 1000 or more, commas will be displayed with the number. The FIXED function is similar, except that it doesn't display a dollar sign ($) with the number. It also has an additional optional parameter, *no_commas*, that lets you suppress commas in the result. If used, the *no_commas* argument requires a logical value of either TRUE or FALSE. A value of TRUE means that all commas will be suppressed. Its syntax is:

FIXED(number, [decimals], [no_commas])

Figure 10.16 shows a few examples of these two functions.

	A	B	C
1	Value	Formula	Formula Result
2	23	=DOLLAR(A2)	$23.00
3	23.456	=DOLLAR(A3)	$23.46
4	23.45	=DOLLAR(23,0)	$23
5	23.45678	=FIXED(A5, 2)	23.46
6	2222.3	=FIXED(A6)	2,222.30
7	2222.3	=FIXED(A7, 2, TRUE)	2222.30

Figure 10.16
DOLLAR and FIXED functions.
Source: Microsoft® Corporation.

The DOLLAR function in row 2 applies standard currency formatting to the value in cell A2. As seen, this includes a dollar sign ($) and two decimal places. The example in row 3 indicates that a value with three decimals is rounded to two decimal places. The

DOLLAR function in row 5 specifies 0 as the decimals argument, which has the effect of rounding the value to an integer. Row 5 illustrates the FIXED function, with a specified value of 2 for the decimals argument. In row 6, we see that for larger numbers, commas are inserted as needed. The example in row 7 specifies a value of TRUE for the *no_commas* argument, so all commas are suppressed.

The TEXT function converts numbers to text in any specified format. In fact, the transformations of the DOLLAR and FIXED functions can also be handled by the TEXT function. The syntax of TEXT is:

TEXT(value, format_text)

The *format_text* argument allows you to create a template of any desired format to display numbers or dates. The rules for formulating this argument are actually quite complex. More than 30 characters can be used to create the template. For example, a number sign (#) specifies that a number should go in that position. A zero (0) adds the requirement that insignificant digits be displayed with a zero if needed. A template of 00# would require a value of 7 to be displayed as 007 rather than merely 7. There are also a large number of formats specific to dates, such as mm to display a two-digit month, and mmm to display the month as a three-character abbreviation such as Jan or Feb. There are numerous other characters that can be used in the template, such as parentheses, plus signs, colons, and so on. The best way to design a template for the *format_text* argument is to view Excel's Help on this function for a full list of options. The examples in Figure 10.17 illustrate some of the possibilities.

	A	B	C
1	Value	Formula	Formula Result
2	23	=TEXT(A2, "#")	23
3	23	=TEXT(A3, "#.0")	23.0
4	23	=TEXT(A4, "000#")	0023
5	2233.4	=TEXT(A5, "$#,##0.00")	$2,233.40
6	2/3/2004	=TEXT(A6, "yyyy/mm/dd")	2004/02/03
7	2/3/2004	=TEXT(A7, "mmm dd, yyyy")	Feb 03, 2004
8	2/3/2004	=TEXT(A8, "ddd")	Tue

Figure 10.17

The TEXT function.

Source: Microsoft® Corporation.

The TEXT function in row 2, using the number sign (#), specifies a basic numeric format without commas or decimal places. The function in row 3 adds a decimal point and one decimal place. The zero to the right of the decimal place indicates that one decimal place will be shown even if it's a zero. The function in row 4 specifies a four-digit number with leading zeros. In row 5, the function adds a dollar sign and comma, as well as two decimal places. The TEXT function in row 6 applies formatting to a date. In row 7, the mmm indicates that a three-character month should be displayed. Finally, the function in row 8 makes use of the ddd format to display the day of the week.

The VALUE function accomplishes the reverse of the TEXT function, turning a text string back to a number. Its syntax is:

VALUE(text)

This function is useful primarily in situations when you've imported text data from a database into Excel and would like to perform a numeric calculation on those values. In order for text to be included in a numeric computation, it first must be converted to a numeric value. As an example, the function VALUE("23") converts the text value "23" to the number 23.

Looking Ahead

In this first of four chapters dealing with Excel functions, we explained the use of functions used to manipulate text. The first set of functions we examined were those that perform case conversion, such as from lowercase to uppercase. We then turned to functions that join text together, using the CONCATENATE function or the ampersand (&) operator. We also examined a related function, REPT, that repeats a single character or group of characters, and that can be used to produce miniature bar graphs within a cell. The next set of text functions we examined allow the analyst to create substrings of text. Functions such as LEFT and RIGHT extract text from the left or right side of a text string. We then showed how to create a nested function, using RIGHT and CONCATENATE in combination, to produce numbers with leading zeros.

The next set of text functions on finding and replacing text explored the use of the SEARCH and SUBSTITUTE functions for that purpose. We then turned to a more complex example with nested functions used to split a single text value into multiple columns. In doing so, we showed how one can either break down a complex formula into intermediate steps, or else utilize a complex nested function in a single column. We closed the chapter with functions that convert numbers to text in a variety of formats, and also perform the reverse procedure. Interestingly, much of this functionality can also be accomplished by modifying the format of a cell, without resorting to the use of functions.

The next chapter moves on from the somewhat mundane topic of text functions to numeric functions—a topic that is much more relevant to business analysis. Text functions can be used to categorize and present data, but the real work of analysis usually requires numeric transformation. We'll examine a number of important classes of numeric functions in the next chapter, including arithmetic, conversion, financial, and date functions.

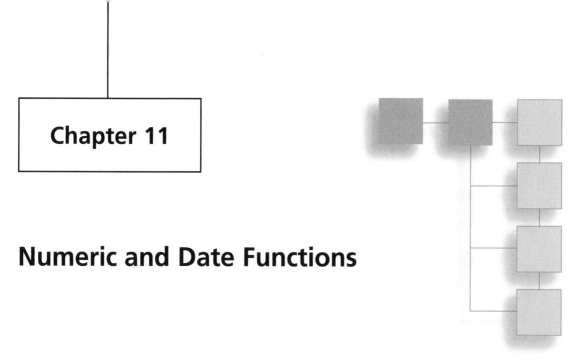

Chapter 11

Numeric and Date Functions

The functions covered in the last chapter dealt with the classification and presentation of textual data. We now turn our attention to functions that involve numeric computations. We begin with functions that perform basic arithmetic computations such as multiplication, exponentiation, and absolute value. We'll also make special note of the importance of logarithms. We'll then talk about rounding or truncating numbers to a desired degree of digits. The next topic will be a special function that allows you to convert units of measurement, such as distances and weights. We'll then turn to a discussion of financial functions and provide examples and explanation of some of the more basic functions of this class. The final topic of this chapter is date and time functions. As you may recall, Excel stores all dates and times as numbers. It is only the presentation layer that displays these numbers as dates. It is therefore fitting to discuss dates along with other numeric functions.

Arithmetic

In Chapter 9, "Formulas," we covered the basic arithmetic operators used for addition, subtraction, multiplication, division, and exponentiation. These operations are indicated, respectively, by the plus sign (+), minus sign (−), asterisk (*), slash (/), and caret (^). Excel provides three functions for multiplication, division, and exponents that allow you to utilize these operations:

- PRODUCT
- QUOTIENT
- POWER

The syntax of these functions is as follows:

PRODUCT(number1, [number2], …)

QUOTIENT(numerator, denominator)

POWER(number, power)

The PRODUCT function multiplies all indicated numbers. It can contain any number of arguments. The QUOTIENT function performs division on two specified arguments, a *numerator* and a *denominator*. The value returned by the function is truncated to an integer value. The POWER function performs an exponential calculation on two arguments, a *number* and the *power* to which it is to be raised. Figure 11.1 illustrates how these three functions can be used for multiplication, division, and exponential calculations.

◢	A	B	C	D
1	Value 1	Value 2	Formula	Formula Result
2	8	5	=PRODUCT(A2, B2)	40
3	8	5	=A3*B3	40
4	7	2	=QUOTIENT(A4, B4)	3
5	7	2	=A5/B5	3.5
6	4	2	=POWER(A6, B6)	16
7	4	2	=4^2	16

Figure 11.1

PRODUCT, QUOTIENT, and POWER functions.

Source: Microsoft® Corporation.

In Figure 11.1, we continue our practice from the prior chapter of displaying the formulas used in a column with text cells and the formula result in another column. The PRODUCT function in row 2 multiplies the values of the cells in A2 and B2, resulting in a value of 40. Row 3 shows the same calculation accomplished with the multiplication (∗) operator. The QUOTIENT function in row 4 divides the value of cell A4 by B4. Although 7 divided by 2 is 3.5, the output of the function is 3, since the QUOTIENT function eliminates any fractional values. Row 5 has the same calculation with the division (/) operator. In this case, the exact value of 3.5 is shown. Row 6 illustrates the POWER function, based on the values in cells A6 and B6. This calculation takes 4 to the second power. Row 7 has the same calculation with the exponentiation (^) operator. Incidentally, the POWER function should not be confused with the EXP function. The EXP function performs an exponential calculation on the irrational number *e*, raising it to a specified power. The EXP function has use in financial calculations involving continuous compounding.

We'll mention three additional arithmetic functions:

- SQRT
- ABS
- LOG

The SQRT function takes the square root of any number. The ABS function takes the absolute value of a number. Thus any number that is negative will be converted to a positive value. The syntax of these functions is:

SQRT(number)

ABS(number)

Figure 11.2 illustrates the SQRT and ABS functions.

	A	B	C
1	Value	Formula	Formula Result
2	25	=SQRT(A2)	5
3	-23.5	=ABS(A3)	23.5
4	38	=ABS(A4)	38
5	-25	=IF(A5 < 0, A5 * -1, A5)	25

Figure 11.2
SQRT and ABS functions.
Source: Microsoft® Corporation.

The SQRT function in row 2 takes the square root of 25, yielding the value 5. The ABS function in row 3 examines the value in cell A2 and converts it to a positive value. Thus, –23.5 becomes 23.5. The example in row 4 takes the absolute value of a positive number. Since 38 is already positive, there is no change in the value. Row 5 illustrates how an absolute value can be computed without the ABS function. Although we haven't yet discussed the IF function, an explanation of how it works is simple. The first argument, A5 < 0, tests to see if the value of cell A5 is less than 0. The second argument, A5 * –1, is executed if the result of the first argument is true. Thus, if A5 is less than 0, the value of A5 will be multiplied by –1. This will turn a negative number into a positive number. The third argument, A5, is executed if the first argument evaluates to false. This means that if A5 is not less than 0, the value of A5 is returned as is.

The LOG function produces the logarithm of a number for base 10. As you may recall, a logarithm is the inverse of an exponential calculation. For example, since 10 to the second power is 100, this means that the logarithm of 100 is 2. In other words, the exponent that must be applied to 10 in order to yield 100 is 2. The syntax of LOG is:

LOG(number, [base])

The *base* argument is optional, and is assumed to equal 10 if not specified. Excel also provides a few additional logarithmic functions that we'll briefly mention. The LOG10 function is the same as the LOG function except that it is always for base 10. The LN function produces the natural log, a value based on the irrational number *e*, and is the inverse of the EXP function. Figure 11.3 illustrates the LOG function.

	A	B	C
1	Value	Formula	Formula Result
2	10	=LOG(A2)	1
3	100	=LOG(A3)	2
4	1000	=LOG(A4)	3
5	325	=LOG(A5)	2.511883361

Figure 11.3
The LOG function.
Source: Microsoft® Corporation.

The LOG function in row 2 shows the logarithm of the value of cell 2. Since the number 10 must be raised to the first power to yield 10, the log is calculated as 1. The function in row 3 shows that the log of 100 is 2. This means that 10 must be raised to the second power to produce 100. Row 4 indicates that the log of 1000 is 3. This is because 10 to the third power is 1000. The LOG function in row 5 results in a fractional value approximately equal to 2.51. Since 325 is between 100 and 1000, it makes sense that its log should be between 2 and 3.

At this point, we want to elaborate further on the value of logs for the business analyst. Basically, logs can be of value when one is interested in the rate of change in a series of numbers. For this reason, stock prices are often displayed on a logarithmic scale. When stocks go up or down in value, we're primarily interested in the rate of change. A stock that doubles in value from 25 to 50 is just as significant as a stock that doubles from 250 to 500. To illustrate what can be done with logs with relation to stock prices, let's look at the data in Figure 11.4.

◢	A	B	C
1	Date	Price	Log
2	1/1/2013	5.00	0.698970004
3	2/1/2013	12.00	1.079181246
4	3/1/2013	25.75	1.410777233
5	4/1/2013	41.50	1.618048097
6	5/1/2013	95.00	1.977723605
7	6/1/2013	225.00	2.352182518

Figure 11.4

Stock prices with logs.

Source: Microsoft® Corporation.

This data shows the price of a specific stock on the first of each month, from 1/1/2013 to 6/1/2013. Column C shows the result of a formula that uses the LOG function. For example, the formula in cell C2 is:

=LOG(B2)

The formulas in the other cells in row C are similar. As expected, the logs of prices under 10 are between 0 and 1. The logs of prices from 10 to 100 are between 1 and 2. The logs of prices from 100 to 1000 are between 2 and 3. As seen, the price of the stock has roughly doubled each month. If we attempt to present this data in a pivot chart, using just rows A and B, the results appear as in Figure 11.5.

Figure 11.5

Pivot chart of stock prices, not using logs.

Source: Microsoft® Corporation.

The trajectory of the line shows the price of the stock has skyrocketed over the course of these five months. While this is true, the complete impact of the stock's rise is not fully explained in this graph. While the graph shows only a very small rise between 1/1/13 and 2/1/13, there is a huge gain between 5/1/13 and 6/1/13. However, the rise in price in January (from $5 to $12) is just as significant for the investor as the rise in price in May (from $95 to $225). This is where logarithms come in. There are two ways that we use logs to present a more meaningful picture of the pricing history. One option is to modify the chart of Figure 11.5 to display the vertical axis on a logarithmic scale. This is accomplished by right-clicking on the vertical axis and selecting the Format Axis contextual command. One then sees a checkbox with an option to display the axis on a logarithmic scale. The chart is then transformed to that shown in Figure 11.6.

Figure 11.6

Pivot chart of stock prices, with a logarithmic scale on the vertical axis.

Source: Microsoft® Corporation.

The image portrayed by this chart provides a much clearer picture as to the value of the stock for an investor. We now see a steady rise in price from $5 on January 1 to $225 on June 1. The logarithmic scale on the vertical axis shows appropriate log values, with markers at 1, 10, 100, and 1000. A second option for utilizing logs is to use the log values that we computed in column C of Figure 11.4. Using the data in columns A and C, we can create a pivot chart without a logarithmic scale that produces the same effect. This is shown in Figure 11.7.

Figure 11.7
Pivot chart of stock prices, using logs.
Source: Microsoft® Corporation.

The line in Figure 11.7 is identical to that in Figure 11.6. The only difference is that this chart does not use a logarithmic scale within the chart itself. Instead, it is using log values calculated by the LOG function. Notice that the vertical axis in Figure 11.7 displays log values, not the actual stock price. This is somewhat of a limitation, but nevertheless serves the purpose of demonstrating the value of logs. Thus, without relying on the logarithmic scale of a chart, logs can be used to transform data into more revealing values.

Rounding

The next set of numeric functions we'll discuss are those that deal with the rounding and truncation of numbers. In some situations, rounding can be accomplished in the presentation layer with the Format Cells command. When one right-clicks on a cell and then selects the Format Cells contextual command, you can specify the number of decimal places a number should contain. If the number has more decimal places than what you specified, Excel will round to that level of significance as it displays the number. However, the real purpose of the Format Cells command relates to how many decimals places are displayed. Any rounding that takes place is incidental. For example, if you specify that the number 23.2 be displayed with three decimal places, it will display as 23.200. If you specify that the number 23.46 be displayed with one decimal place, it will round and display it as 23.5.

The functions covered in this section afford complete control over rounding, without regard to how the number is displayed in the presentation layer. We'll discuss these functions:

- ROUND
- ROUNDUP
- ROUNDDOWN
- TRUNC
- INT
- MROUND
- CEILING
- FLOOR

The ROUND function is the most basic, allowing you to round a number to any specified number of significant digits. The format of the function is:

ROUND(number, num_digits)

The *num_digits* argument can be positive, negative, or zero. Figure 11.8 illustrates how it works.

	A	B	C
1	Value	Formula	Formula Result
2	427.283	=ROUND(A2, 2)	427.28
3	427.283	=ROUND(A3, 1)	427.3
4	427.283	=ROUND(A4, 0)	427
5	427.283	=ROUND(A5, -1)	430
6	427.283	=ROUND(A6, -2)	400
7	-8.62	=ROUND(A7, 1)	-8.6

Figure 11.8
The ROUND function.
Source: Microsoft® Corporation.

The ROUND function in row 2 rounds the value in cell A2 to two decimal digits. The result is 427.28. In rounding, the digit after the significant digit is used to determine how the number rounds. In this case, the digit 3 causes the number to round down to 427.28. In row 3, the *num_digits* argument of 1 causes the number to round to one decimal place, rounding 427.283 up to 427.3. Likewise, the 0 *num_digits* argument in row 4 specifies that there should be no decimal places, so the number is rounded to the nearest integer. Rows 5 and 6 illustrate the effect of a negative number for the *num_digits* argument. In row 6, the –1 means that the number is rounded to the nearest tens place. In row 6, the –2 has the effect of rounding to the nearest hundreds place. Row 7 shows what happens when the number itself is negative. The number –8.62 is rounded to 1 decimal digit, resulting in the value –8.6.

The ROUNDUP, ROUNDDOWN, and TRUNC functions offer a slight variation on ROUND, allowing you to specify whether to round up or down. The syntax of these functions is:

ROUNDUP(number, num_digits)

ROUNDDOWN(number, num_digits)

TRUNC(number, [num_digits])

When rounding the number 12.74 to one decimal place, it would normally be rounded down to 12.7. The ROUNDUP function would force it to round up to 12.8. Whether the number is positive or negative, the ROUNDUP function always rounds the number away from the number 0. Likewise, the number 12.76 would normally be rounded up to 12.8 when rounding one decimal place. The ROUNDDOWN function would force it to round down to 12.7. The TRUNC function is actually identical to ROUNDDOWN, except that it does not require the *num_digits* argument. When the *num_digits* argument is not present in TRUNC, the default is 0. In common usage, truncating a number means to round down. Figure 11.9 shows a few examples.

	A	B	C
1	Value	Formula	Formula Result
2	12.74	=ROUNDUP(A2, 1)	12.8
3	1235	=ROUNDUP(A3, -2)	1300
4	-15.5	=ROUNDUP(A4, 0)	-16
5	12.76	=ROUNDDOWN(A5, 1)	12.7
6	12.76	=TRUNC(A6, 1)	12.7
7	12.76	=TRUNC(A7)	12
8	-15.5	=TRUNC(A8)	-15

Figure 11.9

ROUNDUP, ROUNDDOWN, and TRUNC functions.

Source: Microsoft® Corporation.

The ROUNDUP function in row 2 rounds 12.74 up to a value with one decimal place, resulting in 12.8. The *num_digits* argument in row 3 has a value of –2, which means that it will round up to the nearest hundreds digit, rounding 1235 up to 1300. The ROUNDUP function in row 4 rounds –15.5 up to the nearest integer. Since ROUNDUP always rounds away from 0, this results in –16. Row 5 demonstrates the ROUND-DOWN function, rounding 12.75 down to 12.7. Row 6 has the same values with the TRUNC function, demonstrating that TRUNC is identical to ROUNDDOWN. Finally, the TRUNC functions in rows 7 and 8 show the effect of truncating positive and negative numbers to an integer value. The truncation is always towards the number 0.

The INT function is similar to a TRUNC function with no *num_digits* argument, in that the INT function converts the specified number to an integer. However, whereas the TRUNC function rounds the number towards the number 0, the INT function eliminates all decimal places while rounding towards the next lowest integer. Whereas TRUNC and ROUNDDOWN round down towards the number 0, INT always rounds down in a negative direction. The syntax of INT is:

INT(number)

Figure 11.10 illustrates INT with two examples.

	A	B	C
1	Value	Formula	Formula Result
2	23.4	=INT(A2)	23
3	-23.4	=INT(A3)	-24
4	-23.4	=TRUNC(A4)	-23

Figure 11.10
The INT function.
Source: Microsoft® Corporation.

The INT function in row 2 shows the effect of the function on a positive number. It rounds down towards 0, eliminating all decimal places. In row 3, the INT function is applied to a negative number. This rounds the value –23.4 down to the next lowest integer value, which in this case is –24. Row 4 shows the equivalent formula with the TRUNC function. Unlike INT, the TRUNC function rounds down toward the number 0, resulting in a value of –23.

The final rounding functions we'll examine are MROUND, CEILING, and FLOOR. MROUND rounds to a specified multiple. This, for example, allows you to round a number to the closest multiple of 5. CEILING is the same as MROUND, except that it rounds up towards the nearest multiple, and away from the number 0. Similarly,

FLOOR is the same as MROUND, except that it rounds down towards the closest multiple, and towards the number 0. The syntax of these functions is:

MROUND(number, multiple)

CEILING(number, significance)

FLOOR(number, significance)

In the MROUND function, the *multiple* argument denotes the multiple to which to round. If the number is positive, the *multiple* must also be positive or zero. Likewise, the *multiple* must be negative or zero for negative numbers. For CEILING and FLOOR, the *significance* arguments mean essentially the same thing as the *multiple* argument in MROUND. If the *number* is positive, the *significance* must be positive or zero. However, CEILING and FLOOR allow for any *significance* value for negative numbers. Figure 11.11 illustrates these functions with a few examples.

	A	B	C
1	Value	Formula	Formula Result
2	32	=MROUND(A2, 5)	30
3	17.5	=MROUND(A3, 2)	18
4	38.488	=MROUND(A4, 0.1)	38.5
5	-32	=MROUND(A5, -5)	-30
6	50	=MROUND(A6, 0)	0
7	32	=CEILING(A7, 5)	35
8	32.41	=CEILING(A8, 0.05)	32.45
9	38	=FLOOR(A9, 10)	30

Figure 11.11

MROUND, CEILING, and FLOOR functions.

Source: Microsoft® Corporation.

The MROUND function in row 2 rounds 32 to the nearest multiple of 5, which is 30. In row 3, the value 17.5 is rounded to the closest multiple of 2, which is 18. This is like rounding to the nearest even number. Row 4 rounds 38.488 to the nearest multiple of .1. This has the effect of rounding to one decimal place. In row 5, we round a negative number to a negative multiple. Row 6 illustrates the fact that rounding to a multiple of 0 always produces a result of 0. Thus, this is a meaningless operation. Rows 7 and 8 illustrate the CEILING function. In row 7, 32 is rounded up to the next highest multiple of 5, which is 35. In row 8, we're rounding 32.41 up to the nearest multiple of .05. If you think of the value 32.41 as money, this is like rounding up to the nearest nickel. Finally, row 9 illustrates the FLOOR function, rounding 38 down to a multiple of 10.

Unit Conversion

Excel provides an interesting function, named CONVERT, that allows you to convert one unit of measurement to another. This has applications for a wide variety of measurement types, including distance, weight, time, temperature, volume, area, and speed. For example, this function can convert yards to meters, Celsius to Fahrenheit, or liters to quarts. The types of measurements that can be converted are:

- WEIGHT AND MASS
- DISTANCE
- TIME
- PRESSURE
- FORCE
- ENERGY
- POWER
- MAGNETISM
- TEMPERATURE
- VOLUME
- AREA
- INFORMATION
- SPEED

The full list of each available unit of measurement that be converted can be found by invoking Excel's Help on the function. Each unit of measurement has its own abbreviation. The syntax of the function is:

CONVERT(number, from_unit, to_unit)

Consider these two examples:

CONVERT(30, "m", "ft")
CONVERT(30, B2, C2)

The first example will convert the number 30 from meters (m) to feet (ft). The abbreviations that can be used are found in Excel's Help on the function. The second example will convert the value 30 from the unit of measurement in cell B2 to the unit of measurement in cell C2. Figure 11.12 provides a few additional examples.

	A	B	C	D	E
1	Value	Original Unit of Measure	New Unit of Measure	Formula	Formula Result
2	25	ft	m	=CONVERT(A2, B2, C2)	7.62
3	68	F	C	=CONVERT(A3, B3, C3)	20
4	2000	ft2	m2	=CONVERT(A4, B4, C4)	185.80608
5	5	gal	L	=CONVERT(A5, B5, C5)	18.92705892
6	6105	mn	hr	=CONVERT(A6, B6, C6)	101.75

Figure 11.12

The CONVERT function.

Source: Microsoft® Corporation.

The CONVERT function in row 2 converts 25 feet (ft) to 7.62 meters (m). Row 3 converts 68 degrees Fahrenheit (F) to Celsius (C). In row 4, we're converting square feet (ft2) to square meters (m2). Row 5 converts gallons (gal) to liters (L). Finally, row 6 has a time conversion, translating minutes (mm) to hours (hr).

Financial Analysis

Excel provides more than 50 functions pertaining to financial analysis. The level of financial acumen that would be necessary to discuss these functions in detail is beyond the scope of this book. However, even for the general business analyst, it's useful to have a basic understanding of what some of these functions can accomplish. As such, we'll run through an explanation of these basic financial functions:

- PMT
- RATE
- PV
- NPER
- FV

The first four functions, PMT, RATE, PV, and NPER deal with a basic financial situation where there is a payment made over a specified number of periods for some initial investment or loan amount. A constant rate of interest is applied to all these payments. Thus, there are four variables in the equation: the payment, the interest rate, the present value of the loan or investment, and the number of periods. Each of these four functions solves for one of these variables, given that the other three variables are known. The PMT function solves for the payment amount, given a known interest rate, present value, and number of periods. The RATE function calculates the interest rate for a specified payment amount, present value, and number of periods. The PV function computes what the present value of the loan or investment must be, given a known payment amount, interest rate, and number of periods. Finally, NPER solves for the number of periods, given a known payment amount, interest rate, and present value.

The syntax of the PMT function is:

PMT(rate, nper, pv, [fv], [type])

The *rate, nper,* and *pv* arguments specify, respectively, the interest rate per period, number of periods, and present value of the loan. The *fv* argument is an optional argument that specifies a future value that you would like after all payments are made. If omitted, it is assumed to be zero. *Type* is another optional argument that indicates whether payments are due at the beginning or end of each period. If omitted, the function assumes the end of the period. Figure 11.13 illustrates this function with a few examples.

	A	B	C	D	E	F
1	Annual Rate	Periods	Present Value	Payment Formula	Payment	Total Payments
2	6.0%	36	-10000	=PMT(A2/12, B2, C2)	304.22	10951.90
3	4.0%	36	-10000	=PMT(A3/12, B3, C3)	295.24	10628.63
4	6.0%	48	-10000	=PMT(A4/12, B4, C4)	234.85	11272.81

Figure 11.13

The PMT function.

Source: Microsoft® Corporation.

In this figure, the payment formula is in column D, and the result of that formula is in column E. The formula references values in columns A, B, and C. Column F contains an additional calculation that multiples the number of periods (column B) by the resulting payment (column E) to produce the total payment amount for the loan. The PMT function in row 2 is for a loan at 6% annual interest over 36 months, with a loan amount of 10,000. The formula in column D uses the annual rate of interest in column A and divides it by 12 to yield the interest rate per month. The second argument in the formula, B2, is the number of periods. The third argument, C2, is the present value. The present value is expressed as a negative number since this is a loan being subtracted from one's net worth. The resulting payment produced by the formula is 304.22. The calculation in column F indicates that person will be paying 10,951.90 over the course of the loan, as reimbursement for the 10,000 that was borrowed.

Row 3 changes the scenario to reduce the interest rate to 4%. This has the effect of reducing the payment to 295.24, and total payments to 10,628.63. In row 4, the term of the loan in row 2 is increased from 36 to 48 months. This reduces the payment to 234.85 but increases total payments over the course of the loan to 11,272.81.

The RATE function allows one to determine what interest rate must be obtained to borrow a specified amount of money at a certain interest rate over a set period of time. The syntax of this function is:

RATE(nper, pmt, pv, [fv], [type], [guess])

As with PMT, the optional *fv* argument allows you to specify a future value, and *type* lets you state when the payment is due. The *guess* argument is rarely needed and can be safely ignored. Figure 11.14 illustrates this function.

	A	B	C	D	E
1	Periods	Payment	Present Value	Annual Rate Formula	Annual Rate
2	36	304.22	-10000	=RATE(A2, B2, C2) * 12	6.0%
3	36	295.24	-10000	=RATE(A3, B3, C3) * 12	4.0%

Figure 11.14

The RATE function.

Source: Microsoft® Corporation.

Row 2 of Figure 11.14 reproduces the same data as row 2 of Figure 11.13, except that this time we're solving for the interest rate. The three arguments in the RATE function are the values in columns A, B, and C—namely, the number of periods, the payment amount, and the present value of the loan. Since the RATE function produces the interest rate per period, we must multiply the result by 12 to obtain the annual interest rate. As seen, the result of the calculation is 6%. Row 3 relates to row 3 of Figure 11.13, taking the same situation of a loan amount of 10,000 over 36 months with a payment of 295.24. The RATE function shows that the implied interest rate for this loan is 4%.

The PV function determines the present value of a loan or investment. Its syntax is:

PV(rate, nper, pmt, [fv], [type])

The meaning of its arguments is the same as with PMT and RATE. Figure 11.15 provides two examples.

	A	B	C	D	E
1	Annual Rate	Periods	Payment	Present Value Formula	Present Value
2	6.0%	36	304.22	=PV(A2/12, B2, C2)	-10000.02
3	6.0%	48	300.00	=PV(A3/12, B3, C3)	-12774.10

Figure 11.15

The PV function.

Source: Microsoft® Corporation.

The PV function in row 2 has the same scenario as row 2 in Figures 11.13 and 11.14, except that this time the unknown is the present value. For a 6% loan for 36 months, making payments of 304.22, the corresponding loan amount is 10,000. Note that the loan amount is actually 10000.02, but this difference is due to rounding differences. The PV function is useful in situations where you know what interest rate is available and the payments you can afford, and would like to know how large of a loan can be obtained with those terms. In row 3, we've presented this type of scenario where a payment of 300 for 48 months at 6% interest is specified. The result tells us that the loan that can be obtained with those terms is 12,774.10.

The NPER function computes the number of periods for an investment or loan when the loan amount, payment amount, and interest rate are known. The syntax is:

NPER(rate, pmt, pv, [fv], [type])

These are the same arguments seen in PMT, RATE, and PV. An example of this function is shown in Figure 11.16.

	A	B	C	D	E
1	Annual Rate	Payment	Present Value	Periods Formula	Periods
2	6.0%	304.22	-10000	=NPER(A2/12,B2,C2)	36

Figure 11.16

The NPER function.

Source: Microsoft® Corporation.

Using the same example seen in row 2 of Figures 11.13, 11.14, and 11.15, we're now calculating the number of periods needed for a loan of 10,000 at 6% interest with a monthly payment of 304.22. The result of 36 periods corresponds to the prior examples.

The final financial function we'll discuss is FV, which computes the future value of an investment of period payments with a constant interest rate. The arguments are identical to those in the PV function, except that the *pv* and *fv* arguments are reversed. The syntax of FV is:

FV(rate, nper, pmt, [pv], [type])

The optional *pv* argument lets you specify an amount that the future value of the stream of payments is worth at the present. If omitted, the present value is assumed to be zero. Figure 11.17 gives a few examples of FV.

	A	B	C	D	E	F
1	Annual Rate	Periods	Payment	Future Value Formula	Future Value	Total Gain
2	3.0%	36	-300.00	=FV(A2/12, B2, C2)	11286.17	486.17
3	5.0%	36	-300.00	=FV(A3/12, B3, C3)	11626.00	826.00
4	5.0%	72	-300.00	=FV(A4/12, B4, C4)	25129.28	3529.28
5	5.0%	72	-300.00	=FV(A5/12, B5, C5, -5000)	31874.37	10274.37

Figure 11.17

The FV function.

Source: Microsoft® Corporation.

The FV function in row 2 calculates the future value of a series of investments, where there are 36 monthly payments of 300, earning 3% annual interest. The FV formula, shown in column D, divides the annual rate in column A by 12 as the *rate* argument. The *nper* argument is from column B, and the *pmt* argument is from column C. Note that the payment is a negative amount, indicating that this is outflow of cash for the investor. The result, shown in column E, is 11,286.17. Column F calculates the total gain from the investment. The formula in cell F2 is:

=E2 – (B2 * C2 * –1)

This multiplies the payment by the number of periods, and subtracts it from the future value of this stream of payments to see the total gain. Note that the payment is multiplied by –1 to adjust for the negative value in column C. This calculation indicates that the investor has gained 486.17 from this series of investments.

The data in row 3 is the same, except that the interest rate has been increased to 5%. This results in a larger future value and total gain. In row 4, the interest rate remains at 5%, but the time period is doubled from 36 to 72 months. This results in a much larger future value and corresponding total gain. In row 5, we've added a value for the optional *pv* argument, indicating an initial amount of 5000 in the investment stream. This again increases both the future value and total gain, since that 5000 was an additional amount that earns interest during that 72-month time period.

This survey of financial functions is merely a small sampling of available functions but should give an idea of how they work. The essence of financial functions is that they solve a complex equation for one variable, given known values for other variables.

Dates and Time

In order to make the most out of Excel date and time functions, one first needs to understand how Excel stores dates. All dates and times in Excel are stored as a number. For example, when the date 4/1/2012 is entered into a cell, it is automatically converted and stored as the number 41000. This number is referred to as a *serial number*. The meaning of the number is the number of days that have elapsed since the start of the year 1900. Thus, the date 4/1/2012 is the forty-one thousandth day since Jan 1, 1900. Actually, if you were extremely conscientious and did the arithmetic, you might discover that the number is off by one. This is due to a known bug in Excel that counts 2/29/1900 as a day, even though 1900 wasn't a leap year. In fairness to Microsoft, though, the anecdotal story goes that this was an intentional "feature" that was put in place in the early days of Excel to maintain consistency with a bug that was present in Lotus 1-2-3.

Just as dates are represented as serial numbers, times are represented as the decimal portion of a number. The decimal represents the percent of time that has elapsed in the 24-hour period starting at midnight. Thus, the decimal .5 represents halfway through the day, or 12 PM. The decimal .25 represents one-fourth through the day, or 6 AM. Putting date and times together, if the date Aug 13, 2013 is represented by the serial number 41499, then the serial number 41499.75 represents 6 PM on 8/13/2013.

The serial numbers stored in Excel to represent dates aren't normally visible, unless you explicitly change the format of a date from the Date format to General or Number. The best way to view the serial number of a date is to change the cell to the General format. This displays the number with the correct number of decimal places if there's a time element involved. In terms of how Excel displays dates and times, there are many options. From the Home tab on the Ribbon, Excel provides a drop-down in the Number group of commands that allows you to select Short Date, Long Date, or Time. Additionally, if you right-click on a cell and select the Format Cells contextual command, you can select a Date format, and then choose from numerous date and time formats. If you select the Custom format, you can design your own format using codes such as m or mm for month, yy or yyyy for year, and so on. Excel Help can be consulted for a complete list of available codes. Figure 11.18 illustrates some of the possibilities of how dates can be displayed.

⬚	A	B
1	Value	Format
2	41489	General
3	8/3/2013	Short Date
4	Saturday, August 03, 2013	Long Date
5	08/03/2013	mm/dd/yyyy
6	Aug-2013	mmm-yyyy
7	Sat, Aug 03, 2013	ddd, mmm dd, yyyy

Figure 11.18

Date formats.

Source: Microsoft® Corporation.

In Figure 11.18, we entered the number 41489 in cell A2, and then copied that value to cells A3 through A7. We then modified the format of cells A3 through A7 to the formats indicated in column B. Thus, cell A2 uses the General format. Because of this, it displays 41489 as a number. Cell 3 is in the Short Date format. This has the effect of displaying the number 41489 as a date. Cell A4 uses the Long Date format, which spells out the day of week and month. Cells A5, A6, and A7 use custom formats. The codes shown in column B specify a format for the date. For example, whereas mm causes a two-digit month to be displayed, mmm causes a three-character month abbreviation to be displayed.

The first date and time functions that we'll discuss are:

- TODAY
- NOW
- DATEVALUE
- TIMEVALUE

The TODAY function returns the current date. It has no arguments. Similarly, the NOW function returns the current date and time. The DATEVALUE function can be used to convert a date in a text format to a serial date in the Excel format. This function is often needed when importing dates from an external database. Similarly, the TIMEVALUE function converts the time in a text format to a serial date in the Excel format. Before Excel can utilize any date or time functions with a date, the date must be in the Excel serial date format. The syntax of these four functions is:

TODAY()

NOW()

DATEVALUE(date_text)

TIMEVALUE(time_text)

The TODAY and NOW functions have no arguments. The DATEVALUE and TIME-VALUE have a single argument, being the text value of the date or time. Figure 11.19 provides examples of each function.

	A	B	C
1	Formula	Formula Result	Format of Result
2	=TODAY()	5/15/2013	Short Date
3	=NOW()	5/15/2013 21:36	Custom
4	=DATEVALUE("07/15/2013")	41470	General
5	=TIMEVALUE("7/15/2013 19:21")	0.80625	General

Figure 11.19
TODAY, NOW, DATEVALUE, and TIMEVALUE functions.
Source: Microsoft® Corporation.

In row 2, the TODAY function returns the current date, which was 5/15/2013 at the time the function was executed. The result in column B is shown in the Short Date format. Similarly, the NOW function returns the full date and time, indicating that the time was 9:36 PM. The formula is in a custom format, displaying both the date and time. The DATEVALUE function in row 4 converts the text value "07/15/2013" to an Excel serial date. The result is shown in the General format, so it displays as a number. If we were to switch the format of cell B4 to the short date format, it would display as 07/15/2013. Finally, the TIMEVALUE function in row 5 converts a full date and time text value to the time portion of an Excel serial date. Note that the function ignored the supplied date and converted only the time.

With these preliminaries under our belt, we can now turn to some functions that can assist with date calculations. The next functions we'll examine are:

- YEAR
- MONTH
- DAY
- HOUR
- MINUTE
- SECOND

The purpose of these functions is to take an Excel date or time and extract the component of that date that's of interest. For example, the MONTH function analyzes a date and returns a number between 1 and 12 that represents the month. As will be seen, this functionality is often needed to perform calculations with Excel dates. For example, we may want to add three months to the current date. These functions will assist in that endeavor. The syntax of these functions is:

YEAR(serial_number)

MONTH(serial_number)

DAY(serial_number)

HOUR(serial_number)

MINUTE(serial_number)

SECOND(serial_number)

As seen, all six functions require only one argument, which contains the serial number of the date. Actually, though, these functions also work if you supply a date as a text value. The YEAR function returns a four-digit number representing the year. This is a number greater than or equal to 1900. The MONTH function returns a number between 1 and 12. The DAY function returns a number between 1 and 31. HOUR returns a number between 0 and 23. The MINUTE and SECOND functions return a number between 0 and 59. Figure 11.20 shows examples of the YEAR, MONTH, and DAY functions. The HOUR, MINUTE, and SECOND functions work in a similar fashion.

	A	B	C
1	Value	Formula	Formula Result
2	7/20/2014	=YEAR(A2)	2014
3	41840	=YEAR(A3)	2014
4	7/20/2014	=MONTH(A4)	7
5	7/20/2014	=DAY(A5)	20

Figure 11.20
YEAR, MONTH, and DAY functions.
Source: Microsoft® Corporation.

In row 2, the YEAR function is applied to the date in cell A2. The result is 2014. Row 3 does the same calculation against the number 41840. As it happens, 41840 is the serial number that Excel uses to represent and store the date 7/20/2014, so we get the same result. The argument for the YEAR, MONTH, and DAY functions can be either a serial number or a text date. Row 4 illustrates the MONTH function with the same date. The result is 7, representing July. In row 5, the DAY function returns the value 20.

Up to this point, we haven't yet transformed dates in any meaningful way. The next set of functions will allow you to perform date calculations and do what's referred to as *date arithmetic*. The functions are:

- DATE
- TIME

The DATE function returns a date from specified year, month, and day values. Similarly, the TIME function returns a time from an hour, minute, and second. The syntax of these functions is:

DATE(year, month, day)

TIME(hour, minute, second)

The use of the DATE function will be apparent from the examples shown in Figure 11.21. The TIME function works in a similar manner.

	A	B	C	D	E
1	Year	Month	Day	Formula	Formula Result
2	2014	6	23	=DATE(A2, B2, C2)	6/23/2014
3	2014	6	23	=DATE(A3, B3 - 2, C3)	4/23/2014
4	2014	6	23	=DATE(A4, B4, C4 + 10)	7/3/2014
5	2014	6	23	=DATE(A5, B5 + 1, C5 + 1)	7/24/2014
6	2014	6	23	=DATE(A6, B6, 1)	6/1/2014
7	2014	6	23	=DATE(A7, B7 + 1, 1) - 1	6/30/2014

Figure 11.21

The DATE function.

Source: Microsoft® Corporation.

In Figure 11.21, we first split the date 6/23/2014 into three separate columns with the year, month, and day. The DATE function in row 2 uses the year, month, and day as is to create the date. The value in cell E2 is a trivial result, since we're merely reassembling the individual components of a date back into a full date. In row 3, we apply some arithmetic to the month argument, subtracting 2 from the month. This transforms the date 6/23/2014 to 4/23/2014. Row 3 adds 10 days to the original date, resulting in 7/3/2014. Note that Excel is smart enough to know that there are only 30 days in June. In row 5, we're adding 1 to the month and also 1 to the day. This results in a date that's one month and one day after the original date. Row 6 shows how to calculate the first day of a month. This is accomplished by specifying the value 1 for the *day* argument. Finally, row 7 returns the last day of the month. This is carried out by adding 1 to the *month* argument, and specifying 1 as the day. This produces the first day of the next month. We then subtract 1 from that result, which gives the last day of the current month.

Of course, the demonstration of the DATE function in Figure 11.21 is somewhat unrealistic, in that we would not normally have a situation where the date is already split into the year, month, and day. That's where the YEAR, MONTH, and DAY functions come in. Figure 11.22 shows the same data as in Figure 11.21, except that this time we've specified a single date as the input, and rely on nested functions to calculate the result.

	A	B	C
1	Date	Formula	Formula Result
2	6/23/2013	=DATE(YEAR(A2), MONTH(A2), DAY(A2))	6/23/2013
3	6/23/2013	=DATE(YEAR(A3), MONTH(A3) - 2, DAY(A3))	4/23/2013
4	6/23/2014	=DATE(YEAR(A4), MONTH(A4), DAY(A4) + 10)	7/3/2014
5	6/23/2014	=DATE(YEAR(A5), MONTH(A5) + 1, DAY(A5) + 1)	7/24/2014
6	6/23/2014	=DATE(YEAR(A6), MONTH(A6), 1)	6/1/2014
7	6/23/2014	=DATE(YEAR(A7), MONTH(A7) + 1, 1) - 1	6/30/2014

Figure 11.22
The DATE function with nested functions.
Source: Microsoft® Corporation.

As can be seen, the results in Figure 11.22 are identical to those in Figure 11.21. To understand the difference between the formulas, let's examine the formulas in row 5 of both tables. The formula in Figure 11.22 substitutes the function YEAR(A5) for the A5 of Figure 11.21, MONTH(A5) for B5, and DAY(A5) for C5. Thus, the formulas in Figure 11.21 use nested functions to first parse out the year, month, and day of the date, and then perform appropriate arithmetic before invoking the DATE function to put the date back together.

If you simply want to add or subtract days from a date, you don't need to use the YEAR, MONTH, and DAY functions used in Figure 11.22. Since Excel stores all dates as numbers, you can simply add or subtract a number from any date to add or subtract that number of days. For example, since the date 2/1/2014 is stored as the serial number 41671, you can add 3 days to 2/1/2014 by simply adding 3 to the date. This will result in the number 41674, which is displayed as 2/4/2014. Similarly, you can determine the number of days between any two dates by simply subtracting one date from the other. Since both dates are stored as numbers, this is a simple arithmetic operation which produces a number as the result. Figure 11.23 illustrates these concepts with a few calculations.

	A	B	C	D
1	Date 1	Date 2	Formula	Formula Result
2	4/25/2014		=A2 + 10	5/5/2014
3	4/25/2014		=A3 - 20	4/5/2014
4	4/25/2014	5/5/2014	=B4 - A4	10
5	4/25/2014	5/5/2014	=A5 - B5	-10
6	4/25/2014	5/5/2014	=ABS(A6 - B6)	10

Figure 11.23

Date arithmetic.

Source: Microsoft® Corporation.

The formula in row 2 adds 10 to the date in column A. As mentioned, this calculation doesn't require a function, since all dates are stored internally as numbers. Similarly, the calculation in row 3 subtracts 20 days from the 4/25/2014, yielding 4/5/2014. Rows 4 and 5 show how to find the difference between two dates. In row 4, we're subtracting the date in A4 from the date in B4. Excel does the calculation and returns the value 10. In row 5, we're doing the subtraction in reverse, producing a negative value. Since a negative value may not be desirable, row 6 indicates how to correct that problem, by using the ABS function to take the absolute value of the result. The ABS function guarantees that you'll get a positive number for the difference between two dates, regardless of which date is first.

Looking Ahead

This chapter covered a lot of somewhat varied ground on the use of numeric and date functions. We began with a look at a number of basic arithmetic functions involving multiplication, division, absolute value, exponents, and logarithms. We paid particular attention to the value of logs as it pertains to values expressing a rate of change, and illustrated the relationship between log values and the logarithmic scales available in Excel charts. The next set of functions we examined involved rounding and truncation operations. We explained how to round up and down, as well as how to round to a specified multiple, such as the multiple of 5. We then turned to a brief discussion of an interesting function, CONVERT, that lets you perform unit conversion on a wide variety of unit types, such as distance, weight, and time. Our next topic, financial analysis, provided a brief introduction to the myriad number of ways that interest rates, payments, number of periods, and present and future values can be calculated. The financial functions utilize complex formulas to let you solve for a single value when certain other pieces of financial data are known. Finally, we ended the chapter with a look at date and time functions. We emphasized the importance of understanding that Excel stores all dates and times as numbers. As such, we are able to take advantage of that fact when doing date arithmetic. The most significant function discussed was the DATE function, which, when used in combination with YEAR, MONTH, and DAY, lets you perform complex date calculations.

In our next chapter, "Aggregate and Statistical Functions," we'll take numeric functions to the next level by discussing how powerful aggregate functions can summarize data in a variety of ways. In doing so, we return to the summarization capabilities previously seen in pivot tables, but now applied via functions. We'll also discuss functions that deal with descriptive statistics, such as measures of variability.

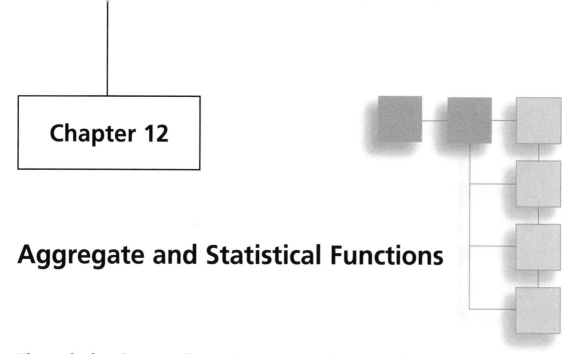

Chapter 12

Aggregate and Statistical Functions

The goal of analysis usually involves a summarization of data in some manner. In Chapter 6, "Pivot Table Calculations," we saw how summarization can be applied to pivot tables via sums, counts, averages, min, max, and more. This same type of quantitative summarization can be applied to worksheet data via a wide variety of functions. The generic term for this type of analysis is *aggregation*. Aggregate functions allow the analyst to apply basic quantitative techniques in order to group or summarize data. The functions discussed in this chapter are found in both the Math & Trig, and the Statistical groups of functions on the Ribbon, under the Formulas tab. Excel categorizes SUM functions in the Math & Trig category but places most of the other functions in this chapter in the Statistical category.

In addition to basic aggregate functions, we'll extend the topic to include some basic statistical functions such as those that compute percentiles, variability, and correlation. This is done to provide you with just a small taste of what can be done with statistics. The general area of statistics is often divided into descriptive statistics and inferential statistics. The topics that we'll touch upon fall firmly under the domain of descriptive statistics. An adequate explanation of inferential statistics lies beyond the scope of this book. For that, you may refer to other texts that deal primarily with statistics.

Sums

The most widely used of all the summarization functions is the SUM function. While simple in concept, the SUM function satisfies the common task of adding up quantities of numbers. We'll discuss three variations of this function:

- SUM
- SUMIF
- SUMIFS

The syntax of the SUM function is:

SUM(number1, [number2], …)

The argument for this function occurs at least once, and can be repeated multiple times. Each argument can be a constant, a cell reference, a range, or a formula. Figure 12.1 illustrates the different ways that the function can be specified. This figure has two ranges of numbers, in columns A and B. We've also defined three names for this worksheet in the Name Manager: VALUES_1 represents cells A2:A6, VALUES_2 represents B2:B6, and ALL_VALUES is for A2:B6.

	A	B	C	D	E
1	Values 1	Values 2		Formula	Formula Result
2	5	2		=SUM(A2:A6)	60
3	5	8		=SUM(A2, A3, A4, A5, A6)	60
4	20	6		=SUM(5, 5, 20, 30)	60
5	cat	dog		=A2 + A3 + A4 + A6	60
6	30	4		=SUM(A2, A3:A6)	60
7				=SUM(A2:B6)	80
8				=SUM(VALUES_1)	60
9				=SUM(VALUES_1, VALUES_2)	80
10				=SUM(ALL_VALUES)	80

Figure 12.1

The SUM function.

Source: Microsoft® Corporation.

In Figure 12.1, as well as in subsequent figures in this chapter, we continue our practice of placing formulas under the Formula Result column, and the text of the formula under the Formula column, allowing you to see both the formula and its result. The SUM function in row 2 sums up values from cells A2 to A6. This results in the value 60. Since the SUM function sums up only numeric quantities, the value "cat" in row 5 is ignored. Row 3 illustrates the fact that these same five values can be indicated as individual arguments in the function, and produce the same output. Row 4 shows that the values can be specified as constants rather than as cell references. In row 5, we've shown the same calculation without the use of the SUM function. While plausible for just a few values, this type of formula would be unwieldy if there were many more values to add.

Row 6 indicates that the SUM function can handle both a cell reference and a range of values. Since these arguments refer to the same cells as before, we get the same outcome. Row 7 sums up all cells in columns A and B, covering the array from A2 to B6. Rows 8, 9, and 10 utilize the names that were set in the Name Manager. Row 8 sums up column A, and rows 9 and 10 each sum up all numbers in columns A and B.

The SUMIF and SUMIFS functions allow the analyst to inject logic into the determination as to what cells are summed. The syntax of these two functions is:

SUMIF(range, criteria, [sum_range])

SUMIFS(sum_range, criteria_range1, criteria1, ...)

For the SUMIF function, the *range* argument specifies the range of cells to be evaluated. The *criteria* argument has the logical expression that's applied to that range. The *sum_range* argument is optional. If specified, then the range to be summed is the *sum_range*. Otherwise, the range that's summed is the *range* argument. The SUMIFS function is similar, except that you always use the *sum_range* argument to specify the range to be summed. It can have multiple *criteria_range* and *criteria* arguments. The data in Figure 12.2 illustrates both of these functions.

	A	B	C	D	E	F
1	Sale Price	Commission	State		Formula	Formula Result
2	500	50	CA		=SUMIF(A2:A6, ">= 200")	1400
3	250	45	NV		=SUMIF(A2:A6, ">= 200", B2:B6)	180
4	300	25	AZ		=SUMIF(C2:C6, "CA", A2:A6)	850
5	350	60	CA		=SUMIFS(A2:A6, C2:C6, "AZ", B2:B6, ">= 25")	300
6	150	5	AZ			

Figure 12.2

SUMIF and SUMIFS functions.

Source: Microsoft® Corporation.

In Figure 12.2, each row in columns A, B, and C represents a sales price and commission paid for a specific item. Column C shows the state where the sale took place. The SUMIF function in row 2 uses A2:A6 as the *range* argument and >= 200 as the *criteria* to be applied to that range. This specifies to sum only those cells where the Sale Price is greater than or equal to 200. The result is 1400, which is the sum of all cells in column A except A6. The formula in row 3 is the same, except that we're adding the range B2:B6 as the *sum_range* argument. This means that we want to sum up only those commission amounts where the corresponding sales price was greater than or equal to 200. The result of 180 is the sum of all rows in column B except row 6. In row 4, we're summing up the Sales Price amounts, where the State equals California (CA). Finally, row 5 illustrates the SUMIFS function. In this formula, we're summing the values in column A where the State equals Arizona (AZ) and the Commission is greater than or equal to 25. The only cell that satisfies both of these criteria is A4, so the result is 300.

Counts

Sometimes, one simply wants to count values rather than sum them. This arises in situations where the analyst wants to count responses, or count rows where some criteria are met in a value or values in that row. These situations are handled by the COUNT function and its variants. The functions we'll look at that deal with counts are:

- COUNT
- COUNTA
- COUNTBLANK
- COUNTIF
- COUNTIFS

The basic COUNT function counts cells in a specified range that contain numbers. COUNTA counts any cells in a range where the cell isn't empty. COUNTBLANK counts blank cells that are empty. The COUNTIF and COUNTIFS functions are similar to SUMIF and SUMIFS, in that they count cells that meet one or more criteria. The syntax of the COUNT, COUNTA, and COUNTBLANK functions is:

COUNT(value1, [value2], …)
COUNTA(value1, [value2], …)
COUNTBLANK(range)

These three functions are illustrated in Figure 12.3.

	A	B	C	D	E
1	Values 1	Values 2		Formula	Formula Result
2	5	2		=COUNT(A2:A6)	3
3	5	8		=COUNTA(A2:A6)	4
4	cat	6		=COUNTBLANK(A2:A6)	1
5		dog		=COUNT(A2:B6)	7
6	30	4			

Figure 12.3
COUNT, COUNTA, and COUNTBLANK functions.
Source: Microsoft® Corporation.

The COUNT function in row 2 counts all numeric quantities in cells A2 to A6. The result is 3. In contrast, the COUNTA function in row 3 includes all cells, unless they are empty. The output of this function is 4, since the value "cat" is now counted. In row 4, the COUNTBLANK function counts only empty cells. The result is 1, for the blank cell in A5. Finally, the COUNT function in row 5 counts the numeric quantities in the array from A2 to B6. There are 7 of these cells.

The COUNTIF and COUNTIFS functions are similar to the SUMIF and SUMIFS functions except that they don't differentiate between the criteria range and a range to count. The syntax of these functions is:

COUNTIF(range, criteria)

COUNTIFS(criteria_range1, criteria1, ...)

Figure 12.4 provides examples of COUNTIF and COUNTIFS.

	A	B	C	D	E	F
1	Sale Price	Commission	State		Formula	Formula Result
2	500	50	CA		=COUNTIF(A2:A6, ">= 200")	4
3	250	45	NV		=COUNTIF(C2:C6, "CA")	2
4	300	25	AZ		=COUNTIFS(C2:C6, "AZ", B2:B6, ">=25")	1
5	350	60	CA			
6	150	5	AZ			

Figure 12.4

COUNTIF and COUNTIFS functions.

Source: Microsoft® Corporation.

Figure 12.4 has the same data previously seen in Figure 12.2. In row 2, the COUNTIF function counts cells in column A with a value greater than or equal to 200. The result is 4. Row 3 counts cells in C2:C6 where the state equals California (CA). In row 4, the COUNTIFS function has two sets of criteria, both of which must be met for the row to be counted. First the State in C2:C6 must equal Arizona (AZ), and second, the Commission in B2:B6 must be greater than or equal to 25. Only one row satisfies both criteria.

Averages

The ability to compute an average logically follows sum and count functions, since an average is nothing more than the sum of a set of numbers divided by the count of those numbers. In statistics, averages are usually referred to as a *measure of central tendency*. For a given set of numbers, the average indicates the central point of those values. In statistical terms, however, there are really three possibilities for computing an average: the mean, the median, and the mode. What's commonly referred to as an average is called the *mean* in statistics. This is the sum of the numbers divided by the count of those numbers. The *median* is the number that represents the middle value of the set. The *mode* is the number (or numbers) that occur most frequently. Excel provides functions for all three of these types of averages. The functions we'll examine are:

- AVERAGE
- AVERAGEA
- MEDIAN
- MODE.SNGL
- MODE.MULT
- AVERAGEIF
- AVERAGEIFS

The syntax of the first three of these functions is:

AVERAGE(number1, [number2], …)
AVERAGEA(value1, [value2], …)
MEDIAN(number1, [number2], …)

As with the SUM and COUNT functions, these three functions must contain at least one argument, but they can have more. Each argument can be a constant, cell reference, range, or formula. Both AVERAGE and AVERAGEA will sum up only numbers in the indicated range or ranges. However, AVERAGEA will also include any cells that have nonnumeric values in the count. The MEDIAN function finds the midpoint of all indicated numbers. The numbers do not have to be in a sorted order. Excel will internally arrange the numbers in sequence to determine the midpoint. If there is an even number of numbers, then there will not be a single midpoint. In that case, MEDIAN will take an average of the two numbers closest to the middle. Figure 12.5 illustrates these functions.

◢	A	B	C	D
1	Value		Formula	Formula Result
2	5		=AVERAGE(A2:A8)	7
3	3		=SUM(A2:A8) / COUNT(A2:A8)	7
4	5		=AVERAGEA(A2:A8)	6
5	7		=MEDIAN(A2:A8)	6
6	apple			
7	12			
8	10			

Figure 12.5

AVERAGE, AVERAGEA, and MEDIAN functions.

Source: Microsoft® Corporation.

The AVERAGE function in row 2 takes a simple average of the numbers in the range from A2 to A8. The text value in cell A6 is ignored. The sum of the numbers is 42 and there are 6 numbers, so the average is 7. The formula in row 3 shows how an average can be restated as the sum of the numbers divided by the count. The result is the same. In row 4, the AVERAGEA function includes the text value in A6 in its count of numbers. The average is computed as 6, since the sum is still 42, but there are now 7 cells in the count. The AVERAGEA function can be useful when you want to include non-responses in an average, such as the situation when a student doesn't take a test, but you still want to count that non-event in his average score. The MEDIAN function in row 5 finds the middle value. Since there are six numbers, the middle values are the third and fourth numbers when the numbers are arranged in sequence. These are 5 and 7. The median is displayed as 6, since the average of 5 and 7 is 6.

Excel provides two functions that compute the mode: MODE.SNGL and MODE.MULT. You may also notice a MODE function in Excel, but this is referred to as a *compatibility* function, meaning that it was replaced by another function and hence may become obsolete in the future. With Excel 2010, Microsoft introduced the MODE.SNGL and MODE.MULT functions to replace MODE, although MODE.SNGL is actually identical to MODE. The suffixes stand for *single* and *multiple*. Their syntax is:

MODE.SNGL(number1, [number2], …)

MODE.MULT(number1, [number2], …)

The reason for these two versions is that the mode can sometimes consist of more than one number. Let's say that our sequence of numbers is: 3, 3, 5, 10, 10, 15. The mode is defined as the number that occurs most frequently in a set of data. However, there can easily be more than one mode. In this case, there are two modes: 3 and 10. Unlike with the median, we can't simply take an average of these numbers, since that would have no real meaning. In the case of multiple modes, it only makes sense to list them all.

The MODE.SNGL lists only one mode, even if there is more than one. The MODE.MULT function can list more than one mode, if necessary. However, to list more than one mode, the MODE.MULT function requires that the function be entered as an *array formula*, which refers to a special way of entering a formula in Excel. When a formula is entered in Excel, it normally produces a single output, and it places that value in the same cell where the formula resides. In contrast, array formulas allow for multiple values as output, and can place those values in more than one cell. To enter an array formula, you must first highlight the cells that you want the formula (and values) to appear in. You enter the formula as normal in the formula bar. Then, rather than hitting the Enter key, you press three keys together: Ctrl+Shift+Enter. After this is done, brackets appear around the formula automatically to indicate that it's an array formula. There are actually two variants of array functions. The type just described allows for multiple values. Another variant, which will be discussed at the end of this chapter, produces only a single value as output. Figure 12.6 demonstrates the use of MODE.SNGL and MODE.MULT.

	A	B	C	D	E
1	Values 1	Values 2		Formula	Formula Result
2	3	3		=MODE.SNGL(A2:A7)	5
3	5	3		=MODE.MULT(A2:A7)	5
4	5	5		=MODE.SNGL(B2:B7)	3
5	7	10			
6	10	10		{=MODE.MULT(B2:B7)}	3
7	15	15		{=MODE.MULT(B2:B7)}	10

Figure 12.6
MODE.SNGL and MODE.MULT functions, and an array formula.
Source: Microsoft® Corporation.

The MODE.SNGL function in row 2 finds the mode of the numbers in column A. Since the number 5 appears twice and all others numbers only once, the result is 5. Row 3 shows that MODE.MULT can be used in place of MODE.SNGL in situations where there is only one mode. Row 4 uses MODE.SNGL against the numbers in column B. Even though there are two modes in column B, 3 and 10, MODE.SNGL can display only one of those values. In rows 6 and 7, we show how to enter MODE.MULT in an array formula to show the two modes in cells B2:B7. This was done by first highlighting cells E6 and E7, and entering the indicated formula, without the brackets, in the formula bar. After pressing Ctrl+Shift+Enter, the brackets appear around the formula, and the result is displayed in cells E6 and E7. The same formula appears in both E6 and E7. Additionally, once an array formula is created, you can't modify individual cells within the array formula. The array exists as a single unit.

The final two average functions we'll examine, AVERAGEIF and AVERAGEIFS, are analogous to the SUMIF and SUMIFS functions. Their syntax is:

AVERAGEIF(range, criteria, [average_range])

AVERAGEIFS(average_range, criteria_range1, criteria1, ...)

Figure 12.7 shows how to use these functions.

	A	B	C	D	E	F
1	Sale Price	Commission	State		Formula	Formula Result
2	500	50	CA		=AVERAGEIF(A2:A6, ">= 200")	350
3	250	45	NV		=AVERAGEIF(A2:A6, ">= 200", B2:B6)	45
4	300	25	AZ		=AVERAGEIF(C2:C6, "CA", A2:A6)	425
5	350	60	CA		=AVERAGEIFS(A2:A6, C2:C6, "AZ", B2:B6, ">= 25")	300
6	150	5	AZ			

Figure 12.7

AVERAGEIF and AVERAGEIFS functions.

Source: Microsoft® Corporation.

Figure 12.7 has the same data previously seen in Figures 12.2 and 12.4. In this case, we're taking an average rather than a sum or count. The AVERAGEIF function in row 2 takes the average of the cells in range A2:A6 that are greater than or equal to 200. This excludes the 150 in cell A6, so the average is 350. Row 3 takes the average of the numbers in column B where the corresponding values in column A are greater than or equal to 200. In row 4, we take the average of the Sale Price where the sale is from California (CA). Finally, row 5 illustrates the AVERAGEIFS function, averaging the Sale Price where the State is AZ and the Commission is greater than or equal to 25. Only cell A4 satisfies both conditions, so the average is the same as the Sale Price, which is 300.

Percentiles and Ranks

Whereas averages tell us something about the center of a set of data, *percentiles* allow us to describe the location of a data element, relative to all other data elements in the set. Percentiles describe relative rank in the data set. A percentile is defined as the percent for which all data elements fall below that value. For example, the 25th percentile is the point for which 25 percent of all other data elements have lower values. The 50th percentile is the same as the median, discussed previously. This is the midpoint of the data set. In common usage, the percentile of a number can have an integer value between 1 and 100. If a number has a percentile of 100, it's like saying that it's the largest number in the set.

A concept related to the percentile is the *quartile*. Whereas percentiles divide a set of numbers into 100 units, quartiles divide a set of numbers into 4 units. Expressed as integer values, it is common to talk about 100 percentiles, but only 4 quartiles. The first quartile is the same as the 25th percentile; the second quartile is like the 50th percentile, and so on. We'll discuss the following functions pertaining to percentile and quartile:

- PERCENTILE.EXC
- PERCENTILE.INC
- QUARTILE.EXC
- QUARTILE.INC
- PERCENTRANK.EXC
- PERCENTRANK.INC

All of these functions come in two variants, with EXC and INC suffixes. These variations are due to differing ways in which percentiles can be calculated. The mathematics behind the algorithms that the PERCENTILE functions utilize behind the scenes is quite complex, and is beyond the scope of this book. The EXC (exclusive) variation is the preferred version and gives a more accurate computation. The only limitation is that the EXC variant won't produce a result if the data point being evaluated is too high or too low, relative to the percentile being calculated. For example, if there are 20 data elements in the array of numbers, and you are asking for something above the 95th percentile, the function will be unable to return a value because it won't be able to make a calculation in the top 1/20 or 5% of the data. However, if the data set has more than 100 data elements, then the EXC functions work just fine. The INC (inclusive) variants of these functions work with any percentile calculation, but may produce a less accurate result. Incidentally, you may also notice older compatibility functions named PERCENTILE, QUARTILE, and RANK. These are equivalent to the newer INC versions of these functions. The syntax of the first four percentile functions we'll examine is:

PERCENTILE.EXC(array, k)

PERCENTILE.INC(array, k)

QUARTILE.EXC(array, quart)

QUARTILE.INC(array, quart)

The PERCENTILE functions have two arguments, *array* and *k*. The *array* specifies the data range of the numbers to be examined. They do not need to be in sequential order. The *k* argument specifies the percentile, as a decimal between 0 and 1. For example, the number .9 represents the 90th percentile. However, the PERCENTILE.EXC is an exclusive function, so you can't specify either 0 or 100. This function corresponds to a strict interpretation of what percentiles mean, so it can never be the case that 100% of numbers are *below* the given value. PERCENTILE.INC allows for any value of *k* between 0 and 1, inclusive of those numbers.

The two QUARTILE functions substitute a *quart* argument for *k*. The *quart* argument in QUARTILE.EXC can have a value of 1 to 3, representing the first, second, or third quartiles. Just as PERCENTILE.EXC doesn't allow you to specify the 100th percentile, QUARTILE.EXC doesn't permit the fourth quartile. However, PERCENTILE.INC also allows for quartile 0, representing the lowest value, and quartile 4, representing the fourth quartile. Figure 12.8 illustrates these functions.

	A	B	C	D	E	F	G
1	33	440	821	15		Formula	Formula Result
2	22	250	334	600		=PERCENTILE.EXC(A1:D5, 0.75)	795
3	487	924	5	599		=PERCENTILE.EXC(A1:D5, 0.95)	968.65
4	586	862	486	801		=PERCENTILE.EXC(A1:D5, 0.96)	#NUM!
5	971	605	123	777		=PERCENTILE.INC(A1:D5, 0.75)	783
6						=PERCENTILE.INC(A1:D5, 1)	971
7						=PERCENTILE.INC(A1:D5, 0)	5
8						=QUARTILE.EXC(A1:D5, 3)	795
9						=QUARTILE.INC(A1:D5, 3)	783
10						=QUARTILE.INC(A1:D5, 4)	971

Figure 12.8
PERCENTILE.EXC, PERCENTILE.INC, QUARTILE.EXC, and QUARTILE.INC functions.
Source: Microsoft® Corporation.

In Figure 12.8, the array of numbers to be evaluated extends from cell A1 to D5. There are 20 numbers, with values that range from 5 to 971. The formulas are in column G, with the text of the formulas shown in column F. The formula in row 2 uses the PERCENTILE.EXC function to calculate the 75th percentile. The output is 795. In row 3, the 95th percentile is calculated as 968.65. Row 4 attempts to calculate the 96th percentile, but the function returns an error because there aren't enough numbers to support this calculation. With only 20 numbers, PERCENTILE.EXC can only calculate percentiles from .05 to .95. The formula in row 5 uses PERCENTILE.INC to compute the 75th percentile. Due to a difference in algorithms used, this results in a slightly different value than when PERCENTILE.EXC was used. Rows 6 and 7 show how PERCENTILE.INC can be used to return percentiles of 100 and 0, returning the highest and lowest number in the array. Row 8 turns to the QUARTILE.EXC function, calculating the third quartile. Note that this gives the same result as the 75th percentile. Rows 9 and 10 use QUARTILE.INC to return the third and fourth quartile. The fourth quartile is the same as the 100th percentile.

The PERCENTRANK functions are the inverse of the PERCENTILE functions. Rather than returning a percentile, this function tells you what value corresponds to a specified percentile. The syntax of these functions is:

PERCENTRANK.EXC(array, x, [significance])

PERCENTRANK.INC(array, x, [significance])

For these functions, the *x* argument is the percentile you want to evaluate, and the optional *significance* argument states the number of decimal places you want to see. Figure 12.9 provides a few examples of these functions.

	A	B	C	D	E	F	G
1	33	440	821	15		Formula	Formula Result
2	22	250	334	600		=PERCENTRANK.EXC(A1:D5, 795)	0.75
3	487	924	5	599		=PERCENTRANK.EXC(A1:D5, 500)	0.482
4	586	862	486	801		=PERCENTRANK.INC(A1:D5, 500)	0.48
5	971	605	123	777		=PERCENTRANK.INC(A1:D5, 971)	1

Figure 12.9

PERCENTRANK.EXC and PERCENTRANK.INC functions.

Source: Microsoft® Corporation.

The array of numbers in Figure 12.9 is the same as in Figure 12.8. The PERCENT-RANK function in row 2 calculates the percentile for the value 795 in the designated array of numbers. The result is .75, which is the decimal equivalent of the 75th percentile. Note that this is the inverse of the formula in row 2 of Figure 12.8, which calculated the 75th percentile as 795. The formula in row 3 calculates the percentile for the value 500. The result is .482. Row 4 uses PERCENTRANK.INC for the same calculation, producing a value of .48. Finally, the PERCENTRANK.INC function in row 5 calculates the percentile of the highest number of 971. The answer is 1, representing the 100th percentile.

Whereas percentiles provide information about the relative rank of a number within a data set, one sometimes wants to know the absolute ranking of a value. To accomplish this, Excel provides these four functions:

- MIN
- MAX
- SMALL
- LARGE

The MIN and MAX functions find the smallest and largest value in a set of numbers. The SMALL and LARGE functions are similar, except that they allow you to locate the kth smallest or largest value. This, for example, would allow you to find the third largest number in an array. The syntax of these functions is:

MIN(number1, [number2], …)

MAX(number1, [number2], …)

SMALL(array, k)

LARGE(array, k)

The arguments in the MIN and MAX functions are a series of numbers, any of which can be an array. The SMALL and LARGE functions require two arguments, an *array* of numbers, and a *k* value that represents the number from the top or bottom to locate. For example, LARGE(A1:B5, 3) specifies to locate the third largest number in the array of numbers from A1 to B5. The examples shown in Figure 12.10 demonstrate the use of these functions.

▲	A	B	C	D	E	F	G
1	33	440	821	15		Formula	Formula Result
2	22	250	334	600		=MIN(A1:D5)	5
3	487	924	5	599		=MAX(A1:D5)	971
4	586	862	486	801		=SMALL(A1:D5,1)	5
5	971	605	123	777		=SMALL(A1:D5,2)	15
6						=LARGE(A1:D5,3)	862

Figure 12.10

MIN, MAX, SMALL, and LARGE functions.

Source: Microsoft® Corporation.

The MIN function in row 2 finds the minimum value of the array of numbers in cells A1 to D5. The smallest number in this set is 5. Likewise, the MAX function in row 3 finds the maximum value, which is 971. The SMALL function in row 4 accomplishes the same result as the MIN function in row 2. The *k* argument has a value of 1, which means that we want to locate the absolute smallest number. The SMALL function in row 5 finds the second smallest number, which is 15. Finally, the LARGE function in row 6 returns the third largest number, which is 862.

Frequencies and Variability

Earlier in this chapter, we discussed various ways of obtaining the average of a set of numbers. In most cases, the term *average* refers to the arithmetic mean, which is the sum of the numbers divided by the count. In statistical lingo, the average provides a measure of central tendency, and the set of numbers in the data set is referred to as a *distribution*. An average provides useful information, but equally important is the ability to understand the amount of variability in a distribution. If one is looking at the returns from a group of 30 stocks and is told that the group had an average return of 10%, it would be important to know how varied the returns were. It might be the case that all 30 stocks had a return of 9, 10, or 11 percent. Or, it might be that some stocks had negative returns, and a few had huge returns of 100% or more. One would want to know how consistent the returns were among all the stocks. To give a more mundane example, it's said that one can drown in a lake that has an average depth of one inch. Knowing the average is nice, but it doesn't always provide sufficient information by itself.

The standard statistic for measuring variability in a data set is referred to as the *standard deviation*. However, before delving into that statistic in detail, we need to turn to the concept of *frequencies* as a means of getting the overall sense of a distribution. When presented with a set of values or measurements, it's often useful as a first step to get a visual picture of what the data looks like. Excel provides the following function to accomplish that task:

■ FREQUENCY

This function is an array function similar to MODE.MULT. The syntax of the function is:

FREQUENCY(data_array, bins_array)

The *data_array* argument contains the numeric values to be analyzed, and the *bins_array* is a vertical array of numbers that defines how the data should be classified. Figure 12.11 illustrates the procedure.

◢	A	B	C	D	E	F	G	H	I
1	2	42	50	68		**Bins**	**Frequencies Formula**	**Description**	**Frequencies**
2	13	46	51	75		10	{=FREQUENCY(A1:D5, F2:F11)}	1-10	1
3	20	48	53	80		20	{=FREQUENCY(A1:D5, F2:F11)}	11-20	2
4	29	49	57	89		30	{=FREQUENCY(A1:D5, F2:F11)}	21-30	1
5	39	50	59	98		40	{=FREQUENCY(A1:D5, F2:F11)}	31-40	1
6						50	{=FREQUENCY(A1:D5, F2:F11)}	41-50	6
7						60	{=FREQUENCY(A1:D5, F2:F11)}	51-60	4
8						70	{=FREQUENCY(A1:D5, F2:F11)}	61-70	1
9						80	{=FREQUENCY(A1:D5, F2:F11)}	71-80	2
10						90	{=FREQUENCY(A1:D5, F2:F11)}	81-90	1
11						100	{=FREQUENCY(A1:D5, F2:F11)}	91-100	1

Figure 12.11

The FREQUENCY function.

Source: Microsoft® Corporation.

In Figure 12.11, the numbers in the array A1:D5 consists of 20 numbers that range in value from 1 to 100. These numbers make up the *data_array* argument. The array in column F from F2 to F11 specifies how we'd like to classify these values, and constitute the *bin_array* argument. Each value in the *bin_array* specifies an upper limit for a range of numbers. For example, the 10 in cell F2 means that the first class (or category) goes from 1 to 10. The 20 in F3 has the cutoff for the second class. The corresponding descriptions for the bin values in column F are found in column H. The formula with the FREQUENCY function is entered in column I, in cells I2 through I11, by highlighting the cells, entering the formula in the formula bar, then pressing Ctrl+Shift+Enter, to signify it as an array formula. The text of this formula is shown in column G.

The result in column I tells us how many values of the original data array fall into each class or category. For example, the value in cell I6 says that there are 6 values between 41 and 50. This is useful information, but one would really want to see this data in chart form to get a clearer picture. This is easily accomplished by highlighting columns H and I and inserting a column chart. The result is shown in Figure 12.12.

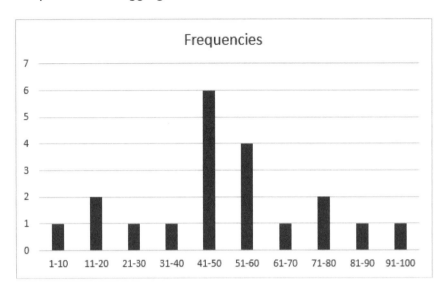

Figure 12.12

A column chart of frequencies.

Source: Microsoft® Corporation.

The frequency distribution chart in Figure 12.12 is referred to as a *histogram* in statistics. By creating classes of data and determining how many values are in each class, we now have an intuitively clear picture of the variability of the data. We can see that most values lie between 41 and 60, and that other values are rather evenly distributed between 1 and 100.

To illustrate the importance of variability, let's repeat the exercise of Figures 12.11 and 12.12 with a different set of data, as seen in Figures 12.13 and 12.14.

	A	B	C	D	E	F	G	H
1	28	42	50	58		**Bins**	**Description**	**Frequencies**
2	64	46	51	55		10	1-10	0
3	40	48	43	62		20	11-20	0
4	41	49	56	65		30	21-30	1
5	39	50	59	72		40	31-40	2
6						50	41-50	8
7						60	51-60	5
8						70	61-70	3
9						80	71-80	1
10						90	81-90	0
11						100	91-100	0

Figure 12.13

The FREQUENCY function.

Source: Microsoft® Corporation.

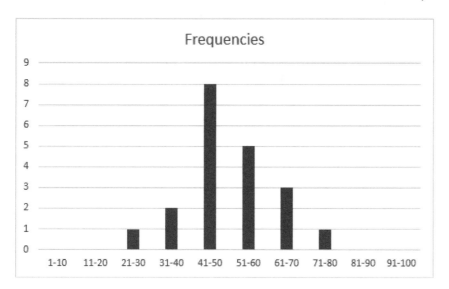

Figure 12.14

A column chart of frequencies.

Source: Microsoft® Corporation.

Figure 12.13 repeats the formulas of Figure 12.11 with a new set of data. In this figure, we've dispensed with the column that shows the text values of the formulas. The FRE-QUENCY function, however, is the same and is found in column H. The resulting chart in Figure 12.14 shows the new frequency distribution, and tells a rather different story. Unlike the original distribution, these data points show much less variability. As before, most values lie between 41 and 60. However, this time there are virtually no values between 1 and 20, or 81 and 100.

Now that we've acquired a general sense of the data via frequency distributions, we can turn to the standard deviation to get a more precise measurement of each data set's variability. As mentioned, the standard deviation is the standard statistic for measuring variability. One sometimes also sees a related statistic called the *variance*. The formulas for these calculations are decidedly more complex than that of the average. Both the standard deviation and the variance start with taking the difference between each value and the mean of the entire data set. Each of these differences is then squared. The squared differences are summed, and then divided by the count of values in the data set. The result of this calculation is the variance. The standard deviation is the square root of the variance. In essence, the standard deviation is similar in concept to an average, except that instead of summing values, we're summing the differences (or deviations) between each value and the mean of the data set. In practical terms, the standard deviation is the more widely used statistic, since it expresses the variance in units that correspond to the original data. Whereas the variance states deviations as squared values, the standard deviation, by taking the square root of the variance, expresses the deviations in the original units of measurement. The variance is important but finds its use primarily as a factor in more complex formulas used in inferential statistics.

As mentioned in the Introduction, this book discusses basic descriptive statistics, but stays away from topics involving inferential statistics. Descriptive statistics deals with ways to describe the data found in a data sample. In contrast, inferential statistics is concerned with producing useful inferences about a larger population from the data found in a sample. This involves making use of probability theory to allow one to make an inference about a population based on information gathered from the sample. This includes the ability to provide a measure of confidence regarding an inference. For example, using inferential statistics, one would be able to state that a sample of 1000 likely voters indicates that 55% of the entire population will vote for a certain candidate, with a 2% margin of error. In this book, we'll utilize descriptive statistics to portray the nature of a sample, and leave the complexities of inferential statistics to other texts. Excel provides two functions that compute the standard deviation:

- STDEV.S
- STDEV.P

The STDEV.S function computes the standard deviation of a sample. STDEV.P calculates the standard deviation of an entire population. The difference between these functions has to do with the denominator of the formula. STDEV.P divides the squared distances from the mean by the number of values in the data set. In contrast, STDEV.S divides by the number of values less one. If there are 100 values in a distribution, STDEV.P will divide by 100, and STDEV.S divides by 99. The reason for this distinction has to do with *degrees of freedom* and *sampling bias*—topics that are beyond the scope of this book. For larger sample sizes, the result of these two functions is almost identical.

The syntax of these functions is:

    STDEV.S(number1, [number2], …)
    STDEV.P(number1, [number2], …)

As with the MIN and MAX functions, the arguments for STDEV.S and STDEV.P are one or more numbers, any of which can be an array. Incidentally, these functions, which were introduced with Excel 2010, are identical to the older compatibility functions STDEV and STDEVP. STDEV.S is identical to STDEV, and STDEV.P is the same as STDEVP. The following examples in Figure 12.15 focus on how to interpret standard deviation values.

	A	B	C	D	E	F	G
1	2	42	50	68		Formula	Formula Result
2	13	46	51	75		=AVERAGE(A1:D5)	50.9
3	20	48	53	80		=STDEV.S(A1:D5)	24.08078509
4	29	49	57	89		=STDEV.P(A1:D5)	23.47104599
5	39	50	59	98			
6							
7	28	42	50	58		=AVERAGE(A7:D11)	50.9
8	64	46	51	55		=STDEV.S(A7:D11)	10.66178616
9	40	48	43	62		=STDEV.P(A7:D11)	10.39182371
10	41	49	56	65			
11	39	50	59	72			

Figure 12.15

STDEV.S and STDEV.P functions.

Source: Microsoft® Corporation.

Figure 12.15 displays the same two sets of data that were seen in Figures 12.11 and 12.13. The data set of Figure 12.11 is found in cells A1 to D5. The data from Figure 12.13 is in A7 to D11. As before, each set contains 20 numbers. The AVERAGE function in row 2 finds the average of A1:D5, which is 50.9. The STDEV.S function in row 3 takes the standard deviation of the same 20 numbers, treating the data as a sample from a larger population. The result is approximately 24.08. The STDEV.P function in row 4 treats the numbers as if they were an entire population. The result is roughly 23.47.

If we perform the same calculations on the second data set in A7:D11, we can observe an interesting comparison. The AVERAGE formula in row 7 shows that the mean (or average) of the second data set is exactly the same as the first. However, the standard deviations in rows 8 and 9 show that the second data set has much lower variability. This meshes with our observations of the frequency distributions in Figures 12.12 and 12.14, which displayed smaller variability in the second data set. The standard deviation statistics quantify that observation, with a standard deviation of 24.08 for the first data set, but only 10.66 for the second data set.

Interpreting the meaning of standard deviation values is less intuitive than a simple average (or mean), but a few observations can be made. First, we note that the standard deviation has an implied connection to the mean. For the first data set, we can say that the mean is 50.9, with a standard deviation of 24.08, when the data is taken as a sample. For a given mean, the smaller the standard deviation, the smaller the variability, and the more confident one can be that most values will be close to the mean.

Furthermore, standard deviations take on a particular importance when the distribution is known to be similar to the *normal distribution*. This distribution, also referred to as a bell shaped curve, allows the statistician to attach specific significance to the standard deviation. If the distribution is a normal one, then roughly 68% of all values will be within 1 standard deviation of the average, 95% will be within 2 standard deviations, and nearly all values will be within 3 standard deviations of the average. Figure 12.16 shows an example of a normal distribution.

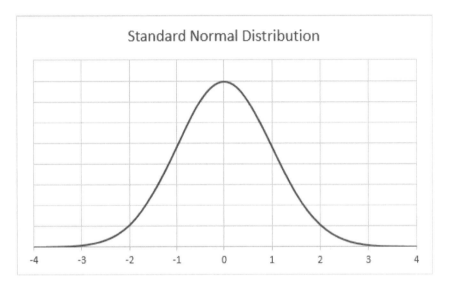

Figure 12.16
Standard normal distribution.
Source: Microsoft® Corporation.

The normal distribution in Figure 12.16 is referred to as the *standard normal distribution*. In this variant, the mean (or average) of all the values is 0, and the horizontal axis shows how many standard deviations each value is from the mean. As seen, nearly all values fall within 3 standard deviations of the mean. This represents the classic bell-shaped normal distribution curve.

Correlation and Regression

The prior calculations of the average and standard deviation of a data set involved a single set of data. However, statistical analysis often involves multiple sets of related data. We'll now look at situations with two sets of data paired with each other. For example, one might want to compare high school grade point averages and SAT scores to see if there is any relationship between the two. This would involve examining data points for students who have taken the SAT and comparing those scores to their grade point average. To give another example, one might want to determine the relationship between advertising expenditures and sales revenue, in hopes of understanding the value of specific advertising campaigns.

After getting a sense of the correlation between two sets of data, we might also want to make predictions based on a variable. For example, we might want to predict an SAT score based on a student's grade point average, or sales revenue based on advertising expenditures. This type of analysis is referred to as linear regression. As a brief introduction with what can be done with correlation and regression in Excel, we'll examine these two functions:

- CORREL

- TREND

The CORREL function compares two arrays of data and calculates a statistic known as the *correlation coefficient*, sometimes also referred to as the *Pearson product-moment coefficient*. This statistic always has a value between -1 and 1. A value of 1 means that there is a perfect positive correlation between the two variables. In other words, as one variable increases in value, the other variable increases in a perfectly similar fashion to maintain the ratio between the two variables. A value of -1 means that there is perfect negative correlation, meaning that as one variable increases, the other decreases. Any value between -1 and 1 indicates that there is a less than perfect relationship between the variables. A relationship of 0 means that there is absolutely no perceived connection between the variables. To illustrate, let's examine the data in Figure 12.17, which has data on a few paperback books written about Excel 2013.

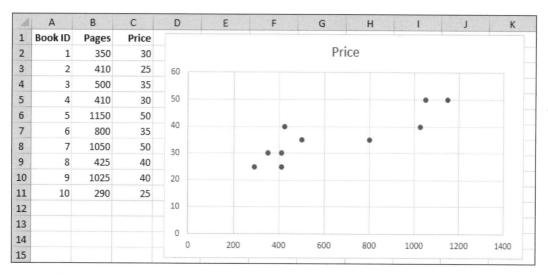

Figure 12.17

Data for correlation analysis.

Source: Microsoft® Corporation.

In Figure 12.17, we see 10 paired data points for two sets of variables: the number of pages in a book, and the corresponding retail price. The values in column A identify each book by an ID number. From the data in columns B and C, we inserted a scatter chart with the number of pages on the x-axis and the price on the y-axis. Each point indicates the pages and price of a single book. As seen, there seems to be a positive relationship between the number of pages and price. In other words, as the number of pages increases, the price tends to increase as well. However, it is not a perfect relationship. If it were perfect, all the points in the chart would be in a straight line.

Now that we have a sense of the correlation between these two variables, we'd like Excel to obtain the correlation coefficient. This will give us a precise measurement of the correlation. To do this, we'll use the CORREL function, which has this syntax:

CORREL(array1, array2)

To make use of this function, we simply specify the two arrays that are in columns B and C. Figure 12.18 shows the original data in Figure 12.17, with an added calculation of the correlation coefficient.

	A	B	C	D	E	F
1	Book ID	Pages	Price		Formula	Formula Result
2	1	350	30		=CORREL(B2:B11, C2:C11)	0.855461373
3	2	410	25			
4	3	500	35			
5	4	410	30			
6	5	1150	50			
7	6	800	35			
8	7	1050	50			
9	8	425	40			
10	9	1025	40			
11	10	290	25			

Figure 12.18

The CORREL function.

Source: Microsoft® Corporation.

As seen in Figure 12.18, the CORREL function computes the correlation coefficient as roughly .85. Being a positive number, this indicates a positive correlation. Since the number is fairly close to 1, it appears that this is a fairly strong relationship. However, it's important to note that the value .85 means nothing in and of itself. One can't say that the relationship between pages in a book and its price is 85%. One can only compare the value .85 to other correlations. However, if we had another experiment where the two variables had a relationship of .5, we could say that the first experiment, with .85, has a stronger correlation than the second experiment with .5. It's also critical to note that a strong correlation has nothing to do with causation. We can't say that the number of pages *causes* a higher price. Similarly, if we were analyzing advertising expenditures and sales revenue, we couldn't say that a large advertising expenditure causes large revenue. Effects of causation fall strictly within the realm of inferential statistics.

Turning to regression analysis, we may want to predict the price of a book, given a known number of pages. The basis of this analysis rests on a regression line that is drawn to represent the best fit for the data elements in the sample. We can actually see the regression line by adding a trendline to the scatter chart of Figure 12.17. This is shown in Figure 12.19.

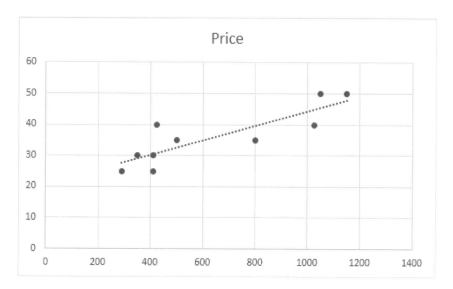

Figure 12.19

A linear trendline in a scatter plot.

Source: Microsoft® Corporation.

The trendline that we inserted in the scatter chart of Figure 12.19 is a linear trendline, and so assumes that the relationship between the two variables is linear in nature. Linear regression lines are computed using a *method of least squares*, which determines the position and slope of the line that minimizes the vertical distances between each point and the resulting line. Once a regression line has been determined, it's a simple calculation to determine the y value for a given x value. Looking at Figure 12.19, it appears that if the trend is followed, a book of 800 pages should be priced at approximately $40. The use of regression analysis assumes that causation has been established. The x values are called the independent variable. The y values are the dependent variable. In this case, we're assuming that the number of pages in a book is the independent variable, and the price of the book is dependent on the number of pages. Let's see if our estimate of $40 for a book of 800 pages is correct. The syntax for the TREND function is:

TREND(known_y's, [known_x's], [new_x's], [const])

In this function, the *known_y's* argument represents the array of dependent variables. The *known_x's* is the array of independent variables. *New_x's* are the values for which we want to compute a y value. The optional *const* argument is an advanced feature that adjusts the constant of the regression equation. Figure 12.20 shows the calculation of price for a book of 800 pages.

	A	B	C	D	E	F
1	Book	Pages	Price		Formula	Formula Result
2	1	350	30		=TREND(C2:C11, B2:B11, 800)	39.73720721
3	2	410	25			
4	3	500	35			
5	4	410	30			
6	5	1150	50			
7	6	800	35			
8	7	1050	50			
9	8	425	40			
10	9	1025	40			
11	10	290	25			

Figure 12.20

The TREND function.

Source: Microsoft® Corporation.

The TREND function in row 2 calculates the y (or dependent) value when x = 800. The *known_x's* array (the independent variable) is B2:B11, representing the array of pages in a book. The *known_y's* array (the dependent variable) is C2:C11, representing the resulting prices in the sample. The TREND function calculates that the price of a book of 800 pages should be $39.73. Note that this is very close to our visual estimation, based on the trendline in Figure 12.19.

At this point, we need to point out that this example is very simplistic, and ignores several significant aspects of a true regression analysis. Basically, we're disregarding the many aspects of regression analysis that rely on statistical inference. In a true regression analysis, we would include additional statistics that explicitly state the probability of error for our predictions. Recognizing that one is working with a sample of data, it's important to utilize inferential statistical methods to deal with the probability of accuracy.

Array Functions and the Sum of Products

When discussing modes earlier in this chapter, we mentioned that the MODE.MULT function is a special type of function referred to as an array function. This type of function can produce output in more than one cell, and is entered by pressing Ctrl+Shift+Enter rather than simply Enter. After doing so, brackets appear around the formula, and the formula is repeated in all selected cells. The MODE.MULT function allows for output in multiple cells, but another variant of the array function places a value in only one cell. We'll illustrate that type of array function with the SUM function. Additionally, we want to mention a related function:

- SUMPRODUCT

The SUMPRODUCT function allows the analyst to sum up the product of numbers in one or more arrays. Its syntax is:

SUMPRODUCT(array1, [array2], [array3], …)

The examples in Figure 12.21 illustrate both the SUM array function and the SUMPRODUCT function, pointing out their similarities.

	A	B	C	D	E	F
1	Quantity	Price	Quantity times Price		Formula	Formula Result
2	2	10	20		=SUM(C2:C6)	110
3	3	5	15		=SUMPRODUCT(A2:A6, B2:B6)	110
4	5	2	10		=(A2*B2)+(A3*B3)+(A4*B4)+(A5*B5)+(A6*B6)	110
5	1	25	25		{=SUM(A2:A6 * B2:B6)}	110
6	4	10	40			

Figure 12.21

The SUMPRODUCT function and a SUM array function.

Source: Microsoft® Corporation.

Figure 12.21 has data on the sale of five items. The values in column A are the quantities, and column B has the price. Our objective is to calculate the total sales for all items. One way of accomplishing this is to multiply Quantity times Price in each row, and then sum up the resulting values. Column C has formulas that multiply Quantity times Price for each row. Thus, we see in row 2 that the total amount sold for that item was 2 times 10, or 20. The SUM function in cell F2 sums up total unit sales in column C, to obtain total sales. As seen, this is a fairly cumbersome solution, as it involves creating formulas in column C, and then summing up those values.

A simpler solution is provided by the SUMPRODUCT function in row 3. This function takes the sum of the products in the two specified arrays, A2:A6 and B2:B6. It first multiplies the corresponding cells in each array, and then sums up the result. Thus, this result is obtained by using only one formula. Note that the SUMPRODUCT function does not require the formulas in column C. The formula in row 4 has the exact equivalent of what the SUMPRODUCT function in row 3 is doing. That is, it multiplies each corresponding pair of values in each array, and then adds up the terms.

A third approach is to use SUM as an array function. This is illustrated in row 5 of Figure 12.20. The indicated SUM function has been entered, with the two arrays as the items to be multiplied, and then added. The Ctrl+Shift+Enter combination is used to turn this into an array function. The result is the same as using SUMPRODUCT. Note the subtle distinction between using SUM as an array function, and the use of MODE.MULT earlier in this chapter. With MODE.MULT, the array refers to the fact that an array of data is produced as output from the function. With SUM, the array is embedded within the function, and there is only a single cell as output.

Looking Ahead

Aggregate and statistical functions are a key element of Excel's capabilities, allowing the analyst to summarize numeric quantities. We began the chapter with an examination of Excel's various sum and count functions. As with pivot tables, SUM and COUNT perform basic aggregations on numeric quantities. The logical versions of these functions—SUMIF, SUMIFS, COUNTIF, and COUNTIFS—allow for the addition of complex logic. In discussing averages, we covered three variants: the mean, the median, and the mode. Of these, the mean is by far the most commonly used and useful. With the mode, we introduced array functions, which allow a function to create output in multiple cells. The remainder of the chapter falls within the realm of descriptive statistics. We discussed percentiles as a device for locating the relative rank of numeric value within a larger data set. The FREQUENCY function is a useful device for categorizing numeric values into defined classes so that the distribution of values can be seen. This provides a nice insight into the variability of one's data. The standard deviation provides a more precise measure of variability. We ended the chapter with a look at correlation and regression, which allow you to understand the relationship between paired data elements. While a true use of some of these statistics requires an understanding of inferential statistics, we have hopefully provided a few insights as to their usefulness.

In the next chapter, "Logical and Lookup Functions," we'll learn about ways to add logic to the many functions that we've already covered. When used in combination with nested functions, these logical functions allow you to combine functions in surprising ways. We'll also examine a number of lookup functions, which provide the analyst with a means of matching data from different ranges or tables.

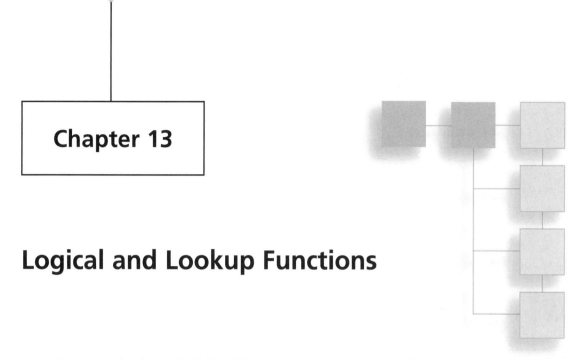

Chapter 13

Logical and Lookup Functions

Functions are the basic building blocks that provide the ability to perform complex calculations in Excel. Each function, by itself, can allow the analyst to execute a transformation that would not be easily accomplished otherwise. Plus, we've seen that increasingly complex formulas can be created with nested functions that combine complementary functions in useful ways. However, even with all of these possibilities for combining functions, we have not yet discussed the application of pure logic to a function.

In this chapter, we'll focus on functions that are logical in nature. This class of functions utilizes *Boolean logic* to evaluate expressions as to whether they are true or false. Boolean logic refers to a class of algebra that uses logic to evaluate operations that involve AND, OR, or NOT conditions. These logical functions, although simple in structure, greatly expand on the analyst's ability to create formulas and calculations that are ever more complex.

We will also examine a number of lookup functions. This set of functions allows you to find matching values in another range or table. For example, this would allow you to retrieve the full name of a state from a lookup table, based on an abbreviation. Since Excel is not a full-fledged relational database, it's not always easy to join data together from multiple tables or data sources. However, lookup functions allow you to do just that.

Logical Functions

Excel provides a number of functions that let you add logic to the criteria that stipulates the values that are selected or displayed in a worksheet cell. The functions we'll peruse in this regard are:

- IF
- AND
- OR
- XOR
- NOT

These functions are all found in the Logical group of functions under the Formulas tab on the Ribbon. The first function that we'll examine is the all-important IF. This function allows you to return values based on an evaluation of an expression as being true or false. Its syntax is:

IF(logical_test), [value_if_true], [value_if_false])

The use of this function is simple and straightforward. The *logical_test* argument contains an expression that is evaluated as true or false. This typically involves using a comparison operation such as equals (=) or greater than (>). This argument can also be a relative reference to another cell that evaluates to true or false. The *value_if_true* and *value_if_false* arguments let you specify the result, depending on whether the *logical_test* is true or false. Figure 13.1 illustrates the IF function with a few examples.

	A	B	C	D	E	F
1	Order ID	State	Quantity Purchased	Price Per Item	Formula	Formula Result
2	1	CO	4	5.00	=IF(B2 = "CO", "Colorado", "Other")	Colorado
3	2	AZ	10	8.00	=IF(B3 = "CO", "Colorado", "Other")	Other
4	3	NM	5	30.00	=IF(C4 * D4 > 100, "Large", "Small")	Large
5	4	TX	3	10.00	=IF(B5 = "UT", "Utah", IF(B5 = "TX", "Texas", "Other"))	Texas
6	5	SC	12	5.00	=IF(C5 * D5 > 50, TRUE, FALSE)	TRUE

Figure 13.1

The IF function.

Source: Microsoft® Corporation.

The data in this table represents orders, showing the state where the order took place, the quantity purchased, and price per item. The IF function in row 2 tests the value of cell B2 to see if it equals CO. If true, it displays "Colorado". Otherwise, it displays "Other". The same function in row 3 returns "Other" since the state in B3 is not equal to CO. The IF function in row 4 demonstrates the use of a different comparison operator, testing a numeric value for a greater-than condition, where the value tested is C4 times D4. Row 5 contains two nested IF functions. The outer function tests B5 to see if it equals UT. If so, it displays "Utah". If false, it then employs another IF to see if it equals TX. If B5 does not equal UT or TX, it displays "Other". Finally, the example in row 6 shows that one can merely display the logical constants TRUE or FALSE in place of numbers or characters.

The IF function creates a useful framework for the evaluation of logical expressions, but the real power of the function becomes evident when it's combined with functions such as AND or OR. The syntax of the next three functions we'll consider is:

AND(logical_1, [logical_2], …)

OR(logical_1, [logical_2], …)

XOR(logical_1, [logical_2], …)

The AND function permits you to evaluate a maximum of 255 logical expressions. Each individual argument is evaluated to determine whether it's true or false. The AND function returns the value TRUE only if all specified arguments are true. Otherwise, it returns FALSE. Similarly, the OR function evaluates up to 255 expressions and determines whether they're true or false. The OR function returns the value TRUE if any of the arguments evaluate to true. If none of the arguments are true, then it returns FALSE.

The XOR function, introduced with Excel 2013, stands for "exclusive or." This function is seldom needed, so we'll comment only briefly on its use. This function, which is normally used with only two arguments, returns a TRUE if only one of the two arguments evaluates as true. If neither logical expression is true or if both expressions are true, then it returns FALSE. If XOR is used in situations where there are more than two arguments, then it will return TRUE if an odd number of the arguments are true; it will return FALSE if an even number of the arguments are true.

Figure 13.2 illustrates the use of the AND function. This table shows customer data, indicating each customer's state and income.

⊿	A	B	C	D	E
1	Customer ID	State	Income	Formula	Formula Result
2	1	CO	55000	=AND(C2 >= 50000, C2 <= 100000)	TRUE
3	2	AZ	38000	=AND(C3 >= 50000, C3 <= 100000)	FALSE
4	1	CO	55000	=IF(AND(C4 >= 50000, C4 <= 100000), "Middle", "Other")	Middle
5	2	AZ	38000	=IF(AND(C5 >= 50000, C5 <= 100000), "Middle", "Other")	Other
6	3	WA	110000	=AND(B6 = "WA", C6 >= 100000)	TRUE
7	4	VT	45000	=AND(B7 = "VT", B7 = "NH")	FALSE

Figure 13.2

The AND function.

Source: Microsoft® Corporation.

The AND function in row 2 evaluates two arguments, one of which tests C2 for being greater than or equal to 50000, and the other which tests it for being less than or equal to 100000. In essence, that means we're testing for values between 50000 and 100000. Since both logical expressions are true, the AND function evaluates to TRUE. The function in row 3 makes the same evaluation against different data. This time, the result is FALSE, since 38000 is not between 50000 and 100000. The AND function in row 4 shows how the AND function in rows 2 and 3 can be combined with an IF function. The entire AND function is substituted for the *logical_test* argument of the IF function, and the values "Middle" and "Other" are used for the *value_if_true* and *value_if_false* arguments. Row 4 has the same data as row 2, so it evaluates to "Middle". Likewise, row 5 has the same data as row 3, so it displays as "Other". Row 6 shows an example where we test two different cells with an AND condition. We're looking to see if the customer is in the state of Washington (WA) and has an income of over 100000. Finally, row 7 shows a test to see if the customer is in both Vermont (VT) and New Hampshire (NH). This is a logical impossibility, so it is of course false.

The examples in Figure 13.3 illustrate the OR function with similar data.

⊿	A	B	C	D	E
1	Customer ID	State	Income	Formula	Formula Result
2	1	SD	55000	=OR(B2 = "SD", B2 = "ND")	TRUE
3	2	AZ	38000	=OR(B3 = "CA", C3 > 100000)	FALSE
4	3	CA	45000	=OR(B4 = "CA", C4 > 100000)	TRUE
5	1	SD	55000	=IF(OR(B2 = "SD", B2 = "ND"), "The Dakotas", "Other")	The Dakotas

Figure 13.3

The OR function.

Source: Microsoft® Corporation.

The OR function in row 2 tests B2 to see if it equals SD or ND. Since it does equal one of these values, the result is displayed as TRUE. In row 3, the test is to see if the State is CA or Income is greater than 100000. Since neither of these is true, the result is FALSE. The same formula in row 4 evaluates to TRUE since the State on this row is CA. Row 5 takes the same formula from row 2 and places it in an IF function. Since the *logical_test* argument of the IF evaluates to TRUE, the value of the *value_if_true* argument is displayed.

As noted, the XOR (exclusive OR) function is seldom needed. Figure 13.4 illustrates its use.

	A	B	C	D	E
1	Customer ID	Checking	Savings	Formula	Formula Result
2	1	yes	no	=XOR(B2 = "yes", C2 = "yes")	TRUE
3	2	no	yes	=XOR(B3 = "yes", C3 = "yes")	TRUE
4	3	no	no	=XOR(B4 = "yes", C4 = "yes")	FALSE
5	4	yes	yes	=XOR(B5 = "yes", C5 = "yes")	FALSE

Figure 13.4

The XOR function.

Source: Microsoft® Corporation.

The data in Figure 13.4 represents four bank customers. Columns B and C indicate if the customer has a savings or checking account. In this example, the bank would like to find customers who have a savings account or a checking account, but not both. This is so they can promote savings accounts to customers who have only a checking account, and vice versa. The formulas in all four rows perform the same test, using the XOR function. The result in row 2 is TRUE because the customer has a checking but not a savings account. Similarly, row 3 is TRUE since the customer has a savings account but not checking. Row 4 returns a FALSE since the customer has neither a savings nor a checking account. Row 5 also returns a FALSE because the customer has both a savings and checking account. If this were an OR function rather than XOR, row 5 would evaluate as TRUE.

The NOT function performs a simple negation of a logical value. It turns TRUE to FALSE, and FALSE to TRUE. The syntax of the function is:

NOT(logical)

The NOT function is normally used in combination with AND or OR, to create a more complex logical expression. Figure 13.5 provides a few examples.

	A	B	C	D	E
1	Customer ID	State	Income	Formula	Formula Result
2	1	SD	55000	=NOT(B2 = "NY")	TRUE
3	2	CA	38000	=NOT(OR(B3 = "IL", B3 = "NY"))	TRUE
4	2	CA	38000	=AND(NOT(B4 = "IL"), NOT(B4 = "NY"))	TRUE

Figure 13.5

The NOT function.

Source: Microsoft® Corporation.

The NOT function in row 2 does a simple negation on a logical expression that tests to see if B2 equals NY. Since the expression evaluates as FALSE, the NOT transforms it into a value of TRUE. The examples in rows 3 and 4 are more typical of how the NOT function is used. In row 3, the inner OR function tests to see if B3 equals IL or NY. This evaluates to FALSE, so the outer NOT function changes it to a TRUE. So, this function returns a TRUE if the state is not IL or NY. In row 4, there are two NOT functions placed within an AND function. This returns a value of TRUE if B4 is not equal to IL and if B4 is not equal to NY. If you think about it, the formulas in rows 3 and 4 are logically identical. No matter what state is placed in cells B3 and B4, assuming they're the same, the logical evaluation of both rows will be identical.

IS Functions

In addition to the logical functions just discussed, Excel provides 12 functions under the Information group that are really logical functions. These are referred to as IS functions, as they all begin with the prefix IS. All of the IS functions have a single argument, and evaluate that argument to determine if the result should be TRUE or FALSE. For example, the ISNUMBER function returns a value of TRUE if the supplied argument is a number. Otherwise, it returns FALSE. These functions can be particularly useful when used in combination with the IF function. Some examples include: ISNUMBER, ISTEXT, ISERROR, and ISBLANK. The two functions that we'll examine are:

■ ISNUMBER

■ ISERROR

The syntax of these functions is:

ISNUMBER(value)

ISERROR(value)

Figure 13.6 explains how the ISNUMBER function can be used.

	A	B	C
1	Test Score	Formula	Formula Result
2	90	=IF(ISNUMBER(A2), A2, 50)	90
3	70	=IF(ISNUMBER(A3), A3, 50)	70
4	86	=IF(ISNUMBER(A4), A4, 50)	86
5		=IF(ISNUMBER(A5), A5, 50)	50
6	90	=IF(ISNUMBER(A6), A6, 50)	90
7			
8		=AVERAGE(A2:A6)	84
9		=AVERAGE(C2:C6)	77.2

Figure 13.6

The ISNUMBER function.

Source: Microsoft® Corporation.

In this example, we see an array of five test scores in cells A2:A6. As seen, there is no value in cell A5. This represents a situation where a student neglected to take a test. The object is to compute an average of all test scores. The average seen in cell C8 is taken of cells A2:A6 as is. This result ignores the blank cell in A5, and essentially acts as if that cell doesn't exist. However, we would like to penalize the student who missed that test by giving him a score of 50. The functions in cells C2:C6 transform the test scores in column A by using the ISNUMBER in combination with the IF function. The ISNUMBER returns a value of TRUE if the value is a number. The IF then takes that result, and assigns either the original number if true, or the value 50 if false. As seen, this results in a transformed value of 50 in cell C5 for the blank cell in A5. As a result, the average of cells C2:C6 is 77.2, reflecting a score of 50 for one of the tests.

We now want to offer a more complex use of the ISNUMBER function, shown in Figure 13.7.

	A	B	C
1	Value	Formula	Formula Result
2	Billings, MT	=SEARCH(" CO", A2)	#VALUE!
3	Denver, CO	=IF(ISNUMBER(SEARCH(" CO", A3)), "Colorado", "Other")	Colorado
4	Denver, CO	=IF(OR(ISNUMBER(SEARCH(" CO", A4)), ISNUMBER(SEARCH(" NM", A4))), "CO/NM", "Other")	CO/NM

Figure 13.7

The ISNUMBER function combined with a SEARCH.

Source: Microsoft® Corporation.

In this example, we want to examine the values in column A and translate the state to an appropriate value. The SEARCH function in row 2 illustrates why the ISNUMBER is necessary in this situation. The function in row 2 is searching the value of cell A2 to see if it equals CO. As you may recall, the SEARCH function returns a number indicating the starting position of the character string, if it is found. Since CO doesn't exist in cell A2, the SEARCH returns #VALUE!, indicating an error. The formula in row 3 circumvents this problem by using ISNUMBER to test for the result of the SEARCH function. The ISNUMBER returns a value of TRUE if the SEARCH successfully returns a number. The result of the ISNUMBER evaluation is then used as the *logical_test* argument of an IF function. If true, it returns the value "Colorado". Row 4 expands upon the formula in row 3 by adding an OR function that tests to see if the state is CO or NM. If the search for CO or NM is successful, the IF function returns the value "CO/NM".

The second IS function we want to discuss is ISERROR. This function checks for any errors in a cell. If there are any, it returns a value of TRUE. We haven't talked much about the errors that can occur when entering formulas in cells, but there are a number of possibilities. Figure 13.8 illustrates the use of the ISERROR function against these four different types of errors: #DIV/0!, #VALUE!, #REF!, and #NAME?. The ISERROR function is typically used in conjunction with IF, to test for an error, and then display an appropriate value if an error is found.

	A	B	C	D
1	Text of Fomula	Formula	Text of ISERROR Function	ISERROR Function
2	=100 / 0	#DIV/0!	=ISERROR(B2)	TRUE
3	=100 / 0	#DIV/0!	=IF(ISERROR(B2), 0, B2)	0
4	="cat" + "dog"	#VALUE!	=ISERROR(B4)	TRUE
5	=100 + Sheet5!A5	#REF!	=ISERROR(B5)	TRUE
6	=roundd(10.5)	#NAME?	=ISERROR(B6)	TRUE

Figure 13.8

The ISERROR function.

Source: Microsoft® Corporation.

In Figure 13.8, we've entered a few invalid formulas in column B. The text of those formulas is shown in column A. The corresponding ISERROR function that tests the formula value is in column D. The text of the ISERROR function is shown in column C. In row 2, we see an attempt to divide 100 by 0. This is, of course, invalid, so we see a #DIV/0! error. The ISERROR function in column D tests cell B2 for the existence of an error, and returns a value of TRUE. In row 3, we show how the ISERROR can be embedded within an IF function to return an appropriate value if an error is found. In this case, we've opted to display a 0. Row 4 illustrates the #VALUE! error, which occurs if an arithmetic operation is attempted with non-numeric values. As before, an error is identified and ISERROR returns TRUE. Row 5 shows the #REF! error, which can occur if there's a reference to a cell that doesn't exist. In this case, we've referenced cell A5 on a non-existent worksheet named Sheet5. The #NAME? error shown in row 6 occurs when an invalid function name is specified. In this case, we typed ROUNDD rather than ROUND.

Three additional errors that the ISERROR function captures aren't illustrated in Figure 13.8: #N/A!, #NUM!, and #NULL!. The #N/A! error occurs when data is missing when invoking a lookup function, such as VLOOKUP. We'll discuss lookup functions in the following section. The #NUM! error comes about when a formula produces a number that's too large for Excel to display. The #NULL! error occurs in rare situations that involve missing commas that are needed to separate arguments in a function.

Lookup Functions

As previously mentioned, Excel is not a relational database. Although Excel can connect to or import from specific tables in a database, it remains largely a free-form tool for the analysis of data. Since the data in Excel is not inherently structured, as would be the case in a desktop database tool such as Access, there is often a need to find a value in a table or array from another cell in Excel. Whereas databases allow data in different tables to be joined together explicitly, Excel relies primarily on a number of lookup functions to accomplish the same trick. We'll discuss the following Excel functions, which are related to this type of activity:

- CHOOSE
- VLOOKUP
- HLOOKUP
- MATCH
- INDEX

The most widely used of these functions, VLOOKUP, allows the analyst to look up values stored in a different location in the Excel workbook. However, before discussing that function, we want to first talk about the CHOOSE function. This function allows you to do a lookup on values that are embedded within the function itself. Its syntax is:

CHOOSE(index_num, value_1, [value_2], …)

The *index_num* argument specifies the value or reference that has the value to be looked up. These values can range from 1 to a positive integer less than or equal to 254. The subsequent arguments (*value_1*, *value_2*, etc.) contain the corresponding translation values that the function will return. The order of these values will necessarily match the value of the *index_num* argument. The examples in Figure 13.9 illustrate how this is done.

◢	A	B	C
1	Value	Function Text	Function
2	3	=CHOOSE(A2,"Sun", "Mon", "Tue", "Wed", "Thur", "Fri", "Sat")	Tue
3	6	=CHOOSE(A3,"Sun", "Mon", "Tue", "Wed", "Thur", "Fri", "Sat")	Fri
4	3.6	=CHOOSE(ROUND(A4 + 1, 0), "F", "D", "C", "B", "A")	A
5	2.4	=CHOOSE(ROUND(A5 + 1, 0), "F", "D", "C", "B", "A")	C

Figure 13.9

The CHOOSE function.

Source: Microsoft® Corporation.

The CHOOSE function in row 2 evaluates the value in cell A2, which contains the number 3. The *index_num* of 3 points to the third item in the list of values contained within the subsequent function arguments. Since the third item (the *num_value_3* argument) has a value of "Tue", that is what is displayed in cell C2. The CHOOSE function in row 3 is very similar, but this time it selects the sixth argument (*num_value_6*), and therefore displays "Fri". Rows 4 and 5 illustrate a slightly more complex use of the function, involving a translation of letter grades (A, B, C, D, and F) to grade point averages with corresponding values of 4, 3, 2, 1, and 0. In this example, the *index_num* argument utilizes the ROUND function to round the value in column A to the nearest integer. The number 1 is also added to the original value since we need to treat a grade of 2, which means a C, as a 3, so the third *num_value* argument can be utilized. In row 4, the value of 3.6 in cell A4 is increased by 1, making it 4.6, and then rounded to 5. The fifth *num_value* argument, "A", is then returned. Row 5 is similar, increasing 2.4 to 3.4, and then rounding to 3, which is a C.

The CHOOSE function is useful with certain types of data, but in most cases you'll need to use the VLOOKUP function to look up values. VLOOKUP and HLOOKUP are nearly identical, except that VLOOKUP arranges lookup values in a vertical fashion, while HLOOKUP has a horizontal orientation. Since the normal convention in Excel is to arrange data in vertical columns, the VLOOKUP is far more prevalently used. The syntax of these functions is:

VLOOKUP(lookup_value, table_array, col_index_num, [range_lookup])

HLOOKUP(lookup_value, table_array, row_index_num, [range_lookup])

In both of these functions, the *lookup_value* argument is the value or reference to a value to be looked up. The *table_array* argument has the array data where the lookup is taken from. The lookup always goes against column 1 of the array. The *col_index_num* states what column in the array has the desired lookup value. Finally, the optional *range_lookup* argument is a logical value that states whether an exact match is returned. The default value is TRUE. If *range_lookup* is TRUE and an exact match is not found, the largest value that's less than the desired lookup value is returned. In this case, the data in the array must be in sorted order, with the sort on the first column. In most cases, you'll want to specify FALSE for this argument. This means that it will return only exact matches, and that the data does not have to be in sorted order.

Figure 13.10 contains an initial example of how to use VLOOKUP.

	A	B	C	D	E	F	G
1	Abbreviation	State		City	State	Full State	Text of Full State Formula
2	NE	Nebraska		Joplin	MO	Missouri	=VLOOKUP(E2, $A$2:$B$5, 2, FALSE)
3	IL	Illinois		Billings	MT	Montana	=VLOOKUP(E3, $A$2:$B$5, 2, FALSE)
4	MO	Missouri		Peoria	IL	Illinois	=VLOOKUP(E4, $A$2:$B$5, 2, FALSE)
5	MT	Montana		Lincoln	NE	Nebraska	=VLOOKUP(E5, $A$2:$B$5, 2, FALSE)
6				St. Louis	MO	Missouri	=VLOOKUP(E6, $A$2:$B$5, 2, FALSE)

Figure 13.10

The VLOOKUP function.

Source: Microsoft® Corporation.

In this figure, we have placed an array of data with lookup values in cells A2:B5. Column A has the abbreviation that will be looked up, and column B has the corresponding state name. The data in the array of cells from D1 to G6 has our primary data that we want to evaluate. Column D has a city name and Column E has a state abbreviation. Our objective is to look up the abbreviation in column E against the data in A1:B5 to retrieve the full state name. The formulas with VLOOKUP are in column F, with column G showing the text value of those formulas.

The VLOOKUP function in row 2 specifies E2 as the *lookup_value* argument. This is what we want to look up in another array. The *table_array* argument is specified as $A$2:$B$5. The use of absolute cell references for this array guarantees that as the formula is copied down the cells in column F, the location of the array won't change. The *col_index_num* argument of 2 means that we want the second column in the lookup array (A2:B5). This is column B, which has the state name. Finally, the *range_lookup* argument value of FALSE means that we want an exact match, and that the data in the lookup array doesn't need to be in sorted order. As seen, this VLOOKUP function returns the value "Missouri", since that is what matches the abbreviation MO. The VLOOKUP functions in rows 3 through 6 are identical, and return the appropriate state names from the lookup table.

In this next example of the VLOOKUP function, rather than look up a static value, we'll look up a value that can easily change. Our objective is to produce an estimate of the hours required to complete a project, and then adjust those hours based on the complexity of the project. Figure 13.11 has the data.

◢	A	B	C	D	E
1	Project ID	Hours	Complexity	Adjusted Hours	Text of Adjusted Hours Formula
2	1	100	High	120	=B2 * VLOOKUP(C2, $A$8:$B$10, 2, FALSE)
3	2	150	Medium	150	=B3 * VLOOKUP(C3, $A$8:$B$10, 2, FALSE)
4	3	80	Low	64	=B4 * VLOOKUP(C4, $A$8:$B$10, 2, FALSE)
5	4	40	Medium	40	=B5 * VLOOKUP(C5, $A$8:$B$10, 2, FALSE)
6					
7	Complexity	Factor			
8	Low	0.8			
9	Medium	1			
10	High	1.2			

Figure 13.11

Another VLOOKUP function.

Source: Microsoft® Corporation.

In Figure 13.11, our lookup table is located in rows 7 through 10, below the primary data elements in the first six rows. For rows 1 through 5, column A is the project ID, column B is our estimate of required hours, and column C describes the complexity of the project. We then place a formula in column D that adjusts the hours based on the complexity. Column E shows the text of these formulas, which multiply the hours in column B by a factor that's found in the lookup table. The lookup is based on the Complexity ranking in column C. The interesting aspect of this use of the VLOOKUP is that we can easily modify the complexity factors in the array in A8:B10, and it will immediately affect the calculation of the adjusted hours. In essence, the values being looked up are a dynamic part of the formula.

The HLOOKUP function is identical to VLOOKUP in every way except for the layout of the lookup table. Figure 13.12 illustrates how it is used.

▲	A	B	C	D
1	NE	IL	MO	MT
2	Nebraska	Illinois	Missouri	Montana
3				
4	City	State	Full State	Text of Full State Formula
5	Joplin	MO	Missouri	=HLOOKUP(B5, $A$1:$E$2, 2, FALSE)
6	Billings	MT	Montana	=HLOOKUP(B6, $A$1:$E$2, 2, FALSE)
7	Peoria	IL	Illinois	=HLOOKUP(B7, $A$1:$E$2, 2, FALSE)
8	Lincoln	NE	Nebraska	=HLOOKUP(B8, $A$1:$E$2, 2, FALSE)
9	St. Louis	MO	Missouri	=HLOOKUP(B9, $A$1:$E$2, 2, FALSE)

Figure 13.12

The HLOOKUP function.

Source: Microsoft® Corporation.

In this example, the lookup table is in the first two rows. As mentioned, this is not the usual way that data is stored. Data is normally arranged with columns representing different attributes and rows containing each instance of the entity. In this case, the attributes are in rows and the instances are in columns. The data in rows 1 and 2 in Figure 13.12 is identical to the data in columns A and B of Figure 13.10. The lookup functions are also identical to those in Figure 13.10, except that the HLOOKUP is referencing a row in the *row_index_num* argument. The results in column C of Figure 13.12 are identical to the similar formulas in column F of Figure 13.10.

One significant limitation of VLOOKUP (or HLOOKUP) is that the key field must be the first column in the lookup array. Our next example will show that it's possible to accomplish the same goal of the VLOOKUP with a combination of the MATCH and INDEX functions. The syntax of these functions is:

MATCH(lookup_value, lookup_array, [match_type])

INDEX(array, row_num, [column_num])

In the MATCH function, the *lookup_value* argument is the value to be looked up. The *lookup_array* is the array where the value is to be found. The *match_type* argument can have three possible values, –1, 0, or 1. A value of 0 means that you want an exact match. In this situation, the lookup doesn't need to be in any particular sorted order. A value of 1 means that the data is sorted in ascending order and that you want the largest value less than or equal to the *lookup_value* argument. A value of –1 means that the data is in descending order and you want the smallest value greater than or equal to *lookup_value*. Unlike VLOOKUP, the MATCH function doesn't return an actual value. It provides only the position of the matching value in the lookup table. If it finds the requested lookup value in the third row of the array, it will return a 3.

The INDEX function returns an actual value. The *array* argument specifies the array of interest. The *row_num* and *column_num* arguments specify the cell whose value is desired. There's actually a second version of the INDEX function with slightly different arguments, but we'll focus on this variant.

Figure 13.13 provides a simple example of how these two functions work.

	A	B	C	D	E
1	State	Abbreviation		Function Text	Function
2	Nebraska	NE		=MATCH("MT", B2:B5, 0)	4
3	Illinois	IL		=INDEX(A2:A5, 4, 1)	Montana
4	Missouri	MO			
5	Montana	MT			

Figure 13.13
MATCH and INDEX functions.
Source: Microsoft® Corporation.

The MATCH function in row 2 searches for the value MT in the array in B2:B5. The *match_type* argument of 0 means that we're looking for an exact match. The function returns the value 4, which indicates that it found MT in the fourth row of the array. The INDEX function in row 3 uses the value of 4 as the *row_num* argument. The specified array is A2:A5, which means that we're only looking for data in column A. The *column_num* value of 1 means that we're only looking at the first column in this array. Of course, since this array has only one column, this value needs to be a 1.

Figure 13.14 shows how the MATCH and INDEX functions can be nested to do a lookup.

	A	B	C	D
1	City	State	Full State	Text of Full State Formula
2	Joplin	MO	Missouri	=INDEX($A$9:$A$12, MATCH(B2, $B$9:$B$12, 0), 1)
3	Billings	MT	Montana	=INDEX($A$9:$A$12, MATCH(B3, $B$9:$B$12, 0), 1)
4	Peoria	IL	Illinois	=INDEX($A$9:$A$12, MATCH(B4, $B$9:$B$12, 0), 1)
5	Lincoln	NE	Nebraska	=INDEX($A$9:$A$12, MATCH(B5, $B$9:$B$12, 0), 1)
6	St. Louis	MO	Missouri	=INDEX($A$9:$A$12, MATCH(B6, $B$9:$B$12, 0), 1)
7				
8	State	Abbreviation		
9	Nebraska	NE		
10	Illinois	IL		
11	Missouri	MO		
12	Montana	MT		

Figure 13.14

Using MATCH and INDEX to do a lookup.

Source: Microsoft® Corporation.

In Figure 13.14, we've placed the lookup table below the data of interest. The formulas in C2:C6 (and displayed as text in column D) utilize a combination of the MATCH and INDEX functions. In row 2, the inner function is a MATCH. This searches for the value B2 in the lookup array B9:B12. In the case of row 2, it would return the value 3, since MO is the third row in the array. The INDEX function then uses this result of 3 as the *row_num* argument. The array for the INDEX function is A9:A12, and the *column_num* is a 1, which means to look in the first column. The INDEX function then returns the value "Missouri", which is the third row of the array. The formulas in rows 3 through 6 work in a similar manner.

The key point to note in this example is that we've been able to do a lookup with a little more flexibility than is afforded by the VLOOKUP function. By using MATCH in combination with INDEX, we can do a lookup where the key value is not the first column in the array.

Looking Ahead

The logical functions discussed in this chapter allow you to add a great deal of power and precision to Excel formulas. By including AND, OR, and NOT functions in nested functions, one can test for a wide variety of logical conditions. When combined with the IF statement, you can specify a course of action for TRUE and FALSE situations. With various combinations of all these functions, the possibilities for complex expressions are virtually limitless. The IS functions provide another way to return a value of TRUE or FALSE, depending on the evaluation of the function. In one of our examples with ISNUMBER, we showed how to combine the function with the SEARCH function to search for a value and use the ISNUMBER function to determine whether the value was found. We rounded out the chapter with a look at a number of lookup functions.

As a practical matter, the ability to look up values is immensely important, and a frequent task of the analyst. In our discussion of relationships and data models in Chapter 6, "Pivot Table Calculations," we saw that pivot tables can include defined relationships that allow data in multiple tables to be joined together. Lookups in Excel are a related concept in that they allow you to retrieve a value in another table or range, based on a field with a value common to both tables. However, unlike databases such as Access, Excel doesn't offer an easy way to relate data in different ranges or tables. In Access, one can simply join tables together in a query to retrieve lookup values. In Excel, this needs to be handled more explicitly via lookup functions. In this regard, our primary focus was on the VLOOKUP function, a commonly used device for performing lookups. We also explored the use of the MATCH and INDEX functions, which when used in combination, can accomplish the same goal.

In our next and final chapter, "Analysis Tools," we'll look at three specific tools provided by Excel that allow you to carry out what-if analysis. These tools focus on the role that the analyst can play in the decision-making process. By looking at a variety of scenarios in a structured manner, one can make an informed decision on the best course of action in a particular situation. In addition to these tools, we'll also examine two important Excel add-ins: Data Analysis and Solver. The Data Analysis add-in is a separate component of Excel that allows you to perform sophisticated statistical analysis. The Solver add-in is a mathematical tool that addresses optimization problems.

Chapter 14

Analysis Tools

The ultimate goal of an analyst is to make a decision. We've talked about a multitude of ways that data can be viewed, transformed, and summarized. This has included crosstab displays of data in pivot tables, viewing data in charts or pivot charts, and utilizing a wide variety of functions. We've explored ways to summarize and aggregate data in pivot tables, as well as using worksheet functions to apply specific transformations to detailed data. However, with all of these tools, nothing has presented itself as a way to come up with a specific answer to a specific question. Of course, one can say that is where human intelligence comes in. By presenting data in a meaningful way, people can look at the results and discern the patterns that lead to a useful course of action.

However, there are other alternatives. In this chapter, we want to look at a number of Excel tools that allow the analyst to more directly reach a solution that can lead to a decision. Three of these tools are found under the What-If Analysis label in the Data Tools section under the Data tab of the Ribbon. These tools are called:

- Data Table
- Scenario Manager
- Goal Seek

The Data Table tool allows for creation of multiple scenarios where there are one or two relevant variables. The Scenario Manager extends the possibilities for saving and comparing more complex scenarios with up to 32 variables. The Goal Seek tool lets you solve for a variable for a specific goal.

We'll also look at two tools that are provided as Excel add-ins:

- Data Analysis
- Solver

The Data Analysis add-in provides ways to do statistical analysis on data without having to use any functions. Unlike the other tools discussed in this chapter, the Data Analysis add-in is not specifically geared towards decision-making, but nevertheless is useful as an added quantitative tool. The Solver add-in provides a useful way to solve a class of models known as optimization problems.

Data Analysis

The Data Analysis add-in is found in the Analysis group of commands under the Data tab of the Ribbon. If you don't see it, that probably means it hasn't been activated. To activate the add-in, you'll need to click on the File tab on the Ribbon, which takes you to the Backstage View. You should then click Options, then Add-Ins, then the Go button next to Manage Excel Add-Ins, select the Analysis ToolPak item, and then click OK.

After selecting the Data Analysis command in the Ribbon, you'll be presented with a dialog box that lets you select from nearly 20 different options, including topics such as descriptive statistics, correlation, regression, histograms, sampling, moving averages, rank and percentile, t-tests, and Fourier analysis. Many of these topics deal with inferential statistics and are subsequently beyond the scope of this book. However, in order to provide a brief introduction to the use of the Data Analysis tools, we'll talk about these options:

- Descriptive Statistics
- Rank and Percentile
- Histogram
- Correlation

After selecting Descriptive Statistics, a dialog box pops up that appears as in Figure 14.1.

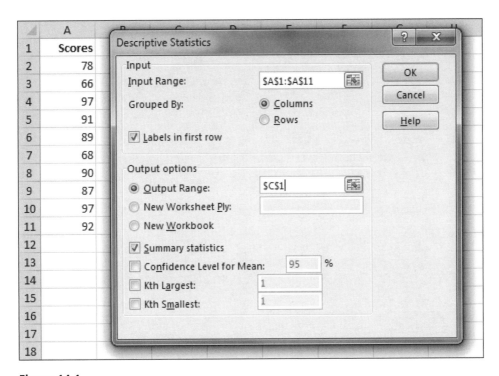

Figure 14.1

Descriptive Statistics dialog box.

Source: Microsoft® Corporation.

In this example, we've already entered some data in column A of the worksheet. This column contains 10 test scores that we'd like to analyze. In the Descriptive Statistics dialog box, we need to specify the input range. In this example, we selected cells A1 through A11. Excel automatically converts this to an absolute reference. We checked the box indicating that there are labels in the first row, and that grouping is by column. We also checked the summary statistics option, which provides basic statistics for the selected data. Under the output options, we specified that the output range should be placed in cell C1. If we had wanted, we could have placed the output in a new worksheet. After clicking OK, the worksheet appears as in Figure 14.2.

	A	B	C	D
1	**Scores**		*Scores*	
2	78			
3	66		Mean	85.5
4	97		Standard Error	3.518996069
5	91		Median	89.5
6	89		Mode	97
7	68		Standard Deviation	11.12804266
8	90		Sample Variance	123.8333333
9	87		Kurtosis	-0.357140658
10	97		Skewness	-0.965151069
11	92		Range	31
12			Minimum	66
13			Maximum	97
14			Sum	855
15			Count	10

Figure 14.2

Descriptive Statistics.

Source: Microsoft® Corporation.

As seen, summary statistics have been added to the worksheet in a range of cells that begins in cell C1. The data is simply text. If you click on any of the added cells, you'll see no formulas behind any of the values. This means that this information is static. If you change any of the test scores in column A, that has no effect on the computed statistics. In this list of basic statistics, we see some of the statistics that were discussed in Chapter 12, "Aggregate and Statistical Functions." This includes the mean, median, mode, and standard deviation, as well as the minimum, maximum, sum, and count. The standard deviation is the sample deviation, the same as calculated from the STDEV.S function. Also, note that if there had been more than one column of data in the original input range, then we'd have additional columns of calculated statistics.

The Rank and Percentile option works very much like Descriptive Statistics. Figure 14.3 shows the dialog box to make the specifications.

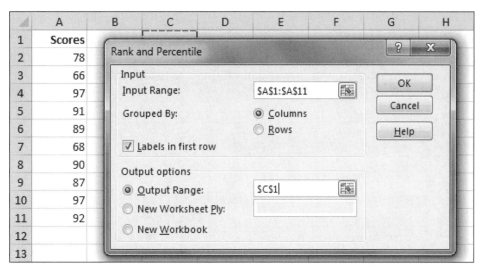

Figure 14.3
Rank and Percentile dialog box.
Source: Microsoft® Corporation.

After clicking OK, the worksheet appears as in Figure 14.4.

	A	B	C	D	E	F
1	**Scores**		*Point*	*Scores*	*Rank*	*Percent*
2	78		3	97	1	88.80%
3	66		9	97	1	88.80%
4	97		10	92	3	77.70%
5	91		4	91	4	66.60%
6	89		7	90	5	55.50%
7	68		5	89	6	44.40%
8	90		8	87	7	33.30%
9	87		1	78	8	22.20%
10	97		6	68	9	11.10%
11	92		2	66	10	0.00%

Figure 14.4
Rank and Percentile.
Source: Microsoft® Corporation.

We now see a ranking of the data, as well as computed percentiles. The Rank column has the rank of the data, the Scores column repeats the original data, but now in order by rank, and the Point column has the original position of each data point. The Percent column has the computed percentile. This percentile is identical to what would be calculated with the PERCENTRANK.INC function.

In Chapter 12, we showed how to create a histogram by using the Frequency function and then generating a chart from the results. The Histogram option of the Data Analysis tool provides a much quicker way to accomplish this task. Figure 14.5 shows the same data as in the above figures, with an added column with the bin values that we want the histogram to reflect.

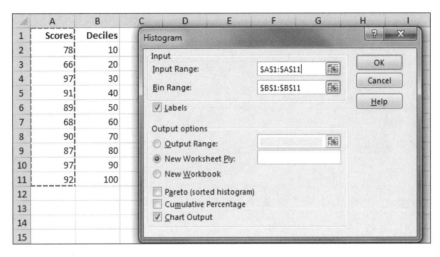

Figure 14.5

Histogram dialog box.

Source: Microsoft® Corporation.

In this dialog box, we've chosen to place the output in a new worksheet. The specified bin range refers to the bin values on the worksheet in column B under the Deciles heading. We checked the Chart Output option in the dialog box, indicating that we want a chart along with the frequencies. The result is shown in Figure 14.6.

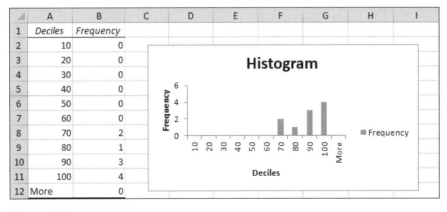

Figure 14.6

Histogram Frequencies and Chart.

Source: Microsoft® Corporation.

This figure contains the newly created worksheet with both the generated frequencies and a chart. As before, the frequency values do not contain any formulas and are thus not directly linked to the underlying data. However, the chart in Figure 14.6 is like any other Excel chart and is linked to frequency data on the same worksheet. This means that the chart can be edited as desired. As seen, this chart displays a histogram of the underlying values, based on the calculated frequencies for each bin. Note that the numbers on the horizontal scale of the chart are really cutoff points. For example, the label of 90 means that these are values greater than 80, but less than or equal to 90.

Our final example of the Data Analysis add-in is with the Correlation option. As you may remember from Chapter 12, the correlation coefficient is a number between –1 and 1 that indicates the strength of the relationship between two variables. A value of 0 means that there is no relationship, a value of 1 means that there is a perfect positive relationship, and a value of –1 means that there is a perfect negative relationship. A nice feature of the correlation option in the Data Analysis add-in is that it easily allows you to look at numerous variables at the same time. The example in Figure 14.7 has statistics on baseball teams in the National League Central division from 2012. Our objective is to get a sense of how these statistics are related to each other.

	A	B	C	D	E	F	G
1	Team	Wins	Runs	Hits	Walks	Home Runs	Stolen Bases
2	Chicago Cubs	61	613	1297	447	137	94
3	Cincinnati Reds	97	669	1377	481	172	87
4	Houston Astros	55	583	1276	463	146	105
5	Milwaukee Brewers	83	776	1442	466	202	158
6	Pittsburgh Pirates	79	651	1313	444	170	73
7	St. Louis Cardinals	88	765	1526	533	159	91
8							
9	Correlation						
10	Input						
11	Input Range:	$B$1:$G$7				OK	
12	Grouped By:	Columns				Cancel	
13		Rows					
14	✓ Labels in first row					Help	
15							
16	Output options						
17	Output Range:						
18	New Worksheet Ply:						
19	New Workbook						
20							

Figure 14.7

Correlation dialog box.

Source: Microsoft® Corporation.

After clicking OK in the Correlation dialog box, we see the results shown in Figure 14.8.

◢	A	B	C	D	E	F	G
1		Wins	Runs	Hits	Walks	Home Runs	Stolen Bases
2	Wins	1					
3	Runs	0.697240485	1				
4	Hits	0.691929892	0.935037815	1			
5	Walks	0.515356064	0.610908359	0.847827486	1		
6	Home Runs	0.63504226	0.721213821	0.480324362	0.055482123	1	
7	Stolen Bases	-0.033603761	0.484763284	0.290541953	-0.032176856	0.604769243	1

Figure 14.8

Correlation.

Source: Microsoft® Corporation.

What we see in Figure 14.8 is a table of correlation coefficients between each of the six statistics in Figure 14.7. There is a diagonal of values running from the upper left to the lower right with values of 1, showing the correlation of each statistic with itself. To avoid clutter, the table shows only coefficient values below this diagonal. From the data, we witness a fairly strong correlation between both runs and wins (.697), and hits and wins (.692). There is a slightly lower correlation between home runs and wins (.635), and an even lower correlation between walks and wins (.515). We see a slightly negative correlation between stolen bases and wins, indicating that these factors are not related. Interestingly, we see a very high correlation between runs and hits (.935), indicating that these statistics are highly related. Again, as noted in Chapter 12, correlation is not the same as causation. We can't necessarily say that a preponderance of runs causes wins. We would need to delve into inferential statistics to make meaningful statements about causation and our degree of confidence as to how these statistics are related to each other.

Data Tables

Data Tables permit you to quickly perform calculations against a wide variety of situations where either one or two variables can change. In essence, Data Tables come in two varieties: one-variable and two-variable. By being able to quickly generate many data points involving these one or two variables, you can more readily come to a decision on your preferred outcome. Like the Scenario Manager and Goal Seek tools discussed later in this chapter, the Data Table tool is found under the What-If Analysis label in the Data Tools group under the Data tab of the Ribbon. These commands are shown in Figure 14.9.

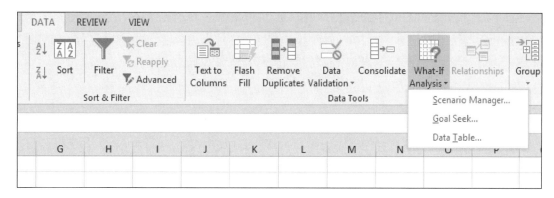

Figure 14.9

What-If Analysis commands.

Source: Microsoft® Corporation.

To set up a Data Table, we'll start with the premise that we want to calculate payments for a number of different interest rates. We'll want to see individual payments as well as total payments over the life of the loan. We also want the ability to produce these numbers for different loan amounts. The data in Figure 14.10 has the basic setup for this situation.

	A	B	C	D	E
1	Loan amount	10000			
2					
3	Interest rate	3 Year Monthly Payment	5 Year Monthly Payment	3 Year Total Payments	5 Year Total Payments
4	4.00%	295.24	184.17	10628.63	11049.91
5	5.00%				
6	6.00%				
7	7.00%				
8	8.00%				

Figure 14.10

Setup for a Data Table.

Source: Microsoft® Corporation.

In Figure 14.10, there are formulas in cells B4 through E4. All other cells have text values as shown. Our objective is to calculate the monthly payments that would be required for both 3- and 5-year loans, at varying interest rates from 4% to 8%. We also want to see the total payments for the life of the loan. The Data Table that we will create will extend from A4 to E8. As seen, many of these cells are currently blank, but after the Data Table is created, these cells will contain values. Our variable for the Data Table is the interest rate, with values shown in column A. This makes it a one-variable Data Table. However, our formulas will also reference another variable outside of the table—namely the loan amount entered in cell B1.

Let's now examine the formulas present in cells B4, C4, D4, and E4. They are, respectively:

=PMT(A4/12, 36, -B1)

=PMT(A4/12, 60, -B1)

=B4*36

=C4*60

The formula in B4 uses the PMT function discussed in Chapter 11, "Numeric and Date Functions," to calculate the payment for the loan. The *rate* argument of the function is the calculation A4/12. For row 4, this is 4% divided by 12. The *nper* (number of periods) argument is 36, representing the number of months in 3 years. The *pv* (present value) argument is the negative of the value in B1, which has the loan amount. The formula in C4 is similar, except that it's for 5 years. The formula in D4 computes the total payment amount as the payment amount in B4 times 36. The formula in E4 is similar, except that it's for 60 months.

Now that we have this setup ready, we can invoke the Data Table tool to fill in all of the blank cells in A4:E8 to contain similar values. The magic of the Data Table tool is that it doesn't require entering any additional formulas. It will load in values based on a few key pieces of information. Before invoking the Data Table command, you must first select the cells in which you want the table to appear. In this case, those are cells A4:E8. Then, after selecting the Data Table command, a dialog box appears as shown in Figure 14.11.

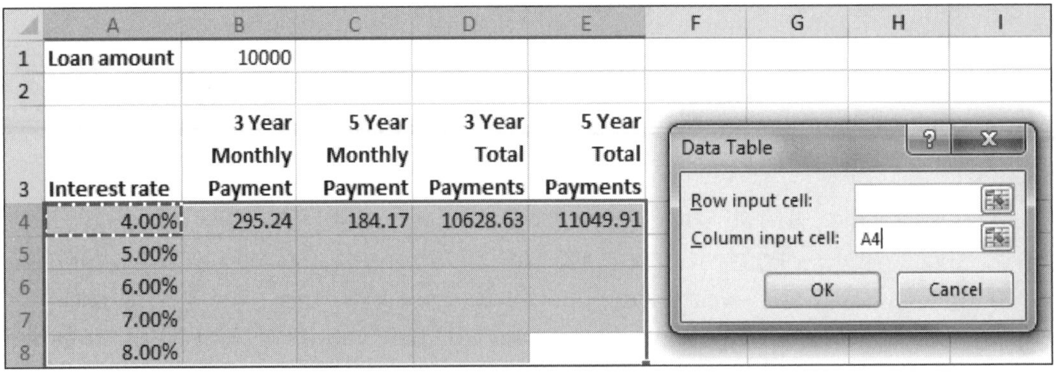

Figure 14.11

Data Table dialog box.

We mentioned that Data Tables are either one-variable or two-variable. In this example, we have a one-variable situation, with the variable being the interest rate, shown in column A. Because we have only one variable that is arranged in a column, we need to make an entry for the Column Input Cell in the dialog box. The appropriate value to enter is A4, since that is the uppermost cell in the column. After clicking OK, the Data Table appears as shown in Figure 14.12.

	A	B	C	D	E
1	Loan amount	10000			
2					
3	Interest rate	3 Year Monthly Payment	5 Year Monthly Payment	3 Year Total Payments	5 Year Total Payments
4	4.00%	295.24	184.17	10628.63	11049.91
5	5.00%	299.70897	188.71234	10789.523	11322.74
6	6.00%	304.21937	193.32802	10951.897	11599.681
7	7.00%	308.77097	198.01199	11115.755	11880.719
8	8.00%	313.36365	202.76394	11281.092	12165.837

Figure 14.12

A Data Table.

Source: Microsoft® Corporation.

If you click on any of the cells in the data table that were previously blank, you'll see this formula:

{=TABLE(,A4)}

This formula indicates that this is an array formula specifying a Data Table based on column cell A4. The power of the Data Table is that it automatically populates all blank cells without requiring any formulas. Note that we also have the ability to modify values by altering the loan amount in cell B1. Since all the formulas directly or indirectly reference cell B1, changing this value will automatically modify all other values.

Scenario Manager

Data Tables work well when only one or two variables are involved. However, you'll likely encounter situations with more than two variables. When that occurs, you can turn to the Scenario Manager. This tool lets you set up a model with up to 32 variables and one more dependent value. The Scenario Manager refers to the cells containing variables as *changing cells*, and the cells with an outcome as *result cells*. We'll illustrate the Scenario Manager with an example that involves determining a budget for meals, with the variables being the price of each type of meal, and the relative percentage that each type of meal is eaten at home versus eaten at a restaurant. Figure 14.13 has the data.

▲	A	B	C	D
1		Daily Cost of Eating at Home	Daily Cost of Eating Out	Percent of Meals Eaten Out
2	Breakfast	2	4	10%
3	Lunch	4	6	25%
4	Dinner	6	12	20%
5				
6	Monthly Food Cost	417.00		

Figure 14.13

Data for Scenario Manager.

Source: Microsoft® Corporation.

In Figure 14.13, we see the average daily cost of eating breakfast, lunch, and dinner, both when the meal is eaten at home and when it is eaten out at a restaurant. These variables contain values provided by the user. In addition, we are specifying the percentage of time that each meal is eaten out. So in total, we have nine variables. The single formula in this worksheet, in cell B6, calculates the monthly food cost, assuming that there are 30 days in the month. The formula in cell B6 is:

=30*((D2*C2) + ((1–D2)*B2) + (D3*C3) + ((1–D3)*B3) + (D4*C4) + ((1–D4)*B4))

There are six terms in this expression, representing the daily cost of eating each of the three meals at home or in a restaurant. For example, D2*C2 represents the cost of eating breakfast out, adjusted for the percent of time that breakfast is eaten out. The term (1–D2)*B2 is the cost of eating breakfast at home, adjusted for the percent of time that meal is taken at home. The six terms are then added together and multiplied by 30. The formula calculates the total monthly food cost in this scenario as 417.

In Figure 14.13, we entered values for each of these nine variables, but now we want to see how the food budget changes if we change some values. However, before modifying anything, we'd like to save our initial results. This is where the Scenario Manager comes in. Our first step is to select the Scenario Manager command under the What-If Analysis label. One then sees the Scenario Manager dialog box shown in Figure 14.14.

Figure 14.14

Scenario Manager dialog box with no scenarios.

Source: Microsoft® Corporation.

The next step is to click the Add button to add our first scenario. After doing so, we see the Edit Scenario dialog box shown in Figure 14.15.

Figure 14.15

Edit Scenario dialog box.

Source: Microsoft® Corporation.

The Edit Scenario dialog box in Figure 14.15 would initially be blank, but we've already added some values. We've given the scenario a name, selected the cells that can change, and provided a comment explaining the selection. The range B2:D4 covers the nine cells that can vary in value. After clicking OK, we see the Scenario Values dialog box shown in Figure 14.16.

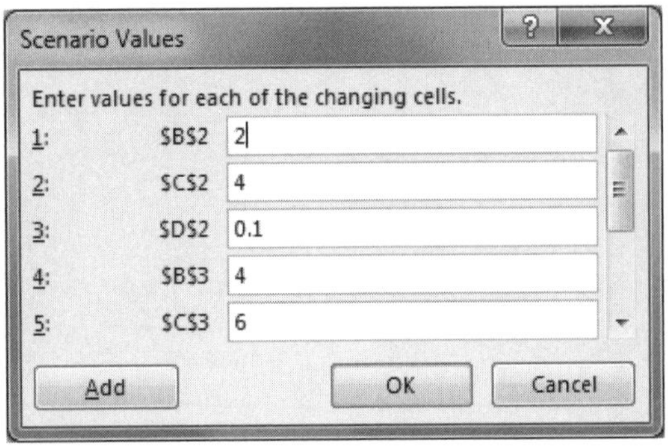

Figure 14.16
Scenario Values dialog box.
Source: Microsoft® Corporation.

This dialog box allows us to modify the values that have been entered for each of the variables. We'll choose to leave them as is. After clicking OK, we see the Scenario Manager dialog box again, this time with one scenario listed. This is shown in Figure 14.17.

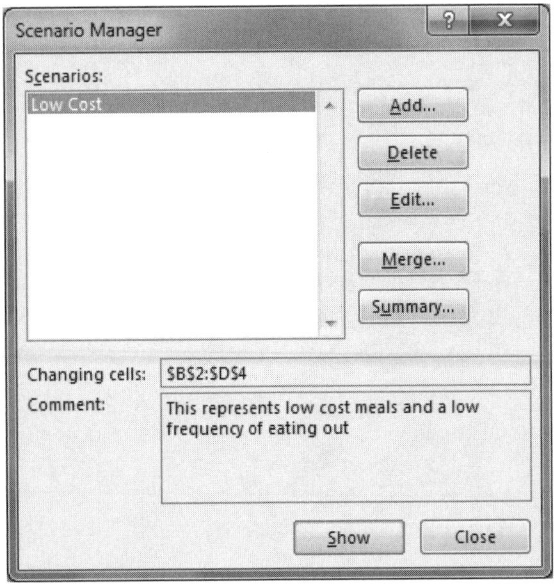

Figure 14.17
Scenario Manager dialog box with one scenario.
Source: Microsoft® Corporation.

At this point, we have several options. We can edit or delete the selected scenario, or merge in a scenario from another worksheet. We can click the Show button to show the selected scenario. We can also click the Summary button to show a summary of all entered scenarios. Or, we can simply close the dialog box and come back to it later. For now, we'll add a new scenario that we'll call Medium Cost. After doing so, the Scenario Manager dialog box appears as in Figure 14.18.

Figure 14.18

Scenario Manager dialog box with two scenarios.

Source: Microsoft® Corporation.

After selecting the Medium Cost scenario in Figure 14.18 and then clicking the Show button, we see the data of Figure 14.19.

	A	B	C	D
1		Daily Cost of Eating at Home	Daily Cost of Eating Out	Percent of Meals Eaten Out
2	Breakfast	2	5	10%
3	Lunch	4	8	25%
4	Dinner	6	15	60%
5				
6	Monthly Food Cost	561.00		

Figure 14.19

Revised data selected by Scenario Manager.

Source: Microsoft® Corporation.

After multiple scenarios have been entered in the Scenario Manager, you can easily switch the numbers on your worksheet by simply selecting the scenario and then clicking the Show button. It's that simple. The next step in using the tool is to display the results of each scenario side by side. This is accomplished by clicking the Summary button in the Scenario Manager dialog box. When this is done, you'll first see the Scenario Summary dialog box shown in Figure 14.20.

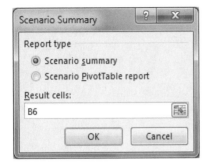

Figure 14.20
Scenario Summary dialog box.
Source: Microsoft® Corporation.

In this dialog box, we'll specify the result cell, which is B6, and then select that we want to see a Scenario Summary. After clicking OK, a new worksheet is created with the data shown in Figure 14.21.

	A	B	C	D	E	F	G
1							
2		**Scenario Summary**					
3				Current Values:	Low Cost	Medium Cost	
5		**Changing Cells:**					
6			$B$2	2	2	2	
7			$C$2	5	4	5	
8			$D$2	10%	10%	10%	
9			$B$3	4	4	4	
10			$C$3	8	6	8	
11			$D$3	25%	25%	25%	
12			$B$4	6	6	6	
13			$C$4	15	12	15	
14			$D$4	60%	20%	60%	
15		**Result Cells:**					
16			$B$6	561.00	417.00	561.00	
17		Notes: Current Values column represents values of changing cells at					
18		time Scenario Summary Report was created. Changing cells for each					
19		scenario are highlighted in gray.					

Figure 14.21
Scenario Summary.
Source: Microsoft® Corporation.

This summary displays both scenarios, Low Cost and Medium Cost, side by side. We also see the current values, which happen to be the same as the Medium Cost scenario. In addition to seeing all specified changing cells, we also see all result cells. In this example, we have only one result cell, but there can be many more. Note also that all cells are identified by reference. If names had been provided for any of the cells via the Name Manager, the name would be shown instead. In fact, this would be an ideal time to use the Name Manager, as it would make the summary considerably more comprehensible.

Goal Seek

The Scenario Manager tool is wonderful at managing a large number of variables and results, and saving the various scenarios so they can be compared. However, nothing in the tool can determine an optimal solution. The next two tools we'll discuss, Goal Seek and Solver, allow you to use the power of mathematics to calculate a scenario that optimizes some particular goal. Goal Seek is the simpler of the two. Essentially, the Goal Seek tool lets you determine the value of a cell that will cause the value of another cell to equal a particular value. The data in Figure 14.22 will be used to illustrate a simple scenario.

	A	B	C
1	Month	Sales	Cumulative Average
2	January	3500	3500
3	February	5000	4250
4	March	2000	3500
5	April	4200	3675
6	May	7200	4380
7	June	0	3650

Figure 14.22

Data for Goal Seek.

Source: Microsoft® Corporation.

In this scenario, we see sales for five months, January through May, and corresponding sales for each month. Assuming that it is now May 31, we'd like to determine the sales that would be required in June to end up with average sales of 5000 per month for the six-month period. Column C shows the cumulative averages for each month. For example, the formula in cell C7 is:

=AVERAGE(B$2:B7)

Incidentally, notice that this formula makes use of absolute cell references to compute a cumulative average. The procedure was to enter the formula AVERAGE(B$2:B2) in cell C2, and then to copy that cell down the column. Since the 2 in cell reference B$2 is absolute, that value doesn't change as the cell is copied to other locations.

The worksheet has a 0 in cell B7 since we don't yet know what June sales will be. We can see that the average for January through May is only 4380, so we obviously need sales over 5000 to achieve our goal. If wanted to determine the amount of sales in June that would cause the six-month average to equal 5000, we could experiment by entering some numbers in cell B7 until we found the number that causes C7 to equal 5000. For example, if we entered 6000 in B7, the formula in C7 would calculate the average as 4650. That would tell us that we need to go higher than 6000. In a few more tries, we could probably figure out the answer. However, Goal Seek can be used to quickly provide the answer without the use of trial and error.

To invoke the tool, we click on the Goal Seek command under the What-If Analysis label on the Ribbon. This causes the dialog box shown in Figure 14.23 to appear.

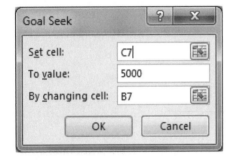

Figure 14.23
Goal Seek dialog box.
Source: Microsoft® Corporation.

This dialog box requires three values: the cell that we set to a value, the value that we want to achieve as a goal, and the cell that will change. The Set Cell value must contain a formula. The dialog box is initially blank, but Figure 14.23 shows values that we subsequently entered. As indicated, we want to set cell C7 to the value 5000 by changing cell B7. After clicking OK, the worksheet appears as in Figure 14.24.

	A	B	C
1	Month	Sales	Cumulative Average
2	January	3500	3500
3	February	5000	4250
4	March	2000	3500
5	April	4200	3675
6	May	7200	4380
7	June	8100	5000

Figure 14.24

Goal Seek result.

Source: Microsoft® Corporation.

As seen, the Goal Seek tool has determined that we need sales of 8100 in June to end up with a six-month average of 5000. Another typical use of the Goal Seek tool is with break-even analysis computations. Figure 14.25 illustrates a basic break-even analysis problem.

	A	B
1	Units sold	0
2	Price per unit	10.25
3	Cost per unit	3.50
4	Fixed cost	10000
5	Profit	-10000

Figure 14.25

Goal Seek break-even analysis.

Source: Microsoft® Corporation.

In this set of data, cells B2:B4 contain parameter values that are entered by the user. The formula in cell B5 computes the profit from the specified number of units sold, the price and cost per unit, and fixed costs. The profit formula is:

=(B1*B2) - (B1*B3) - B4

The first term, B1*B2, represents revenue. The second term, B1*B3, has the variable cost, and the third term, B4, has the fixed cost. The worksheet currently shows a negative profit of -10000, since we haven't yet entered the number of units sold. The Goal Seek tool can be used to compute the break-even point for this product by specifying a profit goal of 0. However, we'll attempt a minor variation on the normal procedure and say that we would like to have a profit of 3500. This is done by entering the values in the Goal Seek dialog box of Figure 14.26. The result is shown in Figure 14.27.

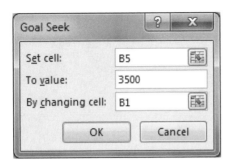

Figure 14.26
Goal Seek dialog box for break-even analysis.
Source: Microsoft® Corporation.

	A	B
1	Units sold	2000
2	Price per unit	10.25
3	Cost per unit	3.50
4	Fixed cost	10000
5	Profit	3500

Figure 14.27
Goal Seek break-even analysis result.
Source: Microsoft® Corporation.

With the goal of setting cell B5 to 3500 by changing cell B1, the Goal Seek tool calculated that the units sold must equal 2000. Again, this rather simple result might have been determined either by trial and error or with a bit of algebra. However, the Goal Seek tool calculates the unknown value with ease.

Solver

The Goal Seek tool is easy to use, but it applies only in situations where there is one formula. However, many problems typically require more than one formula to fully define a model. The Solver is a significantly more complex tool that provides the ability to simultaneously solve multiple formulas to achieve or optimize a goal. Like the Data Analysis tool, the Solver is available as an add-in and can be found in every version of Excel 2013. If it's not visible under the Data tab of the Ribbon, follow the same install notes provided earlier in this chapter for the Data Analysis tool.

The Solver utilizes a class of mathematics known as *linear programming*. This has nothing to do with programming in the traditional sense, but it does deal with linear equations—that is, equations that don't make use of exponents. Using this tool typically requires a certain amount of mathematical acumen, as it involves setting up a series of equations to formulate a problem.

Interestingly, all Goal Seek problems can also be solved by using the Solver. We'll start with a reformulation of the Goal Seek problem shown in Figures 14.22 through 14.24 that determined the sales amount that yielded a desired cumulative average. Even for the mathematically challenged, this use of the Solver tool is no more difficult than using Goal Seek. To use the Solver to address this problem, we'll start with the same data shown in Figure 14.22. The Solver is initiated by clicking the Solver command in the Analysis group under the Data tab of the Ribbon. This brings up the dialog box shown in Figure 14.28.

Figure 14.28
Solver Parameters dialog box.
Source: Microsoft® Corporation.

This dialog box allows you to specify all the data needed for the Solver to create a solution. There are five components in this dialog box:

- An objective
- The type of objective
- Variable cells
- Constraints
- The solving method

The objective is the cell that contains a formula to be optimized. The type of objective can be Max, Min, or Value Of. In most situations, the objective will be either Min or Max. This represents something that you want to minimize or maximize. For example, you may want to maximize profit or minimize costs. The profit or cost to be maximized or minimized is expressed by the formula stated by the objective. However, in a goal-seeking scenario, the objective will be a value that is to be obtained. In our prior example of cumulative averages, we wanted to achieve an average value of 5000.

The variable cells specify the cell or cells that can change in the model. In a goal-seeking situation, this will be a single cell. In more complex models with a Min or Max, this will be multiple cells. For Min or Max models, the constraints are formulas that represent conditions that must be met. For example, if our goal is to maximize profit, the constraints may be formulas that express production limits or design aspects that must be maintained as products are produced. Finally, you'll notice that the dialog box has a drop-down to select a Solving Method. In most cases, this will be Simplex LP, which is the commonly used algorithm for linear programming problems.

Figure 14.29 shows how the Solver Parameters dialog box would be filled out to solve the goal-seeking problem for the data in Figure 14.22.

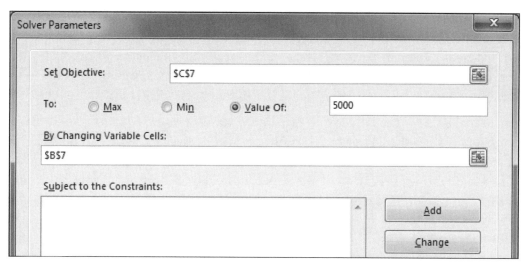

Figure 14.29
Solver Parameters dialog box for Goal Seek problem.
Source: Microsoft® Corporation.

Since this is a goal seek problem, the objective is Value Of rather than Min or Max. The stated objective is a value of 5000. The cell that contains the objective is C7. The cell that we want to change in order to accomplish this objective is B7. There are no constraints. After this model is set up, the result is identical to that shown in Figure 4.25. To achieve a cumulative average of 5000, we need sales of 8100 in June. For this problem, it is decidedly easier to use the Goal Seek tool rather than the Solver. We start with this example merely to indicate that the Solver can do what Goal Seek does, but also much more.

Our next example of how the Solver can be used is considerably more complex and indicates its real power. This example features an objective that we want to maximize, and includes the use of constraints. The relevant facts of our problem are as follows: We can produce three different products, which we'll call products X, Y, and Z. These products are produced from one or more of four different parts, which we'll refer to as parts A, B, C, and D. Product X provides a profit of 90 per unit sold. Products Y and Z have per unit profits of 70 and 60, respectively. Our objective is to maximize profit, subject to a number of constraints. First, there are constraints as to how many of each part we have in inventory. We have available 450 of part A, 250 of part B, 400 of part C, and 450 of part D. Additionally, we have constraints as to how each of the three products is assembled from the four parts. These are:

- Product X requires one part B, one part C, and two of part D
- Product Y requires one part A, two of part B, and one part D
- Product Y requires four of part A, one part C, and one part D

This type of scenario is generally referred to as a *product mix* problem. We have an objective of maximizing profit but need to determine which mix of products will achieve that goal. One can perhaps think of the products as electronic products that can be produced from a mix of common parts. Or, the products might be items to be served in a restaurant, with the parts being the ingredients needed for each recipe.

In order to make use of the Solver tool, we'll need to place some equations in an Excel workbook in a format the Solver tool can understand. However, before we do that, it's helpful to just write down the equations on paper. In the following, we'll let x, y, and z represent the quantities produced of the three products. In algebraic terms, the equations we'll need to solve the problem are:

maximize $90x + 70y + 60z$

subject to these constraints:

$y + 4z <= 450$

$x + 2y <= 250$

$x + z <= 400$

$2x + y + z <= 450$

$x >= 0$

$y >= 0$

$z >= 0$

The first equation is the objective. We want to maximize profit, which is expressed as 90 times the number of product Xs we produce, 60 times product Y, and 30 times product Z. The next four equations represent the constraints for each part. For example, the $y + 4z <= 450$ equation means that we have only 450 of part A in stock, and that one of these parts is required for each product Y, and four for each product Z. The final three equations simply mean that we must end up with non-negative values. We can't produce a negative amount of a product.

The tricky aspect of using the Solver is in placing these equations in an Excel workbook in a suitable format. Figures 14.30 and 14.31 show how these equations might appear in Excel. Figure 14.30 utilizes the Show Formulas command so we can see the formulas behind each cell. Figure 14.31 shows the data without formulas.

	A	B	C	D	E	F
1	Part	Inventory	Part Quantity	Product X	Product Y	Product Z
2	Part A	450	=SUMPRODUCT(D2:F2,D$8:F$8)	0	1	4
3	Part B	250	=SUMPRODUCT(D3:F3,D$8:F$8)	1	2	0
4	Part C	400	=SUMPRODUCT(D4:F4,D$8:F$8)	1	0	1
5	Part D	450	=SUMPRODUCT(D5:F5,D$8:F$8)	2	1	1
6						
7			Per Unit Profit	90	70	60
8			Product Quantity	0	0	0
9						
10			Profit	=SUMPRODUCT(D7:F7,D8:F8)		

Figure 14.30

Setup for a product mix problem, showing formulas.

Source: Microsoft® Corporation.

	A	B	C	D	E	F
1	Part	Inventory	Part Quantity	Product X	Product Y	Product Z
2	Part A	450	0	0	1	4
3	Part B	250	0	1	2	0
4	Part C	400	0	1	0	1
5	Part D	450	0	2	1	1
6						
7			Per Unit Profit	90	70	60
8			Product Quantity	0	0	0
9						
10			Profit	0		

Figure 14.31

Setup for a product mix problem, not showing formulas.

Source: Microsoft® Corporation.

Before getting to the formulas, we can see that column B has the inventories for each part. The numbers in the range D2:F5 express the configuration of products to parts, indicating how many of each part must be in each product. The numbers in row 7 are the profit to be obtained from each product. The zeros in row 8 represent the solution that we are seeking—that is, how many of each product we will produce to maximize profit. The values in C2:C5 are also zeros, representing the number of each part that will be needed in the solution. All these numbers are zero right now, but after running the Solver, we will see numbers appear.

Utilizing the SUMPRODUCT function, the formulas in cells C2:C5 concisely express the inventory constraints discussed previously. As described in Chapter 12, "Aggregate and Statistical Functions," the SUMPRODUCT function multiplies the corresponding cells in each array and then sums up the terms. This means that the formula in cell C2 is equivalent to:

=(D2*D8) + (E2*E8) + (F2*F8)

This equation expresses the total number of Part As that will be used in the final solution. In the Solver tool, we will state that this quantity must be less than or equal to 450, due to inventory constraints. The formulas in cells C3:C5 are similar. The formula in D10 states the profit that will result after the product quantities are determined. This is what we will specify as the objective in the Solver tool. The SUMPRODUCT function in D10 uses the per unit profit amounts in row 7, and is equivalent to this formula:

=(D7*D8) + (E7*E8)*(F7*F8)

Now, let's look at how the Solver Parameters dialog box needs to be filled out to solve the problem. This is shown in Figure 14.32.

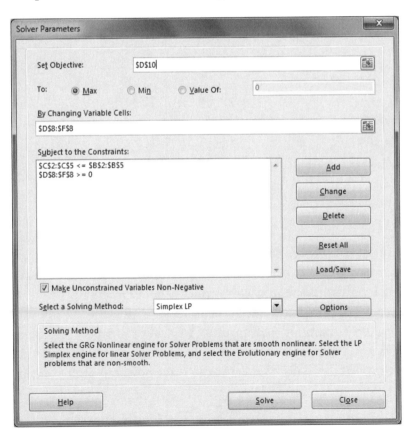

Figure 14.32
Solver Parameters dialog box for a product mix problem.
Source: Microsoft® Corporation.

As seen, the objective is a Max objective that is set to cell D10, which has the formula that expresses profit. The changing variable cells are D8:F8. The Solver will compute these product quantities. Two constraints have been created by clicking the Add button and entering values in an Add Constraint dialog box. This appears as in Figure 14.33.

Figure 14.33
Add Constraint dialog box.
Source: Microsoft® Corporation.

The constraint in Figure 14.33 enforces the fact that the quantity of each part in the final solution must be no greater than the available inventory for that part. The Add Constraint dialog box would be invoked a second time for the set of constraints that says that the product quantities must be greater than or equal to zero. After the constraints are entered, we simply click the Solve button in the Solver Parameters dialog box to view the solution. This is shown in Figure 14.34.

	A	B	C	D	E	F
1	Part	Inventory	Part Quantity	Product X	Product Y	Product Z
2	Part A	450	450	0	1	4
3	Part B	250	250	1	2	0
4	Part C	400	250	1	0	1
5	Part D	450	450	2	1	1
6						
7			Per Unit Profit	90	70	60
8			Product Quantity	150	50	100
9						
10			Profit	23000		

Figure 14.34
Product mix problem solution.
Source: Microsoft® Corporation.

All of the 0 values have now been replaced with positive numbers. The solution indicates that profit is maximized when we produce 150 of product X, 50 of product Y, and 100 of product Z. This requires 450 of part A, 250 of part B, 250 of part C and 450 of part D. Note that we have used all available inventory for every part except for part C. The profit that results from this solution is 23000. This is the maximum possible profit, given our constraints.

One interesting aspect of using the Solver is that, unlike the Data Analysis add-in, the values in the Solver Parameters dialog box are influenced by changes in the underlying values in your worksheet. For example, if you were to add a row between parts B and C in Figure 14.35, the formulas in the Solver Parameters dialog box would automatically adjust, with the assumption that you've added another part.

The types of problems that can be handled by the Solver are many and varied. To give just one more example, one might be interested in solving a personnel scheduling problem that involves determining how many people should work each shift to satisfy the need for personnel during each hour of the day. This can be formulated with a Min objective, where the objective is expressed as the average wage for each shift times the number of workers hired for that shift. The constraints would enforce the requirement that the number of available people at any given time must always be greater than or equal to the need for personnel at that hour.

Final Thoughts

In this chapter, we've covered a number of tools that accomplish some specific analytical goals. The Data Analysis add-in allows the analyst to perform statistical analysis without needing to resort to Excel functions. The downside of this tool is that it doesn't interact with data in your workbooks after being invoked. The tool adds useful statistics to a worksheet, but once created, doesn't change if the underlying data is modified. In our review of the tool, we looked at options related to descriptive statistics, but numerous other features would assist the experienced statistician with inferential statistics.

The Data Table tool lets the analyst construct tables of scenarios, allowing for multiple values for one or two variables. The Scenario Manager is a more robust tool that allows you to modify up to 32 variables and save the results as different scenarios are explored. The beauty of the Scenario Manager is that you can quickly switch between previously saved scenarios, and see side-by-side comparisons. The Goal Seek tool lets you determine the value of a variable when that variable is used in a formula that's set to a specific value. This can be very handy in any situation where you need to determine how to reach a specific goal. In essence, this tool lets you solve complex equations with a single variable.

We ended the chapter with a discussion of the Solver add-in, a mathematical tool that deals with optimization problems. The Solver can be used to maximize or minimize an objective, with any number of specified constraints. The provided example was for a basic product mix problem, but the tool can be used in many other situations. Use of the tool, however, requires the ability to formulate mathematical equations, and then to translate those equations to a format in Excel that the Solver can interpret.

With this book nearly concluded, a few additional thoughts can be expressed. The journey that we've undertaken is one that began with an overview of Excel's basic components. We've made frequent mention of the structural aspects of worksheets and cells, tables, pivot tables, pivot charts, and charts, and of the unique characteristics of each component. This approach was taken to reduce the almost bewildering number of commands and processes in Excel to an understandable framework. The topic of pivot tables was given primary emphasis, as this is an invaluable tool for the business analyst. By providing an easy way to quickly summarize data, the pivot table is perhaps Excel's greatest asset. In fact, we covered pivot tables and pivot charts before delving into the many functions that are available when working solely with worksheets. This correlates with the natural progression of analysis, whereby one frequently wants to summarize a set of data before exploring details.

One of the main challenges of using Excel is that it is not nearly as structured a tool as something like Microsoft Access. Whereas Access forces its user to transform data into a relational structure prior to any analysis against the data, Excel is completely free-form. That is both its greatest virtue and its most significant challenge. The productive use of Excel requires the analyst to think intelligently about his or her goal, and then employ the appropriate tools within Excel to accomplish that objective. It is the author's sincerest hope that this book has helped you gain a higher level of understanding in that regard.

Index

Symbols and Numerics

+ (addition operator), 249
& (ampersand), 250, 278
* (asterisk), 107, 279, 284
: (colon), 249, 251
, (comma), 251
/ (division operator), 249
$ (dollar sign), 44, 232, 289
= (equals sign), 32, 248
= (equal to operator), 250
^ (exponentiation operator), 249
>= (greater than or equal to operator), 250
< (less than operator), 250
<= (less than or equal to operator), 250
* (multiplication operator), 249
<> (not equal to operator), 250
% (percentage operator), 249
+ (plus sign), 249
? (question mark), 107
– (subtraction operator), 249
3-D clustered column chart, 207
100% stacked line charts, 214

A

ABS function, 295, 315
absolute cell references, 252–257
Access
    data imported into pivot table, 70–71
    data imported into table, 70
    Datasheet view, 68
    Design view, 67

    external data from, 66–71
    and Microsoft Query, 89–90
    Sales table, 67
    tables imported from Excel, 19–20
Account command, 56
Accounting formatting command, 43
Add Chart Element label commands, 199
Add Constraint dialog box, 387
Add Criteria dialog box, 85–86
Add Tables dialog box, 81–82
add-ins
    Data Analysis, 23–25
    Solver, 23, 25
addition operator (+), 249
Advanced command, 231
Advanced Filter dialog box, 231–232
advanced filters, 231–233
advanced sorting, 231
Advanced tab, 57
Alignment tab commands, 35
ampersand (&), 250, 278
analysis. *See also* data analysis
    break-even, 379–380
    Data Analysis tool, 362–368
    Data Tables, 368–371
    DAX (data analysis functions), 187
    Goal Seek tool, 377–380
    Scenario Manager tool, 371–377
    Solver tool, 380–388
    What-If Analysis label, 361

Analyze tab, 36
AND function, 346–348
And operator condition, 110–111
AND or OR conditions, 231
area charts, 206
area conversion, 304
arguments, function, 249, 266–267
arithmetic
    date, 314, 316
    functions, 293–299
    operators, 249
Arrange All command, 49–50
Arrange group commands, 52
arrangement, pivot table fields, 121–130
array
    of cells, 3–4
    data arranged into, 6–7
    formulas, 326
    functions, 343–344
ascending sort, 101
asterisk (*), 107, 279, 284
attributes, table, 8
audit formulas, 263–266
auto filters, 107–110
Auto Outline command, 238–239
AutoFit Column Width command, 38–39
AutoFit Height command, 38
AutoSum command, 46
Average command, 166, 235
AVERAGE function, 267–268, 324–325, 337
AVERAGEA function, 324–325
AVERAGEIF function, 324, 327